CLYMER®

HONDA

SHADOW 1100cc • 1985-1996

The world's finest publisher of mechanical how-to manuals

PRIMEDIA
Intertec

P.O. Box 12901, Overland Park, Kansas 66282-2901

Copyright ©1996 PRIMEDIA Intertec

FIRST EDITION
First Printing August, 1991

SECOND EDITION
Revised to include 1991-1995 models
First Printing November, 1994

THIRD EDITION
Revised to include 1996 models
First Printing April, 1996
Second Printing July, 1997
Third Printing November, 1998

Printed in U.S.A.

CLYMER and colophon are registered trademarks of PRIMEDIA Intertec.

ISBN: 0-89287-680-8

Library of Congress: 96-75543

MEMBER

MOTORCYCLE
INDUSTRY
COUNCIL, INC.

Technical photography by Ed Scott.

Technical and photographic assistance by Curt Jordan, Jordan Engineering, Santa Ana, California.

Technical illustrations by Mitzi McCarthy.

COVER: Photographed by Mark Clifford, Mark Clifford Photography, Los Angeles, California.

Chapter One
General Information
1

Chapter Two
Troubleshooting
2

Chapter Three
Lubrication, Maintenance and Tune-up
3

Chapter Four
Engine
4

Chapter Five
Clutch
5

Chapter Six
Transmission and Gearshift Mechanism
6

Chapter Seven
Fuel, Emission Control and Exhaust Systems
7

Chapter Eight
Electrical System
8

Chapter Nine
Cooling System
9

Chapter Ten
Front Suspension and Steering
10

Chapter Eleven
Rear Suspension and Final Drive
11

Chapter Twelve
Brakes
12

Chapter Thirteen
Frame and Repainting
13

Index
14

Wiring Diagrams
15

CONTENTS

QUICK REFERENCE DATA IX

CHAPTER ONE
GENERAL INFORMATION 1

Manual organization
Notes, cautions and warnings
Safety first
Service hints
Washing the bike
Torque specifications
Fasteners
Lubricants

Expendable supplies
Parts replacement
Emission control and battery decals
Basic hand tools
Precision measuring tools
Special tools
Mechanic's tips
Riding safety

CHAPTER TWO
TROUBLESHOOTING 28

Operating requirements
Troubleshooting instruments
Starting the engine
Starting difficulties
Engine starting troubleshooting
Engine performance
Engine noises

Excessive vibration
Clutch
Transmission
Ignition system
Front suspension and steering
Brakes

CHAPTER THREE
LUBRICATION, MAINTENANCE AND TUNE-UP 34

Routine checks
Pre-checks
Service intervals
Tires and wheels
Crankcase breather hose (U.S. models only)
Evaporation emission control
 (California models only)

Battery
Periodic lubrication
Periodic maintenance
Tune-up

CHAPTER FOUR
ENGINE 69

Engine principles
Hydraulic valve adjuster system
Servicing engine in frame
Engine
Cylinder head cover and camshaft
Cylinder heads
Valves and valve components
Rocker arm assemblies
Hydraulic tappets
Cylinder
Piston, piston pin and piston rings

Oil pump drive sprockets and drive chain
Oil pump
Oil pressure relief valve
Primary drive gear
Crankcase
Crankshaft
Connecting rods
Output gear unit
Alternator rotor, starter clutch assembly and
  starter gears
Break-in procedure

CHAPTER FIVE
CLUTCH 153

Clutch
Clutch oil relief valve
Clutch hydraulic system
Clutch master cylinder

Hose replacement
Slave cylinder
Bleeding the clutch
Clutch oil pressure check

CHAPTER SIX
TRANSMISSION AND GEARSHIFT MECHANISM 183

External shift mechanism
Transmission

Internal shift mechanism

CHAPTER SEVEN
FUEL, EMISSION CONTROL AND EXHAUST SYSTEMS 208

Carburetor operation
Carburetor service
Carburetor adjustments
Air filter case
Throttle cable replacement
Choke cable replacement
Fuel shutoff valve
Fuel filter

Fuel pump
Fuel tanks (1985-1986)
Fuel tank (1987-on)
Crankcase breather system (U.S. only)
Evaporative emission control system
  (California models only)
Exhaust system

CHAPTER EIGHT
ELECTRICAL SYSTEM 240

Charging system
Alternator
Voltage regulator/rectifier
Ignition system
Spark unit
Ignition coil
Pulse generator

Starting system
Starter
Starter solenoid
Clutch diode
Lighting system
Switches
Electrical components

CHAPTER NINE
COOLING SYSTEM 273

Cooling system check
Radiator
Cooling fan
Thermostat

Water pump
Coolant pipes
Coolant hoses

CHAPTER TEN
FRONT SUSPENSION AND STEERING 286

Front wheel
Front hub
Wheel balance
Tire changing
Tire repairs

Handlebar
Steering head and stem
Steering head bearing races
Front forks

CHAPTER ELEVEN
REAR SUSPENSION AND FINAL DRIVE 311

Rear wheel
Rear hub
Final drive unit and drive shaft

Universal joint
Swing arm
Shock absorbers

CHAPTER TWELVE
BRAKES 330

Front brake pad replacement
Front master cylinder
Front caliper
Front brake hose replacement

Front brake disc
Bleeding the system
Rear drum brake
Rear brake pedal

CHAPTER THIRTEEN
FRAME AND REPAINTING

FRAME AND REPAINTING 357

Kickstand (sidestand)
Centerstand
Footpegs
Seats

Front fender
Rear fender and grab rail
Frame

INDEX 365

WIRING DIAGRAMS 369

QUICK REFERENCE DATA

TIRE INFLATION PRESSURE (COLD)

Tire size	Air pressure	
	Normal	Maximum load limit*
1985-1986		
Front 110/90-18 61H	32 psi (225 kPa)	32 psi (225 kPa)
Rear 140/90-15 70H	32 psi (225 kPa)	40 psi (280 kPa)
1987-on		
Front 110/90-19 62H	33 psi (225 kPa)	33 psi (225 kPa)
Rear 170/80-15 77H	33 psi (225 kPa)	40 psi (280 kPa)

*Up to maximum load limit of 200 lb. (89 kg) including total weight of motorcycle with accessories, rider(s) and luggage.

FRONT FORK AIR PRESSURE (1985-1986)

Normal	Maximum*
0-6 psi (0-40 kPa)	43 psi (300 kPa)

*Do not exceed the maximum air pressure or internal parts of the fork will be damaged.

MAINTENANCE AND TUNE-UP TORQUE SPECIFICATIONS

Item	N•m	ft.-lb.
Oil drain plug	35	25
Oil filter	18	13
Fork top cap	23	17
Spark plug	14	10

ENGINE OIL CAPACITY

1985-1986	
Oil and filter change	3.3 liters (3.5 U.S. qt., 2.9 Imp. qt.)
At overhaul	3.8 liters (4.0 U.S. qt., 3.3 Imp. qt.)
1987-on	
Oil change only	2.9 liters (3.05 U.S. qt., 2.55 Imp. qt.)
Oil and filter change	3.1 liters (3.26 U.S. qt., 2.73 Imp. qt.)
At overhaul	3.8 liters (4.0 U.S. qt., 3.3 Imp. qt.)

FRONT FORK OIL CAPACITY*

1985-1986	415 cc (14.0 oz.)
1987-1990	442.5-447.5 cc (14.99-15.16 oz.)
1992-on	446.5-451.5 cc (15.10-15.27 oz.)

*Capacity for each fork leg.

ANTIFREEZE PROTECTION AND CAPACITY

Temperature	Antifreeze-to-water ratio
Above –25° F (–32° C)	45:55
Above –34° F (–37° C)	50:50
Above –48° F (–44.5° C)	55:45
Coolant capacity	
Total system	2.20 liters (2.31 U.S. qt., 1.94 Imp. qt.)
Radiator and engine	1.86 liters (1.95 U.S. qt., 1.64 Imp. qt.)
Reserve tank	0.34 liters (0.36 U.S. qt., 0.30 Imp. qt.)

TUNE-UP SPECIFICATIONS

Compression pressure	
(at sea level)	
1985-1986	1,100-1,500 kPa (157-213 psi)
1987-on	981-1,373 kPa (143-199 psi)
Spark plug type	
Standard heat range	ND X22EPR-U9 or NGK DPR7EA-9
Cold weather*	ND X20EPR-U9 or NGK DPR6EA-9
Extended high-speed riding	ND X24EPR-U9 or NGK DPR8EA-9
Spark plug gap	0.8-0.9 mm (0.031-0.035 in.)
Ignition timing	
1985-1986	"F" mark @ idle (5° BTDC)
1987-on	"F" mark @ idle (8° BTDC)
Idle speed	1,000 ±100 rpm

* Cold weather climate—below 41° F (5° C).

REPLACEMENT BULBS

Item	Wattage	Number
Headlight (quartz bulb)	12V 60/55	H4
Tail/brakelight	12V 3/32 cp	SAE No. 1157
Front turn signal and running light	12V 32 cp	SAE No. 1034
Rear turn signal	12V 32 cp	SAE No. 1073
Instrument lights		
1985-1986	12V 3W	—
1987-on	12V 1.7W	—
Indicator lights	12V 3W	—
High beam indicator	12V 3W	—
Turn signal indicator	12V 3W	—
Neutral indicator	12V 3W	—
Overdrive indicator (1985-1986)	12V 3W	—
Oil pressure warning	12V 3W	—

INTRODUCTION

This detailed, comprehensive manual covers the Honda 1100 cc V-Twin Shadow.

The expert text gives complete information on maintenance, tune-up, repair and overhaul. Hundreds of photos and drawings guide you through every step. The book includes all you will need to know to keep your Honda Shadow running right.

A shop manual is a reference. You want to be able to find information fast. As in all Clymer books, this one is designed with you in mind. All chapters are thumb tabbed. Important items are extensively indexed at the rear of the book. All procedures, tables, photos, etc., in this manual are for the reader who may be working on the bike for the first time or using this manual for the first time. All the most frequently used specifications and capacities are summarized in the *Quick Reference Data* pages at the front of the book.

Keep the book handy in your tool box. It will help you better understand how your bike runs, lower repair costs and generally improve your satisfaction with the bike.

CHAPTER ONE

GENERAL INFORMATION

This detailed, comprehensive manual covers the 1985-on Honda 1100 cc V-Twin Shadow.

Troubleshooting, tune-up, maintenance and repair arc not difficult, if you know what tools and equipment to use and what to do. Step-by-step instructions guide you through jobs ranging from simple maintenance to complete engine and suspension overhaul.

This manual can be used by anyone from a first time do-it-yourselfer to a professional mechanic. Detailed drawings and clear photographs give you all the information you need to do the work right.

Some of the procedures in this manual require the use of special tools. The resourceful mechanic can, in many cases, think of acceptable substitutes for special tools—there is always another way. This can be as simple as using a few pieces of threaded rod, washers and nuts to remove or install a bearing or fabricating a tool from scrap material. However, using a substitute for a special tool is not recommended as it can be dangerous and may damage the part. If you find that a tool can be designed and safely made, but will require some type of machine work, you may want to search out a local community college or high school that has a machine shop curriculum. Shop teachers sometimes welcome outside work that can be used as practical shop applications for advanced students.

Table 1 lists model coverage with engine and frame serial numbers.

Metric and U.S. standards are used throughout this manual. U.S. to metric conversion is given in **Table 2**.

Tables 1-5 are found at the end of the chapter.

MANUAL ORGANIZATION

This chapter provides general information and discusses equipment and tools useful both for preventive maintenance and troubleshooting.

Chapter Two provides methods and suggestions for quick and accurate diagnosis and repair of problems. Troubleshooting procedures discuss typical symptoms and logical methods to pinpoint the trouble.

Chapter Three explains all periodic lubrication and routine maintenance necessary to keep your Honda Shadow operating well and competitive. Chapter Three also includes recommended tune-up procedures, eliminating the need to consult other chapters on the various assemblies.

Subsequent chapters describe specific systems such as the engine top end, engine bottom end, clutch, transmission, fuel, exhaust, electrical, cooling system, suspension, steering and brakes. Each chapter provides disassembly, repair, and assembly procedures in simple step-by-step form. If a repair is impractical for a home mechanic, it is so indicated. It is usually faster and less expensive to take such repairs to a Honda dealer or competent repair shop. Specifications concerning a particular system are included at the end of the appropriate chapter.

NOTES, CAUTIONS AND WARNINGS

The terms NOTE, CAUTION and WARNING have specific meanings in this manual. A NOTE provides additional information to make a step or procedure easier or clearer. Disregarding a NOTE could cause inconvenience, but would not cause damage or personal injury.

A CAUTION emphasizes areas where equipment damage could occur. Disregarding a CAUTION could cause permanent mechanical damage; however, personal injury is unlikely.

A WARNING emphasizes areas where personal injury or even death could result from negligence. Mechanical damage may also occur. WARNINGS *are to be taken seriously*. In some cases, serious injury and death has resulted from disregarding similar warnings.

SAFETY FIRST

Professional mechanics can work for years and never sustain a serious injury. If you observe a few rules of common sense and safety, you can enjoy many safe hours servicing your own machine. If you ignore these rules, you can hurt yourself or damage the equipment.

1. *Never* use gasoline as a cleaning solvent.

2. *Never* smoke or use a torch in the vicinity of flammable liquids, such as cleaning solvent, in open containers.

3. If welding or brazing is required on the machine, remove the fuel tank and rear shock to a safe distance, at least 50 feet away.

4. Use the proper sized wrenches to avoid damage to fasteners and injury to yourself.

5. When loosening a tight or stuck nut, be guided by what would happen if the wrench should slip. Be careful: protect yourself accordingly.

6. When replacing a fastener, make sure to use one with the same measurements and strength as the old one. Incorrect or mismatched fasteners can result in damage to the vehicle and possible personal injury. Beware of fastener kits that are filled with cheap and poorly made nuts, bolts, washers and cotter pins. Refer to *Fasteners* in this chapter for additional information.

7. Keep all hand and power tools in good condition. Wipe greasy and oily tools after using them. They are difficult to hold and can cause injury. Replace or repair worn or damaged tools.

8. Keep your work area clean and uncluttered.

9. Wear safety goggles during all operations involving drilling, grinding, the use of a cold chisel or any time you feel unsure about the safety of your eyes. Safety goggles should also be worn any time solvent and compressed air is used to clean a part.

10. Keep an approved fire extinguisher (**Figure 1**) nearby. Be sure it is rated for gasoline (Class B) and electrical (Class C) fires.

11. When drying bearings or other rotating parts with compressed air, never allow the air jet to rotate the bearing or part. The air jet is capable of rotating them at speeds far in excess of those for which they were designed. The bearing or rotating part is very likely to disintegrate and cause serious injury and damage. To prevent bearing damage when using

compressed air, hold the inner bearing race by hand (**Figure 2**).

SERVICE HINTS

Most of the service procedures covered are straightforward and can be performed by anyone reasonably handy with tools. It is suggested, however, that you consider your own capabilities carefully before attempting any operation involving major disassembly of the engine or transmission.

Take your time and do the job right. Do not forget that a newly rebuilt engine must be broken in the same way as a new one. Keep the rpm's within the limits given in your Honda Shadow owner's manual when you get back on the road.

1. "Front," as used in this manual, refers to the front of the motorcycle; the front of any component is the end closest to the front of the motorcycle. The "left-" and "right-hand" sides refer to the position of the parts as viewed by a rider sitting on the seat facing forward. For example, the throttle control is on the right-hand side. These rules are simple, but confusion can cause a major inconvenience during service.

2. Whenever servicing the engine or clutch, or when removing a suspension component, the bike should be secured in a safe manner. An excellent support is a wooden box or stand. A sturdy box can be made with 3/4 in. plywood that will last a long time if constructed well.

WARNING
Never disconnect the positive (+) battery cable unless the negative (−) cable has first been disconnected. Disconnecting the positive cable while the negative cable is still connected may cause a spark. This could ignite hydrogen gas given off by the battery, causing an explosion.

3. Disconnect the negative battery cable when working on or near the electrical, clutch, or starter systems and before disconnecting any electrical wires. On most batteries, the negative terminal will be marked with a minus (−) sign and the positive terminal with a plus (+) sign.

4. Tag all similar internal parts for location and mark all mating parts for position (A, **Figure 3**). Record number and thickness of any shims as they are removed. Small parts such as bolts can be identified by placing them in plastic sandwich bags (B, **Figure 3**). Seal and label them with masking tape.

5. Place parts from a specific area of the engine (e.g. cylinder head, cylinder, clutch, shift mechanism, etc.) into plastic boxes (C, **Figure 3**) to keep them separated.

6. When disassembling transmission shaft assemblies, use an egg flat (the type that restaurants get their eggs in) (D, **Figure 3**) and set the parts from the shaft in one of the depressions in the same order in which it was removed.

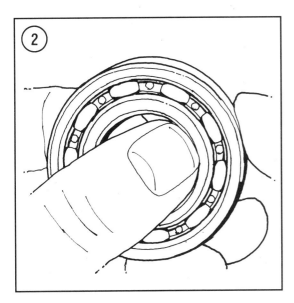

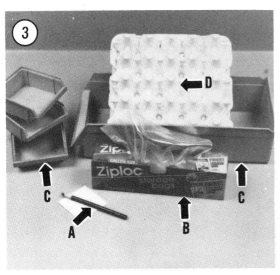

7. Wiring should be tagged with masking tape and marked as each wire is removed. Again, do not rely on memory alone.

8. Finished surfaces should be protected from physical damage or corrosion. Keep gasoline and brake fluid off painted surfaces.

9. Use penetrating oil on frozen or tight bolts, then strike the bolt head a few times with a hammer and punch (use a screwdriver on screws). Avoid the use of heat where possible, as it can warp, melt or affect the temper of parts. Heat also ruins finishes, especially paint and plastics.

10. No parts removed or installed (other than bushings and bearings) in the procedures given in this manual should require unusual force during disassembly or assembly. If a part is difficult to remove or install, find out why before proceeding.

11. Cover all openings after removing parts or components to prevent dirt, small tools, etc. from falling in.

12. Read each procedure *completely* while looking at the actual parts before starting a job. Make sure you *thoroughly* understand what is to be done and then carefully follow the procedure, step by step.

13. Recommendations are occasionally made to refer service or maintenance to a Honda dealer or a specialist in a particular field. In these cases, the work will be done more quickly and economically than if you performed the job yourself.

14. In procedural steps, the term "replace" means to discard a defective part and replace it with a new or exchange unit. "Overhaul" means to remove, disassemble, inspect, measure, repair or replace defective parts, reassemble and install major systems or parts.

15. Some operations require the use of a hydraulic press. It would be wiser to have these operations performed by a shop equipped for such work, rather than to try to do the job yourself with makeshift equipment that may damage your machine.

16. Repairs go much faster and easier if your machine is clean before you begin work. There are many special cleaners on the market, like Bel-Ray Degreaser, for washing the engine and related parts. Follow the manufacturer's directions on the container for the best results. Clean all oily or greasy parts with cleaning solvent as you remove them. See *Washing the Bike* in this chapter.

WARNING
Never use gasoline as a cleaning agent. It presents an extreme fire hazard. Be

sure to work in a well-ventilated area when using cleaning solvent. Keep a fire extinguisher, rated for gasoline fires, handy in any case.

CAUTION
If you use a car wash to clean your bike, don't direct the high pressure water hose at fork seals, steering bearings, carburetor hoses, suspension linkage components, wheel bearings and electrical components (e.g. instrument cluster). The water will flush grease out of the bearings or damage the seals. After washing your bike, remove the wheels and clean the wheel drums (if so equipped) of all water and dirt.

17. Much of the labor charges for repairs made by dealers are for the time involved in the removal, disassembly, assembly, and reinstallation of other parts in order to reach the defective part. It is frequently possible to perform the preliminary operations yourself and then take the defective unit to the dealer for repair at considerable savings.

18. If special tools are required, make arrangements to get them before you start. It is frustrating and time-consuming to get partly into a job and then be unable to complete it.

19. Make diagrams (or take a Polaroid picture) wherever similar-appearing parts are found. For instance, crankcase bolts are often not the same length. You may think you can remember where everything came from—but mistakes are costly. There is also the possibility that you may be sidetracked and not return to work for days or even weeks—in which

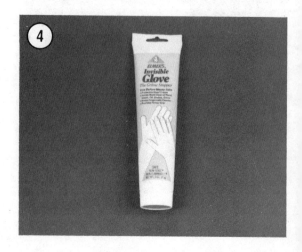

time the carefully laid out parts may have become disturbed.

20. When assembling parts, be sure all shims and washers are replaced exactly as they came out.

21. Whenever a rotating part butts against a stationary part, look for a shim or washer. Use new gaskets if there is any doubt about the condition of the old ones. A thin coat of oil on non-pressure type gaskets may help them seal more effectively.

22. High spots may be sanded off a piston with sandpaper, but fine emery cloth and oil will do a much more professional job.

23. Carbon can be removed from the head, the piston crowns and the exhaust ports with a dull screwdriver. Do *not* scratch machined surfaces. Wipe off the surface with a clean cloth when finished.

24. A baby bottle makes a good measuring device for adding oil to the front forks. Get one that is graduated in fluid ounces and cubic centimeters. After it has been used for this purpose, do *not* let a small child drink out of it as there will always be an oil residue in it.

25. If it is necessary to make a clutch cover or ignition cover gasket and you do not have a suitable old gasket to use as a guide, you can use the outline of the cover and gasket material to make a new gasket. Apply engine oil to the cover gasket surface. Then place the cover on the new gasket material and apply pressure with your hands. The oil will leave a very accurate outline on the gasket material that can be cut around.

CAUTION
When purchasing gasket material to make a gasket, measure the thickness of the old gasket and purchase gasket ma-

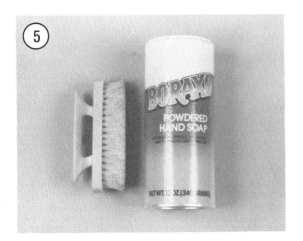

terial with the same approximate thickness.

26. Heavy grease can be used to hold small parts in place if they tend to fall out during assembly. However, keep grease and oil away from electrical and brake components.

27. The carburetors are best cleaned by disassembling them and soaking the parts in a commercial carburetor cleaner. Never soak gaskets and rubber parts in these cleaners. Never use wire to clean out jets and air passages. They are easily damaged. Use compressed air to blow out the carburetor only if the float has been removed first.

28. There are many items available that can be used on your hands before and after working on your bike. A little preparation prior to getting "all greased up" will help when cleaning up later. Before starting, work Vaseline, soap or a product such as Invisible Glove (**Figure 4**) onto your forearms, into your hands and under your fingernails and cuticles. This will make cleanup a lot easier. For cleanup, use a waterless hand soap such as Sta-Lube and then finish with powdered Boraxo and a fingernail brush (**Figure 5**).

WASHING THE BIKE

Even though the Honda Shadow is a street bike and not ridden off-road you should keep it clean. It will make maintenance and service procedures quick and easy. More important, proper cleaning will prevent dirt from falling into critical areas undetected. Failing to clean the bike or cleaning it incorrectly will add to your maintenance costs and shop time because dirty parts wear out prematurely. It's unthinkable that your bike could break because of improper cleaning, but it can happen.

When cleaning your Honda, you will need a few tools, shop rags, scrub brush, bucket, liquid cleaner and access to water. Many riders use a coin-operated car wash. Coin-operated car washes are convenient and quick, but with improper use, the high water pressures can do more damage than good to your bike.

NOTE
A safe biodegradable, non-toxic and non-flammable liquid cleaner that works well for washing your bike as well as for removing grease and oil from

engine and suspension parts is Simple Green. Simple Green can be purchased through some supermarkets, hardware, garden and discount supply houses. Follow the directions on the container for recommended dilution ratios.

When cleaning your bike, and especially when using a spray type degreaser, remember that what goes on the bike will rinse off and drip onto your driveway or into your yard. If you can, use a degreaser at a coin-operated car wash. If you are cleaning your bike at home, place thick cardboard or newspapers underneath the bike to catch the oil and grease deposits that are rinsed off.

1. Place the bike on a stand.
2. Check the following before washing the bike:
   a. Make sure the gas filler cap seals tightly.
   b. Make sure the oil fill cap is tight.
   c. Plug both muffler openings with a large cork or rag.
3. Wash the bike from top to bottom with soapy water. Use the scrub brush to get excess dirt out of the wheel rims and engine crannies. Concentrate on the upper controls, engine, side panels and gas tank during this wash cycle. Don't forget to wash dirt and mud from underneath the fenders and engine crankcase.
4. Remove the side panels and seat. Wrap a plastic bag around the ignition coils and CDI unit. Concentrate the second wash cycle on the frame tube members, outer airbox areas, suspension linkage, rear shock and swing arm.
5. Direct the hose underneath the engine and swing arm. Wash this area thoroughly. If this area is extremely dirty, you may want to lay the bike on its side. Protect the finish when laying the bike down.
6. The final wash is the rinse. Use cold water without soap and spray the entire motorcycle again. Use as much time and care when rinsing the bike as when washing it. Built up soap deposits will quickly corrode electrical connections and remove the natural oils from tires, causing premature cracks and wear. Make sure you thoroughly rinse the bike off.
7. Tip the bike from side-to-side to allow any water that has collected on horizontal surfaces to drain off.
8. If you are washing the bike at home, start the engine. Idle the engine to burn off any internal moisture.
9. Before taking the bike into the garage, wipe it dry with a soft cloth or chamois. Inspect the machine as

you dry it for further signs of dirt and grime. Make a quick visual inspection of the frame and other painted pieces. Spray any worn-down spots with WD-40 or Bel-Ray 6-in-1 to prevent rust from building on the bare metal. When the bike is back at your work area you can repaint the bare areas with touch-up paint after wiping off the WD-40. A quick shot from a touch-up paint can each time you work on the bike will keep it looking sharp and stop rust from building and weakening parts.

TORQUE SPECIFICATIONS

Torque specifications throughout this manual are given in Newton-meters (N•m) and foot-pounds (ft.-lb.).

Existing torque wrenches calibrated in meter kilograms can be used by performing a simple conversion. All you have to do is move the decimal point

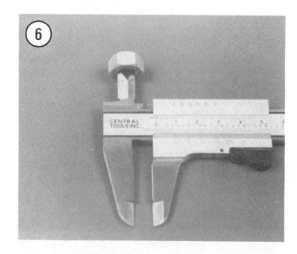

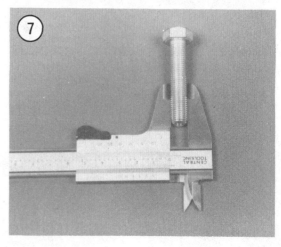

one place to the right: for example, 3.5 mkg = 35 N•m. This conversion is accurate enough for mechanical work even though the exact mathematical conversion is 3.5 mkg = 34.3 N•m.

Refer to **Table 3** for standard torque specifications for various size screws, bolts and nuts that may not be listed in the respective chapters. To use the table, first determine the size of the bolt or nut. Use a vernier caliper and measure the inside dimension of the threads of the nut (**Figure 6**) and across the threads for a bolt (**Figure 7**).

FASTENERS

The materials and designs of the various fasteners used on your Honda are not arrived at by chance or accident. Fastener design determines the type of tool required to work the fastener. Fastener material is carefully selected to decrease the possibility of physical failure.

Nuts, bolts and screws are manufactured in a wide range of thread patterns. To join a nut and bolt, the diameter of the bolt and the diameter of the hole in the nut must be the same. It is just as important that the threads on both be properly matched.

The best way to tell if the threads on 2 fasteners are matched is to turn the nut on the bolt (or the bolt into the threaded hole in a piece of equipment) with fingers only. Be sure both pieces are clean. If much force is required, check the thread condition on each fastener. If the thread condition is good but the fasteners jam, the threads are not compatible. A thread pitch gauge (**Figure 8**) can also be used to determine pitch. Honda motorcycles are manufactured with ISO (International Organization for Standardization) metric fasteners. The threads are cut differently from those of American fasteners (**Figure 9**).

Most threads are cut so that the fastener must be turned clockwise to tighten it. These are called right-hand threads. Some fasteners have left-hand threads; they must be turned counterclockwise to be tightened. Left-hand threads are used in locations where normal rotation of the equipment would tend to loosen a right-hand threaded fastener.

ISO Metric Screw Threads

ISO (International Organization for Standardization) metric threads come in 3 standard thread sizes: coarse, fine and constant pitch. The ISO coarse pitch is used for most all common fastener applications. The fine pitch thread is used on certain precision tools and instruments. The constant pitch thread is used mainly on machine parts and not for fasteners. The constant pitch thread, however, is used on all metric thread spark plugs.

ISO metric threads are specified by the capital letter M followed by the diameter in millimeters and the pitch (or the distance between each thread) in millimeters separated by the sign ×. For example: an M8 × 1.25 bolt is one that has a diameter of 8 millimeters with a distance of 1.25 millimeters between each thread. The measurement across 2 flats on the head of the bolt (**Figure 10**) indicates the proper wrench size to be used. **Figure 11** shows how to determine bolt diameter.

NOTE
When purchasing a bolt from a dealer or parts store, it is important to know how to specify bolt length. The correct

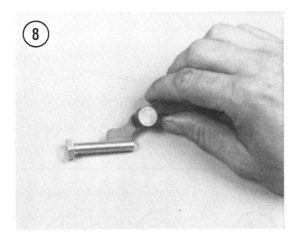

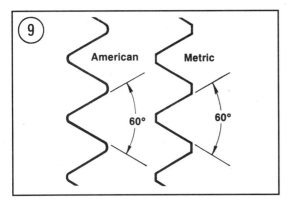

*way to measure bolt length is by measuring the length starting from underneath the bolt head to the end of the bolt (**Figure 12**). Always measure bolt length in this manner to avoid purchasing bolts that are too long.*

Machine Screws

There are many different types of machine screws. **Figure 13** shows a number of screw heads requiring different types of turning tools. Heads are also designed to protrude above the metal (round) or to be slightly recessed in the metal (flat). See **Figure 14**.

Bolts

Commonly called bolts, the technical name for these fasteners is cap screws. Metric bolts are de-

scribed by the diameter and pitch (or the distance between each thread). For example: an M8 × 1.25 bolt is one that has a diameter of 8 millimeters and a distance of 1.25 millimeters between each thread. The measurement across 2 flats on the head of the bolt (**Figure 10**) indicates the proper wrench size to

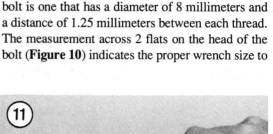

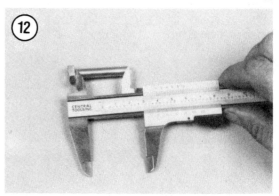

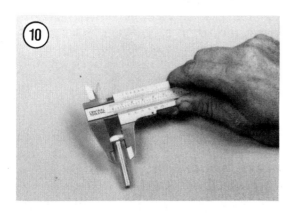

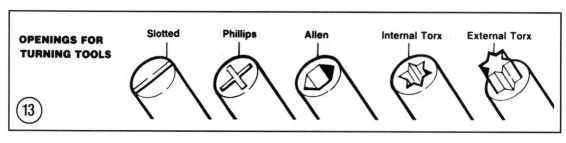

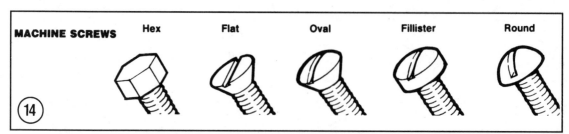

be used. Use a vernier caliper and measure across the threads (**Figure 11**) to determine the bolt diameter and to measure the length (**Figure 12**).

Nuts

Nuts are manufactured in a variety of types and sizes. Most are hexagonal (6-sided) and fit on bolts, screws and studs with the same diameter and pitch.

Figure 15 shows several types of nuts. The common nut is generally used with a lockwasher. Self-locking nuts have a nylon insert which prevents the nut from loosening; no lockwasher is required. Wing nuts are designed for fast removal by hand. Wing nuts are used for convenience in non-critical locations.

To indicate the size of a metric nut, manufacturers specify the diameter of the opening and the thread pitch. This is similar to bolt specifications, but without the length dimension. The measurement across 2 flats on the nut indicates the proper wrench size to be used (**Figure 16**).

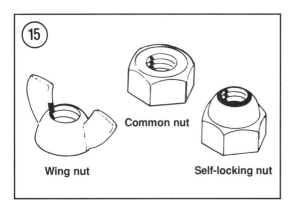

Wing nut   Common nut   Self-locking nut

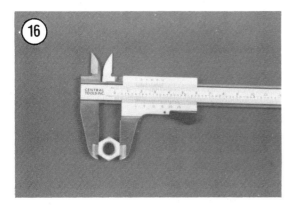

Prevailing Torque Fasteners

Several types of bolts, screws and nuts incorporate a system that develops an interference between the bolt, screw, nut or tapped hole threads. Interference is achieved in various ways: by distorting threads, coating threads with dry adhesive or nylon, distorting the top of an all-metal nut, using a nylon insert in the center or at the top of a nut, etc.

Prevailing torque fasteners offer greater holding strength and better vibration resistance. Some prevailing torque fasteners can be reused if in good condition. Others, like the nylon insert nut, form an initial locking condition when the nut is first installed; the nylon forms closely to the bolt thread pattern, thus reducing any tendency for the nut to loosen. When the nut is removed, the locking efficiency is greatly reduced. For greatest safety, it is recommended that you install new prevailing torque fasteners whenever they are removed.

Washers

There are 2 basic types of washers: flat washers and lockwashers. Flat washers are simple discs with a hole to fit a screw or bolt. Lockwashers are designed to prevent a fastener from working loose due to vibration, expansion and contraction. **Figure 17** shows several types of washers. Washers are also used in the following functions:

    a. As spacers.

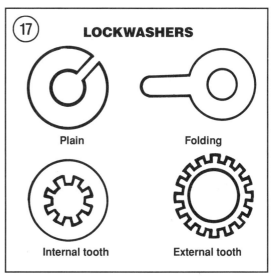

LOCKWASHERS

Plain   Folding

Internal tooth   External tooth

b. To prevent galling or damage of the equipment by the fastener.

c. To help distribute fastener load during torquing.

d. As seals.

Note that flat washers are often used between a lockwasher and a fastener to provide a smooth bearing surface. This allows the fastener to be turned easily with a tool.

Cotter Pins

Cotter pins (**Figure 18**) are used to secure special kinds of fasteners. The threaded stud must have a hole in it; the nut or nut lock piece has castellations around which the cotter pin ends wrap. Cotter pins should not be reused after removal.

Circlips

Circlips can be internal or external design. They are used to retain items on shafts (external type) or within tubes (internal type). In some applications, circlips of varying thicknesses are used to control the end play of parts assemblies. These are often called selective circlips. Circlips should be replaced during installation, as removal weakens and deforms them.

Two basic styles of circlips are available: machined and stamped circlips. Machined circlips (**Figure 19**) can be installed in either direction (shaft or housing) because both faces are machined, thus creating two sharp edges. Stamped circlips (**Figure 20**) are manufactured with one sharp edge and one rounded edge. When installing stamped circlips in a thrust situation (transmission shafts, fork tubes, etc.), the sharp edge must face away from the part producing the thrust. When installing circlips, observe the following:

a. Compress or expand circlips only enough to install them.

b. After the circlip is installed, make sure it is completely seated in its groove.

Transmission circlips become worn with use and increase side play. For this reason, always use new circlips whenever a transmission is being reassembled.

LUBRICANTS

Periodic lubrication assures long life for any type of equipment. The *type* of lubricant used is just as important as the lubrication service itself, although in an emergency the wrong type of lubricant is better than none at all. The following paragraphs describe

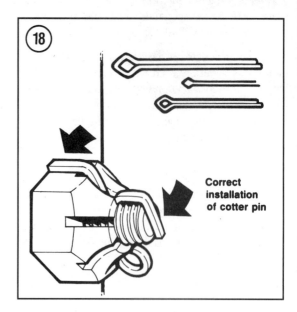

Correct installation of cotter pin

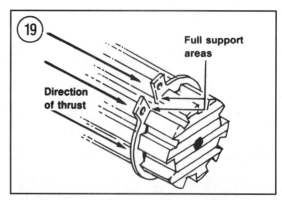

Full support areas

Direction of thrust

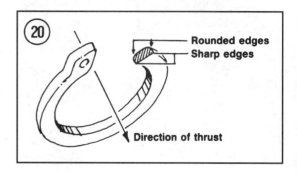

Rounded edges
Sharp edges

Direction of thrust

the types of lubricants most often used on motorcycle equipment. Be sure to follow the manufacturer's recommendations for lubricant types.

Generally, all liquid lubricants are called "oil." They may be mineral-based (including petroleum bases), natural-based (vegetable and animal bases), synthetic-based or emulsions (mixtures). "Grease" is an oil to which a thickening base has been added so that the end product is semi-solid. Grease is often classified by the type of thickener added; lithium soap is commonly used.

Engine Oil

Four-cycle oil for motorcycle and automotive engines is graded by the American Petroleum Institute

(API) and the Society of Automotive Engineers (SAE) in several categories. Oil containers display these ratings on the top or label.

API oil grade is indicated by letters; oils for gasoline engines are identified by an "S." Honda models described in this manual require SE or SF graded oil (A, **Figure 21**).

Viscosity is an indication of the oil's thickness. The SAE uses numbers to indicate viscosity; thin oils have low numbers while thick oils have high numbers (B, **Figure 21**). A "W" after the number indicates that the viscosity testing was done at low temperature to simulate cold-weather operation. Engine oils fall into the 5W-30 and 20W-50 range.

Multi-grade oils (for example 10W-40) are less viscous (thinner) at low temperatures and more viscous (thicker) at high temperatures. This allows the oil to perform efficiently across a wide range of engine operating conditions. The lower the number, the better the engine will start in cold climates. Higher numbers are usually recommended for engines running in hot weather conditions.

Grease

Greases are graded by the National Lubricating Grease Institute (NLGI). Greases are graded by number according to the consistency of the grease; these range from No. 000 to No. 6, with No. 6 being the most solid. A typical multipurpose grease is NLGI No. 2. For specific applications, equipment manufacturers may require grease with an additive such as molybdenum disulfide (MOS2)

EXPENDABLE SUPPLIES

Certain expendable supplies are required during maintenance and repair work. These include grease, oil, gasket cement, wiping rags and cleaning solvent. Ask your dealer for the special locking compounds, silicone lubricants and other products (**Figure 22**) which make vehicle maintenance simpler and easier. Cleaning solvent or kerosene is available at some service stations or hardware stores.

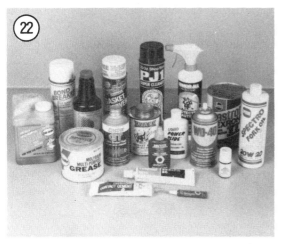

WARNING
Having a stack of clean shop rags on hand is important when performing engine and suspension service work. However, to prevent the possibility of

fire damage from spontaneous combustion from a pile of solvent soaked rags, store them in a lid sealed metal container until they can be washed or discarded.

> **NOTE**
> *To avoid absorbing solvent and other chemicals into your skin while cleaning parts, wear a pair of petroleum-resistant rubber gloves. These can be purchased through industrial supply houses or well-equipped hardware stores.*

PARTS REPLACEMENT

Honda makes frequent changes during a model year, some minor, some relatively major. When you order parts from the dealer or other parts distributor, always order by frame and engine numbers. The frame serial number is stamped on the right-hand side of the steering head pipe (**Figure 23**). The vehicle identification number is stamped on the left-hand side of the steering head pipe. The engine number is stamped on a raised pad on the right-hand side of the crankcase below the rear cylinder (**Figure 24**). The carburetor number (**Figure 25**) is on the intake side of the carburetor body just above the float bowl.

The paint color label is located in the following locations:

a. 1985 models: on top of the rear fender under the seat.

b. 1986 models: on the left-hand side of the fuel tank (**Figure 26**) behind the frame side cover.

c. 1987-on models: on the right-hand side of the air filter case.

Write the numbers down and carry them with you. Compare new parts to old before purchasing them. If they are not alike, have the parts manager explain the difference to you. **Table 1** lists engine and frame serial numbers for the models covered in this manual.

> **NOTE**
> *If your Honda was purchased second-hand and you are not sure of its model year, use the bike's engine serial number and the information listed in **Table 1**. Read your bike's engine serial number. Then compare the number with the en-*

*gine serial numbers listed in **Table 1**. If your bike's serial number is listed in **Table 1**, cross-reference the number with the adjacent model number and year.*

EMISSION CONTROL AND BATTERY DECALS

On models so equipped, a vehicle emission control information decal is fixed to the backside of the frame's left-hand side cover. This decal lists all emission control related tune-up information.

On California models, an emission hose routing label is also fixed to the back of the side cover.

BASIC HAND TOOLS

Many of the procedures in this manual can be carried out with simple hand tools and test equipment familiar to the average home mechanic. Keep your tools clean and in a tool box. Keep them organ-

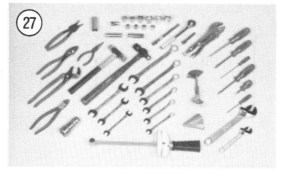

ized with the sockets and related drives together, the open-end combination wrenches together, etc. After using a tool, wipe off dirt and grease with a clean cloth and return the tool to its correct place.

Top-quality tools are essential; they are also more economical in the long run. If you are now starting to build your tool collection, stay away from the "advertised specials" featured at some parts houses, discount stores and chain drug stores. These are usually a poor grade tool that can be sold cheaply and that is exactly what they are—*cheap*. They are usually made of inferior material, and are thick, heavy and clumsy. Their rough finish makes them difficult to clean and they usually don't last very long. If it is ever your misfortune to use such tools, you will probably find out that the wrenches do not fit the heads of bolts and nuts correctly and damage the fastener.

Quality tools are made of alloy steel and are heat treated for greater strength. They are lighter and better balanced than cheap ones. Their surface is smooth, making them a pleasure to work with and easy to clean. The initial cost of good-quality tools may be more but they are cheaper in the long run. Don't try to buy everything in all sizes in the beginning; do it a little at a time until you have the necessary tools.

The following tools are required to perform virtually any repair job on a bike. Each tool is described and the recommended size given for starting a tool collection. **Table 4** includes the tools that should be on hand for simple home repairs and/or major overhaul as shown in **Figure 27**. Additional tools and some duplicates may be added as you become more familiar with the bike. Almost all motorcycles and bikes (with the exception of the U.S. built Harley and some English bikes) use metric size bolts and nuts. If you are starting your collection now, buy metric sizes.

Screwdrivers

The screwdriver is a very basic tool, but if used improperly it will do more damage than good. The slot on a screw has a definite dimension and shape. A screwdriver must be selected to conform with that shape. Use a small screwdriver for small screws and a large one for large screws or the screw head will be damaged.

Two basic types of screwdrivers are required: common (flat-blade) screwdrivers (**Figure 28**) and Phillips screwdrivers (**Figure 29**).

Screwdrivers are available in sets which often include an assortment of common and Phillips blades. If you buy them individually, buy at least the following:

    a. Common screwdriver—5/16 × 6 in. blade.

    b. Common screwdriver—3/8 × 12 in. blade.

    c. Phillips screwdriver—size 2 tip, 6 in. blade.

Use screwdrivers only for driving screws. Never use a screwdriver for prying or chiseling metal. Do not try to remove a Phillips or Allen head screw with a common screwdriver (unless the screw has a combination head that will accept either type); you can damage the head so that the proper tool will be unable to remove it.

Keep screwdrivers in the proper condition and they will last longer and perform better. Always keep the tip of a common screwdriver in good condition. **Figure 30** shows how to grind the tip to the proper shape if it becomes damaged. Note the symmetrical sides of the tip.

Pliers

Pliers come in a wide range of types and sizes. Pliers are useful for cutting, bending and crimping. They should never be used to cut hardened objects

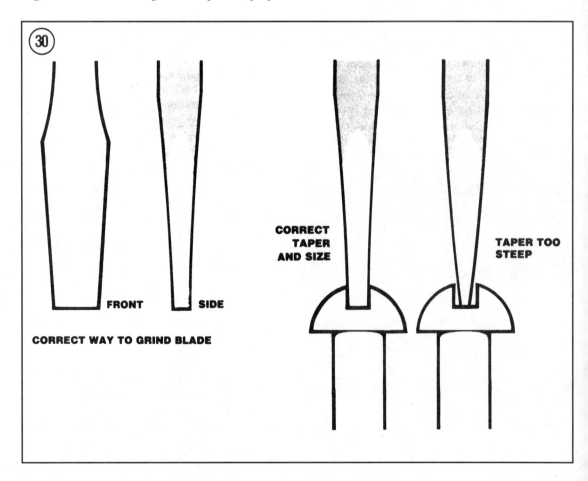

CORRECT TAPER AND SIZE

TAPER TOO STEEP

FRONT   SIDE

CORRECT WAY TO GRIND BLADE

or to turn bolts or nuts. **Figure 31** shows several pliers useful in motorcycle repairs.

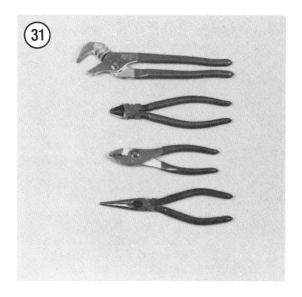

Each type of pliers has a specialized function. Slip-joint pliers are general-purpose pliers and are used mainly for holding things and for bending.

Needlenose pliers are used to hold or bend small objects. Channel-lock pliers can be adjusted to hold various sizes of objects; the jaws remain parallel to grip around objects such as pipe or tubing. There are many more types of pliers. The ones described here are most suitable for bike repairs.

Vise-grip Pliers

Vise-grip pliers (**Figure 32**) are used to hold objects very tightly like a vise. But avoid using them unless absolutely necessary since their sharp jaws will permanently scar any objects which are held. Vise-grip pliers are available in many types for more specific tasks.

Circlip Pliers

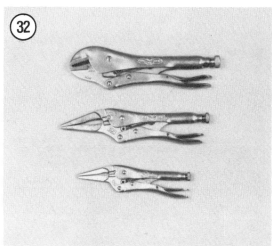

Circlip pliers (**Figure 33**) are special in that they are only used to remove circlips from shafts or within engine or suspension housings. When purchasing circlip pliers, there are two kinds to distinguish from. External pliers (spreading) are used to remove circlips that fit on the outside of a shaft. Internal pliers (squeezing) are used to remove circlips which fit inside a gear or housing.

> *WARNING*
> *Because circlips can sometimes slip and "fly off" during removal and installation, always wear safety glasses.*

Box-end, Open-end and Combination Wrenches

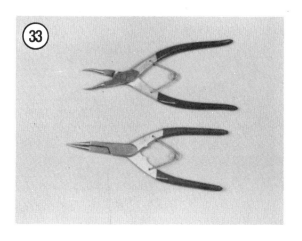

Box-end, open-end and combination wrenches are available in sets or separately in a variety of sizes. On open-end and box-end wrenches, the number stamped near the end refers to the distance between 2 parallel flats on the hex head bolt or nut. On combination wrenches, the number is stamped near the center.

Open-end wrenches are speedy and work best in areas with limited overhead access. Their wide flat jaws make them unstable for situations where the bolt or nut is sunken in a well or close to the edge of a casting. These wrenches grip only two flats of a fastener so if either the fastener head or the wrench jaws are worn, the wrench may slip off.

Box-end wrenches require clear overhead access to the fastener but can work well in situations where the fastener head is close to another part. They grip on all six edges of a fastener for a very secure grip. They are available in either 6-point or 12-point. The 6-point gives superior holding power and durability but requires a greater swinging radius. The 12-point works better in situations with limited swinging radius.

Combination wrenches (**Figure 34**) have open-end on one side and box-end on the other with both ends being the same size. These wrenches are favored by professionals because of their versatility.

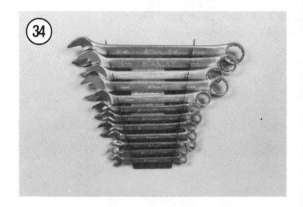

Adjustable (Crescent) Wrenches

An adjustable wrench (sometimes called crescent wrench) can be adjusted to fit nearly any nut or bolt head which has clear access around its entire perimeter. Adjustable wrenches (**Figure 35**) are best used as a backup wrench to keep a large nut or bolt from turning while the other end is being loosened or tightened with a proper wrench.

Adjustable wrenches have only two gripping surfaces which make them more subject to slipping off the fastener and damaging the part and possibly injuring your hand. The fact that one jaw is adjustable only aggravates this shortcoming.

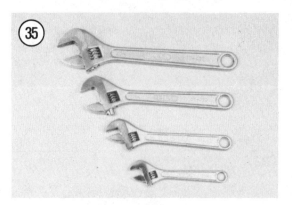

These wrenches are directional; the solid jaw must be the one transmitting the force. If you use the adjustable jaw to transmit the force, it will loosen and possibly slip off.

Adjustable wrenches come in all sizes but something in the 6 to 8 in. range is recommended as an all-purpose wrench.

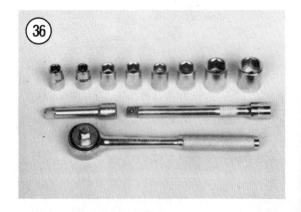

Socket Wrenches

This type is undoubtedly the fastest, safest and most convenient to use. Sockets which attach to a ratchet handle (**Figure 36**) are available with 6-point or 12-point openings and 1/4, 3/8, 1/2 and 3/4 in. drives. The drive size indicates the size of the square hole which mates with the ratchet handle (**Figure 37**).

Several large sockets are required for the disassembly of the engine. These large sockets are not

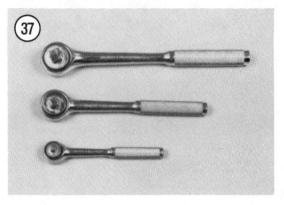

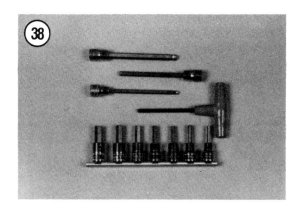

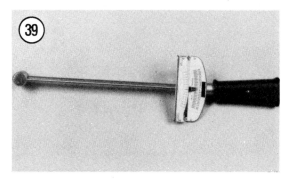

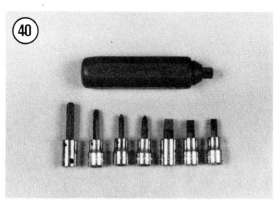

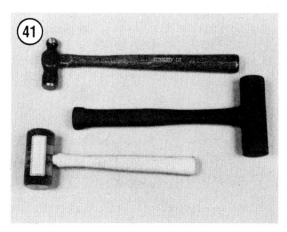

usually included in standard socket sets. These sizes are a must and are as follows:

   a. Balancer gear nut and clutch nut: 30 mm.

   b. Primary gear nut: 36 mm.

Allen Wrenches

Allen wrenches are available in sets or separately in a variety of sizes. These sets come in SAE and metric size, so be sure to buy a metric set. Allen bolts are sometimes called socket bolts. Sometimes the bolts are difficult to reach and it is suggested that a variety of Allen wrenches be purchased (e.g. socket driven, T-handle and extension type) as shown in **Figure 38**.

Torque Wrench

A torque wrench is used with a socket to measure how tightly a nut or bolt is installed. They come in a wide price range and with either 3/8 or 1/2 in. square drive (**Figure 39**). The drive size indicates the size of the square drive which mates with the socket. Purchase one that measures 0-280 N•m (0-200 ft.-lb.).

Impact Driver

This tool might have been designed with the bike in mind. This tool makes removal of fasteners easy and eliminates damage to bolts and screw slots. Impact drivers and interchangeable bits (**Figure 40**) are available at most large hardware, motorcycle or auto parts stores. Don't purchase a cheap one as they do not work as well and require more force (the "use a larger hammer" syndrome) than a moderately priced one. Sockets can also be used with a hand impact driver. However, make sure that the socket is designed for use with an impact driver or air tool. Do not use regular hand sockets, as they may shatter during use.

Hammers

The correct hammer (**Figure 41**) is necessary for repairs. Use only a hammer with a face (or head) of rubber or plastic or the soft-faced type that is filled with buckshot. These are sometimes necessary in engine teardowns. *Never* use a metal-faced hammer on engine or suspension parts, as severe damage will result in most cases. You can always produce the same amount of force with a soft-faced hammer. A metal-faced hammer, however, will be required when using a hand impact driver.

PRECISION MEASURING TOOLS

Measurement is an important part of motorcycle service. When performing many of the service procedures in this manual, you will be required to make a number of measurements. These include basic checks such as valve clearance, engine compression and spark plug gap. As you get deeper into engine disassembly and service, measurements will be required to determine the size and condition of the piston and cylinder bore, valve and guide wear, camshaft wear, crankshaft runout and so on. When making these measurements, the degree of accuracy will dictate which tool is required. Precision measuring tools are expensive. If this is your first experience at engine or suspension service, it may be more worthwhile to have the checks made at a Honda dealer or machine shop. However, as your skills and enthusiasm increase for doing your own service work, you may want to begin purchasing some of these specialized tools. The following is a description of the measuring tools required during engine and suspension overhaul.

Feeler Gauge

Feeler gauges come in assorted sets and types (**Figure 42**). The feeler gauge is made of either a piece of a flat or round hardened steel of a specified thickness. Wire gauges are used to measure spark plug gap. Flat gauges are used for all other measurements. Feeler gauges are also designed for specialized uses, such as for measuring valve clearances. On these gauges, the gauge end is usually small enough and angled so as to make checking valve clearances easier.

Vernier Caliper

This tool (**Figure 43**) is invaluable when reading inside, outside and depth measurements to within close precision. It can be used to measure clutch

spring length and the thickness of clutch plates, shims and thrust washers.

Outside Micrometers

One of the most reliable tools used for precision measurement is the outside micrometer (**Figure 44**). Outside micrometers will be required to measure valve shim thickness, piston diameter and valve stem diameter. Outside micrometers are also used

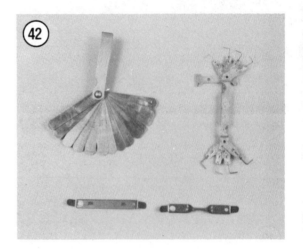

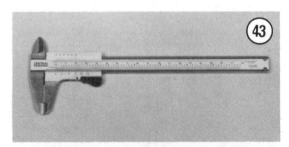

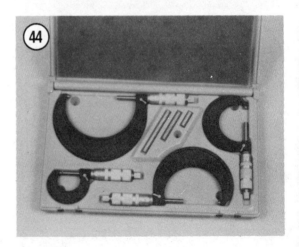

with other tools to measure the cylinder bore and the valve guide inside diameters. Micrometers can be purchased individually or as a set.

Dial Indicator

Dial indicators (**Figure 45**) are precision tools used to check dimension variations on machined parts such as transmission shafts and axles and to check crankshaft and axle shaft end play. Dial indicators are available with various dial types for different measuring requirements. For motorcycle repair, select a dial indicator with a continuous dial (**Figure 46**).

Cylinder Bore Gauge

The cylinder bore gauge is a very specialized precision tool. The gauge set shown in **Figure 47** is comprised of a dial indicator, handle and a number of length adapters to adapt the gauge to different bore sizes. The bore gauge can be used to make cylinder bore measurements such as bore size, taper and out-of-round. Depending on the bore gauge, it can sometimes be used to measure brake caliper and master cylinder bore sizes. An outside micrometer must be used together with the bore gauge to determine bore dimensions.

Small Hole Gauges

A set of small hole gauges allows you to measure a hole, groove or slot ranging in size up to 13 mm (0.500 in.). A small hole gauge will be required to measure valve guide, brake caliper and brake master cylinder bore diameters. An outside micrometer must be used together with the small hole gauge to determine bore dimensions.

Compression Gauge

An engine with low compression cannot be properly tuned and will not develop full power. A compression gauge (**Figure 48**) measures engine compression. The one shown has a flexible stem

(45)

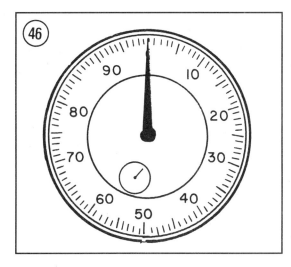

(46)

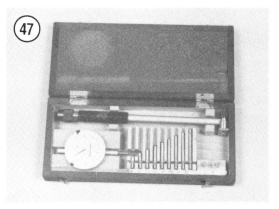

(47)

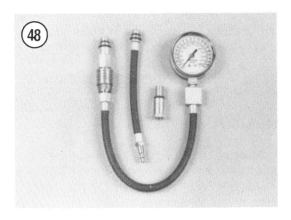

(48)

with an extension that can allow you to hold it while kicking the engine over. Open the throttle all the way when checking engine compression. See Chapter Three.

Strobe Timing Light

This instrument is useful for checking ignition timing. By flashing a light at the precise instant the spark plug fires, the position of the timing mark can be seen. The flashing light makes a moving mark appear to stand still opposite a stationary mark.

Suitable lights range from inexpensive neon bulb types to powerful xenon strobe lights (**Figure 49**). A light with an inductive pickup is recommended to eliminate any possible damage to ignition wiring. Use according to manufacturer's instructions.

Multimeter or VOM

This instrument (**Figure 50**) is invaluable for electrical system troubleshooting. See *Electrical Troubleshooting* in Chapter Eight for its use.

Battery Hydrometer

A hydrometer (**Figure 51**) is the best way to check a battery's state of charge. A hydrometer measures the weight or density of the sulfuric acid in the battery's electrolyte in specific gravity.

Screw Pitch Gauge

A screw pitch gauge (**Figure 52**) determines the thread pitch of bolts, screws, studs, etc. The gauge is made up of a number of thin plates. Each plate has a thread shape cut on one edge to match one thread pitch. When using a screw pitch gauge to determine a thread pitch size, try to fit different blade sizes onto the bolt thread until both threads match (**Figure 53**).

Magnetic Stand

A magnetic stand (**Figure 54**) is used to hold a dial indicator securely when checking the runout of a round object or when checking the end play of a shaft.

V-Blocks

V-blocks (**Figure 55**) are precision ground blocks used to hold a round object when checking its runout or condition. In motorcycle repair, V-blocks can be used when checking the runout of such items as valve stems, camshaft, balancer shaft, crankshaft, wheel axles and fork tubes.

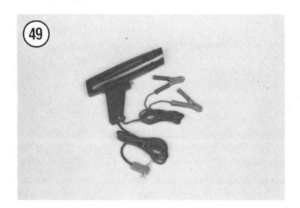

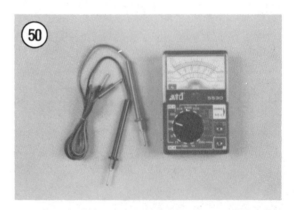

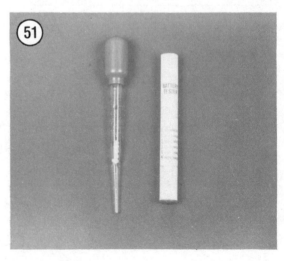

SPECIAL TOOLS

A few special tools may be required for major service. These are described in the appropriate chapters and are available either from a Honda dealer or other manufacturers as indicated.

This section describes special tools unique to motorcycle service and repair.

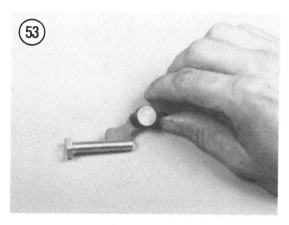

The Grabbit

The Grabbit (**Figure 56**) is a special tool used to hold the clutch boss when removing the clutch nut.

Tire Levers

To prevent damaging the wheel rim during tire changing, purchase a good set of tire levers (**Figure 57**). Never use a screwdriver in place of a tire lever; refer to Chapter Ten for its use. Before using a tire lever, check the working end of the tool and remove any burrs. Don't use a tire lever for prying anything but tires.

Alternator Rotor Puller

A rotor puller (**Figure 58**) will be required whenever it is necessary to remove the rotor and service the stator plate assembly or when adjusting the ignition timing. In addition, when disassembling the engine, the rotor must be removed before the crank-

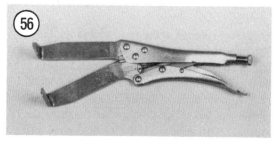

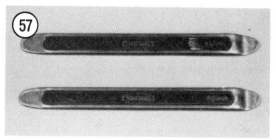

cases can be split. There is no satisfactory substitute for this tool. Because the rotor is a taper fit on the crankshaft, makeshift removal often results in crankshaft and rotor damage. Don't think about removing the rotor without this tool.

MECHANIC'S TIPS

Removing Frozen Nuts and Screws

When a fastener rusts and cannot be removed, several methods may be used to loosen it. First, apply penetrating oil such as Liquid Wrench or WD-40 (available at hardware or auto supply stores). Apply it liberally and let it penetrate for 10-15 minutes. Rap the fastener several times with a small hammer; do not hit it hard enough to cause damage. Reapply the penetrating oil if necessary.

For frozen screws, apply penetrating oil as described, then insert a screwdriver in the slot and rap the top of the screwdriver with a hammer. This loosens the rust so the screw can be removed in the normal way. If the screw head is too chewed up to use this method, grip the head with Vise-grip pliers and twist the screw out.

Avoid applying heat unless specifically instructed, as it may melt, warp or remove the temper from parts.

Removing Broken Screws or Bolts

When the head breaks off a screw or bolt, several methods are available for removing the remaining portion.

If a large portion of the remainder projects out, try gripping it with Vise-grip pliers. If the projecting portion is too small, file it to fit a wrench or cut a slot in it to fit a screwdriver. See **Figure 59**.

If the head breaks off flush, use a screw extractor. To do this, centerpunch the exact center of the remaining portion of the screw or bolt. Drill a small hole in the screw and tap the extractor into the hole. Back the screw out with a wrench on the extractor. See **Figure 60**.

Remedying Stripped Threads

Occasionally, threads are stripped through carelessness or impact damage. Often the threads can be cleaned up by running a tap (for internal threads on nuts) or die (for external threads on bolts) through the threads. See **Figure 61**. To clean or repair spark plug threads, a spark plug tap can be used (**Figure 62**).

> *NOTE*
> *Tap and dies can be purchased individually or in a set as shown in **Figure 63**.*

If an internal thread is damaged, it may be necessary to install a Helicoil (**Figure 64**) or some other type of thread insert. Follow the manufacturer's instructions when installing their insert.

RIDING SAFETY

General Tips

1. Read your owner's manual and know your machine.
2. Check the throttle and brake controls before starting the engine.

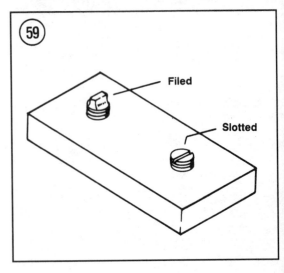

Filed

Slotted

3. Know how to make an emergency stop.

4. Never add fuel while anyone is smoking in the area or when the engine is running.

5. Never wear loose scarves, belts or boot laces that could catch on moving parts.

6. Always wear eye and head protection and protective clothing to protect your *entire* body. Today's riding apparel is very stylish and you will be ready for action as well as being well protected.

7. Riding in the winter months requires a good set of clothes to keep your body dry and warm, otherwise your entire trip may be miserable. If you dress properly, moisture will evaporate from your body. If you become too hot and if your clothes trap the moisture, you will become cold. Even mild temperatures can be very uncomfortable and dangerous when combined with a strong wind or traveling at high speed. See **Table 5** for wind chill factors. Al-

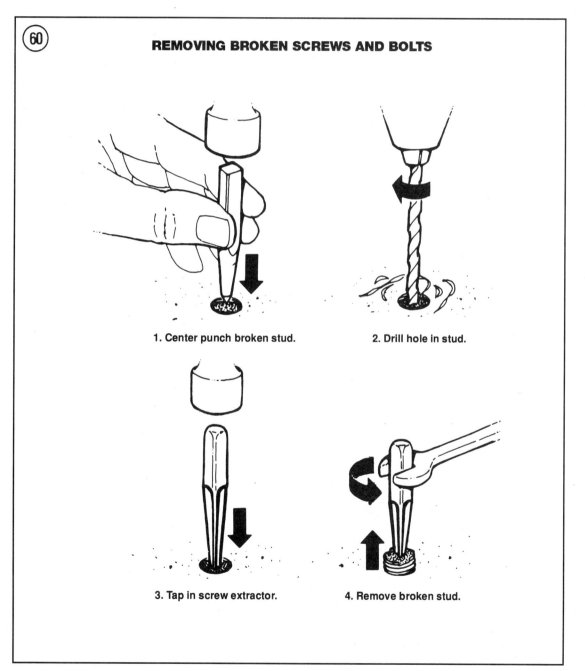

REMOVING BROKEN SCREWS AND BOLTS

1. Center punch broken stud.

2. Drill hole in stud.

3. Tap in screw extractor.

4. Remove broken stud.

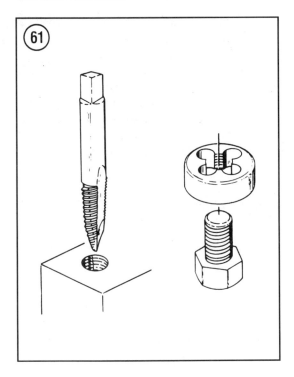

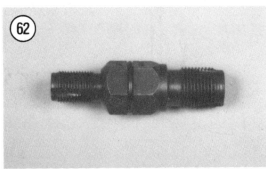

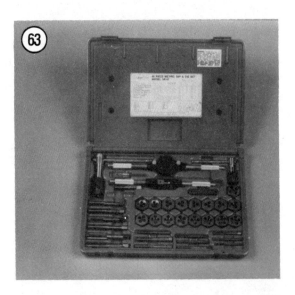

ways dress according to what the wind chill factor is, not the ambient temperature.

8. Never allow anyone to operate the bike without proper instruction. This is for their bodily protection and to keep your machine from damage or destruction.

9. Use the "buddy system" for long trips, just in case you have a problem or run out of gas.

10. Never attempt to repair your machine with the engine running except when necessary for certain tune-up procedures.

11. Check all of the machine components and hardware frequently, especially the wheels and the steering.

Operating Tips

1. Avoid dangerous terrain.

2. Keep the headlight, turn signal lights and taillight free of dirt.

3. Always steer with both hands.

4. Be aware of the terrain and avoid operating the bike at excessive speed.

5. Do not panic if the throttle sticks. Turn the engine stop switch to the OFF position.

6. Do not tailgate. Rear end collisions can cause injury and machine damage.

7. Do not mix alcoholic beverages or drugs with riding—*ride straight*.

8. Check your fuel supply regularly. Do not travel farther than your fuel supply will permit you to arrive at the next fuel stop.

Table 1 ENGINE AND CHASSIS NUMBERS

Year	Engine serial No. start to end	Frame serial No.start to end
1985		
49-state	SC18E-2000078-2006602	SC180-FA002276-006775
California	SC18E-2000058-2004920	SC181-FA002001-005150
1986		
49-state	SC18E-2100014-on	SC180-GA100100-on
California	SC18E-2100382-on	SC181-GA102191-on
1987		
49-state	SC18E-2200048-2204876	SC180-HA200101-204915
California	SC18E-2200051-2202477	SC181-HA200104-204610
1988		
49-state	SC18E-2300001-2304945	SC180-JA300101-304552
California	SC18E-2300025-2305071	SC181-JA300101-300703
1989		
49-state	SC18E-2400001-2403014	SC180-KA400001-402630
California	SC18E-2400851-2401814	SC181-KA400001-400580
1990		
49-state	SC18E-2500001-on	SC180-LA500001-on
California	SC18E-2500361-on	SC181-LA500001-on
1991	*	
1992	SC18E-2600001-on	SC181-NA600001-on
1993	SC18E-2700001-on	SC181-PA700001-on
1994	SC18E-2800001-on	SC181-RA800001-on
1995		
49-state	SC18E-2900001-on	SC180-SA900001-on
California	SC18E-2900001-on	SC181-SA900001-on
1996		
49-state	SC18E-3000001-on	SC180-TA000001-on
California	SC18E-3000001-on	SC181-TA000001-on

*Discontinued

Table 4 DECIMAL AND METRIC EQUIVALENTS

Fractions	Decimal in.	Metric mm	Fractions	Decimal in.	Metric mm
1/64	0.015625	0.39688	25/64	0.390625	9.92187
1/32	0.03125	0.79375	13/32	0.40625	10.31875
3/64	0.046875	1.19062	27/64	0.421875	10.71562
1/16	0.0625	1.58750	7/16	0.4375	11.11250
5/64	0.078125	1.98437	29/64	0.453125	11.50937
3/32	0.09375	2.38125	15/32	0.46875	11.90625
7/64	0.109375	2.77812	31/64	0.484375	12.30312
1/8	0.125	3.1750	1/2	0.500	12.70000
9/64	0.140625	3.57187	33/64	0.515625	13.09687
5/32	0.15625	3.96875	17/32	0.53125	13.49375
11/64	0.171875	4.36562	35/64	0.546875	13.89062
3/16	0.1875	4.76250	9/16	0.5625	14.28750
13/64	0.203125	5.15937	37/64	0.578125	14.68437
7/32	0.21875	5.55625	19/32	0.59375	15.08125
15/64	0.234375	5.95312	39/64	0.609375	15.47812
1/4	0.250	6.35000	5/8	0.625	15.87500
17/64	0.265625	6.74687	41/64	0.640625	16.27187
9/32	0.28125	7.14375	21/32	0.65625	16.66875
19/64	0.296875	7.54062	43/64	0.671875	17.06562
5/16	0.3125	7.93750	11/16	0.6875	17.46250
21/64	0.328125	8.33437	45/64	0.703125	17.85937
11/32	0.34375	8.73125	23/32	0.71875	18.25625
23/64	0.359375	9.12812	47/64	0.734375	18.65312
3/8	0.375	9.52500	3/4	0.750	19.05000

Table 4 DECIMAL AND METRIC EQUIVALENTS (continued)

Fractions	Decimal in.	Metric mm	Fractions	Decimal in.	Metric mm
49/64	0.765625	19.44687	57/64	0.890625	22.62187
25/32	0.78125	19.84375	29/32	0.90625	23.01875
51/64	0.796875	20.24062	59/64	0.921875	23.41562
13/16	0.8125	20.63750	15/16	0.9375	23.81250
53/64	0.828125	21.03437	61/64	0.953125	24.20937
27/32	0.84375	21.43125	31/32	0.96875	24.60625
55/64	0.859375	22.82812	63/64	0.984375	25.00312
7/8	0.875	22.22500	1	1.00	25.40000

Table 3 GENERAL SPECIFICATIONS*

Thread size	N·m	ft.-lb.
Bolt or nut		
5 mm	5	3.6
6 mm	10	7.2
8 mm	22	16
10 mm	35	25
12 mm	55	40
Flange bolt or nut		
6 mm	12	9
8 mm	27	20
10 mm	40	29
Screw		
5 mm	4	2.9
6 mm, 6 mm bolt with 8 mm head	9	6.5

*Use these torque figures for all fasteners not individually listed.

Table 4 WORKSHOP TOOLS

Tool	Size or specification
Screwdriver	
Common	1/8 × 4 in. blade
Common	5/16 × 8 in. blade
Common	3/8 × 12 in. blade
Phillips	Size 2 tip, 6 in. overall
Pliers	
Slip joint	6 in. overall
Vise-grips	10 in. overall
Needlenose	6 in. overall
Channel lock	12 in. overall
Snap ring	Assorted
Wrenches	
Box-end set	Assorted
Open-end set	Assorted
Crescent	6 in. and 12 in. overall
Socket set	1/2 in. drive ratchet with assorted metric sockets
Socket drive extensions	1/2 in. drive, 2 in., 4 in. and 6 in.
Socket universal joint	1/2 in. drive
Allen	Socket driven (long and short), T-handle drive and 90°
Hammers	
Soft faced	—
Plastic faced	—
Metal faced	—
Other special tools	
Impact driver	1/2 in. drive with assorted bits
Torque wrench	1/2 in. driver (ft.-lb.)
Flat feeler gauge	Metric set

Table 5 WINDCHILL FACTOR

Estimated Wind Speed in MPH	Actual Thermometer Reading (° F)											
	50	40	30	20	10	0	–10	–20	–30	–40	–50	–60
	Equivalent Temperature (° F)											
Calm	50	40	30	20	10	0	–10	–20	–30	–40	–50	–60
5	48	37	27	16	6	–5	–15	–26	–36	–47	–57	–68
10	40	28	16	4	–9	–21	–33	–46	–58	–70	–83	–95
15	36	22	9	–5	–18	–36	–45	–58	–72	–85	–99	–112
20	32	18	4	–10	–25	–39	–53	–67	–82	–96	–110	–124
25	30	16	0	–15	–29	–44	–59	–74	–88	–104	–118	–133
30	28	13	–2	–18	–33	–48	–63	–79	–94	–109	–125	–140
35	27	11	–4	–20	–35	–49	–67	–82	–98	–113	–129	–145
40	26	10	–6	–21	–37	–53	–69	–85	–100	–116	–132	–148

*

Little Danger
(for properly clothed person)

Increasing Danger | **Great Danger**

• Danger from freezing of exposed flesh •

* Wind speeds greater than 40 mph have little additional effect

CHAPTER TWO

TROUBLESHOOTING

Diagnosing mechanical problems is relatively simple if you use orderly procedures and keep a few basic principles in mind. The first step in any troubleshooting procedure is to define the symptoms as closely as possible and then localize the problem. Subsequent steps involve testing and analyzing those areas which could cause the symptoms. A haphazard approach may eventually solve the problem, but it can be very costly in terms of wasted time and unnecessary parts replacement.

Proper lubrication, maintenance and periodic tune-ups as described in Chapter Three will reduce the necessity for troubleshooting. Even with the best of care, however, a motorcycle is prone to problems which will require troubleshooting.

Never assume anything. Do not overlook the obvious. If you are riding along and the engine suddenly quits, check the easiest, most accessible problem spots first. Is there gasoline in the tank? Is the fuel shutoff valve in the ON position? Has one of the spark plug wires fallen off?

If nothing obvious turns up in a quick check, look a little further. Learning to recognize and describe symptoms will make repairs easier for you or a mechanic at the shop. Describe problems accurately and fully. Saying "it won't run" isn't the same thing as saying "it quit climbing a hill and won't start," or

"it sat in my garage for 3 months and then wouldn't start."

Gather as many symptoms as possible to aid in diagnosis. Note whether the engine lost power gradually or all at once, what color smoke came from the exhaust and so on. Remember that the more complicated a machine is, the easier it is to troubleshoot because symptoms point to specific problems.

After the symptoms are defined, areas which could cause problems are tested and analyzed. Guessing at the cause of a problem may provide the solution, but it can easily lead to frustration, wasted time and a series of expensive, unnecessary parts replacements.

You do not need fancy equipment or complicated test gear to determine whether repairs can be attempted at home. A few simple checks could save a large repair bill and lost time while the bike sits in a dealer's service department. On the other hand, be realistic and do not attempt repairs beyond your abilities. Service departments tend to charge heavily for putting together a disassembled engine that may have been abused. Some won't even take on such a job—so use common sense, don't get in over your head.

OPERATING REQUIREMENTS

An engine needs 3 basics to run properly: correct fuel/air mixture, compression and a spark at the right time. If one basic requirement is missing, the engine will not run. Four-stroke engine operating principles are described in Chapter Four under *Engine Principles*. The ignition system is the weakest link of the 3 basics. More problems result from ignition breakdowns than from any other source. Keep that in mind before you begin tampering with carburetor adjustments and the like.

If a bike has been sitting for any length of time and refuses to start, check and clean the spark plugs. Check the condition of the battery to make sure it has an adequate charge. If these are okay, then look to the gasoline delivery system. This includes the tank, fuel shutoff valve, fuel pump and fuel lines to the carburetors. If your bike has a steel tank, rust may have formed in the tank, obstructing fuel flow. Gasoline deposits may have gummed up carburetor jets and air passages. Gasoline tends to lose its potency after standing for long periods. Condensation may contaminate it with water. Drain the old gas and try starting with a fresh tankful.

TROUBLESHOOTING INSTRUMENTS

Chapter One lists the instruments needed and detailed instruction on their use.

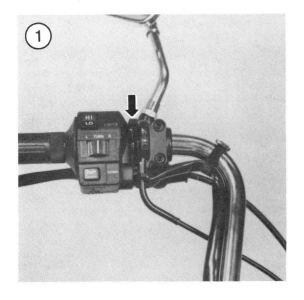

STARTING THE ENGINE

When your engine refuses to start, frustration can cause you to forget basic starting principles and procedures. The following outline will guide you through basic starting procedures.

An ignition control system is installed on all 1100 Shadow models that consists of an ignition control unit, neutral indicator light, neutral switch and a sidestand switch. When the ignition switch and the engine stop switch are ON, the ignition will produce a spark for starting only if the following conditions exist:

    a. The sidestand is up (the sidestand switch is ON). The engine will start if the transmission is in gear and the clutch lever is pulled in.

    b. The transmission is in neutral (the neutral switch is ON).

Always allow the engine to warm up sufficiently before riding off. Do not rev or accelerate hard with a cold engine as this may cause premature engine wear.

Starting a Cold Engine

1. Shift the transmission into NEUTRAL.
2. Turn the fuel valve to ON.
3. Open the choke (**Figure 1**), move the lever to the down position.
4. Turn the ignition key to ON.
5. Turn the engine stop switch to the RUN position.
6. Position the sidestand up.
7. With the throttle completely *closed*, press the start button.
8. When the engine starts, work the throttle slightly to keep it running.
9. Idle the engine approximately for a minute or until the throttle responds cleanly and the choke can be closed.

Starting a Warm or Hot Engine

1. Shift the transmission into NEUTRAL.
2. Turn the fuel valve to ON.
3. Make sure the choke (**Figure 1**) is closed, move the lever to the up position.
4. Turn the ignition key to ON and the engine stop switch to the RUN position.
5. Position the sidestand up.

6. Open the throttle slightly and press the start button. If the engine does not start, try again with the throttle opened approximately 1/4 to 1/2.

Starting a Flooded Engine

If the engine is flooded, open the throttle all the way and press the start button to turn the engine over until it starts. If the engine refuses to start, check the carburetor overflow hose attached to the fitting at the bottom of the float bowl. If fuel is running out of the hose, the float needle may be stuck open.

STARTING DIFFICULTIES

When the bike is difficult to start, or won't start at all, it does not help to wear down the battery or overheat the starter. Check for obvious problems even before getting out your tools. Go down the following list step-by-step. Do each one. If the bike still will not start, refer to the appropriate troubleshooting procedures which follow in this chapter.

1. Is there fuel in the tank? Remove the filler cap and rock the bike from side to side. Listen for fuel sloshing around.

> *WARNING*
> *Do not use an open flame to check in the tank. A serious explosion is certain to result.*

2. Make sure the fuel pump is operating correctly. Refer to *Fuel Pump Testing* in Chapter Seven. Also make sure the fuel filter is not clogged; replace if necessary.

3. If the engine is getting fuel, is the starter motor turning at its normal speed? If the starter motor is operating properly (adequate engine compression), proceed to Step 4. However, if the starter motor is operating unusually fast or slow, perform the *Compression Test* under *Tune-Up* in Chapter Three.

4. Check that the engine stop switch is in the RUN position. If necessary, test the switch as described under *Switches* in Chapter Eight.

5. Make sure all 4 spark plug wires are on tight (**Figure 2**). Push each one on and slightly rotate it to clean the electrical connection between the plug and the connector.

6. Is the choke lever in the correct position? Refer to *Starting the Engine* in this chapter.

ENGINE STARTING TROUBLESHOOTING

An engine that refuses to start or is difficult to start is very frustrating. More often than not, the problem is very minor and can be found with a simple and logical troubleshooting approach.

The following items show a beginning point from which to isolate engine starting problems.

Engine Fails to Start

Perform the following spark test to determine if the ignition system is operating properly.

> *CAUTION*
> *Before removing the spark plug in Step 1, clean all dirt and debris from the plug base. Dirt that falls into the cylinder will cause rapid piston, piston ring and cylinder wear.*

1. Remove one of the spark plugs from one of the cylinders.

2. Connect the spark plug wire connector to the spark plug and touch the spark plug base to the cylinder head to ground it. Position the spark plug so you can see the electrode.

3. Turn the ignition key to ON and the engine stop switch to RUN.

> *WARNING*
> *Do not hold the spark plug, wire or connector or a serious electrical shock*

may result. If it is necessary to hold the high voltage lead, do so with an insulated pair of pliers. The high voltage generated by the ignition system could produce serious or fatal shocks.

4. Crank the engine over with the starter. A fat blue spark should be evident across the spark plug electrode.

5. If the spark is good, check for one or more of the following possible malfunctions:
   a. Obstructed fuel line(s) or fuel filter.
   b. Leaking head or cylinder base gasket(s).
   c. Low compression.
   d. Engine flooded with fuel.
   e. Choke not operating correctly.
   f. Throttle not operating correctly.

6. If spark is not good, check for one or more of the following:
   a. Weak ignition coil(s).
   b. Weak pulse generator unit(s).
   c. Weak spark unit.
   d. Broken or shorted high tension lead to the spark plug(s).
   e. Loose electrical connections.
   f. Dirty electrical connections.
   g. Loose or broken ignition coil ground wire.

Engine is Difficult to Start

Check for one or more of the following possible malfunctions:
   a. Fouled spark plug(s)
   b. Improperly operating choke.
   c. Contaminated fuel system.
   d. Improperly adjusted carburetor(s)
   e. Loose electrical connections.
   f. Dirty electrical connections.
   g. Weak ignition coil(s).
   h. Weak pulse generator unit(s).
   i. Weak spark unit.
   j. Poor compression.

Engine Will Not Crank

If the engine will not crank because of a mechanical problem, check for one or more of the following possible malfunctions.
   a. Discharged battery.
   b. Defective starter and/or starter gear.

c. Seized piston(s).
d. Seized crankshaft bearings.
e. Broken connecting rod(s).
f. Locked-up transmission or clutch assembly.

ENGINE PERFORMANCE

In the following check list, it is assumed that the engine runs, but is not operating at peak performance. This will serve as a starting point from which to isolate a performance malfunction.

The possible causes for each malfunction are listed in a logical sequence and in order of probability.

Engine Will Not Idle

   a. Carburetor(s) incorrectly adjusted (too lean or too rich).
   b. Fouled or improperly gapped spark plug(s).
   c. Leaking head gasket(s) or vacuum leak.
   d. Ignition timing incorrect.
   e. Weak or faulty spark unit(s) or pulse generator(s).
   f. Improper valve timing.
   g. Obstructed fuel line or fuel shutoff valve.
   h. Low engine compression.
   i. Slow air cutoff valve faulty.
   j. Starter valve (choke) stuck in the open position.
   k. Incorrect pilot screw adjustment.
   l. Clogged air filter element.
   m. Improper valve clearance.

Engine Misses at High Speed

   a. Fouled or improperly gapped spark plugs.
   b. Improper ignition timing.
   c. Improper main jet selection in carburetor(s).
   d. Clogged jets in the carburetor(s).
   e. Weak ignition coil.
   f. Weak or faulty spark unit(s) or pulse generator(s).
   g. Improper valve timing.
   h. Obstructed fuel line or fuel shutoff valve.

Engine Overheating

   a. Coolant level low.

b. Faulty temperature gauge or gauge sensor.

c. Thermostat stuck in the closed position.

d. Faulty radiator cap.

e. Passages blocked in the radiator, hoses or water jackets in the engine.

f. Fan blades cracked or missing.

g. Faulty fan motor.

h. Improper ignition timing.

i. Improper spark plug heat range.

j. Dragging brake(s).

Smokey Exhaust and Engine Runs Roughly

a. Clogged air filter element.

b. Carburetor adjustment incorrect—mixture too rich.

c. Carburetor floats damaged or incorrectly adjusted.

d. Choke not operating correctly.

e. Water or other contaminants in fuel.

f. Clogged fuel line.

g. Excessive piston-to-cylinder clearance.

h. Valve component wear.

Engine Loses Power

a. Carburetor(s) incorrectly adjusted.

b. Engine overheating.

c. Improper ignition timing.

d. Ignition timing incorrect due to ignition system malfunction.

e. Incorrectly gapped spark plugs.

f. Weak ignition coil(s).

g. Weak spark unit.

h. Weak pulse generator(s).

i. Obstructed muffler(s).

j. Dragging brake(s).

k. Improper valve clearance.

Engine Lacks Acceleration

a. Carburetor adjustment incorrect (too lean).

b. Clogged fuel line.

c. Ignition timing incorrect due to ignition system malfunction.

d. Dragging brake(s).

Engine Backfires

a. Improper ignition timing.

b. Carburetor(s) improperly adjusted.

c. Lean fuel mixture.

Engine Misfires During Acceleration

a. Improper ignition timing.

b. Lean fuel mixture.

ENGINE NOISES

1. *Knocking or pinging during acceleration*—Caused by using a lower octane fuel than recommended. May also be caused by poor fuel available at some "discount" gasoline stations. Pinging can also be caused by a spark plug of the wrong heat range and incorrect carburetor jetting. Refer to *Correct Spark Plug Heat Range* in Chapter Three.

2. *Slapping or rattling noises at low speed or during acceleration*— May be caused by piston slap, i.e., excessive piston-to-cylinder wall clearance.

3. *Knocking or rapping while decelerating*— Usually caused by excessive rod bearing clearance.

4. *Persistent knocking and vibration*— Usually caused by worn main bearings.

5. *Rapid on-off squeal*— Compression leak around cylinder head gasket(s) or spark plug(s).

EXCESSIVE VIBRATION

This can be difficult to find without disassembling the engine. Usually this is caused by loose engine or suspension mounting hardware.

CLUTCH

The three basic clutch troubles are:

a. Clutch noise.

b. Clutch slipping.

c. Improper clutch disengagement.

All clutch troubles, except adjustments, require partial engine disassembly to identify and cure the problem. Refer to Chapter Five for procedures.

TRANSMISSION

The basic transmission troubles are:

a. Excessive gear noise.

b. Difficult shifting.

c. Gears pop out of mesh.

d. Incorrect shift lever operation.

Transmission symptoms are sometimes hard to distinguish from clutch symptoms. Be sure that the clutch is not causing the trouble before working on the transmission.

IGNITION SYSTEM

All Shadow models are equipped with a capacitor discharge ignition (CDI) system. This solid state system uses no contact breaker point or other moving parts. Because of the solid state design, problems with the capacitor discharge system are relatively few. However, when problems arise they stem from one of the following:

a. Weak spark.

b. No spark.

It is possible to check CDI systems that:

a. Do not spark.

b. Have broken or damaged wires.

c. Have a weak spark.

It is difficult to check CDI system that malfunction due to:

a. Vibration problems.

b. Components that malfunction only when the engine is hot or under a load.

1. Disconnect the engine stop switch and see if the problem still exists.

2. Make sure that the alternator stator plate screws are tight. If the screws are loose, recheck the ignition timing as described in Chapter Three.

3. Make sure the connectors are connected properly. If necessary, clean the connectors with aerosol electrical contact cleaner.

4. Check the alternator stator plate for cracks or damage that would cause the coils to be out of alignment.

5. If you cannot locate the problem, refer to *Ignition System Troubleshooting* in Chapter Eight.

FRONT SUSPENSION AND STEERING

Poor handling may be caused by improper front or rear tire pressure, a damaged or bent frame or front steering components, worn swing arm bushings, worn wheel bearings or dragging brakes.

BRAKES

Front Disc Brake

The front disc brake is critical to riding performance and safety. It should be inspected frequently and any problems located and repaired immediately. When replacing or refilling the brake fluid, use only DOT 4 brake fluid from a closed and sealed container. See Chapter Twelve for additional information concerning brake fluid and disc brake service.

CHAPTER THREE

LUBRICATION, MAINTENANCE AND TUNE-UP

A motorcycle, even in normal use, is subjected to tremendous heat, stress and vibration. When neglected, any bike becomes unreliable and actually dangerous to ride.

To gain the utmost in safety, performance and useful life from the Honda Shadow, it is necessary to make periodic inspections and adjustments. Frequently minor problems are found during these inspections that are simple and inexpensive to correct at the time. If they are not found and corrected at this time, they could lead to major and more expensive problems later on.

Start by doing simple tune-up, lubrication and maintenance. Tackle more involved jobs as you become more acquainted with the bike.

This chapter explains lubrication, maintenance and tune-up procedures required for the Honda 1100 cc Shadow V-Twin.

Table 1 is a suggested factory maintenance schedule. **Tables 1-9** are located at the end of this chapter.

ROUTINE CHECKS

The following simple checks should be performed at each stop at a service station for gas.

Engine Oil Level

Refer to *Engine Oil Level Check* under *Periodic Lubrication* in this chapter.

Coolant Level

Check the coolant level when the engine has warmed up to normal operating temperature.

Check the level in the coolant reserve tank. The level should be between the "UPPER" and "LOWER" marks (**Figure 1**). If necessary, add coolant to the reserve tank fill cap (not the radiator filler cap) so the level is to the "UPPER" mark.

General Inspection

1. Quickly inspect the engine for signs of oil, fuel or coolant leakage.

2. Check the tires for embedded stones. Pry them out with a suitable tool from your tool kit.

3. Make sure all lights work.

NOTE
At least check the brake light. It can burn out at any time. Motorists cannot

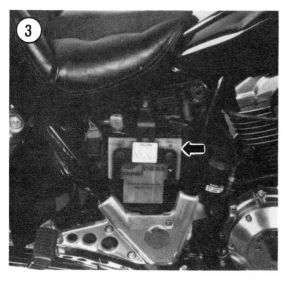

stop as quickly as you and need all the warning you can give.

Tire Pressure

Tire pressure must be checked with the tires cold. Correct tire pressure varies with the load you are carrying. See **Table 2**.

Battery

Remove the frame right-hand side cover (**Figure 2**) and check the battery electrolyte level. The level must be between the upper and lower level marks on the case (**Figure 3**).

For complete details see *Battery Removal, Installation and Electrolyte Level Check* in this chapter.

Check the level more frequently in hot weather; electrolyte will evaporate rapidly as heat increases.

Lights and Horn

With the engine running, check the following.
1. Pull the front brake lever on and check that the brake light comes on.
2. Push the rear brake pedal down and check that the brake light comes on soon after you have begun depressing the pedal.
3. Press the headlight dimmer switch to both the HI and LO positions and check to see that both headlight elements are working.
4. Turn the turn signal switch to the left and right positions and check that all 4 turn signals are working.
5. Push the horn button and make sure that the horn blows loudly.
6. If the horn or any of the lights failed to operate properly, refer to Chapter Eight.

PRE-CHECKS

The following checks should be performed prior to the first ride of the day.
1. Inspect all fuel lines and fittings for wetness.
2. Make sure the fuel tank is full of fresh gasoline.
3. Make sure the engine oil level is correct.
4. Inspect the coolant level in the coolant reserve tank.

5. Check the operation of the clutch and if necessary, add hydraulic fluid to the clutch master cylinder, or bleed the system as described in Chapter Five.

6. Check the operation of the front brake. Add hydraulic fluid to the front brake master cylinder if necessary as described in this chapter.

7. Check the rear brake, make sure it operates properly with no binding. Add hydraulic fluid to the rear brake master cylinder if necessary as described in this chapter.

8. Check the throttle, make sure it operates properly with no binding.

9. Inspect the front and rear suspension; make sure it has a good solid feel with no looseness.

10. Check tire pressure. Refer to **Table 2**.

11. On 1985-1986 models, check the air pressure in the front forks. Refer to **Table 3**.

12. Check the exhaust system for damage.

13. Check the tightness of all fasteners, especially engine mounting hardware.

SERVICE INTERVALS

The services and intervals shown in **Table 1** are recommended by the Honda factory. Strict adherence to these recommendations will ensure long service from the Honda. If the bike is run in an area of high humidity, the lubrication services must be done more frequently to prevent possible rust damage.

For convenience when maintaining your motorcycle, most of the services shown in **Table 1** are described in this chapter. However, some procedures which require more than minor disassembly or adjustment are covered elsewhere in the appropriate chapter.

TIRES AND WHEELS

Tire Pressure

Tire pressure should be checked and adjusted to maintain the smoothness of the tire, good traction and handling and to get the maximum life out of the tire. A simple, accurate gauge (**Figure 4**) can be purchased for a few dollars and should be carried in your motorcycle tool kit. The appropriate tire pressures are shown in **Table 2**.

NOTE
*After checking and adjusting the air pressure, make sure to reinstall the valve stem cap (**Figure 5**). The cap prevents small pebbles and dirt from collecting in the valve stem; this could allow air leakage or result in incorrect tire pressure readings.*

Tire Inspection

The tires take a lot of punishment so inspect them periodically for excessive wear, cuts, abrasions, etc. If you find a nail or other object in the tire, mark its location with a light crayon prior to removing it. This will help locate the hole for repair. Refer to Chapter Ten for tire changing, repair and balancing information.

Check local traffic regulations concerning minimum tread depth. Measure the tread depth at the

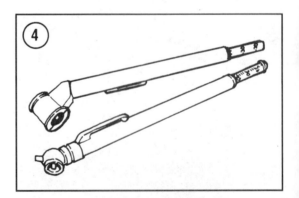

center of the tire and to the center of the tire tread (**Figure 6**) using a tread depth gauge (**Figure 7**) or small ruler. Honda recommends that original equipment tires be replaced when the front tire tread depth is 1.5 mm (1/16 in.) or less, when the rear tread depth is 2.0 mm (3/32 in.) or less or when tread wear indicators appear across the tire indicating the minimum tread depth.

Rim Inspection

Frequently inspect the wheel rims. If a rim has been damaged, it might have been enough to knock it out of alignment. Improper wheel alignment can

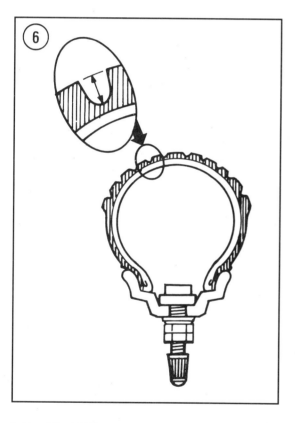

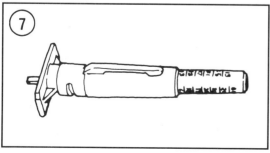

cause severe vibration and result in an unsafe riding condition. If the rim portion of the cast alloy wheel is damaged, the wheel must be replaced as it cannot be repaired.

CRANKCASE BREATHER HOSE (U.S. MODELS ONLY)

Inspect the breather hoses for cracks and deterioration and make sure that all hose clamps are tight.

EVAPORATION EMISSION CONTROL (CALIFORNIA MODELS ONLY)

Inspect the hoses for cracks, kinks and deterioration. Make sure that all hoses are tight where they attach to the various components. For correct hose routing, refer to Chapter Seven.

BATTERY

The battery is an important component in your Honda's electrical system. It is also the one most frequently neglected. In addition to checking and correcting the battery electrolyte level on a weekly basis, the battery should be cleaned and inspected at periodic intervals.

The battery used on your Honda should be checked periodically for electrolyte level, state of charge and corrosion. During hot weather periods, frequent checks are recommended. If the electrolyte level is below the fill line, add distilled water as required. To assure proper mixing of the water and acid, operate the engine immediately after adding water. *Never* add battery acid instead of water; this will shorten the battery's life.

NOTE
Recycle your old battery. When you replace the old battery, be sure to turn in the old battery at that time. The lead plates and the plastic case can be recycled. Most motorcycle dealers will accept your old battery in trade when you purchase a new one, but if they will not, many automotive supply stores certainly will. Never place an old battery in your household trash since it is illegal, in most states, to place any acid or lead (heavy metal) contents in landfills. There is also the danger of the battery

being crushed in the trash truck and spraying acid on the truck operator.

Removal/Electrolyte Level Check/Installation

The battery is the heart of the electrical system. It should be checked and serviced as indicated in **Table 1**. The majority of electrical system troubles can be attributed to neglect of this vital component.

The electrolyte level should be maintained between the 2 marks on the battery case (**Figure 3**). If the electrolyte level is low, remove the battery from the bike so it can be thoroughly serviced and checked.

1. Remove the right-hand side cover (**Figure 2**).
2. Remove the bolt (A, **Figure 8**) securing the battery holder bracket.
3. Swing the holder bracket down (B, **Figure 8**) and out of the way.
4. Disconnect the battery negative (–) lead (A, **Figure 9**) and then the positive (+) lead (B, **Figure 9**) from the battery.
5. Unhook the battery vent tube (C, **Figure 9**) from the battery. Leave it routed through the bike's frame.
6. Lay several layers of old newspapers on top of your workbench where you intend to place the battery. This will protect the workbench surface if there is electrolyte residue on the sides and bottom of the battery case.
7. Carefully slide the battery out of the frame.
8. Set the battery on the newspapers (**Figure 10**).
9. Wipe off any of the highly corrosive residue that may have dripped from the battery and onto the frame during removal.

> *WARNING*
> *Protect your eyes, skin and clothing. If electrolyte gets into your eyes, flush your eyes thoroughly with clean water and get prompt medical attention.*

> *CAUTION*
> *Be careful not to spill battery electrolyte on painted or polished surfaces. The liquid contains sulfuric acid that is highly corrosive and will damage the finish. If it is spilled, wash it off immediately with soapy water and thoroughly rinse with clean water.*

10. Remove the filler caps (**Figure 11**) from the battery cells and add distilled water to correct the

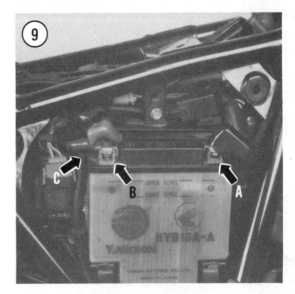

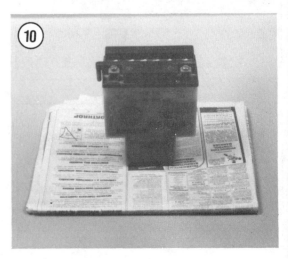

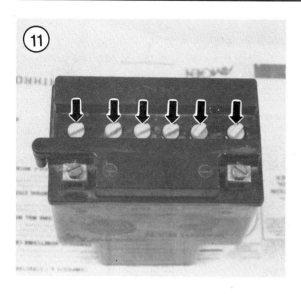

fluid level (**Figure 12**). Never add electrolyte (acid) to correct the level.

NOTE
If distilled water has been added, rein-stall the battery caps and gently shake the battery for several minutes to mix the existing electrolyte with the new water.

CAUTION
*If distilled water is going to be added to a battery in freezing or near freezing weather; add it to the battery, dress real warm and then ride the bike for a **mini-mum of 30 minutes**. This will help mix the just added water into the electrolyte in the battery. Distilled water is lighter than electrolyte and will float on top of the electrolyte if it is not mixed in prop-erly. If the water stays on the top, it may freeze and fracture the battery case, ruining the battery.*

11. After the fluid level has been corrected and the battery allowed to stand a few minutes, remove the battery caps and check the specific gravity of the electrolyte in each cell with a hydrometer. See *Bat-tery Testing* in this chapter.

12. After the battery has been refilled, recharged or replaced, install it by reversing these removal steps. Note the following during installation.

13. Clean both battery terminals (**Figure 13**), elec-trical cable connectors and surrounding case and install the battery in the frame.

14. Coat the battery terminals with Vaseline or pro-tective spray (**Figure 14**) to retard the corrosion and decomposition of the terminals.

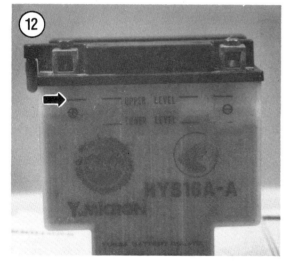

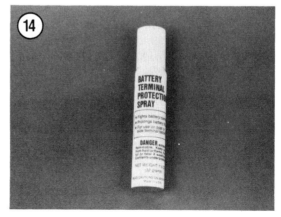

Testing

Hydrometer testing is the best way to check battery condition. Use a hydrometer with numbered graduations from 1.100 to 1.300 rather than one with color-coded bands. To use the hydrometer, perform the following:

1. Remove the battery filler caps (**Figure 11**).
2. Squeeze the rubber ball, insert the tip into the cell and release the pressure on the ball.
3. Draw enough electrolyte to float the weighted float inside the hydrometer. Note the number in line with the surface of the electrolyte (**Figure 15**); this is the specific gravity for this cell.

   a. The specific gravity of the electrolyte in each battery cell is an excellent indication of that cell's condition. A fully charged cell will read from 1.265-1.280, while a cell in good condition reads from 1.225-1.265 and anything below 1.125 is practically dead. Refer to **Figure 16**.

   b. If the cells test in the poor range, the battery requires recharging. The hydrometer is useful for checking the progress of the charging operation. **Table 4** shows approximate state of charge.

4. Squeeze the rubber ball again and return the electrolyte to the cell from which it came.
5. Install the cap onto each cell and tighten securely.

Charging

1. Connect the positive (+) charger lead to the positive (+) battery terminal (or lead) and the negative (–) charger lead to the negative (–) battery terminal (or lead).
2. Remove all filler caps (**Figure 11**) from the battery, set the charger at 12 volts and switch the charger on. If the output of the charger is variable, it is best to select a low setting—1 1/2 to 2 amps.

3. After the battery has been charged for about 8 hours, turn the charger off, disconnect the leads and check the specific gravity. It should be within the limits specified in **Table 4**. If it is, and remains stable for 1 hour, the battery is considered charged.
4. Clean the battery terminals (**Figure 13**), electrical cable connectors and surrounding case and tray and reinstall them in the bike, reversing the removal

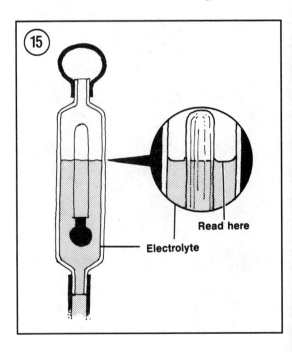

steps. Coat the battery terminals with Vaseline or protective spray (**Figure 14**) to retard corrosion and decomposition of the terminals.

> *CAUTION*
> *Route the breather tube so that it does not drain onto any part of the bike's frame. The tube must be free of bends or twists as any restriction may pressurize the battery and damage it.*

Battery Electrical Cable Connectors

To ensure good electrical contact between the battery and the electrical cables, the cables must be clean and free of corrosion.

1. If the electrical cable terminals are badly corroded, disconnect them from the bike's electrical system.
2. Thoroughly clean each connector with a wire brush and then with a baking soda solution. Wipe dry with a clean cloth.
3. After cleaning, apply a very thin coating of petroleum jelly such as Vaseline or a light mineral grease to the battery terminals before reattaching the cables.
4. If disconnected, connect the electrical cables to the bike's electrical system.
5. After connecting the electrical cables, apply a light coating of Vaseline or protective spray (**Figure 14**) to the electrical terminals of the battery to retard corrosion and decomposition of the terminals.

New Battery Installation

When replacing the old battery with a new one, be sure to charge it completely (specific gravity 1.260-1.280) before installing it in the bike. Failure to do so or using the battery with a low electrolyte level will permanently damage the new battery.

PERIODIC LUBRICATION

Oil

Oil is graded according to its viscosity, which is an indication of how thick it is. The Society of Automotive Engineers (SAE) system distinguishes oil viscosity by numbers. Thick oils have higher viscosity numbers than thin oils. For example, an SAE 5 oil is a thin oil while a SAE 90 oil is relatively thick.

Grease

A good-quality grease (preferably waterproof) should be used. Water does not wash grease off parts as easily as it washes oil off. In addition, grease maintains its lubricating qualities better than oil on long and strenuous rides. In a pinch, though, the wrong lubricant is better than none at all. Correct the situation as soon as possible.

In many cases in this book a special grease called molybdenum disulfide grease is specified. It is used on some parts during engine reassembly and some suspension components. Whenever this type of grease is specified, it should be used as it has special lubricating qualities.

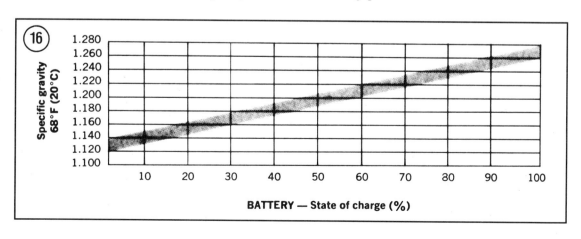

Engine Oil Level Check

Engine oil level is checked with the dipstick located on the right-hand crankcase/clutch cover (**Figure 17**).

1. Place the bike on level ground and on the centerstand.

2. Start the engine and let it idle for 2-3 minutes.

3. Shut off the engine and let the oil settle.

4. Unscrew the dipstick/filler cap and wipe it clean with a lint-free cloth. Reinsert the dipstick/filler cap onto the threads in the hole; do *not* screw it in.

5. Remove the dipstick/filler cap and check the oil level.

6. The level should be between the 2 lines (**Figure 18**) and not above the upper one. If the level is below the lower line, add the recommended type engine oil to correct the level.

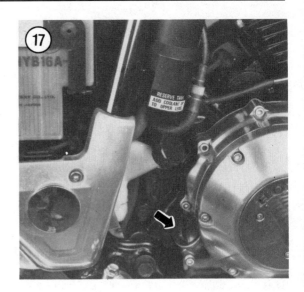

Engine Oil and Filter Change

The factory-recommended oil and filter change interval is listed in **Table 1**. This assumes that the motorcycle is operated in moderate climates. In extreme climates, oil should be changed every 30 days. The time interval is more important than the mileage interval because acids formed by combustion blowby will contaminate the oil even if the motorcycle is not run for several months. If the motorcycle is operated under dusty conditions, the oil will get dirty more quickly and should be changed more frequently than recommended.

Use only a high-quality detergent motor oil with an API rating of SE or SF. The quality rating is stamped or printed on top of the can or plastic bottle (**Figure 19**). Try to use the same brand of oil at each change. Use of oil additives is not recommended as it may cause clutch slippage. Refer to **Figure 20** for correct oil viscosity to use under anticipated ambient temperatures (not engine oil temperature).

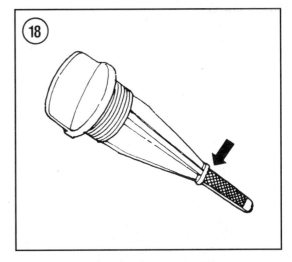

> ### CAUTION
> *Do not add any friction-reducing additives to the oil as they will cause clutch slippage. Also do not use an engine oil with graphite added. The use of graphite oil will void any applicable Honda warranty. It is not established at this time if graphite will build up on the clutch friction plates and cause clutch problems. Until further testing is done*

by the oil and motorcycle industries, do not use this type of oil.

To change the engine oil and filter, you will need the following:

a. Drain pan.

b. Funnel.

c. Can opener or pour spout (oil in cans).

d. 17 mm wrench (drain plug).

e. Strap wrench for the oil filter.

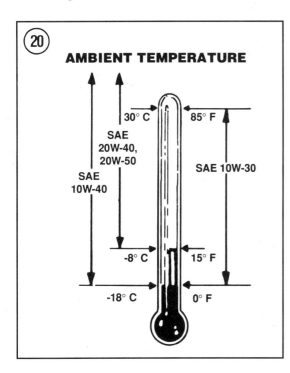

f. 4 quarts of oil.

g. New oil filter.

There are a number of ways to discard the old oil safely. Some service stations and oil retailers will accept your used oil for recycling; some may even give you money for it. Never drain the oil onto the ground.

NOTE
Some service stations and oil retailers will accept your used oil for recycling. Do not discard oil in your household trash or pour it onto the ground. Never add fork oil, brake fluid or any other type of petroleum based fluid to any engine oil that you want to recycle. Most oil retailers may not accept the oil if other fluids have been combined with it.

NOTE
Warming the engine allows the oil to heat up; thus it flows freely and carries contamination and any sludge buildup out with it.

1. Start the engine and let it reach operating temperature; 15-20 minutes of stop-and-go riding is usually sufficient.

2. Turn the engine off and place the bike on the centerstand.

3. Place a drain pan under the left-hand side of the engine so it is under the oil pan drain plug and oil filter.

NOTE
***Figure 21** is shown with some components removed from the engine for clarity. It is not necessary to remove any of these components to gain access to the oil drain plug.*

4. Remove the oil drain plug (A, **Figure 21**).

5. Remove the dipstick/oil filler cap (**Figure 17**); this will speed up the flow of oil.

6. Let it drain for at least 15-20 minutes.

7. Using a nail and hammer, carefully punch a couple of holes in the bottom of the oil filter and allow the oil to drain out of the filter.

8. Inspect the sealing washer on the cylinder block oil drain plug. Replace if its condition is in doubt.

9. Install the oil drain plug and tighten to the torque specification listed in **Table 5**.

NOTE
Before removing the oil filter, thoroughly clean off all road dirt and oil around it.

10. Move the drain pan under the oil filter.

11. Use a strap wrench and unscrew the oil filter (B, **Figure 21**) from the crankcase. Place the used filter in a heavy plastic bag to contain any residual oil. Close off the bag to prevent oil from draining out and properly discard the old filter and bag.

NOTE
Prior to installing the oil filter, clean off the mating surface of the crankcase—do not allow any road dirt to enter into the oil system.

12. Apply a light coat of new engine oil to the rubber seal (**Figure 22**) on the new oil filter and screw on the oil filter. Tighten the filter to the torque specification listed in **Table 5**.

13. Move the drain pan out of the way and pour the used oil into a container as previously mentioned.

14. Insert a funnel into the oil fill hole and fill the engine with the recommended quantity of oil. Refer to **Table 6**.

15. Screw in the dipstick/oil filler cap securely.

16. Start the engine; the oil warning light should go *out* within 1-3 seconds. If it stays on, shut off the engine immediately and locate the problem. Do not run the engine with the oil warning light on.

17. Let the engine run at moderate speed and check for leaks.

18. Turn the engine off and check for correct oil level; adjust as necessary.

Final Drive Oil Level Check

The final drive case should be cool. If the bike has been run, allow it to cool down (minimum of 10 minutes), then check the oil level. When checking or changing the final drive oil, do not allow any dirt or foreign matter to enter the case opening.

1. Place the bike on the centerstand on a level surface.

2. Wipe the area around the oil filler cap clean and unscrew the oil filler cap (A, **Figure 23**).

3. The oil level is correct if the oil is up to the lower edge of the filler cap hole. If the oil level is low, add

SAE 80 hypoid gear oil rated API GL-5 until the oil level is correct.

4. Inspect the O-ring seal on the oil filler cap. If it is deteriorated or starting to harden, it must be replaced.

5. Install the oil filler cap.

Final Drive Oil Change

The factory-recommended oil change interval is listed in **Table 1**.

To drain the oil you will need the following:

a. Drain pan.

b. Funnel.

c. Approximately 130 cc (4.4 oz.) of hypoid gear oil.

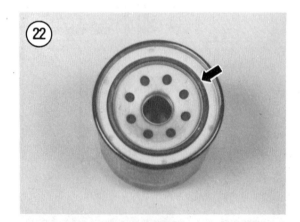

1. Ride the bike until normal operating temperature is obtained. Usually 15-20 minutes of stop-and-go riding is sufficient.

2. Place the bike on the centerstand.

3. Place a drain pan under the drain plug.

4. Remove the oil filler cap (A, **Figure 23**) and the drain plug (B, **Figure 23**).

5. Let the oil drain for at least 15-20 minutes to ensure that the majority of the oil has drained out.

NOTE
Discard old oil as outlined under Engine Oil and Filter Change in this chapter.

6. Inspect the sealing washer on the drain plug; replace the sealing washer if necessary.

7. Install the drain plug and tighten it securely.

8. Insert a funnel into the oil filler cap hole.

9. Add approximately 130 cc (4.4 oz.) of SAE 80 hypoid gear oil.

NOTE
In order to measure the correct amount of fluid, use a plastic baby bottle. These have measurements in cubic centimeters (cc) and fluid ounces (oz.) on the side.

WARNING
*After it has been used for this purpose, do **not** let a small child drink out of it as there will always be an oil residue in it.*

10. Install the oil filler cap.

11. Test ride the bike and check for oil leaks. After the test ride, recheck the oil level as described in this chapter and readjust if necessary.

Front Fork Oil Change

1. On 1985-1986 models, perform the following:

   a. Unscrew each fork top cap cover.

WARNING
Always bleed off all air pressure; failure to do so may cause personal injury when disassembling the fork.

NOTE
Release the air pressure gradually. If released too fast, fork oil will spurt out with the air. Protect your eyes and clothing accordingly.

   b. Insert the tip of a screwdriver on the valve stem (A, **Figure 24**) and bleed off *all* air pressure from both forks.

2. Jack up the bike and place wood block(s) under the engine to support it securely with the front wheel off the ground.

3. Unscrew the fork top cap (B, **Figure 24**) slowly as it is under spring pressure from the fork spring.

4. Place a drain pan under the drain screw (**Figure 25**) and remove the drain screw. Allow the oil to drain for at least 5 minutes. *Never* reuse the oil.

CAUTION
Do not allow the fork oil to come into contact with any of the brake components.

5. Inspect the gasket on the drain screw; replace it if necessary. Install the drain screw and gasket and tighten securely.

6. Place a clean shop cloth around the top of the fork tube and remove the spacer, the spring seat and the fork spring. This will make it easier to refill the fork tube.

7. Repeat Steps 2-6 for the other fork.

8. Refill each fork leg with the specified quantity of DEXRON automatic transmission fluid (ATF) or 10W fork oil. Refer to **Table 7** for specified quantity.

NOTE
In order to measure the correct amount of fluid, use a plastic baby bottle. These have measurements in cubic centimeters (cc) and fluid ounces (oz.) on the side.

WARNING
*After it has been used for this purpose, do **not** let a small child drink out of it as there will always be an oil residue in it.*

9A. On 1985-1986 models, position the fork spring with the closer wound coils toward the bottom and install the fork spring into the fork tube.

9B. On 1987-on models, position the fork spring with the tapered coils at the bottom end and install the fork spring into the fork tube.

10. Install the spring seat and the spacer into the fork tube.

11. Inspect the O-ring seal (**Figure 26**) on the fork top cap; replace if necessary.

12. Install the fork top cap while pushing down on the spring. Start the fork top cap slowly; don't cross thread it. Tighten fork top cap to the torque specification listed in **Table 5**.

WARNING
Never use any type of compressed gas as an explosion may be lethal. Never heat the fork assembly with a torch or place it near an open flame or extreme heat as this will also result in an explosion.

13. On 1985-1986 models, inflate the front forks to the pressure listed in **Table 3**. Do not use compressed air; only use a small hand-operated air pump (**Figure 27**). Install the air valve cap.

14. Road test the bike and check for leaks.

Throttle Control and Choke Cables Lubrication

The throttle control cables and choke cable should be lubricated at the interval indicated in **Table 1**. They should also be inspected at this time for fraying and the cable sheath should be checked for chafing. The cables are relatively inexpensive and should be replaced when found to be faulty.

The cables can be lubricated either with oil or with any of the popular cable lubricants and a cable lubricator. The first method requires more time and complete lubrication of the entire cable is less certain.

Examine the exposed end of the inner cable. If it is dirty or the cable feels gritty when moved up and down in its housing, first spray it with a lubricant/solvent such as LPS-25 or WD-40. Let this solvent drain out, then proceed with the following steps.

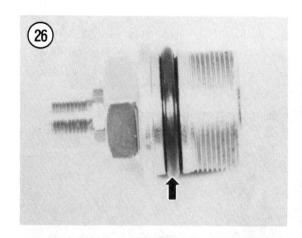

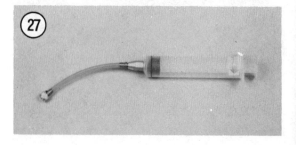

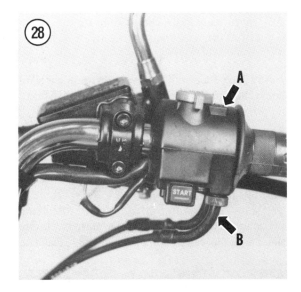

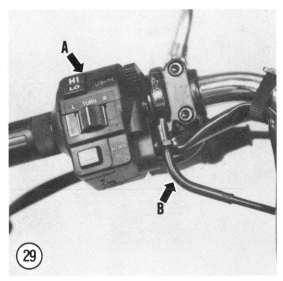

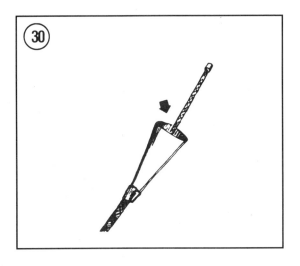

Oil method

1. Remove the screws that clamp the throttle control/switch housing (A, **Figure 28**) together to gain access to the cable ends. Disconnect the cables (B, **Figure 28**) from the throttle grip assembly.

2. Remove the screws that clamp the left-hand switch housing (A, **Figure 29**) together to gain access to the cable end. Disconnect the cable (B, **Figure 29**) from the choke control lever.

3. Make a cone of stiff paper and tape it to the end of the cable sheath (**Figure 30**).

4. Hold the cable upright and pour a small amount of thin oil (SAE 10W-30) into the cone. Work the cable in and out of the sheath for several minutes to help the oil work its way down to the end of the cable.

NOTE
To avoid a mess, place a shop cloth at the end of the cable to catch the oil as it runs out.

5. Remove the cone, reconnect the choke cable and throttle cables and adjust the cables as described in this chapter.

Lubricator method

1. Remove the screws that clamp the throttle control/switch housing (A, **Figure 28**) together to gain access to the cable ends. Disconnect the cables (B, **Figure 28**) from the throttle grip assembly.

2. Remove the screws that clamp the left-hand switch housing (A, **Figure 29**) together to gain access to the cable end. Disconnect the cable (B, **Figure 29**) from the choke control lever.

3. Attach a lubricator following the manufacturer's instructions.

4. Insert the nozzle of the lubricant can into the lubricator, press the button on the can and hold it down until the lubricant begins to flow out of the other end of the cable.

NOTE
Place a shop cloth at the end of the cables to catch all excess lubricant that will flow out.

5. Remove the lubricator, reconnect the cables and adjust the cables as described in this chapter.

Speedometer Cable Lubrication

Lubricate the speedometer cable every year or whenever needle operation becomes erratic.

1. Unscrew the retaining collar (**Figure 31**) and remove the cable from the instrument.

2. Pull the speedometer cable from the cable sheath.

3. If the grease on the cable is contaminated, thoroughly clean off all old grease.

4. Thoroughly coat the cable with a good grade of multipurpose grease and reinstall the cable into the sheath.

5. Make sure the cable is correctly seated into the drive unit in the wheel. It may be necessary to rotate the front wheel slightly in order to seat the cable in the drive unit.

6. Insert the cable into the instrument and screw the retaining collar on securely.

PERIODIC MAINTENANCE

Disc Brake Fluid Level

The fluid level in the reservoir should be up to the upper line (A, **Figure 32**) on the rear master cylinder. If the brake fluid level reaches the lower level mark, the fluid level must be corrected by adding fresh brake fluid.

1. Place the bike on level ground and position the handlebars so the front master cylinder reservoir is level.

2. Clean any dirt from the area around the top cover prior to removing the cover.

3. Remove the screws securing the top cover and remove the top cover (B, **Figure 32**), set plate and the diaphragm.

> *WARNING*
> *Use brake fluid from a sealed container and clearly marked DOT 4 only (specified for disc brakes). Others may vaporize and cause brake failure. Do not intermix different brands or types of brake fluid as they may not be compatible. Do not intermix a silicone based (DOT 5) brake fluid as it can cause brake component damage leading to brake system failure.*

> *CAUTION*
> *Be careful when handling brake fluid. Do not spill it on painted or plated*

surfaces as it will destroy the surface. Wash the area immediately with soapy water and thoroughly rinse it off.

4. Add brake fluid until the level is to the upper level line within the master cylinder body. Use fresh brake fluid from a sealed brake fluid container.

5. Reinstall the diaphragm, set plate and the top cover. Tighten the screws securely.

Disc Brake Lines

Check brake lines between the master cylinder and the brake caliper(s). If there is any leakage,

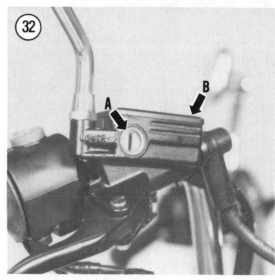

tighten the connections and bleed the brakes as described under *Bleeding the System* in Chapter Twelve. If this does not stop the leak or if a brake line is obviously damaged, cracked or chafed, replace the brake line and bleed the system.

Disc Brake Pad Wear

Inspect the brake pads for excessive or uneven wear, scoring and oil or grease on the friction surface. Look at the pads through top slot at the rear of the caliper assembly. Replace the pads if the wear line (**Figure 33**) on the pads reaches the brake disc.

> *NOTE*
> *Always replace both pads in one or both front caliper assemblies at the same time.*

If any of these conditions exist, replace the pads as described under *Front Brake Pad Replacement* in Chapter Twelve.

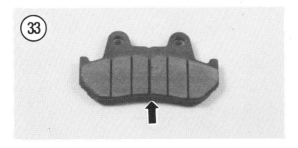

Disc Brake Fluid Change

Every time the reservoir cover is removed, a small amount of dirt and moisture enters the brake fluid. The same thing happens if a leak occurs or any part of the hydraulic system is loosened or disconnected. Dirt can clog the system and cause unnecessary wear. Water in the brake fluid vaporizes at high temperature, impairing the hydraulic action and reducing the brake's stopping ability.

To maintain peak performance, change the brake fluid as indicated in **Table 1**. To change brake fluid, follow the *Bleeding the System* procedure in Chapter Twelve. Continue adding new fluid to the master cylinder and bleeding out at the calipers until the fluid leaving the calipers is clean and free of contaminants.

> *WARNING*
> *Use brake fluid from a sealed container and clearly marked DOT 4 only (specified for disc brakes). Others may vaporize and cause brake failure. Do not intermix different brands or types of brake fluid as they may not be compatible. Do not intermix a silicone based (DOT 5) brake fluid as it can cause brake component damage leading to brake system failure.*

Rear Brake Pedal Height Adjustment

The rear brake pedal should be adjusted as indicated in **Table 1**.

1. Place the bike on the centerstand.

2. Check that the brake pedal is in the at-rest position.

3A. On 1985-1986 models, adjust the pedal height so that the brake pedal is 20 mm (3/4 in.) above the top surface of the front footpeg (**Figure 34**).

3B. On 1987-on models, adjust the pedal height so that the brake pedal is 35 mm (1 3/8 in.) above the top surface of the front footpeg.

4. To change height position, loosen the locknut and turn the adjuster bolt. Tighten the locknut.

Rear Brake Pedal Free Play

Free play is the distance the rear brake pedal travels from the at-rest position to the applied position when the pedal is depressed.

1. Place the bike on the centerstand with the rear wheel off the ground.

2. Adjust the brake pedal to the correct height as described in this chapter.

3. Turn the adjust nut on the end of the brake rod (**Figure 35**) until the pedal has 20-30 mm (3/4-1 1/4 in.) free play.

4. Rotate the rear wheel and check for brake drag.

5. Operate the brake pedal several times to make sure the pedal returns to the at-rest position immediately after release.

Clutch Fluid Level Check

The clutch is hydraulically operated and requires no routine adjustment.

The hydraulic fluid in the clutch master cylinder should be checked as listed in **Table 1** or whenever the level drops, whichever comes first. Bleeding the clutch system and servicing clutch components are covered in Chapter Five.

> *CAUTION*
> *If the clutch operates correctly when the engine is cold or in cool weather, but operates erratically (or not at all) after the engine warms-up or when riding in hot weather, there is air in the hydraulic line and the clutch system must be bled. Refer to Chapter Five.*

The fluid level in the reservoir should be up to the upper mark within the reservoir. This upper level mark is only visible when the master cylinder top cover is removed. If the fluid level reaches the lower level mark (A, **Figure 36**), visible through the viewing port in the master cylinder reservoir, the fluid level must be corrected by adding fresh hydraulic (brake) fluid.

1. Place the bike on level ground and position the handlebars so the master cylinder reservoir is level.

2. Clean any dirt from the area around the top cover prior to removing the cover.

3. Remove the screws securing the top cover and remove the top cover (B, **Figure 36**), set plate and the diaphragm.

> *WARNING*
> *Use hydraulic fluid from a sealed container and clearly marked DOT 4 only. Do not intermix different brands or types of hydraulic fluid as they may not be compatible. Do not intermix a silicone based (DOT 5) hydraulic fluid as it can cause clutch component damage leading to clutch release system failure.*

> *CAUTION*
> *Be careful when handling hydraulic fluid. Do not spill it on painted or plated surfaces as it will destroy the surface. Wash the area immediately with soapy water and thoroughly rinse it off.*

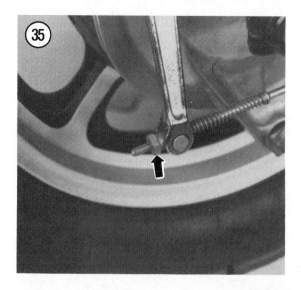

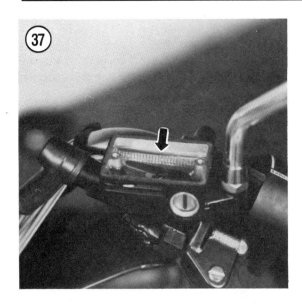

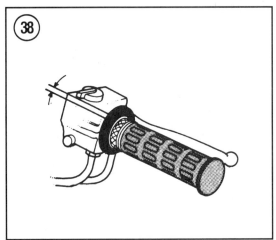

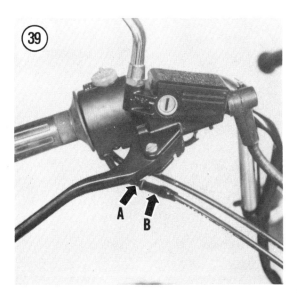

4. Add clutch fluid until the level is to the upper level line (**Figure 37**) within the master cylinder body. Use fresh hydraulic fluid from a sealed hydraulic fluid container.

5. Reinstall the diaphragm, set plate and the top cover. Tighten the screws securely.

Clutch Hydraulic Lines

Check clutch lines between the master cylinder and the clutch slave cylinder. If there is any leakage, tighten the connections and bleed the clutch as described under *Bleeding the System* in Chapter Five. If this does not stop the leak or if a clutch line is obviously damaged, cracked or chafed, replace the clutch line and bleed the system as described in Chapter Five.

Throttle Adjustment and Operation

The throttle grip should have 2-6 mm (1/8-1/4 in.) rotational free play (**Figure 38**).

If minor adjustment is necessary, loosen the locknut and turn the cable adjuster at the throttle grip in or out to achieve proper free play rotation. Tighten the locknut.

Minor adjustment is made at the upper end of the throttle cable as follows:

1. Loosen the locknut (A, **Figure 39**) and turn the adjuster (B, **Figure 39**) at the upper end of the cable to achieve proper free play rotation.

2. Tighten the locknut.

If major adjustment is necessary, perform the following:

1. Remove the screws securing the throttle linkage cover and remove the cover.

2. Loosen the locknut and turn the adjuster at the carburetor end of the cable to achieve proper free play rotation.

3. Tighten the locknut.

Check the throttle cables from grip to carburetor. Make sure they are not kinked or chafed. Replace as necessary.

Make sure the throttle grip rotates freely from a fully closed to fully open position. Check with the handlebar at center, at full right and at full left. If necessary, remove the throttle grip and apply a lithium base grease to all sliding or rotating parts.

Air Filter Element Replacement

The air filter element should be removed and cleaned as indicated in **Table 1**.

The air filter removes dust and abrasive particles from the air before the air enters the carburetors and engine. Without the air filter, very fine particles could enter into the engine and cause rapid wear of the piston rings, cylinder and bearings and might clog small passages in the carburetors. Never run the bike without the air filter element installed.

Proper air filter servicing can do more to ensure long service from your engine than almost any other single item.

1. On 1985-1986 models, perform the following:
   a. Remove the bolts securing the fuel tank cover.
   b. Lift the cover up and disconnect the electrical connectors from the gauges in the cover.
   c. Remove the fuel tank cover.

   NOTE
   Figure 40 is shown with the fuel tank assembly removed for clarity. It is only necessary to remove the fuel tank cover to gain access to the air filter.

   d. Remove the screws securing the air filter cover (**Figure 40**) and remove the cover.
   e. Remove the air filter element from the air box (**Figure 41**).
2. On 1987-on models, perform the following:
   a. Remove both seats as described under *Seat Removal/Installation* in Chapter Thirteen.
   b. Remove the screws securing the air filter cover and remove the cover.
   c. Remove the air filter element from the air box.
3. Discard the air filter element. Honda does not recommend cleaning the air filter element; it must be replaced.
4. Wipe out the interior of the air box with a shop rag dampened with cleaning solvent. Remove any foreign matter that may have passed through a broken element.
5. Install the air filter element into the air box.
6. Make sure the rubber gasket is snug against the mating surface of the air box.
7. Inspect the gasket on the air filter cover. If it is damaged in any way, replace the gasket.
8. Install the air filter cover and secure it with the screws. Tighten the screws securely.
9A. On 1985-1986 models, perform the following:

   a. Position the fuel tank cover next to the fuel tank.
   b. Connect the electrical connectors onto the gauges in the cover. Make sure the connectors are free of corrosion and are tight.
   c. Install the cover and tighten the bolts securely.
9B. On 1987-on models, install both seats as described under *Seat Removal/Installation* in Chapter Thirteen.

Fuel Filter Replacement
(1985-1986)

The inline fuel filter removes particles in the fuel which might otherwise enter the carburetors. This

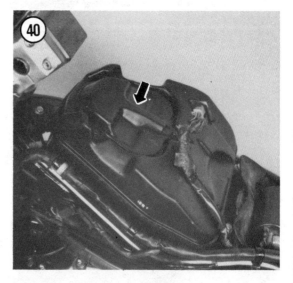

could cause the float needle(s) to stay in the open position or clog one of the jets.

1. Turn the fuel shutoff valve to the OFF position.

2. Remove the left-hand side cover.

3. Remove the voltage regulator/rectifier from its mounting bracket as described under *Voltage Regulator/Rectifier Removal/Installation (1985-1986)* in Chapter Eight.

4. Disconnect the fuel *inlet line* from the fuel pump.

5. Remove the mounting nut securing the fuel filter holder to the bottom of the auxiliary fuel tank.

6. Carefully pull the fuel filter out of the holder.

7. Disconnect the fuel lines from the fuel filter and plug the ends of the fuel lines with golf tees.

8. Remove the golf tees and install the new fuel filter with the directional arrow pointing toward the outlet side or toward the fuel pump.

9. Reinstall the fuel filter into the holder on the bottom of the auxiliary fuel tank.

10. Install the mounting nut securing the fuel filter holder to the bottom of the auxiliary fuel tank. Tighten the nut securely.

11. Turn the fuel shutoff valve to the ON position.

12. Start the engine and check for leaks.

13. Install the left-hand side cover.

Fuel Filter Replacement (1987-on)

The inline fuel filter removes particles in the fuel which might otherwise enter the carburetors. This could cause the float needle(s) to stay in the open position or clog one of the jets.

1. Turn the fuel shutoff valve to the OFF position.

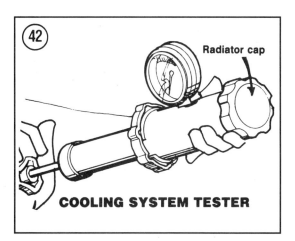

42

Radiator cap

COOLING SYSTEM TESTER

2. Remove the exhaust system as described under *Exhaust System Removal/Installation (1987-on)* in Chapter Seven.

3. Carefully pull the fuel filter out of the rubber mount.

4. Disconnect the fuel lines from the fuel filter and plug the fuel lines with golf tees.

5. Remove the golf tees and install the new fuel filter with the smaller end pointing toward the fuel shutoff valve.

6. Reinstall the fuel filter into the rubber mount.

7. Turn the fuel shutoff valve to the ON position.

8. Start the engine and check for leaks.

9. Install the exhaust system as described under *Exhaust System Removal/Installation (1987-on)* in Chapter Seven.

Fuel Line Inspection

Inspect the fuel lines from the fuel tank to the carburetors. If any are cracked or starting to deteriorate, they must be replaced. Make sure the small hose clamps are in place and holding securely.

> *WARNING*
> *A damaged or deteriorated fuel line presents a very dangerous fire hazard to both the rider and the bike if fuel should spill onto a hot engine or exhaust pipe.*

Cooling System Inspection

At the interval indicated in **Table 1**, the following items should be checked. If you do not have the test equipment, the tests can be done by a Honda dealer, automobile dealer, radiator shop or service station.

1. Have the radiator cap pressure tested (**Figure 42**). The specified radiator cap relief pressure is 73.5-103 kPa (10.7-14.9 psi). The cap must be able to sustain this pressure for a minimum of 6 seconds. Replace the radiator cap if it does not hold pressure or if the relief pressure is too high or too low.

> *CAUTION*
> *If test pressure exceeds the specifications, the radiator may be damaged.*

2. Leave the radiator cap off and have the entire cooling system pressure tested (**Figure 43**). The entire cooling system should be pressurized up to, but not exceeding, 103 kPa (14.9 psi). The system

must be able to sustain this pressure for 6 seconds. Replace or repair any components that fail this test.

3. Test the specific gravity of the coolant with an anti-freeze tester (**Figure 44**) to ensure adequate temperature and corrosion protection. The system must have at least a 50:50 mixture of antifreeze and distilled water. Never let the mixture become less than 40% antifreeze or corrosion protection will be impaired.

4. Check all cooling system hoses for damage or deterioration. Replace any hose that is questionable. Make sure all hose clamps are tight.

5. Carefully clean any road dirt, bugs, mud, etc. from the radiator core. Use a whisk broom, compressed air or low-pressure water. If the radiator has been hit by a small rock or other item, *carefully* straighten out the fins with a screwdriver.

> *NOTE*
> *If the radiator has been damaged across approximately 20% or more of the frontal area, the radiator should be recored or replaced as described under **Radiator Removal/Installation** in Chapter Nine.*

Coolant Change

> *WARNING*
> *Antifreeze has been classified as an environmental toxic waste by the EPA and cannot be legally disposed of by flushing down a drain or pouring onto the ground. Treat antifreeze that is to be discarded as you treat engine oil. Put it in suitable containers and dispose of it according to local regulations.*

> *WARNING*
> *Antifreeze is poisonous and may attract animals. Do not store the drained coolant where it is accessible to children or pets.*

The cooling system should be completely drained and refilled at the interval indicated in **Table 1**.

It is sometimes necessary to remove the radiator or drain the coolant from the system in order to perform a service procedure on some parts of the bike. If the coolant is still in good condition (not time to replace the coolant), the coolant can be reused if it is kept clean. Drain the coolant into a *clean* drain pan and pour it into a *clean* sealable container like a plastic milk or bleach bottle. This coolant can then be reused if it is still clean.

> *CAUTION*
> *Use only a high quality ethylene glycol antifreeze specifically labeled for use with aluminum engines. Do not use an alcohol-based antifreeze.*

In areas where freezing temperatures occur, add a higher percentage of antifreeze to protect the system to temperatures far below those likely to occur. **Table 8** lists the recommended amount of antifreeze for protection at various ambient temperatures.

The following procedure must be performed when the engine is cool.

> *CAUTION*
> *Be careful not to spill antifreeze on painted surfaces as it will destroy the surface. Wash immediately with soapy water and rinse thoroughly with clean water.*

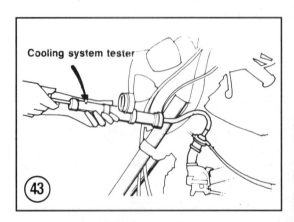
Cooling system tester

(43)

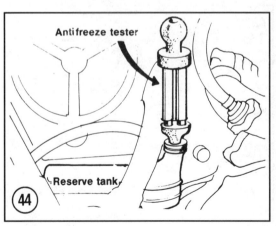
Antifreeze tester

Reserve tank

(44)

1. Place the bike on the centerstand.

2A. On 1985-1986 models, remove the radiator cap cover.

2B. On 1987-on models, perform the following:

    a. Remove the fuel tank as described under *Fuel Tank Removal/Installation (1987-on)* in Chapter Seven.

    b. Remove the right-hand steering head cover.

3. Remove the radiator cap (**Figure 45**). This will speed up the draining process.

NOTE
Figure 46 is shown with some components removed from the engine for clarity. These components do not have to be removed for this procedure.

4. Place a drain pan under the water pump cover. Remove the drain bolt (**Figure 46**).

5. Do not install the drain bolt yet.

6. Take the bike off the centerstand and tip the bike from side to side to drain any residual coolant from the cooling system. Place the bike back onto the centerstand.

7. Install the drain bolt and washer on the water pump cover and tighten securely.

8. Refill the radiator. Add the coolant through the radiator filler neck, not the reserve tank. Use the recommended mixture of antifreeze and distilled water; see **Table 8**. Do not install the radiator cap at this time.

9. Start the engine and let it run at idle speed until the engine reaches normal operating temperature. Make sure there are no air bubbles in the coolant and that the coolant level stabilizes at the correct level. Add coolant as necessary.

10. Install the radiator cap.

11. Add coolant to the reserve tank to the correct level.

12A. On 1985-1986 models, install the radiator cap cover.

12B. On 1987-on models, perform the following:

    a. Install the right-hand steering head cover.

    b. Install the fuel tank as described under *Fuel Tank Removal/Installation (1987-on)* in Chapter Seven.

13. Test ride the bike and readjust the coolant level in the reserve tank if necessary.

Wheel Bearings

There is no factory-recommended mileage interval for inspecting the wheel bearings. They should be checked whenever the wheel(s) is removed or whenever there is the likelihood of water contamination. The correct service procedures are covered in Chapter Ten and Chapter Eleven.

Steering Head Adjustment Check

The steering head is fitted with either loose or assembled bearings. It should be checked as indicated in **Table 1**.

Place the bike up on wood block(s) so that the front wheel is off the ground. Hold onto the front fork tubes and gently rock the fork assembly back and forth. If you can feel looseness, the steering stem must be disassembled and adjusted; refer to *Steering Head and Stem Assembly* in Chapter Ten.

Front Suspension Check

1. Apply the front brake and pump the forks up and down as vigorously as possible. Check for smooth operation and check for any oil leaks.

2. Make sure the upper and lower fork bridge bolts (**Figure 47**) are tight.

3. Make sure the handlebar holder (**Figure 48**) bolts are tight.

4. Make sure the front axle holder nuts (**Figure 49**) or bolt are tight on each side.

> *CAUTION*
> *If any of the previously mentioned bolts and nuts are loose, refer to Chapter Ten for correct procedures and torque specifications.*

Rear Suspension Check

1. Place the bike on the centerstand.

2. Push hard on the rear wheel (sideways) to check for side play in the rear swing arm bushings.

3. Check the tightness of the shock absorber's upper and lower shock absorber mounting bolts and nuts (**Figure 50**).

4. Make sure the rear axle nut (**Figure 51**) and pinch bolt (**Figure 52**) are tight.

> *CAUTION*
> *If any of the previously mentioned bolts and nuts are loose, refer to Chapter Eleven for correct procedures and torque specifications.*

Nuts, Bolts and Other Fasteners

Constant vibration can loosen many of the fasteners on the motorcycle. Check the tightness of all fasteners, especially those on:

    a. Engine mounting hardware.

    b. Handlebar and front forks.

    c. Gearshift lever.

    d. Brake pedal and lever.

    e. Exhaust system.

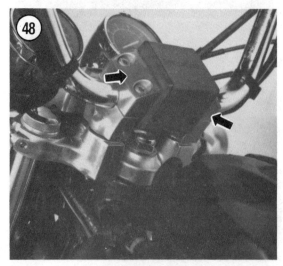

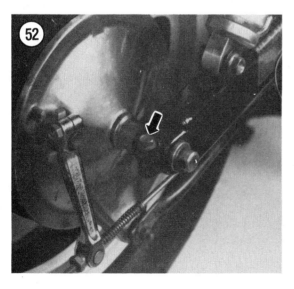

Sidestand Rubber

The rubber pad on the sidestand kicks the sidestand up if you should forget. If it wears down to the molded line, it will no longer be effective and must be replaced.

Remove the bolt and replace the rubber pad with a new one. Be sure the new rubber pad is marked "Over 260 lbs. Only."

Crankcase Breather (U.S. Models Only)

At the interval indicated in **Table 1** or sooner if a considerable amount of riding is done at full throttle or in the rain, the residue in the breather storage tank should be drained.

1. Remove the drain tube from the clamp on the frame.

2. Remove the cap in the end of the breather tube and drain out all residue.

3. Install the cap and make sure the clamp is tight.

TUNE-UP

A complete tune-up should be performed at the interval indicated in **Table 1** for normal riding. More frequent tune-ups may be required if the bike is ridden primarily in stop-and-go traffic. The purpose of the tune-up is to restore the performance lost due to normal wear and deterioration of parts.

Table 9 summarizes tune-up specifications.

The spark plugs should be routinely replaced at every tune-up. Have the new parts on hand before you begin.

The cam chain tensioners are completely automatic and do not require any periodic adjustment. There are no provisions for tensioner adjustment on the engine.

The engine is equipped with a hydraulic valve adjuster train system and requires no periodic valve adjustment. The only time any type of adjustment is necessary is after a cylinder head overhaul; see Chapter Four.

The air filter element should be replaced prior to doing other tune-up procedures, as described in this chapter.

Because different systems in an engine interact, the procedure should be done in the following order:

  a. Replace the air filter element.

  b. Replace the spark plugs.

c. Run a compression test.

d. Synchronize the carburetors.

e. Adjust the carburetor idle speed.

To perform a tune-up on your Honda, you will need the following tools:

a. 18 mm spark plug wrench.

b. Socket wrench and assorted sockets.

c. Compression gauge.

d. Spark plug wire feeler gauge and gaper tool.

e. Ignition timing light.

f. Tune-up tachometer.

g. Manometer (carburetor synchronization tool).

Spark Plug Selection

Spark plugs are available in various heat ranges, hotter or colder than plugs originally installed at the factory.

Select plugs of a heat range designed for the loads and temperature conditions under which the bike will be run. The use of *incorrect* heat ranges can cause seized pistons, scored cylinder walls or damaged piston crowns.

> *NOTE*
> *Higher plug numbers designate colder plugs; lower plug numbers designate hotter plugs. For example, an NGK BP8ES plug is colder than an NGK BP7ES plug.*

In general, use a hot plug for low speeds, low engine loads and low temperatures. Use a cold plug for high speeds, high engine loads and high temperatures. The plug should operate hot enough to burn off unwanted deposits, but not so hot that it is damaged or causes preignition. A spark plug of the correct heat range will show a light tan color on the portion of the insulator within the cylinder after the plug has been in service.

In areas where seasonal temperature variations are great, the factory recommends a "2-plug system"— cold plugs for hard summer riding and hot plugs for slower winter operation.

The reach (length) of a plug is also important. A longer than normal plug could interfere with the valves and pistons, causing permanent and severe damage. Refer to **Figure 53**. The recommended spark plugs are listed in **Table 9**.

Spark Plug Removal/Cleaning

1. Grasp the spark plug lead (**Figure 54**) as near to the plug as possible and pull it off the plug. If the boot is stuck to the plug, twist it slightly back and forth to break it loose.

2. Blow away any dirt that has accumulated in the spark plug wells.

> *CAUTION*
> *The dirt could fall into the cylinders when the plugs are removed, causing serious engine damage.*

3. Remove all spark plugs with an 18 mm spark plug wrench.

> *NOTE*
> *If plugs are difficult to remove, apply penetrating oil around base of plugs and let it soak in about 10-20 minutes.*

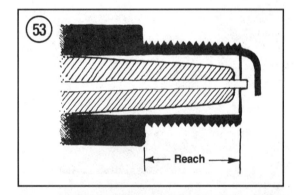

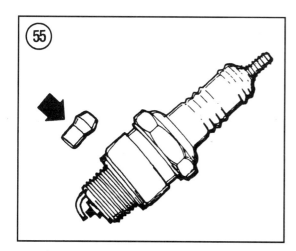

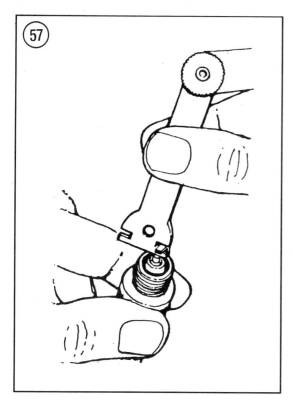

4. Inspect spark plug carefully. Look for a plug with broken center porcelain, excessively eroded electrodes and excessive carbon or oil fouling. Replace such plugs. If deposits are light, the plug may be cleaned in solvent with a wire brush or in a special spark plug sandblast cleaner. Regap the plug as explained in this chapter.

Spark Plug Gapping and Installation

New plugs should be carefully gapped to ensure a reliable, consistent spark. You must use a special spark plug gapping tool with a wire feeler gauge.

Be sure to replace all 4 spark plugs at the same time; all 4 plugs must be of the same heat range.

1. Remove the new plugs from the box. Do *not* screw on the small piece that is loose in each box (**Figure 55**); it is not used.

2. Insert a wire feeler gauge between the center and the side electrode of each plug (**Figure 56**). The correct gap is listed in **Table 9**. If the gap is correct, you will feel a slight drag as you pull the wire through. If there is no drag or the gauge won't pass through, bend the side electrode *with the gapping tool* (**Figure 57**) to set the proper gap.

3. Put a *small* drop of oil or aluminum anti-seize lubricant (**Figure 58**) on the threads of each spark plug.

4. Install the spark plug into a spark plug wrench and extension.

5. Screw each spark plug in by hand until it seats. Very little effort is required. If force is necessary, you have a plug cross-threaded; unscrew it and try again.

6. Tighten the spark plugs an additional 1/2 turn after the gasket has made contact with the head. If you are

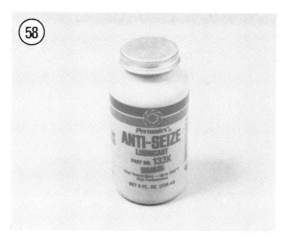

reinstalling old, regapped plugs and are reusing the old gasket, only tighten an additional 1/4 turn.

NOTE
Do not overtighten. This will only squash the gasket and destroy its sealing ability.

7. Install each spark plug lead; make sure the lead is on tight.

Reading Spark Plugs

Much information about engine and spark plug performance can be determined by careful examination of the spark plugs. This information is only valid after performing the following steps.

1. Ride the bike a short distance at full throttle in any gear.

2. Turn the engine kill switch to the OFF position before closing the throttle and simultaneously pull in the clutch or shift to NEUTRAL; coast and brake to a stop.

3. Remove the spark plugs and examine them. Compare them to **Figure 59**. If the insulator is white or burned, the plug is too hot and should be replaced with a colder one.

A too-cold plug will have sooty or oily deposits ranging in color from dark brown to black. Replace with a hotter plug and check for too-rich carburetion or evidence of oil blowby at the piston rings.

If the plug has a light tan or gray colored deposit and no abnormal gap wear or electrode erosion is evident, the plug and the engine are running properly.

If the plug exhibits a black insulator tip, a damp and oily film over the firing end and a carbon layer over the entire nose, it is oil fouled. An oil fouled plug can be cleaned, but it is better to replace it.

If any one plug is found unsatisfactory, discard and replace all plugs.

Ignition Timing

The Honda V-Twin Shadows are equipped with a digital transistorized ignition system. This system uses no breaker points and is non-adjustable and there are no provisions for inspecting ignition timing.

If any component of the ignition system is not functioning correctly, it can cause a drastic loss of engine performance and efficiency. It may also cause overheating.

If you feel that any portion of the ignition system is not operating correctly, check all electrical connections related to the ignition system. Make sure all connections are tight and free of corrosion and that all ground connections are tight.

If the system is still not operating correctly, refer to Chapter Eight and check the spark unit(s) and the pulse generator. There is no method for adjusting ignition timing.

Compression Test

At every other tune-up, check cylinder compression. Record the results and compare them at the next tune-up. A running record will show trends in deterioration so that corrective action can be taken before complete failure.

The results, when properly interpreted, can indicate general cylinder, piston ring and valve condition.

1. Warm the engine to normal operating temperature. Shut the engine off. Make sure that the choke valve is completely open and that the engine stop switch is in the OFF position.

2. Place the bike on the centerstand.

3. Disconnect the spark plug wires from *all 4 spark plugs*.

4. Remove one of the spark plugs from each cylinder.

5. Connect the compression tester to one cylinder following manufacturer's instructions.

6. Open the throttle completely and using the starter, crank the engine over until there is no further rise in pressure. Maximum pressure is usually reached within 4-7 seconds of engine cranking.

CAUTION
Do not turn the engine over more than absolutely necessary. When spark plug leads are disconnected, the electronic ignition will produce the highest voltage possible and the ignition coils may overheat and be damaged.

7. Remove the tester and record the reading.

8. Repeat Steps 5-7 for the other cylinder.

⑤⑨

SPARK PLUG CONDITION

NORMAL

- Identified by light tan or gray deposits on the firing tip.
- Can be cleaned.

GAP BRIDGED

- Identified by deposit buildup closing gap between electrodes.
- Caused by oil or carbon fouling. If deposits are not excessive, the plug can be cleaned.

OIL FOULED

- Identified by wet black deposits on the insulator shell bore and electrodes.
- Caused by excessive oil entering combustion chamber through worn rings and pistons, excessive clearance between valve guides and stems, or worn or loose bearings. Can be cleaned. If engine is not repaired, use a hotter plug.

CARBON FOULED

- Identified by black, dry fluffy carbon deposits on insulator tips, exposed shell surfaces and electrodes.
- Caused by too cold a plug, weak ignition, dirty air cleaner, too rich a fuel mixture, or excessive idling. Can be cleaned.

LEAD FOULED

- Identified by dark gray, black, yellow, or tan deposits or a fused glazed coating on the insulator tip.
- Caused by highly leaded gasoline. Can be cleaned.

WORN

- Identified by severely eroded or worn electrodes.
- Caused by normal wear. Should be replaced.

FUSED SPOT DEPOSIT

- Identified by melted or spotty deposits resembling bubbles or blisters.
- Caused by sudden acceleration. Can be cleaned.

OVERHEATING

- Identified by a white or light gray insulator with small black or gray brown spots and with bluish-burnt appearance of electrodes.
- Caused by engine overheating, wrong type of fuel, loose spark plugs, too hot a plug, or incorrect ignition timing. Replace the plug.

PREIGNITION

- Identified by melted electrodes and possibly blistered insulator. Metallic deposits on insulator indicate engine damage.
- Caused by wrong type of fuel, incorrect ignition timing or advance, too hot a plug, burned valves, or engine overheating. Replace the plug.

3

9. Install the 4 spark plugs as described in this chapter and connect the spark plug wires.

When interpreting the results, actual readings are not as important as the difference between the readings. Standard compression pressures are listed in **Table 9**. A maximum difference of 100 kPa (14 psi) between the cylinders is acceptable. Greater pressure differences indicate worn or broken rings, leaking or sticking valves, blown head gasket(s) or a combination of all.

If compression readings do not differ between the cylinders by more than 70 kPa (10 psi), the rings and valves are in good condition.

If a low reading (10% or more) is obtained on one of the cylinders, it indicates valve or ring trouble. To determine which, insert a small funnel into the spark plug hole and pour about a teaspoon of engine oil through it onto the top of the piston. Turn the engine over once to clear some of the excess oil, then take another compression test and record the reading. If the compression returns to normal, the valves are good but the rings are defective on that cylinder. If compression does not increase, the valves require servicing. A valve could be hanging open or a piece of carbon could be on a valve seat.

Carburetor Idle Mixture

The idle mixture (pilot screw) is preset at the factory and *is not to be reset*. This pertains to both carburetors. Do not adjust the pilot screws unless the carburetors have been overhauled; refer to *Pilot Screw Adjustment* in Chapter Seven.

Carburetor Synchronization

When the carburetors are properly synchronized, the engine will warm up faster and there will be an improvement in throttle response, performance and mileage.

Prior to synchronizing the carburetors, the air filter element must be clean.

This procedure requires special tools. You will need a mercury manometer (carb-sync tool). This is a tool that measures the manifold vacuum for both cylinders simultaneously. A carb-sync tool can be purchased from a Honda dealer, motorcycle supply store or mail order firm.

NOTE
When purchasing this tool, check that it is equipped with restrictors. These restrictors keep the mercury from being drawn into the engine when engine rpm is increased during the adjustment procedure. If the mercury is drawn into the engine, the tool will have to be replaced.

One additional special tool needed is the carburetor pilot screw adjusting wrench (Honda part No. 07908-KE70000 or 07908-4730000). This tool is used to turn the synchronization screw that is very difficult, if not impossible, to reach with a screwdriver.

1. Start the engine and let it warm up to normal operating temperature. Ten minutes of stop-and-go riding is usually sufficient. Shut the engine off.

2. Place the bike on the centerstand.

3. On 1985-1986 models, perform the following:

   a. Remove the seats as described in Chapter Thirteen.

   b. Remove the bolts securing the fuel tank—do not remove the fuel tank.

   c. Raise the *front* of the fuel tank up and place it on wood block(s).

4. Remove the vacuum plug, consisting of a screw and flat washer (**Figure 60**), from each cylinder head.

5. Connect the vacuum lines from the carb-sync tool, following the manufacturer's instructions. Be sure to route the vacuum lines to the correct cylinder. Most carb-sync tools have the cylinder number in-

dicated on them next to each tube containing mercury.

NOTE
Most carb-sync tools are made for 4-cylinder engines. Use the vacuum lines for No. 1 (front cylinder) and No. 2 (rear cylinder).

NOTE
The No. 1 carburetor has no synchronization screw. The No. 2 carburetor must be synchronized to it.

6. Start the engine and let it idle at the idle speed listed in **Table 9**. If necessary, adjust the idle speed as described under *Idle Speed Adjustment* in this chapter.

7. If the difference in gauge readings is 40 mm Hg (1.6 in. Hg) or less between the 2 cylinders, the carburetors are considered synchronized. If not, proceed as follows.

NOTE
***Figure 61** is shown with the carburetor assembly removed for clarity. Do not remove the carburetor assembly for this procedure.*

8. Turn the synchronization adjusting screw (**Figure 61**).

CAUTION
If your carb-sync tool is not equipped with restrictors, open and close the

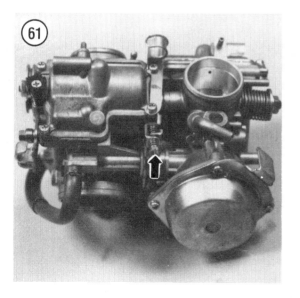

(61)

throttle very gently to avoid sucking mercury into the engine. If this happens, it will not harm the engine but will render the tool useless.

NOTE
To gain the utmost in performance and efficiency from the engine, adjust the carburetors so that the gauge readings are as close to each other as possible.

9. Shut off the engine and remove the vacuum lines and adapters. Install the screws and washers into the vacuum ports in the cylinder heads. Make sure they are in tight to prevent a vacuum leak.

10. On 1985-1986 models, perform the following:

    a. Lower the fuel tank into position and install the bolts and tighten securely.

    b. Install the seats as described in Chapter Thirteen.

11. Restart the engine and readjust the idle speed, if necessary, as described in this chapter.

Idle Speed Adjustment

Before making this adjustment, the air filter element must be clean, the carburetors must be synchronized and the engine must have adequate compression. Otherwise, this procedure cannot be done properly.

1. Attach a portable tachometer following the manufacturer's instructions.

NOTE
The bike's tachometer is not accurate enough in the low rpm range for this adjustment.

2. Start the engine and let it warm up to normal operating temperature.

NOTE
***Figure 62** is shown with the carburetor assembly removed for clarity. Do not remove the carburetor assembly to perform this procedure.*

3. Set the idle speed by turning the idle speed stop screw (**Figure 62**) in to increase or out to decrease idle speed. The correct idle speed is listed in **Table 9**.

4. Open and close the throttle a couple of times; check for variations in idle speed. Readjust if necessary.

> *WARNING*
> *With the engine idling, move the handlebar from side to side. If idle speed increases during this movement, the throttle cables may need adjusting or they may be incorrectly routed through the frame. Correct this problem immediately. Do **not** ride the bike in this unsafe condition.*

5. Shut the engine off and disconnect the portable tachometer.

Table 1 SERVICE INTERVALS*

Every 600 miles (1,000 km) or 6 months	Check engine oil level Check battery specific gravity and electrolyte level Check hydraulic fluid level in brake master cylinder Check hydraulic fluid level in clutch master cylinder Lubricate rear brake pedal and shift lever Lubricate side and centerstand pivot points Inspect front steering for looseness Check wheel bearings for smooth operation Check wheel runout
Every 4,000 miles (6,400 km)	Replace spark plugs Check and adjust idle speed Check and adjust throttle operation and free play Adjust rear brake pedal height and free play Check hydraulic fluid level in brake master cylinder Check hydraulic fluid level in clutch master cylinder Inspect brake pads and linings for wear Inspect crankcase breather hose for cracks or loose hose clamps; drain out all residue Inspect fuel line for chafed, cracked or swollen ends Check engine mounting bolts for tightness Check all suspension components
Every 8,000 miles (12,800 km)	Check ignition timing Replace the air filter element (1985) Check and adjust the carburetors Check and synchronize the carburetors Check and adjust the choke Run a compression test Change engine oil and filter Inspect fuel lines for wetness or damage Inspect the radiator for damage or leakage Inspect entire brake system for leaks or damage Inspect oil level in final drive unit Inspect wheel bearings Inspect the steering head bearings, repack if necessary Inspect evaporative emission control system (1985) Lubricate the speedometer drive cable Lubricate final drive splines Check brake light switch operation Check and adjust headlight aim
Every 12,000 miles (19,200 km)	Replace air cleaner element (1986-on) Inspect evaporative emission control system (1986-on) Change front fork oil Change hydraulic fluid in clutch master cylinder** Change hydraulic fluid in brake master cylinder**
Every 24,000 miles (38,000 km)	Replace fuel filter Change oil in final drive unit Change hydraulic fluid in clutch master cylinder Change coolant***

(continued)

Table 1 SERVICE INTERVALS* (continued)

Every 4 years	Replace all hydraulic brake hose(s) Replace the hydraulic clutch hose assembly

* This Honda factory maintenance schedule should be considered as a guide to general maintenance and lubrication intervals. Harder than normal use and exposure to mud, water, sand, high humidity, etc. will naturally dictate more frequent attention to most maintenance items.
** Change the hydraulic fluid in the brake and clutch system every 12,000 miles (19,200 km) or every 2 years, whichever comes first.
*** Change the coolant every 24,000 miles (38,000 km) or every 2 years, whichever comes first.

Table 2 TIRE INFLATION PRESSURE (COLD)

Tire size	Air pressure	
	Normal	Maximum load limit*
1985-1986 Front 110/90-18 61H Rear 140/90-15 70H	32 psi (225 kPa) 32 psi (225 kPa)	32 psi (225 kPa) 40 psi (280 kPa)
1987-on Front 110/90-19 62H Rear 170/80-15 77H	33 psi (225 kPa) 33 psi (225 kPa)	33 psi (225 kPa) 40 psi (280 kPa)

* Up to maximum load limit of 200 lbs (89 kg) including total weight of motorcycle with accessories, rider(s) and luggage.

Table 3 FRONT FORK AIR PRESSURE (1985-1986)

Normal	Maximum*
0-6 psi (0-40 kPa)	43 psi (300 kPa)

* Do not exceed the maximum air pressure or internal parts of the fork will be damaged.

Table 4 STATE OF CHARGE

Specific Gravity	State of Charge
1.110-1.130	Discharged
1.140-1.160	Almost discharged
1.170-1.190	One-quarter charged
1.200-1.220	One-half charged
1.230-1.250	Three-quarters charged
1.260-1.280	Fully charged

Table 5 MAINTENANCE AND TUNE-UP TORQUE SPECIFICATIONS

Item	N·m	ft.-lb.
Oil drain plug	35	25
Oil filter	18	13
Fork top cap	23	17
Spark plug	14	10

3

Table 6 ENGINE OIL CAPACITY

1985-1986	
Oil and filter change	3.3 liter (3.5 U.S. qt., 2.9 Imp. qt.)
At overhaul	3.8 liter (4.0 U.S. qt., 3.3 Imp. qt.)
1987-on	
Oil change only	2.9 liter (3.05 U.S. qt., 2.55 Imp. qt.)
Oil and filter change	3.1 liter (3.26 U.S. qt., 2.73 Imp. qt.)
At overhaul	3.8 liter (4.0 U.S. qt., 3.3 Imp. qt.)

Table 7 FRONT FORK OIL CAPACITY*

1985-1986	415 cc (14.0 oz.)
1987-1990	442.5-447.5 cc (14.99-15.16 oz.)
1992-on	446.5-451.5 cc (15.10-15.27 oz.)
*Capacity for each fork leg.	

Table 8 ANTIFREEZE PROTECTION AND CAPACITY

Temperature	Antifreeze-to-water ratio
Above –25° F (–32° C)	45:55
Above –34° F (–37° C)	50:50
Above –48° F (–44.5° C)	55:45
Coolant capacity	
Total system	2.20 liters (2.31 U.S. qt., 1.94 Imp. qt.)
Radiator and engine	1.86 liters (1.95 U.S. qt., 1.64 Imp. qt.)
Reserve tank	0.34 liters (0.36 U.S. qt., 0.30 Imp. qt.)

Table 9 TUNE-UP SPECIFICATIONS

Compression pressure	
(at sea level)	
1985-1986	1,100-1,500 kPa (157-213 psi)
1987-on	981-1,373 kPa (143-199 psi)
Spark plug type	
Standard heat range	ND X22EPR-U9 or NGK DPR7EA-9
Cold weather*	ND X20EPR-U9 or NGK DPR6EA-9
Extended high-speed riding	ND X24EPR-U9 or NGK DPR8EA-9
Spark plug gap	0.8-0.9 mm (0.031-0.035 in.)
Ignition timing	
1985-1986	"F" mark @ idle (5° BTDC)
1987-on	"F" mark @ idle (8° BTDC)
Idle speed	1,000 ±100 rpm

* Cold weather climate—below 41° F (5° C).

CHAPTER FOUR

ENGINE

The engine in the Honda 1100 cc V-Twins is a water-cooled, 4-stroke engine with a single overhead camshaft per cylinder. The crankshaft is supported by 2 main bearings and the camshafts are chain-driven from the sprockets on each end of the crankshaft. The camshafts operate rocker arms above each of the 3 valves per cylinder. There is a hydraulic valve adjuster system that eliminates the need for valve adjustment.

Engine lubrication is by wet sump, with the oil supply housed in the crankcase. The chain-driven oil pump supplies oil under pressure throughout the engine.

The starter motor is located just behind the rear cylinder and drives the starter clutch on the alternator side of the engine.

This chapter provides complete service and overhaul procedures for the Honda 1100 cc V-Twin engine. Although the clutch and the transmission are located within the engine, they are covered separately in Chapter Five and Chapter Six to simplify the presentation of this material.

Service procedures for all models are virtually the same. Where differences occur, they are identified.

Table 1 provides complete engine specifications. Tables 1-7 are located at the end of this chapter.

ENGINE PRINCIPLES

Figure 1 explains how the engine works. This will be helpful when troubleshooting or repairing your engine.

HYDRAULIC VALVE ADJUSTER SYSTEM

The hydraulic valve adjuster system is designed to create an automatic zero valve clearance setting throughout the engine's rpm range and to eliminate any routine valve adjustment. Valve clearance remains the same when the engine is cold or hot. The system is basically a tensioning system and does not contain hydraulic valve lifters like those used in many automobile engines.

Each rocker arm is installed on an eccentric rocker arm shaft. The rocker arm shaft has a notch on the top of it where an assist shaft and spring are positioned. There is also a notch on the bottom of the rocker arm shaft that accepts the hydraulic tappet.

①

4-STROKE OPERATING PRINCIPLES

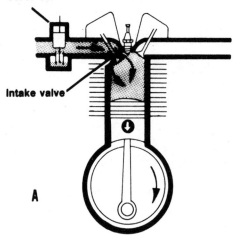

A

As the piston travels downward, the exhaust valve is closed and the intake valve opens, allowing the new air-fuel mixture from the carburetor to be drawn into the cylinder. When the piston reaches the bottom of its travel (BDC), the intake valve closes and remains closed for the next 1 1/2 revolutions of the crankshaft.

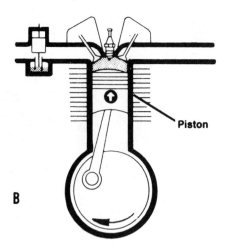

B

While the crankshaft continues to rotate, the piston moves upward, compressing the air-fuel mixture.

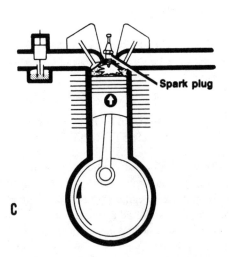

C

As the piston almost reaches the top of its travel, the spark plug fires, igniting the compressed air-fuel mixture. The piston continues to top dead center (TDC) and is pushed downward by the expanding gases.

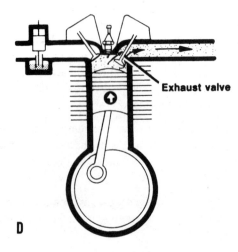

D

When the piston almost reaches BDC, the exhaust valve opens and remains open until the piston is near TDC. The upward travel of the piston forces the exhaust gases out of the cylinder. After the piston has reached TDC, the exhaust valve closes and the cycle starts all over again.

The hydraulic tappets are supplied with air-bled engine oil from the de-foaming chambers in the cylinder head cover. The combined effect of these components is to maintain zero valve clearance.

Refer to **Figure 2** for the following description of the system:

a. When there is no cam lift on the rocker arm, the hydraulic tappet, assist shaft and spring are in the at-rest position (A, **Figure 2**).

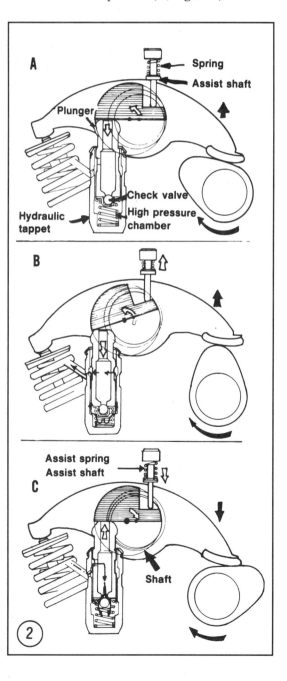

b. As the cam lobe starts to lift the rocker arm, the eccentric rocker arm shaft also moves.

c. This movement of the rocker arm begins to compress the hydraulic tappet, the assist shaft and the spring.

d. When the hydraulic tappet is compressed, the oil pressure in the tappet high-pressure chamber increases and moves the check ball onto its seat and to the closed position.

e. When the cam lobe reaches its maximum lift, the oil pressure within the tappet high-pressure chamber is very high and keeps the check ball closed.

f. As the rocker arm is pressing on the tappet, some of the oil within the high pressure chamber is forced out. This allows the plunger in the tappet to absorb some of the load when the cam lobe is at its maximum lift (B, **Figure 2**).

g. As the cam lobe moves past its maximum lift, the valve springs apply force on the other end of the rocker arm and move the rocker arm back in the other direction.

h. As the rocker arm shaft moves back in the other direction, the springs within the tappet push the plunger upward (C, **Figure 2**).

i. The oil pressure within the high-pressure chamber has now decreased, allowing the check ball to leave its seat. This allows the oil to re-enter the high-pressure chamber.

j. The sequence then starts all over.

SERVICING ENGINE IN FRAME

The following components can be serviced while the engine is mounted in the frame (the bike's frame is a great holding fixture for breaking loose stubborn bolts and nuts):

a. Partial clutch assembly.

b. Alternator and starter gears.

c. Carburetor assembly.

ENGINE

Removal/Installation

WARNING
The engine weighs 92 kg (202 lb.). Due to this weight it is essential that a minimum of 2, preferably 3, people be avail-

able for the removal and installation procedure.

1. Place the bike on the centerstand and remove the seats and the side covers.

2. Disconnect the battery negative and positive leads.

3A. On 1985-1986 models, remove the main fuel tank as described in Chapter Seven.

3B. On 1987-on models, remove the fuel tank as described in Chapter Seven.

4. Drain the engine oil as described in Chapter Three.

5. Drain the engine coolant as described in Chapter Three.

6. Remove the radiator as described in Chapter Nine.

7. Disconnect the spark plug wires and tie them up out of the way.

8. Remove the rear brake pedal assembly as described in Chapter Twelve.

9. Remove the exhaust system as described in Chapter Seven.

10. Remove the carburetor assembly as described in Chapter Seven. After the carburetor assembly has been removed, insert a clean shop cloth into the intake ports to prevent the entry of foreign matter and coolant.

11. Disconnect the coolant pipe (**Figure 3**) from both the front and rear cylinder heads.

12. Disconnect the engine breather hose from the rear cylinder head cover.

13. Remove the ignition coils as described in Chapter Eight.

14. Remove the alternator as described in this chapter and Chapter Eight.

15. Remove all clutch components that can be removed with the engine in the frame; refer to Chapter Five.

16. Remove the clutch slave cylinder as described in Chapter Five.

CAUTION
Do not try to remove the engine with the gearshift spindle still installed in the crankcase. The gearshift spindle sticks out too far and makes engine removal impossible. If it is left in place, it will either be damaged or the crankcase will be damaged in the area surrounding the gearshift spindle.

NOTE
The gearshift spindle guide plug may be very difficult to remove as it is very close to the frame tube. Work it loose and remove it out from the bottom of the engine.

17. Use a large screwdriver on the pry point on each side of the gearshift spindle guide plug (**Figure 4**) and remove the plug. This is a metal plug with an O-ring seal and in most cases is difficult to remove.

18. Partially pull the gearshift spindle (A, **Figure 5**) out of the crankcase and remove the gearshift spindle along with the starter gear (B, **Figure 5**).

19. Disconnect the engine ground strap, the thermo sensor wire, the neutral/OD switch wire, the oil pressure sender wire, the pulse generator and the tachometer sending unit wire connectors.

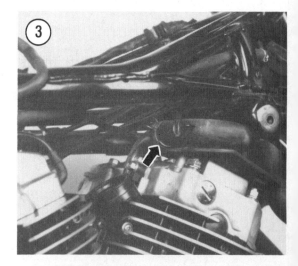

20. On models so equipped, disconnect all tubes relating to the fuel evaporation canister. Refer to Chapter Seven.

21. Take a final look all over the engine to make sure everything has been disconnected.

22. Remove the front through bolt (**Figure 6**) and remove the bolt and spacers (**Figure 7**). Reinstall the spacers and nut onto the bolt to avoid misplacing them.

23. On 1987-on models, remove the 4 bolts securing the front cylinder head to the frame down tubes.

24. Remove the bolts (**Figure 8**) securing the sub-frame and remove the sub-frame.

25. Place a jack under the crankcase. Place a piece of plywood or 2 × 4 piece of wood between the jack pad and the engine to protect the crankcase.

26. Loosen, but do not remove, the rear through bolts and nuts (**Figure 9**).

27. Apply a slight amount of jack pressure up on the engine.

> *WARNING*
> *Due to the weight of the engine, the following steps must be taken slowly and carefully to avoid dropping the engine out of the frame, causing damage not only to the engine but to yourself and your helpers.*

28. Remove the upper and then the lower rear through bolt nuts and then withdraw the through bolts. The engine should now be resting on the jack.

> *CAUTION*
> *The engine assembly is very heavy. This final step requires a minimum of 2, preferably 3, people to remove the engine from the frame safely.*

NOTE
Engine removal from the frame is very tricky. The clearance between the engine and the frame is very close. It will take a lot of "jockeying around" of the engine within the frame in order to get it free from the frame. Take your time and be careful not to drop the engine out of the frame.

29. Carefully and slowly pivot the engine (on the jack) out of the right-hand side of the frame in order to gain access to all sides. Move it out far enough so that everyone can get a good hand-hold on the engine.

30. Slide the engine out of the open frame area on the right-hand side.

31. Place the engine in an engine stand or take it to a work bench for further disassembly.

32. Install by reversing these removal steps while noting the following.

NOTE
Due to the weight of the complete engine assembly, it is suggested that all components removed for engine removal be left off until the crankcase assembly is reinstalled into the frame. If you choose to install a completed engine assembly, it requires a minimum of 3 people.

33. Install all through bolts from the left-hand side.

34. Be sure to install the right- and left-hand spacers (**Figure 7**) on the front through bolt.

35. Tighten the bolts and nuts to the torque specifications listed in **Table 2**.

36. Fill the crankcase with the recommended type and quantity of engine oil and coolant. Refer to Chapter Three.

37. Start the engine and check for leaks.

CYLINDER HEAD COVER AND CAMSHAFT

There are 2 camshafts and 2 cam chains. Each cylinder has one camshaft that operates all 3 valves for that cylinder. There are 2 intake valves and one exhaust valve per cylinder.

There is a cam chain sprocket on the left-hand side of the crankshaft and a separate cam chain sprocket that is splined onto the crankshaft on the right-hand side. Both cam chains are the Hy-Vo type and the engine must be removed and disassembled to remove the chains.

The gaskets used on the upper covers are not the reusable type. The gaskets on the cylinder head cover and cam sprocket cover have an adhesive coating on each side and "self-destruct" when any part is removed from the engine. Purchase these gaskets prior to doing any upper-end service on the engine.

Either cylinder head cover and camshaft can be removed without removing these items from the other cylinder. If both cylinders are going to be disassembled, perform the procedures in the order given.

Refer to **Figure 10** for this procedure.

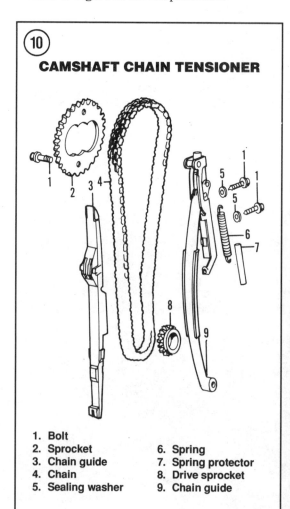

CAMSHAFT CHAIN TENSIONER

1. Bolt
2. Sprocket
3. Chain guide
4. Chain
5. Sealing washer
6. Spring
7. Spring protector
8. Drive sprocket
9. Chain guide

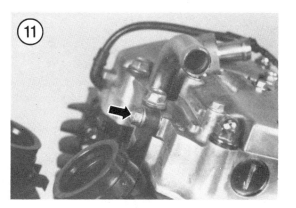

Rear Cylinder Head Cover
and Camshaft Removal

1. Remove the engine as described in this chapter.

2. If not already installed, place a clean shop cloth into the intake ports of both cylinders to prevent the entry of small parts and foreign matter.

3. Remove the bolts (**Figure 11**) securing the external oil pipe to each cylinder head and to the crankcase (A, **Figure 12**). Don't lose the sealing washers on each side of the fitting where the bolts attach. Remove the oil pipe (B, **Figure 12**).

4. Remove the bolts (**Figure 13**) securing the coolant pipe to each cylinder head and remove both coolant pipes.

NOTE
The spark plug sleeve must be removed for cam chain removal. The sleeve can be removed 2 different ways depending on what tools are available.

5A. To remove the spark plug sleeve (**Figure 14**) on each cylinder head without using a special tool:

   a. Select an extra bolt that is 1 1/16 in. across the flats of the head.

   b. Install the bolt head into the sleeve with the threaded portion sticking out.

   c. Attach Vise-grip pliers to the bolt threads and unscrew the sleeve from the cylinder head.

5B. To remove the spark plug sleeve (**Figure 14**) on each cylinder head with the special tool:

   a. Use a K & N rotor puller (**Figure 15**), part No. 82-0150.

   b. Install the puller *backwards* into the sleeve (**Figure 16**).

   c. Use an open-end wrench on the puller to unscrew the sleeve from the cylinder head.

6. Remove the bolts, cap nuts and washers securing the cam sprocket cover and remove the cover and gasket. Refer to **Figure 17** for 1985-1986 models or **Figure 18** for 1987-on models. Don't lose the locating dowels.

7. Remove the bolts, cap nuts and washers securing the cylinder head cover (**Figure 19**) and remove the cover and gasket. Discard the gasket.

8A. If the camshaft holder is going to be disassembled, remove the springs and assist shafts (A, **Figure 20**) from the camshaft holder.

8B. If the camshaft holder is not going to be disassembled, leave the springs and assist shafts (A, **Figure 20**) in the camshaft holder. This will make installation easier.

9. Remove all 4 spark plugs. This will make it easier to rotate the engine by hand in the following steps.

10. Remove the cover cap from the timing hole (A, **Figure 21**).

11. Using a 17 mm socket, rotate the engine using the primary drive gear bolt (B, **Figure 21**).

12. Rotate the engine *clockwise* until the "RT" mark aligns with the fixed pointer on the crankcase cover (**Figure 22**).

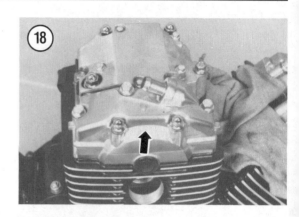

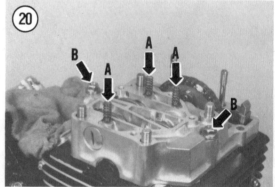

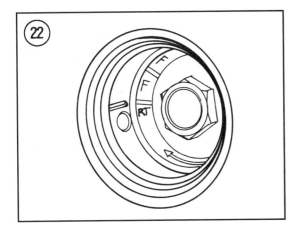

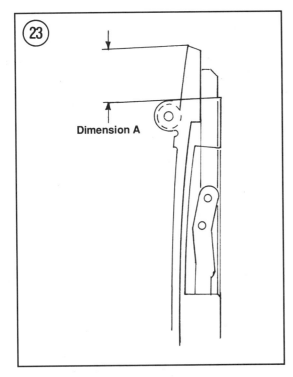

Dimension A

13. Prior to removing any parts, perform the following to inspect cam chain length:

   a. Measure the amount (dimension A) that wedge B protrudes above the top surface of the cam chain tensioner (**Figure 23**).

   b. If dimension "A" exceeds 9.0 mm (0.35 in.), the cam chain has stretched and must be replaced.

14. To achieve the minimum amount of cam chain tension for cam removal and installation, perform the following:

   a. Push wedge B down and pull wedge A straight up until the hole in wedge A is exposed.

   b. Install a 2 mm pin or piece of wire in the hole in wedge A. This will hold wedge A in the raised position.

15. Remove the cap nuts, bolts and washers (B, **Figure 20**) securing the camshaft holder.

16. Partially pull the camshaft holder up.

17. Look between the camshaft holder and the cylinder head and locate the 3 hydraulic tappets. They are next to 3 of the crankcase studs. Carefully remove the camshaft holder but keep the hydraulic tappets and shims in place in the cylinder head.

> *CAUTION*
> *If the hydraulic tappets and any shims come out of their receptacle in the cylinder head, reinstall them into their correct receptacle in the cylinder head. They must be kept in their respective pairs; otherwise, the **Hydraulic Tappet Adjustment** procedure in this chapter will have to be performed before the camshaft holder can be installed.*

18. Remove the hydraulic tappets and shim(s) (A, **Figure 24**) from the cylinder head. Place each tappet and its shim(s) into a container and mark its location—i.e. intake/left-hand side, intake/right-hand side and exhaust. Remember the right-hand side refers to the engine as it sits in the bike's frame not as it sits on your workbench.

> *NOTE*
> *The shims will be either stuck to the base of the tappet or in the receptacle in the cylinder head. Make sure no shims are left in the cylinder head. The receptacle in the cylinder head has a machined recessed dimple in it. If you look into the receptacle and it looks*

4

smooth, chances are the shim is still in place.

19. Remove the dowel pins (B, **Figure 24**) from the crankcase studs in the cylinder head.

20. Remove the rubber grommets (A, **Figure 25**) at each end of the camshaft from the cylinder head.

21. Remove the exposed cam sprocket bolt (B, **Figure 25**).

22. Rotate the engine *clockwise* 360° and remove the other exposed sprocket bolt.

23. Rotate the engine *clockwise* 180°.

24. Slide the cam sprocket and cam chain off the shoulder on the cam.

25. Slide the cam out of the cam sprocket and remove the cam.

26. Remove the cam sprocket and tie a piece of wire to the cam chain. Tie the other end of the wire to an external part of the engine so the cam chain will not fall down into the crankcase.

> *CAUTION*
> *If the crankshaft must be rotated when the camshafts are removed, pull up on the cam chains and keep them taut while rotating the crankshaft. Make certain that the chains are positioned onto the crankshaft sprockets. If this is not done, the chains may become kinked and may damage both the chains and the sprockets on the crankshaft.*

Front Cylinder Head Cover and Camshaft Removal

1. Perform Steps 1-4 of *Rear Cylinder Head Cover and Camshaft Removal* in this chapter.

> *NOTE*
> *The spark plug sleeve must be removed for cam chain removal. The sleeve can be removed 2 different ways depending on what tools are available.*

2A. To remove the spark plug sleeve (**Figure 26**) on each cylinder head without using a special tool:

  a. Select an extra bolt that is 1 1/16 in. across the flats of the head.

  b. Install the bolt head into the sleeve with the threaded portion sticking out.

  c. Attach Vise-grip pliers to the bolt threads and unscrew the sleeve from the cylinder head.

2B. To remove the spark plug sleeve (**Figure 26**) on each cylinder head with the special tool:

  a. Use a K & N rotor puller (**Figure 15**), part No. 82-0150.

  b. Install the puller *backwards* into the sleeve (**Figure 16**).

  c. Use an open-end wrench on the puller to unscrew the sleeve from the cylinder head.

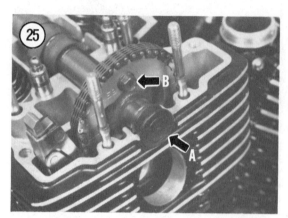

3. Remove the bolts, cap nuts and washers securing the cam sprocket cover (**Figure 27**) and remove the cover and gasket. Don't lose the locating dowels.

4. Remove the bolts, cap nuts and washers securing the cylinder head cover (**Figure 28**) and remove the cover and gasket.

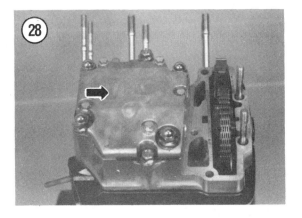

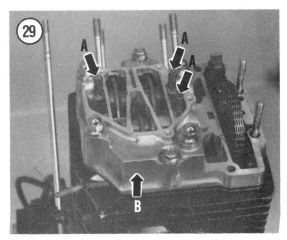

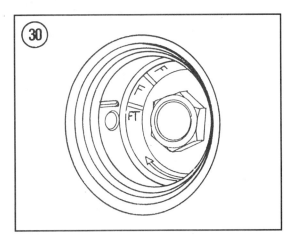

5A. If the camshaft holder is going to be disassembled, remove the springs and assist shafts (A, **Figure 29**) from the camshaft holder.

5B. If the camshaft holder is not going to be disassembled, leave the springs and assist shafts (A, **Figure 29**) in the camshaft holder. This will make installation easier.

6. Remove all 4 spark plugs (this will make it easier to rotate the engine by hand).

7. Remove the cap from the timing hole cover (A, **Figure 21**).

8. Using a 17 mm socket, rotate the engine using the primary drive gear bolt (B, **Figure 21**).

9. Rotate the engine *clockwise* until the "FT" mark (**Figure 30**) aligns with the fixed pointer on the crankcase cover.

10. Prior to removing any parts, perform the following to inspect cam chain length:

    a. Measure the amount (dimension A) that wedge B protrudes above the top surface of the cam chain tensioner (**Figure 23**).

    b. If dimension "A" exceeds 9.0 mm (0.35 in.), the cam chain has stretched and must be replaced.

11. To achieve the minimum amount of cam chain tension for cam removal and installation, perform the following:

    a. Push wedge B down and pull wedge A straight up until the hole in wedge A is exposed.

    b. Install a 2 mm pin or piece of wire in the hole in wedge A. This will hold wedge A in the raised position.

12. Remove the cap nuts, bolts and washers securing the camshaft holder (B, **Figure 29**).

13. Partially pull the camshaft holder up.

14. Look between the camshaft holder and the cylinder head and locate the 3 hydraulic tappets. They are next to 3 of the crankcase studs. Carefully remove the camshaft holder but keep the hydraulic tappets and shims in place in the cylinder head.

CAUTION
*If the hydraulic tappets and any shims come out during the camshaft holder removal, reinstall them into their correct receptacle in the cylinder head. They must be kept in their respective pairs; otherwise, the **Hydraulic Tappet Adjustment** procedure will have to be performed before the cylinder head cover can be installed.*

15. Remove the hydraulic tappets and shim(s) (A, **Figure 31**) from the cylinder head. Place each tappet and its shim(s) into a container and mark its location—i.e. intake/left-hand side, intake/right-hand side and exhaust. Remember the right-hand side refers to the engine as it sits in the bike's frame, not as it sits on your workbench.

NOTE
The shims will be stuck to the base of the tappet or in the receptacle in the cylinder head. Make sure no shims are left in the cylinder head. The receptacle in the cylinder head has a machined recessed dimple in it. If you look into the receptacle and it looks smooth, chances are the shim is still in place.

16. Remove the locating dowels (B, **Figure 31**) from the crankcase studs in the cylinder head.
17. Remove the rubber grommets (A, **Figure 32**) at each end of the camshaft from the cylinder head.
18. Remove the exposed cam sprocket bolt (B, **Figure 32**).

CAUTION
If the rear cylinder head cover and camshaft are removed, Step 19 and Step 20 will require the aid of a helper. When rotating the engine in the following steps, have the helper pull up on the cam chain for the rear cylinder and keep it properly meshed with the sprocket on the crankshaft. This is necessary to avoid letting the chain bunch up and damage the crankcase and chain.

19. Rotate the engine *clockwise* 360° and remove the other exposed sprocket bolt.
20. Rotate the engine *clockwise* 180°.
21. Slide the cam sprocket and cam chain off the shoulder on the cam.
22. Slide the cam out of the cam sprocket and remove the cam.
23. Remove the cam sprocket and tie a piece of wire to the cam chain. Tie the other end of the wire to an external part of the engine so the cam chain will not fall down into the crankcase.

CAUTION
If the crankshaft must be rotated when the camshafts are removed, pull up on the cam chains and keep them taut while rotating the crankshaft. Make certain

that the chains are positioned onto the crankshaft sprockets. If this is not done, the chains may become kinked and may damage both the chains and the sprockets on the crankshaft.

Inspection

1. Check the camshaft bearing journals (A, **Figure 33**) for wear and scoring.

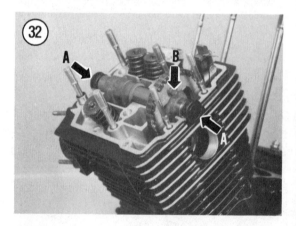

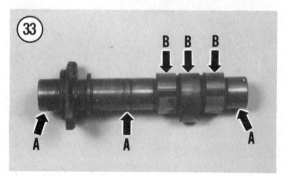

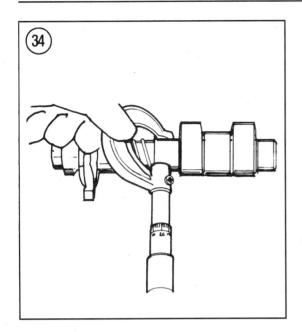

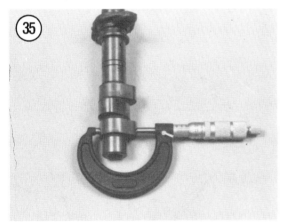

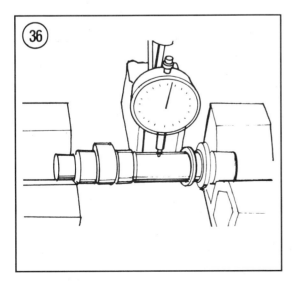

2. Even if the camshaft bearing journal surface appears to be satisfactory, with no visible signs of wear, the camshaft bearing journal must be measured with a micrometer as shown in **Figure 34**. Replace the camshaft(s) if worn beyond the service limits listed in **Table 1**.

3. Check the camshaft lobes for wear (B, **Figure 33**). The lobes should not be scored and the edges should be square. Slight damage may be removed with a silicone carbide oilstone. Use No. 100-200 grit initially, then polish with a No. 280-320 grit.

4. Even if the camshaft lobe surface appears to be satisfactory, with no visible signs of wear, the camshaft lobes must be measured with a micrometer as shown in **Figure 35**. Replace the camshaft(s) if worn beyond the service limits listed in **Table 1**.

5. Measure the runout of the camshaft with a dial indicator and V-blocks as shown in **Figure 36**. Use 1/2 of the total runout and compare to the service limits listed in **Table 1**.

6. Check the camshaft bearing journals in the cylinder head (**Figure 37**) and camshaft holder (**Figure 38**) for wear and scoring. They should not be scored or excessively worn. If necessary, replace the cylinder head and cam holder as a matched pair.

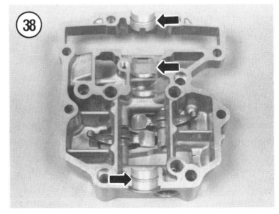

4

7. Inspect the sprocket mounting flanges (**Figure 39**) on the camshaft for fractures or wear, replace if necessary.

8. Inspect the cam sprockets for wear; replace if necessary.

Camshaft Bearing
Clearance Measurement

This procedure requires the use of a Plastigage set. The camshaft must be installed into the head. Prior to installation, wipe all oil residue from each cam bearing journal and bearing surface in the head and all camshaft holders.

Perform this measurement on one cylinder at a time.

1. Install the camshaft into the cylinder head with the lobes facing down.

2. Install all camshaft holder locating dowels into position in the cylinder head.

3. Wipe all oil from cam bearing journals prior to using the Plastigage material.

4. Place a strip of Plastigage material on top of each cam bearing journal, parallel to the cam, as shown in **Figure 40**.

5. Carefully place the camshaft holder into position.

6. Install all camshaft holder bolts and nuts. Install finger-tight at first, then tighten in a crisscross pattern to the final torque specification listed in **Table 2**.

7. Install the cylinder head cover and camshaft sprocket cover.

8. Install all cylinder head cover and camshaft sprocket cover bolts and nuts. Install finger-tight at first, then tighten in a crisscross pattern to the final torque specification listed in **Table 2**.

NOTE
Do not rotate the camshaft with the Plastigage material in place.

9. Gradually remove the bolts and nuts in a crisscross pattern. Remove the cylinder head cover, camshaft sprocket cover and the camshaft holder carefully.

10. Measure the width of the flattened Plastigage according to manufacturer's instructions (**Figure 41**).

11. If the clearance exceeds the wear limit in **Table 1**, measure the camshaft bearing journals with a micrometer and compare to the wear limits in **Table 1**. If the camshaft bearing journal is less than the

dimension specified, replace the cam. If the cam is within specifications, the cylinder head and camshaft holders must be replaced as a matched set.

CAUTION
Remove all particles of Plastigage from all camshaft bearing journals and the camshaft holder. Be sure to clean the camshaft holder groove. This material

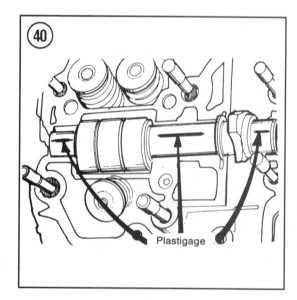

Plastigage

must not be left in the engine as it can plug up an oil control orifice and cause severe engine damage.

Front Cylinder Head Cover and Camshaft Installation

If both cylinder head covers and camshaft holders have been removed, install the *front* camshaft and holder first, then the rear. Each camshaft is marked with an "F" (front) (**Figure 42**) or "R" (rear) on the sprocket boss. Be sure to install the camshaft into the correct cylinder head.

CAUTION
If the rear cylinder head cover and camshaft have been removed, the following

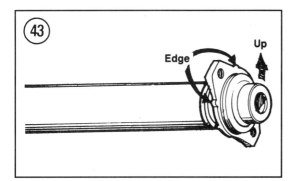

steps will require the aid of a helper. When rotating the engine in the following steps, have the helper pull up on the cam chain for the rear cylinder and keep it properly meshed with the sprocket on the crankshaft. This is necessary to avoid letting the chain bunch up and damage the crankcase and chain.

1. Coat all camshaft lobes and bearing journals with molybdenum disulfide grease or assembly oil.

2. Also coat the bearing surfaces in the cylinder head and camshaft bearing holders.

3. Position the cam sprocket with the index marks facing toward the left-hand side and positioned up and down (90° from the top surface of the cylinder head).

4. Temporarily install the cam chain onto the cam sprocket.

5. Install the cam into the sprocket and cam chain and fill the cam lobe oil cavity in the cylinder head with fresh engine oil.

6. Position the cam with the lobes facing down and the raised edges on the cam sprocket mounting flange facing up (**Figure 43**).

CAUTION
If the rear cylinder head cover and camshaft have been removed, the following steps will require the aid of a helper. When rotating the engine in the following steps, have the helper pull up on the rear cam chain and keep it properly meshed with the sprocket on the crankshaft. This is necessary to avoid causing damage to the crankcase and chain.

7. Using a 17 mm socket on the primary gear bolt (B, **Figure 21**), rotate the engine *clockwise* until the "FT" mark (**Figure 30**) aligns with the fixed pointer on the crankcase cover.

8. Carefully pull the cam chain off of the cam sprocket and rotate the cam sprocket until the index marks are parallel to the top surface of the cylinder head (A, **Figure 44**).

9. Pull the cam chain and sprocket up onto the shoulder on the camshaft. Again check the alignment of the index marks as noted in Step 8. If the alignment is incorrect, correct it at this time.

10. Temporarily install the sprocket bolt into the exposed hole (B, **Figure 44**).

11. Rotate the engine *clockwise* 360° and install the other cam sprocket bolt.

12. Rotate the engine *clockwise* 360° and check for correct cam sprocket alignment as described in Step 7 and Step 8. Readjust if necessary.

CAUTION
Very expensive damage could result from improper camshaft and chain alignment. Recheck your work several times to be sure alignment is correct.

13. Remove the exposed cam sprocket bolt and apply red Loctite (No. 271) to the bolt threads and to the underside of the bolt head. Install the bolt and tighten to the torque specifications listed in **Table 2**.

14. Rotate the engine *clockwise* one full turn (360°). Remove the exposed cam sprocket bolt and apply red Loctite (No. 271) to the bolt threads and to the underside of the bolt head. Install this bolt and tighten to the torque specifications listed in **Table 2**.

15. Clean all oil residue from the rubber grommets and apply a light coat of liquid gasket seal to the portion that seats in the cylinder head.

16. Install the rubber grommets in the cylinder at each end of the camshaft (A, **Figure 32**).

17. Place wood blocks under the crankcase so the front cylinder head is almost horizontal.

CAUTION
The hydraulic tappets must be bled of all air prior to installation or they will not function properly.

18. Inspect and bleed the hydraulic tappets as described in this chapter.

19. Install the tappet shim(s) into their correct receptacle in the cylinder head (**Figure 45**).

20. Keep the hydraulic tappet vertical and install the tappets into their correct receptacles in the cylinder head (A, **Figure 31**).

21. Install the locating dowels (B, **Figure 31**) onto the crankcase studs in the cylinder head.

CAUTION
*In the following step, do **not** apply the liquid gasket sealer to the area around each hydraulic tappet receptacle (**Figure 46**).*

22. Clean the mating surfaces of the cylinder head and the camshaft holder with aerosol electrical con-

tact cleaner. Apply a light coat of liquid gasket sealer to the mating surface of the camshaft holder.

23. Install the camshaft holder, 8 mm bolts, 10 mm cap nuts and washers. Tighten the bolts and nuts in a crisscross pattern in 2-3 stages to the torque specifications listed in **Table 2**.

24. Make sure the assist shafts and springs (A, **Figure 47**) are in place.

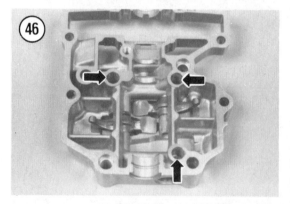

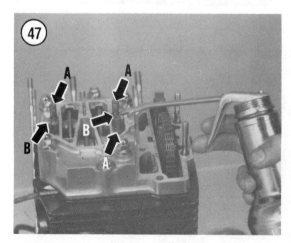

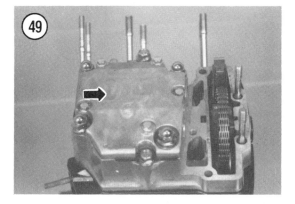

25. Fill both de-foaming chambers with fresh engine oil (B, **Figure 47**). These chambers must be full of oil so the bleed hole in each tappet will be covered with oil. This is necessary so that air will not enter the high pressure chamber in the tappet.

26. Clean any oil residue from the mating surfaces of the cylinder head cover and the camshaft holder with contact cleaner.

27. Remove the protective sheet from each side of the new gasket and install the gasket (**Figure 48**).

28. Install the cylinder head cover (**Figure 49**) and tighten the 6 mm bolts in a crisscross pattern in 2-3 stages to the torque specification listed in **Table 2**.

29. Install the locating dowels and then the camshaft sprocket cover (**Figure 50**) on the chain side. Install the 8 mm bolts, cap nuts and washers and tighten in a crisscross pattern in 2-3 stages to the torque specification listed in **Table 2**.

30. If the rear cylinder was *not* disassembled, perform Steps 30-37 of *Rear Cylinder Head Cover and Camshaft Installation*.

Rear Cylinder Head Cover and Camshaft Installation

Each camshaft is marked with an "F" (front) or "R" (rear) (**Figure 51**) on the sprocket boss. Be sure to install the camshaft in the correct cylinder head.

1. Coat all camshaft lobes and bearing journals with molybdenum disulfide grease or assembly oil. Also coat the bearing surfaces in the cylinder head and camshaft bearing holders.

2. Position the cam sprocket with the index marks facing toward the left-hand side and positioned up and down (90° from the top surface of the cylinder head).

3. Temporarily install the cam chain onto the cam sprocket.

4. Install the cam into the sprocket and cam chain and fill the cam lobe oil cavity in the cylinder head with fresh engine oil.

5. Position the cam with the lobes facing down (**Figure 52**) and the raised edges on the cam sprocket mounting flange facing up (**Figure 43**).

6. Using a 17 mm socket, rotate the engine using the primary drive gear bolt (**Figure 53**).

7. Rotate the engine *clockwise* until the "RT" mark (**Figure 54**) aligns with the fixed pointer on the crankcase cover.

8. Carefully pull the cam chain off of the cam sprocket and rotate the cam sprocket until the index marks are parallel to the top surface of the cylinder head (A, **Figure 55**).

9. Pull the cam chain and sprocket up onto the shoulder on the camshaft. Again check the alignment of the index marks as noted in Step 8. If the alignment is incorrect, correct it at this time.

10. Temporarily install the sprocket bolt into the exposed hole (B, **Figure 55**).

11. Rotate the engine *clockwise* 360° and install the other cam sprocket bolt (**Figure 56**).

12. Rotate the engine *clockwise* 360° and check for correct cam sprocket alignment as described in Step 7 and Step 8. Readjust if necessary.

CAUTION
Very expensive damage could result from improper camshaft and chain alignment. Recheck your work several times to be sure alignment is correct.

13. Remove the exposed cam sprocket bolt and apply red Loctite (No. 271) to the bolt threads and to the underside of the bolt head. Install this bolt and tighten to the torque specifications listed in **Table 2**.

14. Rotate the engine *clockwise* one full turn (360°). Remove the exposed cam sprocket bolt and apply red Loctite (No. 271) to the bolt threads and to the underside of the bolt head. Install this bolt and tighten to the torque specifications listed in **Table 2**.

15. Clean all oil residue from the rubber grommets and apply a light coat of liquid gasket seal to the portion that seats into the cylinder head.

16. Install the rubber grommets in the cylinder at each end of the camshaft.

17. Place wood blocks under the crankcase so the rear cylinder head is almost horizontal.

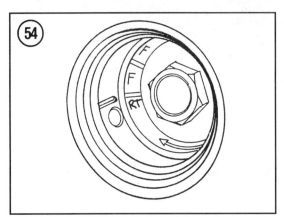

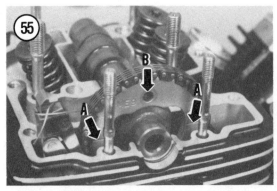

NOTE
When the crankcase is blocked up this way, some of the oil in the de-foaming chambers of the front cylinder will run out. Don't worry; the small loss of oil will not affect the front cylinder's hydraulic tappets.

CAUTION
The hydraulic tappets must be bled of all air prior to installation or they will not function properly.

18. Inspect and bleed the hydraulic tappets as described in this chapter.

19. Install the tappet shim(s) into their correct receptacle in the cylinder head (**Figure 57**).

20. Keep the hydraulic tappet vertical and install the tappets into their correct receptacles in the cylinder head (A, **Figure 58**).

21. Install the locating dowels (B, **Figure 58**) onto the crankcase studs in the cylinder head.

CAUTION
*In the following step, do **not** apply the liquid gasket sealer to the area around each hydraulic tappet receptacle (**Figure 59**).*

22. Clean the mating surfaces of the cylinder head and the camshaft holder with aerosol electrical contact cleaner. Apply a light coat of liquid gasket sealer to the mating surface of the camshaft holder.

23. Install the camshaft holder, bolts and washers. Tighten the bolts to the torque specifications listed in **Table 2**.

24. Make sure the assist shafts and springs (A, **Figure 60**) are in place.

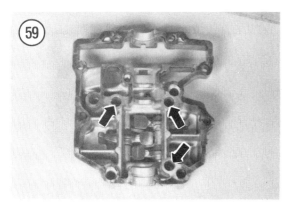

25. Fill both de-foaming chambers with fresh engine oil (B, **Figure 60**). These chambers must be full of oil so the bleed hole in each tappet will be covered with oil. This is necessary so that air will not enter the high-pressure chamber in the tappet.

26. Clean the mating surfaces of the cylinder head cover and the camshaft holder with contact cleaner.

27. Remove the protective sheets from each side of the new gasket and install the gasket (**Figure 61**).

28. Install the cylinder head cover (**Figure 62**) and tighten cap nut and the 6 mm bolts in a crisscross pattern in 2-3 stages to the torque specification listed in **Table 2**.

29. Install the locating dowels (**Figure 63**) and then the camshaft holder on the chain side. Install the 8 mm bolts, cap nuts and washers and tighten in a crisscross pattern in 2-3 stages to the torque specification listed in **Table 2**.

NOTE
*Steps 30-37 pertain to **both** the front and rear cylinders.*

30. Inspect the O-ring seals (**Figure 64**) on the spark plug sleeve. Replace if they are hard or starting to deteriorate.

31. Install the spark plug sleeve into the cylinder head and tighten securely. Use the same tool set-up used for removal.

32. Install the external oil pipe on each cylinder head and crankcase.

NOTE
*Refer to (**Figure 65**) for correct location of the external oil line bolt locations.*

33. Install the 10 mm union bolt (A, **Figure 66**) and sealing washers securing the external oil pipe (B, **Figure 66**) to the crankcase. Tighten the 10 mm bolt to the torque specification listed in **Table 2**.

NOTE
*The 6 mm oil bolts used to attach the oil pipe to the cylinder heads are unique. They have a raised rib on each side which locates the bolt within the fitting as shown in **Figure 67**. These ribs locate the bolts and also allow oil to flow past them to enter the cylinder head.*

CAUTION
Do not substitute another type of 6 mm bolt for these special 6 mm oil bolts as

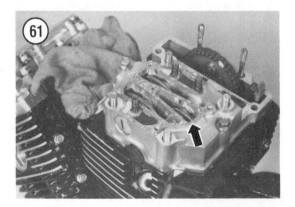

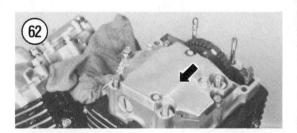

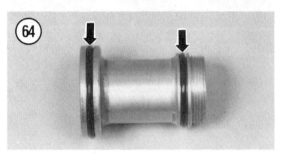

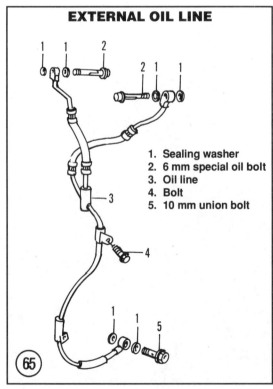

EXTERNAL OIL LINE

1. Sealing washer
2. 6 mm special oil bolt
3. Oil line
4. Bolt
5. 10 mm union bolt

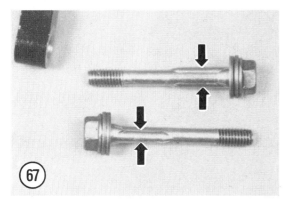

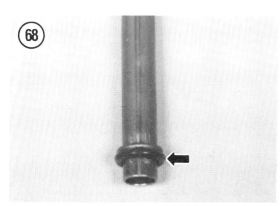

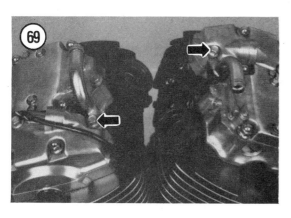

*oil flow to the cylinder head may be obstructed—**resulting in extensive engine damage**.*

34. Install a sealing washer on each side of the fitting where the bolts attach to the cylinder heads. Tighten the special 6 mm oil bolts to the torque specification listed in **Table 2**.

35. Inspect the O-ring seals (**Figure 68**) on the end of the coolant pipe where it fits into the cylinder. If they have started to harden or deteriorate, replace with new ones.

36. Install a coolant pipe into each cylinder head. Install the bolts (**Figure 69**) securing the coolant pipe and tighten securely.

37. Install the engine as described in this chapter.

CYLINDER HEADS

Removal/Installation

Either cylinder head can be removed without first removing the other cylinder head. If both cylinder heads are going to be removed, either cylinder head can be removed first. This procedure pertains to both cylinder heads.

1. Remove the engine as described in this chapter.

2. Remove the cylinder head cover, camshaft holder and camshaft for the specific cylinder as described in this chapter.

3. Remove the bolts (A, **Figure 70**) securing the cam chain tensioner and pull the cam chain tensioner assembly (B, **Figure 70**) up and out of the cylinder head.

4. Loosen the head by tapping around the perimeter with a rubber or plastic mallet.

CAUTION
Remember, the fins on the cylinder head are fragile and may be damaged if tapped or pried too hard. Never use a metal hammer. These fins are more for cosmetic value than cooling. They are not as fragile as those on an air-cooled engine but they still may break.

5. Untie the wire securing the cam chain and retie it to the cylinder head. Lift the cylinder head (**Figure 71**) straight up and off the crankcase studs. Pull the cam chain and wire through the opening in the cylinder head and retie the cam chain to one of the crankcase studs.

NOTE
*If both heads are going to be removed, mark them with an "F" (front cylinder) or "R" (rear cylinder) so they will be reinstalled onto the correct position on the engine. On some models, the cylinder heads have a cast-in mark "R" or "L" (**Figure 72**).*

6. Remove the head gasket, dowel pins and the cam chain guide.

7. Place a clean shop rag into the cam chain opening in the cylinder to prevent entry of foreign matter.

8. Install by reversing these removal steps while noting the following.

9. Clean the cylinder head mating surfaces of any gasket material.

10. Install a new head gasket (A, **Figure 73**) and the old locating dowels (B, **Figure 73**).

11. Install the cam chain guide (C, **Figure 73**).

12. Install the cylinder head and push it down until it seats completely.

13. Install the cam chain tensioner (B, **Figure 70**).

14. Install the bolts (A, **Figure 70**) securing the cam chain tensioner and tighten the bolts securely.

15. Repeat this procedure for the other cylinder head if necessary.

Inspection

1. If necessary, remove the bolts securing the decorative cooling fins (**Figure 74**) to the cylinder head and remove them from each side of the cylinder head.

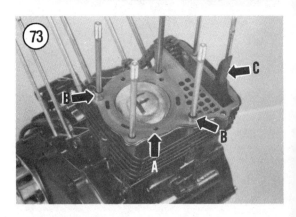

2. Remove all traces of gasket material from the cylinder head (A, **Figure 75**) and the cylinder mating surfaces.

3. *Without* removing the valves, remove all carbon deposits from the combustion chamber (B, **Figure 75**) with a wire brush. A blunt screwdriver or chisel may be used if care is taken not to damage the head, valves and spark plug threads.

4. After all carbon is removed from the combustion chambers and intake and exhaust ports, clean the entire head in solvent.

5. Clean away all carbon on the piston crowns. Do not remove the carbon ridge at the top of the cylinder bore.

6. Check for cracks in the combustion chamber and exhaust ports. A cracked head must be replaced.

7. After the head has been thoroughly cleaned, place a straightedge across the gasket surface (**Figure 76**) at several points. Measure warp by inserting a flat feeler gauge between the straightedge and the cylinder head at each location. There should be no warpage; if a small amount is present, the head can be resurfaced by a Honda dealer or qualified machine shop.

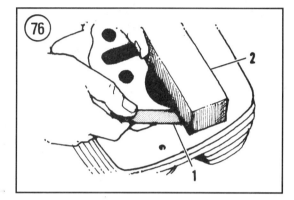

8. Check the valves and valve guides as described in this chapter.

9. Inspect the cam chain tensioner and cam chain guide for wear (**Figure 77**).

10. Inspect the spring and all moving parts of the cam chain tensioner assembly (**Figure 78**) for wear or damage. If any parts are worn, the assembly must be replaced.

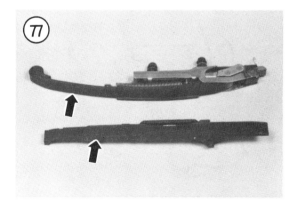

VALVES AND VALVE COMPONENTS

Removal

Refer to **Figure 79** for this procedure.

1. Remove the cylinder head(s) as described in this chapter.

> *CAUTION*
> *To avoid loss of spring tension, do not compress the springs any more than necessary to remove the keepers.*

2. Compress springs with a valve spring compressor tool (**Figure 80**). Remove the valve keepers and release compression.

3. Remove the valve compressor tool.

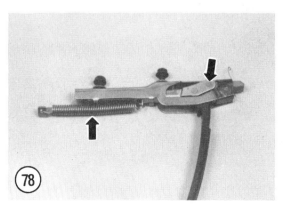

4. Prior to removing the valves, remove any burrs from the valve stem (**Figure 81**). Otherwise, the valve guides will be damaged.

5. Remove the valve keepers, valve spring retainer and both inner and outer springs (**Figure 82**).

6. Remove the valve seal/ring and the valve spring seat.

Inspection

1. Clean all valves with a wire brush and solvent.

2. Inspect the contact surface of each valve for burning. Minor roughness and pitting can be removed by lapping the valve as described in this chapter. Excessive unevenness of the contact surface is an indication that the valve is not serviceable.

3. Measure each valve seating face for wear (**Figure 83**). If worn to the service limit in **Table 1** or less, the valve must be replaced.

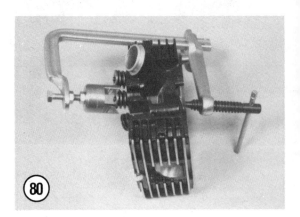

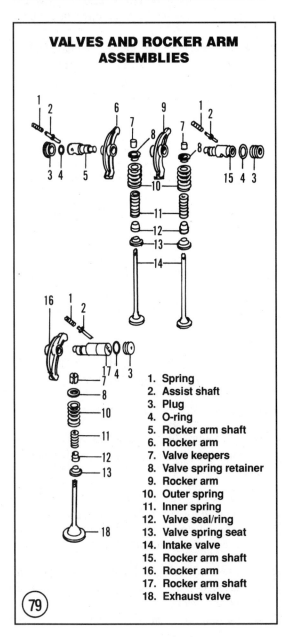

VALVES AND ROCKER ARM ASSEMBLIES

1. Spring
2. Assist shaft
3. Plug
4. O-ring
5. Rocker arm shaft
6. Rocker arm
7. Valve keepers
8. Valve spring retainer
9. Rocker arm
10. Outer spring
11. Inner spring
12. Valve seal/ring
13. Valve spring seat
14. Intake valve
15. Rocker arm shaft
16. Rocker arm
17. Rocker arm shaft
18. Exhaust valve

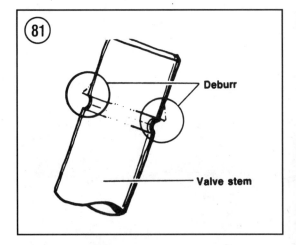

Deburr
Valve stem

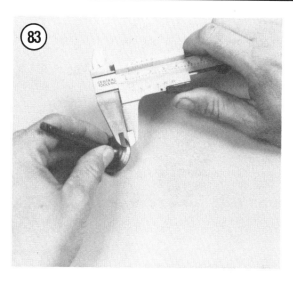

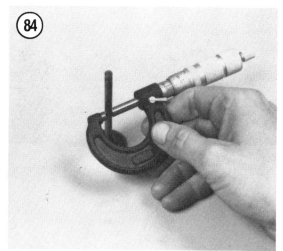

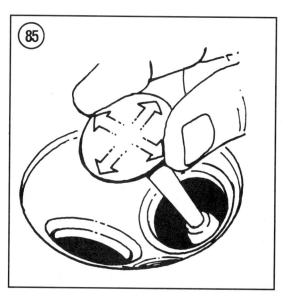

NOTE
*The contact surface of the valve **cannot** be ground; the valve must be replaced if this area shows more than slight damage.*

4. Measure valve stems for wear with a micrometer (**Figure 84**). Compare with specifications in **Table 1**.

5. Remove all carbon and varnish from the valve guides with a stiff spiral wire brush.

NOTE
The next step assumes that all valve stems are within specifications.

6. Insert each valve in its guide. Hold the valve just slightly off its seat and rock it sideways in 2 directions (**Figure 85**). If it rocks more than slightly, the guide is probably worn and should be replaced. If a dial indicator is available, a more accurate measurement can be made as shown in **Figure 86**. Replace any guides that exceed the valve stem-to-guide clearance specified in **Table 1**. If the guides must be replaced, take the cylinder head to a dealer or machine shop.

7. Measure the valve spring heights with a vernier caliper (**Figure 87**). All should be the length speci-

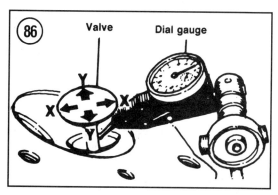

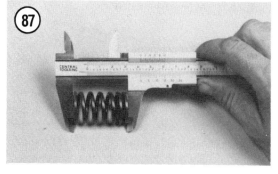

fied in **Table 1** with no bends or other distortion. Replace defective springs as a set.

8. Inspect each set of valve springs (**Figure 88**) for wear, distortion or damage. Replace as a set if necessary.

9. Check the valve spring retainer and valve keepers. If they are in good condition, they may be reused.

10. Inspect valve seats. If worn or burned, they must be reconditioned. This should be performed by your dealer or a qualified machine shop. Seats and valves in near-perfect condition can be reconditioned by lapping with a fine carborundum paste. Lapping, however, is always inferior to precision grinding.

Installation

1. Install the valve spring seat (A, **Figure 89**).

2. Remove the ring from the valve seal. This will make valve seal installation much easier.

3. Install a new valve seal (B, **Figure 89**) and then install the ring onto the valve seal.

4. Coat the valve stems with molybdenum disulfide grease. To avoid damage to the valve stem seal, turn the valve slowly while inserting the valve into the cylinder head.

5. Install the valve springs with the narrow pitch end (end with coils closest together) facing the head (**Figure 90**). Install the upper valve spring retainers.

> *CAUTION*
> *To avoid loss of spring tension, do not compress the springs any more than necessary to install the keepers.*

6. Push down on upper valve spring retainers with the valve spring compressor and install valve keepers.

7. After all keepers have been installed, gently tap the valve stems with a plastic mallet to make sure the keepers are properly seated.

Valve Guide Replacement

When valve guides are worn so that there is excessive valve stem-to-guide clearance or valve tipping, the guides must be replaced. This job should only be done by a dealer as special tools are required as well as considerable expertise. If the valve guide is replaced, also replace the respective valve.

The following procedure is provided if you choose to perform this task yourself.

1. Remove the valve assemblies (A, **Figure 91**) as described in this chapter.

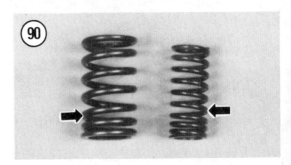

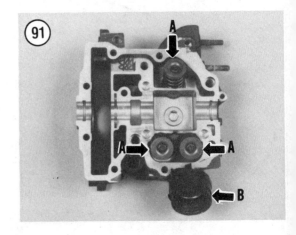

2. Remove the clamping screw securing the intake pipe (B, **Figure 91**) onto the cylinder head. Remove the intake pipe prior to placing the cylinder head in the oven.

CAUTION
*There **may** be a residual oil or solvent odor left in the oven after heating the cylinder head. If you use a household oven, first check with the person who uses the oven for food preparation to avoid getting into trouble.*

3. The valve guides are installed with a slight interference fit. Place the cylinder head in a heated oven (or on a hot plate). Heat the cylinder head to a temperature between 100-150° C (212-300° F). An

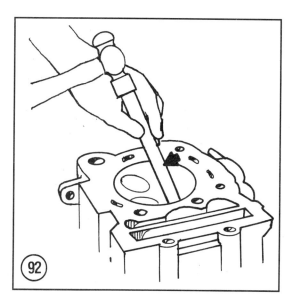
(92)

easy way to check for the proper temperature is to drop tiny drops of water on the cylinder head; if they sizzle and evaporate immediately, the temperature is correct.

CAUTION
Do not heat the cylinder head with a torch (propane or acetylene); never bring a flame into contact with the cylinder head or valve guide. The direct heat will destroy the case hardening of the valve guide and will likely cause warpage of the cylinder head.

4. Remove the cylinder head from the oven and hold onto it with kitchen pot holders, heavy gloves or heavy shop cloths—*it is very hot.*

5. While heating up the cylinder head, place the new valve guides in a freezer (or refrigerator) if possible. Chilling them will slightly reduce their overall diameter while the hot cylinder head is slightly larger due to heat expansion. This will make valve guide installation much easier.

6. Turn the cylinder head upside down on wood blocks. Make sure the cylinder head is properly supported on the wood blocks.

7. From the combustion chamber side of the cylinder head, drive out the old valve guide with a hammer and valve guide remover (**Figure 92**). Use Honda special tool, Valve Guide Remover, part No. 07742-0010200. Remove the special tool.

8. Remove and discard the valve guide. *Never* reinstall a valve guide that has been removed as it is no longer true nor within tolerances.

9. Apply fresh engine oil to the new valve guide and the valve guide hole in the cylinder head.

CAUTION
Failure to apply fresh engine oil to both the valve guide and the valve guide hole in the cylinder head will result in damage to the cylinder head and/or the new valve guide.

CAUTION
The cylinder head must still be at the temperature indicated in Step 3 in order to install the new valve guide.

10. From the top side (rocker arm side) of the cylinder head, drive in the new valve guide. Use Honda special tool, Valve Guide Installer, part No. 07743-0020000 and a hammer (**Figure 93**). Drive the new

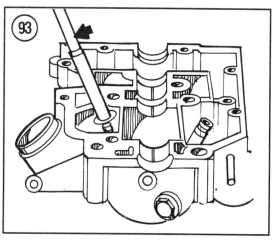
(93)

4

guide in until it protrudes up 0.90-1.10 mm (0.035-0.059 in.) above the top surface of the cylinder head adjacent to the valve guide (**Figure 94**).

11. Allow the cylinder head to cool to room temperature.

12. After installation, ream the new valve guide as follows:

    a. Apply cutting oil to both the new valve guide and the valve guide reamer.

    b. Use Honda special tools, Valve Guide Reamer, part No. 07984-5110000 and a holder similar to a thread tap holder (**Figure 95**).

> *CAUTION*
> **Always** *rotate the valve guide reamer* **clockwise** *when installing and removing. If the reamer is rotated counterclockwise, damage to a good valve guide will occur.*

    c. Rotate the reamer *clockwise*. Continue to rotate the reamer and work it down through the entire length of the new valve guide. Apply additional cutting oil during this procedure.

    d. While rotating the reamer *clockwise*, withdraw the reamer from the valve guide. Remove the reamer.

13. If necessary, repeat Steps 1-12 for any other valve guides.

14. Thoroughly clean the cylinder head and valve guides with solvent to wash out all metal particles. Dry with compressed air.

15. Reface the valve seats as described in this chapter.

16. Install all items removed.

Valve Seat Inspection

1. Remove the valves as described in this chapter.

> *NOTE*
> *The contact surface of the valve **cannot be ground**; the valve must be replaced if this area is damaged.*

2. The most accurate method for checking the valve seal is to use Prussian Blue or machinist's dye, available from auto parts stores or machine shops. To check the valve seal with Prussian Blue or machinist's dye, perform the following:

    a. Thoroughly clean off all carbon deposits from the valve face with solvent or detergent, then thoroughly dry.

    b. Spread a thin layer of Prussian Blue or machinist's dye evenly on the valve face.

    c. Moisten the end of a suction cup valve tool (**Figure 96**) and attach it to the valve. Insert the valve into the guide.

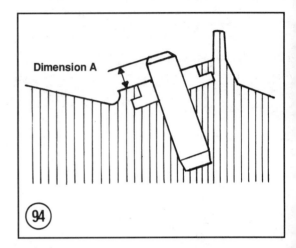

Dimension A

94

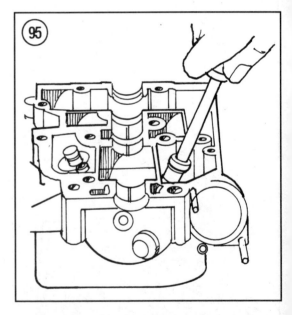

95

96

d. Using the suction cup tool, *tap* the valve up and down in the cylinder head. Do *not* rotate the valve or a false indication will result.

e. Remove the valve and examine the impression left by the Prussian Blue or machinist's dye. If the impression left in the dye (on the valve or in the cylinder head) is not even and continuous and the valve seat width (**Figure 97**) is not within specified tolerance listed in **Table 1**, the cylinder head valve seat must be reconditioned.

3. Closely examine the valve seat in the cylinder head. It should be smooth and even with a polished seating surface.

4. If the valve seat is okay, install the valves as described in this chapter.

5. If the valve seat is not correct, recondition the valve seat as described in this chapter.

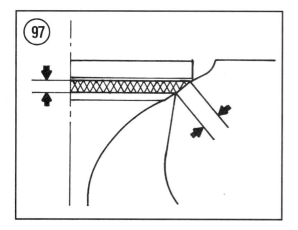

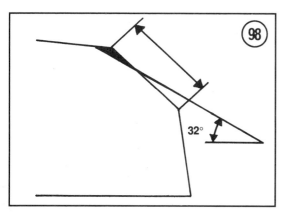

Valve Seat Reconditioning

Special valve cutter tools and considerable expertise are required to recondition the valve seats in the cylinder head properly. You can save considerable money by removing the cylinder head(s) and taking just the cylinder head(s) to a dealer or machine shop and have the valve seats ground.

The following procedure is provided if you choose to perform this task yourself.

The valve seat cutters are available from a Honda dealer or from machine shop supply outlets. Follow the manufacturer's instruction in regard to operating the cutters. You will need the following cutters:

a. 32°.

b. 45°.

c. 60°.

You will also need a T-handle and the solid pilot.

The valve seat for both the intake valves and exhaust valves are machined to the same angles— but *different* diameters. The valve contact surface is cut to a 45° angle and the area above the contact surface (closest to the combustion chamber) is cut to a 32° angle. The area below the contact surface (closest to the valve) is cut to a 60° angle.

1. Carefully rotate and insert the solid pilot into the valve guide. Make sure the pilot is correctly seated.

2. Using the 45° angle side of the cutter, install the cutter and the T-handle onto the solid pilot.

3. Using the 45° cutter, descale and clean the valve seat with one or two turns.

> *CAUTION*
> *Measure the valve seat contact area in the cylinder head after each cut to make sure the contact area is correct and to prevent removing too much material. If too much material is removed, the cylinder head must be replaced.*

4. If the seat is still pitted or burned, perform the following:

a. Use the 32° cutter and remove a *small* amount of the top portion of the valve seat (**Figure 98**). Remove the 32 mm cutter.

b. Use the 60° cutter and remove a *small* amount of the bottom portion of the valve seat (**Figure 99**). Remove the 60° cutter.

c. Finally use the 45° cutter to achieve the valve face surface of the desired width as shown in **Figure 100**. Refer to the previous CAUTION to avoid removing too much material from the cylinder head.

5. Remove the valve cutter, T-handle and solid pilot from the cylinder head.

6. Inspect the valve seat-to-valve face impression as follows:

    a. Spread a thin layer of Prussian Blue or machinist's dye evenly on the valve face.

    b. Moisten the end of a suction cup valve tool (**Figure 96**) and attach it to the valve. Insert the valve into the guide.

    c. Using the suction cup tool, tap the valve up and down in the cylinder head. Do *not* rotate the valve or a false indication will result.

    d. Remove the valve and examine the impression left by the Prussian Blue or machinist's dye.

    e. Measure the valve seat width as shown in **Figure 97**. Refer to **Table 1** for the seat width.

7. After the final cut has been made, apply valve lapping compound and lap the valve using light pressure as described in this chapter.

8. Check that the finish has a smooth and velvety surface, it should *not* be shiny or highly polished. The final seating will take place when the engine is first run.

9. Repeat Steps 1-8 for all remaining valve seats.

10. Thoroughly clean the cylinder head and all valve components in solvent or detergent and hot water.

11. After the lapping has been completed and the valve assemblies have been reinstalled into the head, the valve seal should be tested. Check the seal of each valve by pouring solvent into each of the intake and exhaust ports. The solvent should not flow past the valve seat and the valve head. Perform on all sets of valves. If fluid leaks past any of the seats, disassemble that valve assembly and repeat the lapping procedure until there is no leakage.

12. If the cylinder head and valve components were cleaned in detergent and hot water, apply a light coat of engine oil to all bare metal surfaces to prevent any rust formations.

Valve Lapping

Valve lapping is a simple operation which can restore the valve seal without machining if the amount of wear or distortion is not too great.

1. Coat the valve seating area in the head with a lapping compound such as Carborundum or Clover Brand.

2. Insert the valve into the cylinder head.

3. Wet the suction cup (**Figure 96**) of the lapping stick and stick it onto the head of the valve. Lap the

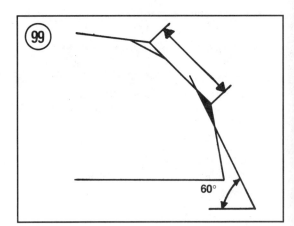

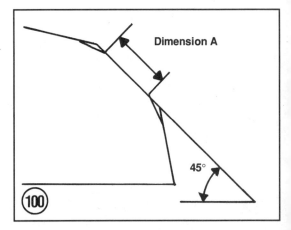

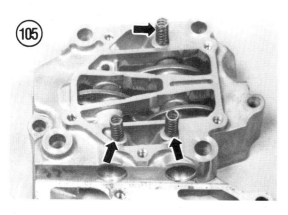

valve to the seat by rotating the lapping stick in both directions (**Figure 101**). Every 5 to 10 seconds, rotate the valve 180° in the valve seat; continue lapping until the contact surfaces of the valve and the valve seat are a uniform grey. Stop as soon as they are, to avoid removing too much material.

4. Thoroughly clean the cylinder head and all valve components in solvent or detergent and hot water to remove all grinding compound. Any compound left on the valves or the cylinder head will end up in the engine and will cause damage.

5. After the lapping has been completed and the valve assemblies have been reinstalled into the head, the valve seal should be tested. Check the seal of each valve by pouring solvent into each of the intake and exhaust ports. The solvent should not flow past the valve seat and the valve head. Perform on all sets of valves. If fluid leaks past any of the seats, disassemble that valve assembly and repeat the lapping procedure until there is no leakage.

6. If the cylinder head and valve components were cleaned in detergent and hot water, apply a light coat of engine oil to all bare metal surfaces to prevent any rust formations.

ROCKER ARM ASSEMBLIES

The rocker arm assemblies (rocker arms, shafts and camshaft holder) for the front and rear cylinders are identical (same Honda part No.) but they will develop different wear patterns during use. It is recommended that the rocker arm assemblies from one head be disassembled, inspected and then assembled to avoid the intermixing of parts.

Disassembly

1. Remove the camshaft and camshaft holder as described in this chapter.

2. Unscrew the plug from the camshaft holder (**Figure 102**) from the side opposite the cam chain.

3. On the side next to the cam chain, screw in a 6 mm bolt (**Figure 103**) into each plug and remove both rocker arm holder plugs (**Figure 104**).

4. Remove the assist shafts and springs (**Figure 105**).

5. Using a rubber mallet, tap on the end of the camshaft holder and the rocker arm shafts will partially work their way out of the camshaft holder.

6. Withdraw each rocker arm shaft and rocker arm (**Figure 106**). Place each set in a container and keep them separate as they must be reinstalled in the correct position. Mark the exhaust, intake (away from the cam chain) and intake (next to cam chain).

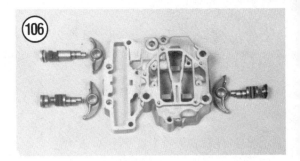

Inspection

1. Wash all parts in cleaning solvent and thoroughly dry.

2. Inspect the rocker arm pad where it rides on the cam lobe and where it rides on the valve stem (**Figure 107**). If the pad is scratched or unevenly worn, inspect the cam lobe for scoring, chipping or flat spots. Replace the rocker arm if defective.

3. Measure the inside diameter of the rocker arm (A, **Figure 108**) with an inside micrometer and check against dimensions in **Table 1**. Replace if worn to the service limit or greater.

> *NOTE*
> *Even though the 3 rocker arm shafts are different in appearance, the inspection dimension is the same.*

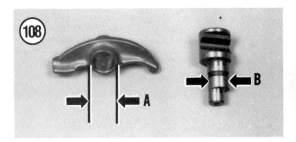

4. Inspect the rocker arm shaft for signs of wear or scoring. Measure the outside diameter where the rocker arm rides (not the larger portion that rides in the camshaft holder) (B, **Figure 108**) with a micrometer and check against dimensions in **Table 1**. Replace if worn to the service limit or less.

5. Inspect each assist shaft (**Figure 109**) for wear or bending. Replace as necessary.

6. Measure the free length of each assist spring. Replace if less than the service limit dimension listed in **Table 1**. Replace all 3 as a set even if only one has sagged to the service limit dimension.

7. Inspect the oil flow holes (**Figure 110**) in the cylinder head cover and the camshaft holder (**Figure 111**). Blow them out with compressed air to make sure they are open. They must be clean for proper oil flow to the assist shafts and springs.

8. Inspect the O-ring seal on each plug. Replace if they have started to harden or deteriorate.

Assembly

1. Coat the rocker arm shaft and rocker arm bore with molybdenum disulfide grease.

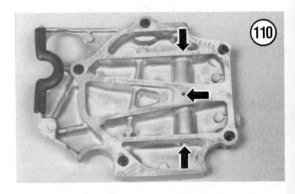

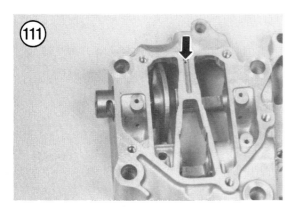

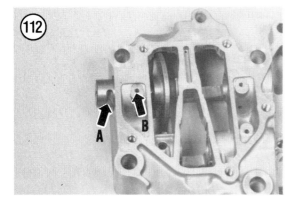

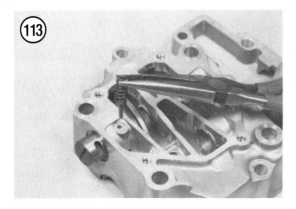

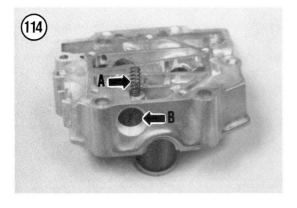

CAUTION
In the following steps be sure to install the correct rocker arm into the correct position in the camshaft holder. Refer to **Figure 106**.

2. Starting with the intake valve rocker arm assembly *farthest* from the cam chain, perform the following:

   a. Partially install the intake rocker arm shaft and align the rocker arm with the shaft. Push the rocker arm shaft in sufficiently to hold the rocker arm in place.

   b. Align the assist shaft notch (A, **Figure 112**) in the rocker arm with the assist shaft hole (B, **Figure 112**) in the camshaft holder.

   c. Recheck the alignment (**Figure 113**) and push the rocker arm shaft in all the way.

   d. Install the assist shaft and assist spring (A, **Figure 114**).

   e. After the assist shaft and spring are installed, use a screwdriver in the slot in the end of the rocker arm shaft to turn the rocker arm shaft (B, **Figure 114**) carefully back and forth about 8-12° from the 1 o'clock position (**Figure 115**). Check that the rocker arm shaft and rocker arm move correctly and that the assist shaft and spring move up and down.

   f. Move the slot in the end of the rocker arm shaft to the 1 o'clock position. At this point, the assist shaft should be in the down position.

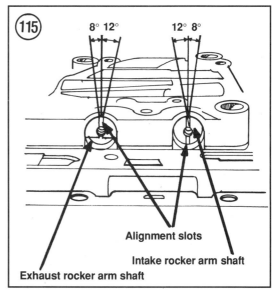

3. On the intake valve rocker arm assembly *next* to the cam chain, perform the following:

   a. Partially install the rocker arm shaft and align the rocker arm with the shaft. Push the rocker arm shaft in sufficiently to hold the rocker arm in place.

   b. Align the assist shaft notch (A, **Figure 116**) in the rocker arm with the assist shaft hole (B, **Figure 116**) in the camshaft holder.

   c. Recheck the alignment and push the rocker arm shaft in all the way.

   d. Install the assist shaft and assist spring (A, **Figure 117**).

   e. After the assist shaft and spring are installed, use a screwdriver in the slot in the end of the rocker arm shaft to turn the rocker arm shaft (B, **Figure 117**) carefully back and forth about 8-12° from the 11 o'clock position (**Figure 115**). Check that the rocker arm shaft and rocker arm move correctly and that the assist shaft and spring move up and down.

   f. Move the slot in the end of the rocker arm shaft to the 11 o'clock position. At this point, the assist shaft should be in the down position.

4. On the exhaust valve rocker arm assembly, perform the following:

   a. Partially install the exhaust rocker arm shaft and align the rocker arm with the shaft. Push the rocker arm shaft in sufficiently to hold the rocker arm in place.

   b. Align the assist shaft notch (A, **Figure 118**) in the rocker arm with the assist shaft hole (B, **Figure 118**) in the camshaft holder.

   c. Recheck the alignment and push the rocker arm shaft in all the way.

   d. Install the assist shaft and assist spring (**Figure 119**).

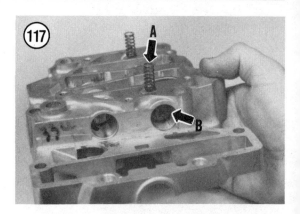

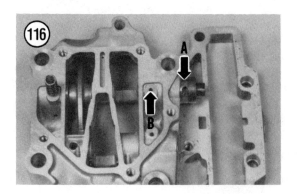

e. After the assist shaft and spring are installed, use a screwdriver in the slot in the end of the rocker arm shaft to turn the rocker arm shaft (**Figure 120**) carefully back and forth about 8-12° from the 1 o'clock position (**Figure 115**). Check that the rocker arm shaft and rocker arm move correctly and that the assist shaft and spring move up and down.

f. Move the slot in the end of the rocker arm shaft to the 1 o'clock position. At this point, the assist shaft should be in the down position.

5. Repeat the disassembly, inspection and assembly procedures for the other cylinder head rocker arm assembly.

HYDRAULIC TAPPETS

Inspection

1. Inspect the exterior of the tappet for wear or damage, replace if necessary.

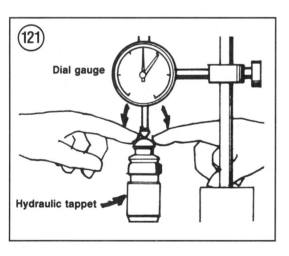

Dial gauge

Hydraulic tappet

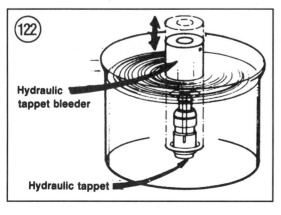

Hydraulic tappet bleeder

Hydraulic tappet

2. Measure the free length of the tappet as follows:
a. Bleed the tappet as described in this chapter.
b. Remove the tappet from the container used for bleeding.
c. Keep the tappet upright and place it on a flat surface under a dial gauge.
d. Still keeping the tappet upright, try to compress the tappet quickly with your fingers (**Figure 121**).
e. You should be able to compress the tappet between 0-0.2 mm (0-0.0078 in.). If it compresses more than the specified dimension, the tappet must be replaced.

3. If the tappet is okay, it must be bled again prior to installation.

Bleeding

For proper operation, the hydraulic tappets must be free of air in the high-pressure chamber. A special Honda tool (Hydraulic Tappet Bleeder, Honda part No. 07973-MJ00000) or an improvised tool set-up may be used.

CAUTION
Be sure to note the correct location in the cylinder head from which the tappet and shim(s) were removed.

1. Remove the tappet and shim(s) from the cylinder head as described in this chapter.
2. Fill a plastic or glass jar (it must be transparent) with kerosene. Fill the jar with enough kerosene so the tappet is completely covered.

CAUTION
The tappet must be kept submerged and upright during this procedure.

3A. If the special tool is used, perform the following:
a. Place the tappet right side up within the special tool.
b. Place the special tool and tappet into the jar filled with kerosene.
c. Holding the tappet and special tool upright, push down on the special tool and pump the tappet as shown in **Figure 122**.
d. Continue to pump until air bubbles stop coming from the high-pressure chamber in the tappet.

3B. If the special tool is not available, perform the following:

a. Insert a 1/16 in. drill bit into the opening in the top of the tappet.

b. Place the tappet and drill bit into the jar filled with kerosene (**Figure 123**).

c. Holding the tappet upright, push down on the drill bit with a piece of metal or wood dowel and pump the tappet as shown in **Figure 124**.

d. Continue to pump until air bubbles stop coming from the high-pressure chamber in the tappet.

NOTE
The small amount of kerosene left in the high pressure chamber of the tappet will not contaminate the engine's oil.

4. Remove the tappet from the jar filled with kerosene and keep the tappet in the upright position. If the tappet is laid down at an angle or on its side, air will enter the high-pressure chamber and the tappet will have to be bled again.

5. Reinstall the tappet and shim(s) into the correct receptacle in the cylinder head as described in this chapter.

6. Repeat this procedure for all tappets.

Tappet Adjustment

In order to achieve a zero clearance in the valve train, the tappet must provide the correct amount of pressure on the rocker arm. To compensate for manufacturing tolerances in various parts, shims are added to the base of each tappet. Measuring the stroke of the assist shaft will determine the number of shim(s) required to achieve the correct pressure.

This procedure is *not* a routine adjustment but has to be performed *only* when any of the following parts are replaced:

a. Camshaft holder.

b. Cylinder head.

c. Valve or valve guide replaced or valve seat reground.

d. Rocker arm and rocker arm shaft.

e. Camshaft.

1. Remove the camshaft cover as described in this chapter.

2. Remove the tappets as described in this chapter.

3. Bleed the tappets as described in this chapter.

4. Remove all shims from the receptacles in the cylinder head.

5. Install the tappets (**Figure 125**) into their correct receptacles in the cylinder head.

6. Install the camshaft holder (A, **Figure 126**) and secure it with the 8 mm bolts and 10 mm cap nuts. Tighten the bolts and nuts to the torque specifications listed in **Table 2**.

7. If installed, remove the assist shaft springs (B, **Figure 126**).

8. Using the 17 mm bolt (**Figure 127**) on the primary drive gear, rotate the engine *clockwise* until the timing marks align with the fixed pointer on the crankcase cover. Refer to the following:

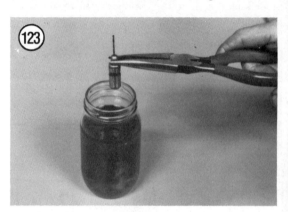

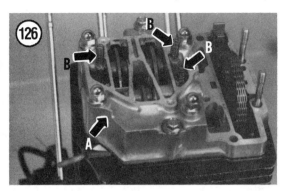

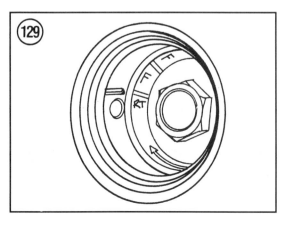

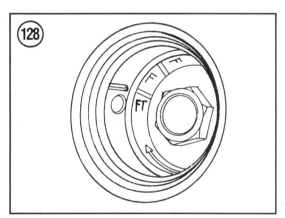

a. **Figure 128**: front cylinder "FT."

b. **Figure 129**: rear cylinder "RT."

9. Install a dial gauge to the camshaft holder.

10. Install one of the assist shafts into the hole in the camshaft holder.

11. Place the dial indicator over the assist shaft and place the pointer of the dial indicator onto the top of the assist shaft (**Figure 130**).

12. Zero the dial on the dial indicator.

13. Have an assistant rotate the crankshaft 2 complete revolutions using the 17 mm bolt on the primary drive gear.

14. Record the stroke dimension of the assist shaft during these 2 revolutions.

15. Refer to the dimensions listed in **Table 3** to determine the number of shim(s) required under that tappet.

16. Repeat this procedure for all tappets affected by any replaced parts.

17. After the shims have been added to all tappets in one cylinder head, repeat this procedure and check that the stroke is within the 0-1.20 mm (0-0.047 in.) range.

CYLINDER

Removal

1. Remove the cylinder head as described in this chapter.

2. If both cylinders are going to be removed, they should be marked with an "F" (front cylinder) or "R"

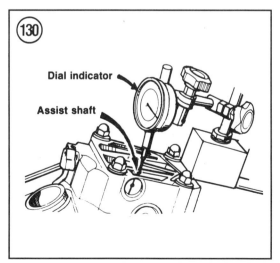

(rear cylinder) as shown in **Figure 131**. This will avoid any mix-up upon installation.

3. Loosen the cylinder by tapping around the perimeter with a rubber or plastic mallet. If necessary, *gently* pry the cylinder loose with a broad-tipped screwdriver.

4. Pull the cylinder straight up and off of the crankcase studs. Work the cam chain wire through the opening in the cylinder.

5. Remove the cylinder base gasket and discard it. Remove the dowel pins from the crankcase studs.

6. Install a piston holding fixture under the piston (**Figure 132**) to protect the piston skirt from damage. This fixture may be purchased or may be a homemade unit of wood. See **Figure 133** for dimensions.

Inspection

The following procedure requires the use of highly specialized and expensive measuring instruments. If such equipment is not readily available, have the measurements performed by a dealer or qualified machine shop.

1. Do not remove or damage the carbon ridge around the top of the cylinder bore. If the cylinders, pistons and rings are found to be dimensionally correct and can be reused, removal of the carbon ridge from the top of the cylinder bores or the ring from the top of pistons will cause excessive oil consumption.

2. Soak with solvent any old cylinder head gasket material on the cylinder mating surface (**Figure 134**) and the cylinder base mating surface (**Figure 135**). Use a broad-tipped *dull* chisel and gently scrape off all gasket residue. Do not gouge the sealing surface as oil and air leaks will result.

3. Measure the cylinder bore with a cylinder gauge or inside micrometer at the points shown in **Figure**

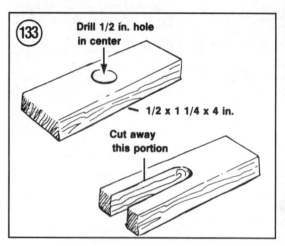

Drill 1/2 in. hole in center

1/2 x 1 1/4 x 4 in.

Cut away this portion

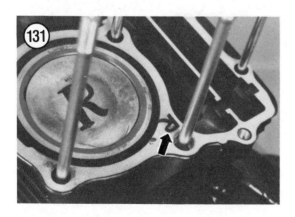

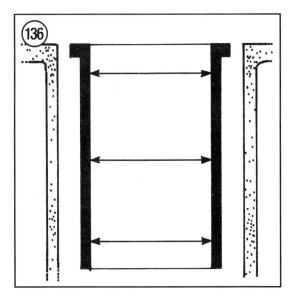

136. Measure in 2 axes—in line with the piston pin and at 90° to the pin. If the taper or out-of-round is 0.10 mm (0.004 in.) or greater, the cylinder must be rebored to the next oversize and a new piston installed. There are 2 oversize piston sizes available (0.25 mm and 0.50 mm).

NOTE
The new piston should be obtained before the cylinder is rebored so that the piston can be measured; slight manufacturing tolerances must be taken into account to determine the actual size and working clearance.

4. Check the cylinder wall (**Figure 137**) for scratches; if evident, the cylinder should be rebored.

NOTE
*The maximum wear limit on the cylinder is listed in **Table 1**. If the cylinder is worn to this limit, it must be replaced. Never rebore a cylinder if the finished rebore diameter will be this dimension or greater.*

Installation

1. Check that the top surface of the crankcase and the bottom surface of the cylinder are clean prior to installing a new base gasket.
2. Install a new cylinder base gasket (A, **Figure 138**) and locating dowels (B, **Figure 138**) to either the crankcase or to the base of the cylinder.
3. Make sure the piston holding fixture is still under the piston (C, **Figure 138**).
4. Make sure the end gaps of the piston rings are *not* lined up with each other—they must be staggered. Lightly oil the piston rings and the inside of the cylinder bores with assembly oil.
5. Install the cylinder and slide it down onto the crankcase studs (**Figure 139**).

WARNING
The edges of all piston rings are very sharp, especially the flat rings of the oil ring assembly. Be careful when handling them to avoid cut fingers.

CAUTION
The side rings of the oil ring assembly are very thin. Be very careful that the

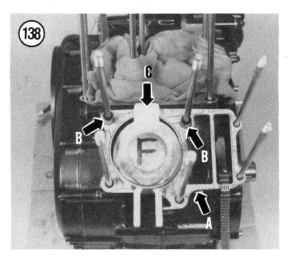

cylinder does not snag one of these rings during installation.

6. Start the cylinder down over the piston. Compress each piston ring with your fingers as it enters the cylinder.

7. Slide the cylinder down until it bottoms on the piston holding fixture (**Figure 140**).

8. Remove the piston holding fixture and slide the cylinder down into place on the crankcase.

9. Carefully feed the cam chain and wire up through the opening in the cylinder and tie it to the engine (**Figure 141**).

10. Install the cylinder head as described in this chapter.

11. Follow the *Break-in Procedure* in this chapter if the cylinder was rebored or honed or a new piston or piston rings were installed.

12. Repeat this procedure for the other cylinder if necessary.

PISTON, PISTON PIN AND PISTON RINGS

The piston is made of an aluminum alloy and is fitted with 2 compression rings and one oil control ring.

Piston Removal

1. Remove the cylinder head as described in this chapter.

2. Mark the top of each piston with an "F" (front cylinder) or "R" (rear cylinder) so they will be reinstalled in their correct cylinder. Refer to **Figure 142**.

3. Remove the cylinder as described in this chapter.

4. Remove the piston rings as described in this chapter.

NOTE
*Wrap a clean shop cloth (**Figure 143**) under the piston so the piston pin clip will not fall into the crankcase.*

5. Remove the piston pin clips (**Figure 144**) from each side of the piston with a small screwdriver or scribe. Hold your thumb over one edge of the clip when removing it to prevent it from springing out.

6. Use a proper size wooden dowel or socket extension and push out the piston pin.

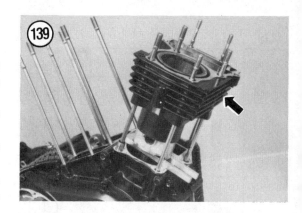

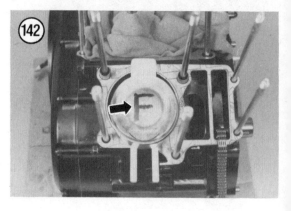

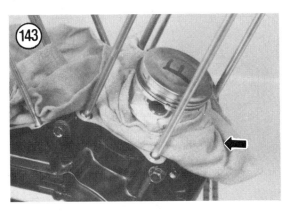

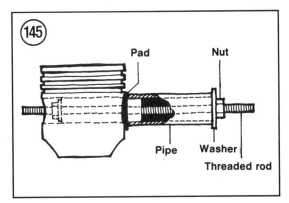

Pad   Nut

Pipe   Washer

Threaded rod

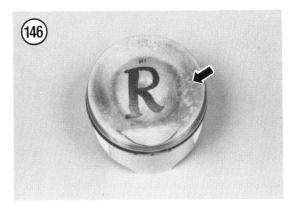

CAUTION
Be careful when removing the pin to avoid damaging the connecting rod. If it is necessary to tap the pin gently to remove it, be sure that the piston is properly supported.

7. If the piston pin is difficult to remove, heat the piston and pin with a small butane torch. The pin will probably push right out. If not, heat the piston to about 60° C (140° F), i.e., until it is too warm to touch, but not excessively hot. If the pin is still difficult to push out, use a special tool as shown in **Figure 145**.

Piston Inspection

1. Carefully clean the carbon from the piston crown (**Figure 146**) with a chemical remover or with a soft scraper. Do not remove or damage the carbon ridge around the circumference of the piston above the top ring. If the pistons, rings and cylinders are found to be dimensionally correct and can be reused, removal of the carbon ring from the top of pistons or carbon ridge from the top of cylinder bores will cause excessive oil consumption.

CAUTION
Do not wire brush piston skirts.

2. Examine each ring groove for burrs, dented edges and wide wear. Pay particular attention to the top compression ring groove, as it usually wears more than the others.
3. Measure piston-to-cylinder clearance as described in this chapter. If damage or wear indicates piston replacement, select a new piston as described under *Piston Clearance Measurement* in this chapter.
4. Oil the piston pin and install it in the connecting rod bearing. Slowly rotate the piston pin and check for radial and axial play (**Figure 147**). If there is play, the piston pin should be replaced, providing the rod bore is in good condition.
5. Measure the piston pin bore (**Figure 148**) with a snap gauge and measure the outside diameter of the piston pin with a micrometer (**Figure 149**). Compare against dimensions given in **Table 1**. A machinist can do this for you if you do not have the measuring tools. Replace the piston and piston pin as a set if either are worn.

6. Check the piston skirt (**Figure 150**) for galling and abrasion which may have been caused by piston seizure. If light galling is present, smooth the affected area with No. 400 emery cloth and oil or a fine oilstone. However, if galling is severe or if the piston is deeply scored, replace it.

Piston Clearance Measurement

1. Make sure the piston and cylinder walls are clean and dry.

2. Measure the inside diameter of the cylinder bore at a point 13 mm (1/2 in.) from the upper edge with a bore gauge.

3. Measure the outside diameter of the piston across the skirt (**Figure 151**) at right angles to the piston pin. Measure at a distance 10 mm (0.4 in.) up from the bottom of the piston skirt.

4. Piston clearance is the difference between the maximum piston diameter and the minimum cylinder diameter. Subtract the dimension of the piston from the cylinder dimension. If the clearance exceeds the dimension listed in **Table 1**, the cylinder should be rebored to the next oversize and a new piston installed.

> *NOTE*
> *The new piston should be obtained before the cylinder is rebored so that the piston can be measured; slight manufacturing tolerances must be taken into account to determine the actual size and working clearance.*

5. To establish a final overbore dimension with a new piston, add the new piston skirt measurement to the specified piston-to-cylinder clearance. This will determine the dimension for the cylinder overbore size.

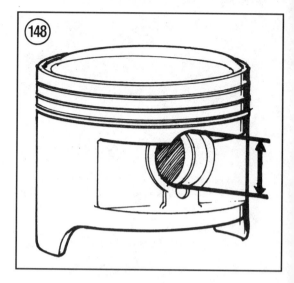

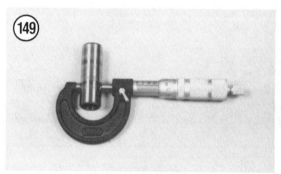

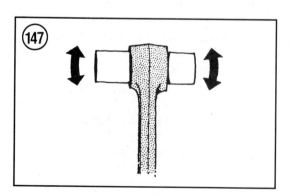

Remember, do not exceed the cylinder maximum inside diameter listed in **Table 1**.

6. There are 2 oversize piston sizes available (0.25 mm and 0.50 mm).

Piston Installation

1. Apply molybdenum disulfide grease to the inside surface of the connecting rod small end. Apply fresh engine oil to the piston pin and piston pin bore.

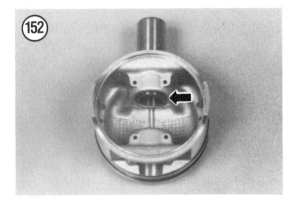

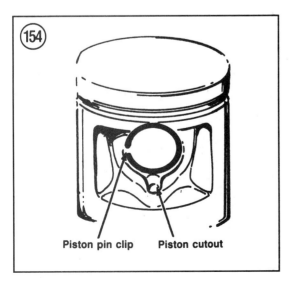

Piston pin clip   Piston cutout

2. Insert the piston pin into the piston until its end extends slightly beyond the inside of the boss (**Figure 152**).

3. Align the piston with the "IN" mark (**Figure 153**) toward the other cylinder (facing toward the carburetors).

4. Be sure to install the piston to the correct connecting rod as marked during removal. Line up the piston pin with the holes in the piston and connecting rod and push the pin into the piston until its ends are even with the clip grooves.

> *NOTE*
> *If the piston pin does not slide in easily, heat the piston until it is too warm to touch but not excessively hot (60° C/140° F). Continue to drive the piston pin while holding the piston so the rod does not have to take any shock. Drive the piston pin in until it is centered in the rod. If the pin is still difficult to install, use the special tool used during the removal sequence.*

> *NOTE*
> *In the next step, install the clips with the gap away from the cutout in the piston (**Figure 154**).*

5. Install new piston pin clips in the ends of the pin boss (**Figure 144**). Make sure they are seated in the grooves.

6. Check installation by rocking the piston back and forth around the pin axis and from side to side along the axis. It should rotate freely back and forth but not from side to side.

7. Repeat for the piston in the other cylinder.

8. Install the rings as described in this chapter.

9. Install the cylinders and cylinder heads as described in this chapter.

**Piston Ring Removal/
Inspection/Installation**

> *WARNING*
> *The edges of all piston rings are very sharp, especially the flat rings of the oil ring assembly. Be careful when handling them to avoid cut fingers.*

1. Measure the side clearance of each ring in its groove with a flat feeler gauge (**Figure 155**) and compare with dimensions listed in **Table 1**. If the

clearance is greater than specified, the rings must be replaced. If the clearance is still excessive with the new rings, the piston must be replaced.

2. Remove the top ring with a ring expander tool or by spreading the ring ends with your thumbs and lifting the ring up and over the piston (**Figure 156**). Repeat for the remaining rings.

3. Carefully remove all carbon from the ring grooves with a ring groove cleaner or a piece of a broken ring. Inspect grooves carefully for burrs, nicks or broken and cracked lands. Recondition or replace the piston if necessary.

4. Roll each ring around its piston groove as shown in **Figure 157** to check for binding. Minor binding may be cleaned up with a fine-cut file.

5. Measure the rings for wear as shown in **Figure 158**:

a. Place each ring, one at a time, into the cylinder and push it in about 20 mm (3/4 in.) with the crown of the piston to ensure that the ring is square in the cylinder bore.

b. Measure the gap with a flat feeler gauge and compare with dimensions listed in **Table 1**. If the gap is greater than specified, the ring(s) should be replaced.

c. When installing new rings, measure their end gap in the same manner. If the gap is less than specified, carefully file the ends with a fine-cut file until the gap is correct.

6. Install the piston rings in the order shown in **Figure 159**.

> *NOTE*
> *Install all rings with their markings fac-*
> *ing up.*

7. Install the piston rings—first the bottom, then the middle, then the top ring—by carefully spreading

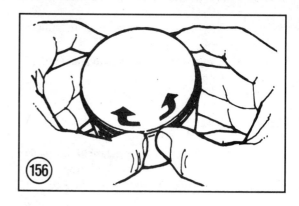

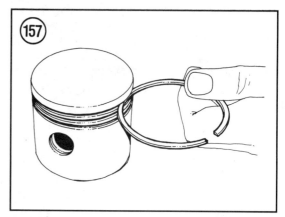

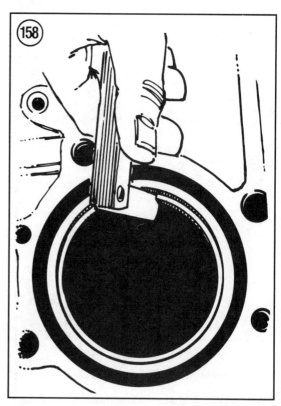

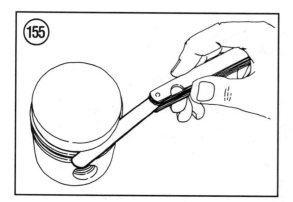

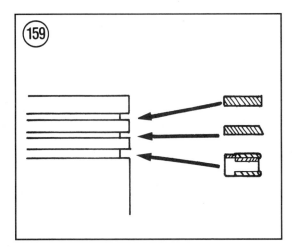

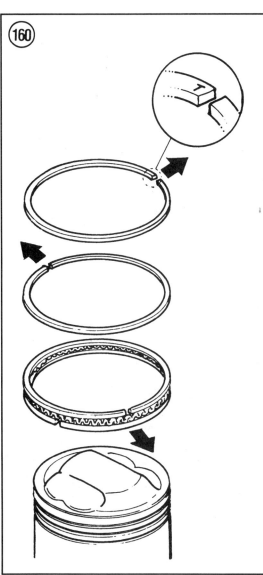

the ends with your thumbs and slipping the ring over the top of the piston. Remember that the piston rings must be installed with the marks on them facing up toward the top of the piston.

8. Make sure the rings are seated completely in their grooves all the way around the piston and that the end gaps are distributed around the piston as shown in **Figure 160**. The important thing is that the ring gaps are not aligned with each other when installed.

9. If new rings are installed, measure the side clearance of each ring in its groove with a flat feeler gauge (**Figure 155**) and compare to dimensions listed in **Table 1**.

OIL PUMP DRIVE SPROCKETS AND DRIVE CHAIN

Removal/Inspection

Refer to **Figure 161** for this procedure.

1. Remove the clutch as described in Chapter Five.

2. Remove the internal oil line (**Figure 162**) from the crankcase. Don't lose the O-ring seals on each end of the line.

NOTE
If the O-rings are not on the oil line when it is removed, check the receptacles in the crankcase. Remove them and install them onto the oil line to prevent misplacing them.

3. Remove the bolt and washer (**Figure 163**) securing the oil pump driven sprocket.

4. Remove the oil pump driven sprocket (A, **Figure 164**) and the drive chain (B, **Figure 164**).

5. Remove the oil pump drive sprocket (**Figure 165**), the clutch outer housing bushing (**Figure 166**) and the distance collar (**Figure 167**).

6. Inspect the drive chain and both sprockets for wear or damage. Refer to **Figure 168** and **Figure 169**. Replace as a set if necessary.

Installation

1. Install the distance collar (**Figure 167**) and the clutch outer housing bushing (**Figure 166**) onto the transmission main shaft prior to installing the sprockets and drive chain.

2. Position the oil pump drive sprocket with the long pins (**Figure 170**) facing out toward the clutch outer

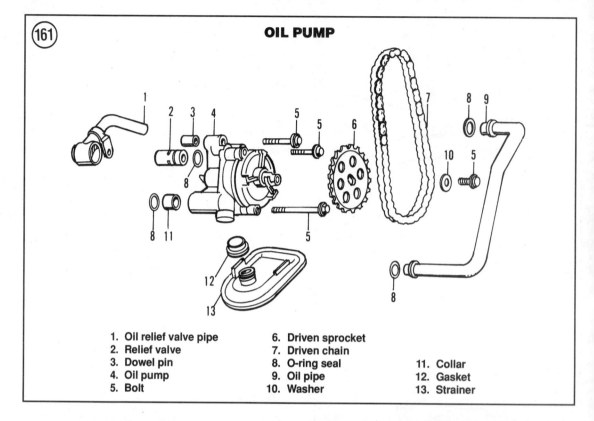

OIL PUMP

1. Oil relief valve pipe
2. Relief valve
3. Dowel pin
4. Oil pump
5. Bolt
6. Driven sprocket
7. Driven chain
8. O-ring seal
9. Oil pipe
10. Washer
11. Collar
12. Gasket
13. Strainer

housing. This is necessary so they will index into the receptacles in the backside of the clutch outer housing for proper clutch operation.

3. Install the oil pump drive sprocket (**Figure 165**).

4. Install the oil pump driven sprocket (A, **Figure 164**) and the drive chain (B, **Figure 164**).

5. Engage the drive chain with the drive sprocket (**Figure 171**).

6. Align the flats on the driven sprocket with the flats on the oil pump shaft.

7. Install the oil pump driven sprocket bolt and washer (**Figure 163**). Tighten the bolt to the torque specification listed in **Table 2**.

8. Install a new O-ring seal (**Figure 172**) onto each end of the internal oil line.

9. Install the oil line (**Figure 162**) into the receptacles in the crankcase. Push the oil line in until it bottoms out.

10. Install the clutch as described in Chapter Five.

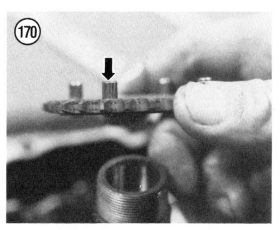

OIL PUMP

The oil pump is mounted within the crankcase. The engine must be removed from the frame and the crankcase disassembled to gain access to the oil pump.

Refer to **Figure 161** for this procedure.

Removal

1. Remove the engine as described in this chapter.
2. Separate the crankcase as described in this chapter.

> *NOTE*
> *Figure 173 is shown with the crankshaft and transmission assemblies removed for clarity. It is not necessary to remove any of these assemblies for this procedure.*

3. Remove the bolts (**Figure 173**) securing the oil pump assembly to the left-hand crankcase.
4. Remove the locating dowel and O-ring seal (**Figure 174**) from the left-hand crankcase.
5. Remove the oil strainer, O-ring seal and the oil pump relief valve pipe from oil pump assembly.

Installation

1. To prime the oil pump, pour clean engine oil into one of the openings in the oil pump. Add oil until the oil drains out of the other opening.
2. Install the O-ring seal (**Figure 175**) onto the oil strainer and then install the oil strainer (**Figure 176**) onto the oil pump. Make sure the locating tabs (A, **Figure 177**) are aligned correctly on the oil pump.

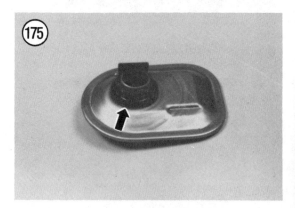

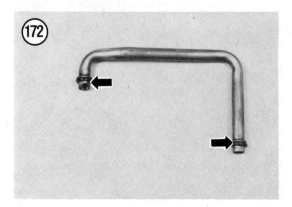

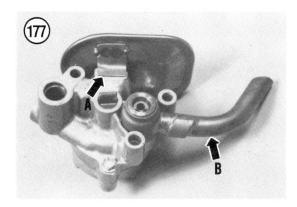

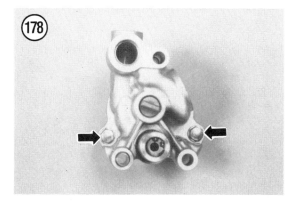

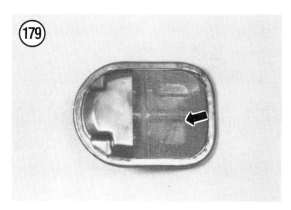

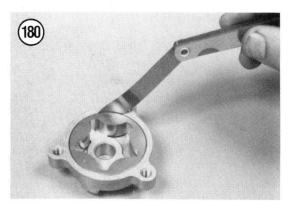

3. Install the oil pump relief valve pipe (B, **Figure 177**) onto the oil pump body.

4. Install a new O-ring seal onto the locating dowel and install the dowel into the crankcase (**Figure 174**).

5. Install the oil pump assembly into the left-hand crankcase.

6. Install the mounting bolts and tighten to the torque specifications listed in **Table 2**.

7. Assemble the crankcase and install the engine as described in this chapter.

8. Refill the engine with the recommended viscosity and quantity of engine oil as described in Chapter Three.

9. Start the engine and check for leaks.

Disassembly/Inspection/
Assembly

> *NOTE*
> *Replacement parts are not available for the oil pump. If any of the external or internal components are worn or damaged, the entire oil pump assembly must be replaced.*

1. Inspect the outer cover and body for cracks.

2. Remove the bolts (**Figure 178**) securing the pump cover to the pump body. Remove the pump cover.

3. Withdraw the oil pump drive shaft, spacer and pin. Don't lose the pin; it will slide out of the shaft.

4. Remove the inner and outer rotors. Check all parts for scratches and abrasion.

5. Clean all parts in solvent and thoroughly dry with compressed air. Carefully scrub the strainer screen with a soft toothbrush; do not damage the screen.

6. Coat all parts with fresh oil prior to installation.

7. Inspect the interior passageways of the oil pump body. Make sure that all oil sludge and foreign matter is removed.

8. Inspect the strainer screen for broken areas (**Figure 179**). This would allow small foreign particles to enter the oil pump and cause damage. If broken in any area, replace the strainer.

9. Install the outer rotor into the pump cover.

10. Check the clearance between the outer rotor and the body (**Figure 180**) with a flat feeler gauge. If the clearance is greater than the service limit in **Table 1**, the oil pump must be replaced.

11. Install the inner rotor, the oil pump drive shaft and pin (**Figure 181**). Mesh the pin into the groove in the inner rotor and install the spacer onto the shaft.

12. Check the clearance between the inner tip and outer rotor (**Figure 182**) with a flat feeler gauge. If the clearance is greater than the service limit in **Table 1**, the oil pump must be replaced.

13. Check the rotor end clearance with a straightedge and flat feeler gauge. If the clearance is greater than the service limit in **Table 1**, the oil pump must be replaced.

14. Install the locating dowel (**Figure 183**) into the cover.

15. Install the body and tighten the screws (**Figure 178**) securely.

16. After the oil pump is assembled, turn the shaft and make sure the oil pump turns freely with no binding.

17. Install the oil pump as described in this chapter.

NOTE
If the condition of the oil pump is doubt-ful, run the Oil Pump Pressure Test described in this chapter.

Oil Pump Pressure Test

If the oil pump output is doubtful, the following test can be performed.

1. Warm the engine up to normal operating temperature (80° C/176° F). Shut off the engine.

2. Place the bike on the centerstand.

3. Check the engine oil level. It must be to the upper line; add oil if necessary. Do not run this test with the oil level low or the test readings will be false.

4. Pull the rubber boot back from the oil pressure switch.

5. Remove the electrical wire (**Figure 184**) from the oil pressure switch.

6. Remove the oil pressure switch from the crank-case.

7. Screw a portable oil pressure gauge into the switch hole in the crankcase.

NOTE
These can be purchased in an automo-tive or motorcycle supply store or from a Honda dealer. The Honda parts are No. 07506-3000000 (Oil Pressure Gauge) and No. 07510-4220100 (Oil Pressure Gauge Attachment).

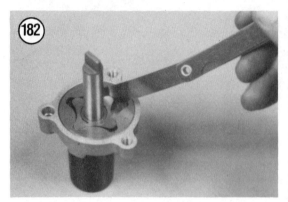

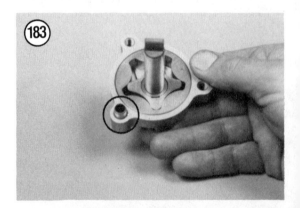

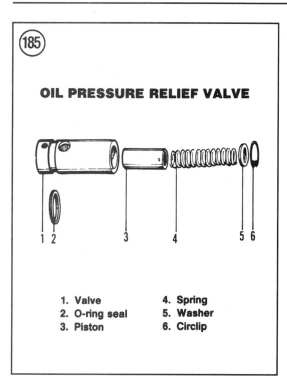

OIL PRESSURE RELIEF VALVE

1. Valve
2. O-ring seal
3. Piston
4. Spring
5. Washer
6. Circlip

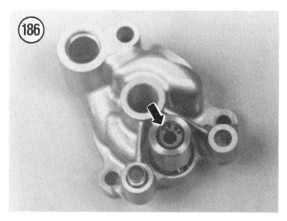

8. With the engine at normal operating temperature, start the engine and run it at 6,000 rpm. The standard pressure is as follows:

a. 1985-1986: 4.7-6.1 kg/cm^2 (66.7-86.6 psi).
b. 1987-on: 4.5 kg/cm^2 (64 psi).

If the pressure is less than specified the oil pump must be replaced.

9. Remove the portable oil pressure gauge.

10. Apply Three-Bond No. 1211 or equivalent to the switch threads prior to installation. Tighten the switch to the torque specifications listed in **Table 2**.

11. Install the electrical wire to the top of the switch. This connection must be free of oil to make good electrical contact.

12. Slide the rubber boot back into place on the switch.

OIL PRESSURE RELIEF VALVE

Disassembly/Inspection/Assembly

Refer to **Figure 185** for this procedure.

1. Remove the oil pump as described in this chapter.

2. Remove the circlip (**Figure 186**) securing the pressure relief valve.

3. Remove the washer, spring and check valve.

4. Wash all parts in solvent and thoroughly dry with compressed air.

5. Inspect the check valve and the cylinder that it rides in for scratches or wear. Replace if defective.

6. Make sure the spring is not broken or distorted; replace if necessary.

7. Make sure the holes in the valve are not clogged.

8. Install the check valve, spring, washer and circlip.

9. Install the oil pump as described in this chapter.

PRIMARY DRIVE GEAR

Removal/Installation

1. Remove the engine from the frame as described in this chapter.

2. Remove the bolts securing the right-hand crankcase cover (**Figure 187**) and remove the cover and gasket. Don't lose the locating dowels.

3. To keep the primary drive gear from turning, insert a copper washer into mesh with the primary drive gear and the clutch outer housing gear.

4

4. Remove the bolt (A, **Figure 188**) securing the pulse generator plate and the primary drive gear.

5. Remove the pulse generator plate (B, **Figure 188**).

6. Insert a flat-bladed screwdriver into the primary drive gear (A, **Figure 189**) and align the sub-gear teeth.

7. Slide the primary drive gear (B, **Figure 189**) up and off of the crankshaft.

8. Inspect the primary drive gear as described in this chapter.

9. Install by reversing these removal steps while noting the following.

10. Prior to installing the pulse generator plate, fill in the timing marks with white grease pencil or typewriter white correction fluid. This will make it easier to see the timing marks.

11. Align the flat on the crankshaft splines with the flat section on the primary drive gear and the pulse generator plate and install both parts.

12. Use the same tool set-up used in Step 5 to keep the primary drive gear from turning and tighten the bolt to the torque specifications listed in **Table 2**.

Inspection

1. Inspect the sub-gear springs (**Figure 190**) for wear or damage. Replace the gear if necessary.

2. Inspect the inner splines (**Figure 191**) for wear or damage. Replace the gear if necessary.

3. Inspect the gear for chipped or missing teeth (**Figure 192**). Replace the gear if necessary.

CRANKCASE

Disassembly of the crankcase (splitting the cases) and removal of the crankshaft assembly requires that the engine be removed from the frame.

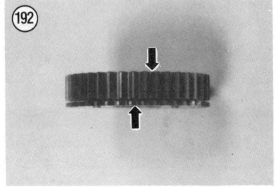

The crankcase is made in 2 halves of precision die cast aluminum alloy and is of the "thin-walled" type. To avoid damage, do not hammer or pry on any of the interior or exterior projected walls. These areas are easily damaged. The cases are assembled with a coat of gasket sealer between the 2 halves and dowel pins align the halves when they are bolted together.

The procedure which follows is presented as a complete, step-by-step major lower-end rebuild that should be followed if an engine is to be completely

reconditioned. However, if you're replacing a known failed part, the disassembly should be carried out only until the failed part is accessible; there's no need to disassemble the engine beyond that point so long as you know the remaining components are in good condition and that they were not affected by the failed part.

Disassembly

1. Remove the engine as described in this chapter.
2. Remove all exterior engine assemblies as described in this chapter and other related chapters:
    a. Cylinder heads (this chapter).
    b. Cylinders (this chapter).
    c. Pistons and piston pins (this chapter).
    d. Alternator (this chapter).
    e. External shift mechanism (Chapter Six).
    f. Water pump (Chapter Nine).
    g. Starter gears (this chapter).
    h. Starter motor (Chapter Eight).

> *NOTE*
> *Wedge a soft copper washer between the primary drive gear and the gear on the clutch outer housing to keep the primary drive gear from rotating during removal and installation of the bolt.*

3. Prior to removing the clutch, loosen the bolt (**Figure 193**) securing the primary drive gear to the end of the crankshaft.
4. Remove the clutch as described in Chapter Five.

> *NOTE*
> *Install the drive shaft universal joint onto the splined end of the output gear shaft (**Figure 194**). Place a large screwdriver or drift between the 2 sections of the universal joint. Hold onto the screwdriver or large drift to prevent the gears from moving while you remove the bolt and washer on the output gear shaft.*

5. Remove the bolt and washer (**Figure 195**) securing the output gear shaft.
6. Remove the front cylinder cam chain (**Figure 196**) from the timing gear on the crankshaft and remove the chain.
7. Remove the rear cylinder cam chain from the timing sprocket (**Figure 197**) and remove the chain.

8. Slide the rear cylinder timing sprocket (**Figure 198**) off of the crankshaft.

9. Loosen, then remove, the left-hand crankcase bolts:

    a. 8 mm flange bolt (**Figure 199**).

    b. 8 mm Allen bolt (**Figure 200**).

    c. 6 mm flange bolt (**Figure 201**).

> *NOTE*
> *Note the location of the washer on the*
> *bolt (W, Figure 202).*

10. Loosen the right-hand crankcase 6 mm and 8 mm bolts (**Figure 202**) in the torque pattern shown and in 2-3 steps. Remove the bolts.

11. Lay the crankcase assembly on 2 blocks of wood with the left-hand crankcase side up.

12. Using a soft-faced mallet, tap around the perimeter of the crankcase half and on the end of the crankshaft while pulling up on the right-hand crankcase half. Continue to tap until the crankcase halves separate.

13. Remove the left-hand crankcase half.

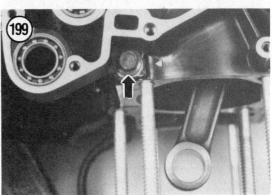

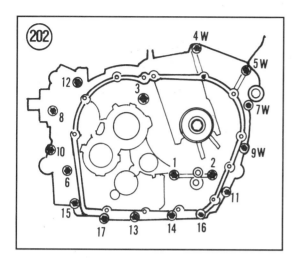

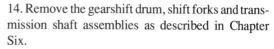

14. Remove the gearshift drum, shift forks and transmission shaft assemblies as described in Chapter Six.

15. Pull the crankshaft assembly straight up and out of the right-hand crankcase half.

16. Remove the oil pump assembly as described in this chapter.

17. Remove the oil jet (**Figure 203**) from each crankcase half.

18. Remove the output gear case as described in this chapter.

19. Remove the oil control orifice (**Figure 204**) for the final drive unit to avoid misplacing it.

20. If necessary, remove the neutral and the overdrive (OD) indicator switches (**Figure 205**), the oil pressure switch (**Figure 206**) and the oil control bolt (**Figure 207**) from the left-hand crankcase half.

Crankcase Inspection

1. Clean both crankcase halves inside and out with cleaning solvent. Thoroughly dry with compressed air and wipe off with a clean shop cloth. Be sure to remove all traces of the old gasket material from the mating surfaces.

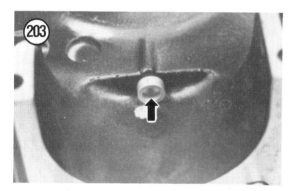

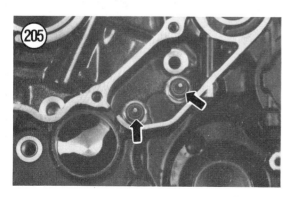

2. Check the transmission, shift drum and output gear ball bearings for roughness and play by rotating them slowly by hand. Refer to **Figure 208** and **Figure 209**. If any roughness or play can be felt in a bearing, it must be replaced. Refer to *Crankcase Ball Bearing Replacement* in this chapter for the correct procedure.

NOTE
Inspection of the crankshaft main bearing is covered under **Crankshaft Inspection** *in this chapter.*

3. Carefully examine the cases (A, **Figure 210**) for cracks and fractures. Also check the areas around the stiffening ribs, bearing bosses and threaded holes. If any damage is found, have it repaired by a shop specializing in the repair of precision aluminum castings or replace the crankcase halves as a set.

4. Make sure the crankcase studs (B, **Figure 210**) are tight. If any are loose, tighten them securely.

5. Inspect the camshaft drive chain and sprockets (**Figure 211**) for each cylinder. Check the sprockets for chipped or missing teeth; replace if necessary. If one of the sprockets is damaged, chances are the drive chain will also be damaged. If any one of the 3 parts is worn or damaged, replace all 3 parts as a set.

Crankcase Ball Bearing Replacement

The following special Honda tools may be required for bearing removal from the left-hand crankcase half:

   a. Bearing remover (20 mm): Honda part No. 07936-3710600.
   b. Remover handle: Honda part No. 07936-3710100.
   c. Remover weight: Honda part No. 07936-3710200.

1. On the right-hand crankcase half, remove the screws securing the bearing retainers (**Figure 212**) and remove the bearing retainers.

2. The bearings are installed with a slight interference fit. The crankcase must be heated in an oven to about 100° C (212° F). An easy way to check for the proper temperature is to drop tiny drops of water on the case; if they sizzle and evaporate immediately, the temperature is correct. Heat only one case half at a time.

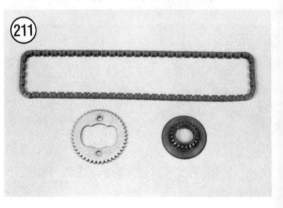

3. Remove the case from the oven and hold onto the crankcase with a kitchen potholder, heavy gloves or heavy shop cloths—*it is hot.*

4. Hold the case with the bearing side down and tap it squarely on a piece of soft wood. Continue to tap until the bearing(s) fall out. Repeat for the other half.

5A. On the right-hand crankcase half, if the bearings are difficult to remove, they can be gently tapped out with a socket or piece of pipe the same size as the bearing outer race.

5B. On the left-hand crankcase half, if the bearings are difficult to remove, special tools are required as

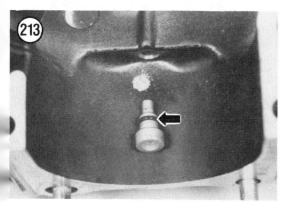

the bearings are not accessible from the other side of the crankcase. Use the special Honda tools described in the introduction to this procedure:

    a. Attach the bearing remover to the bearing.

    b. Attach the remover handle and remover weight to the bearing remover.

    c. Move the weight up and down on the remover handle (similar to a body shop slide hammer) until the bearing is removed from the crank-case.

    d. If necessary, repeat this step for the other bearing.

6. While heating the crankcase halves, place new bearings in a freezer if possible. Chilling them will slightly reduce their overall diameter while the hot crankcase is slightly larger due to heat expansion. This will make installation easier.

7. Install the new bearing(s) in the heated cases. Press each bearing in by hand until it is completely seated. Do not hammer it in. If a bearing will not seat, remove it and cool it. Reheat the case and install the bearing again.

8. On bearings so equipped, install the bearing retainer and tighten the screws securely.

Assembly

Assemble all components into the right-hand crankcase half.

1. If removed, install the neutral and OD indicator switches (**Figure 205**) and the oil control bolt (**Figure 207**).

2. If removed, apply a coat of Three-Bond No. 1211, or equivalent to the threads of the oil pressure switch. Install the switch (**Figure 206**) and tighten to the torque specification listed in **Table 2**.

3. Install the output gear case oil control orifice (**Figure 204**) into the left-hand crankcase half.

4. Install a new O-ring seal (**Figure 213**) on each oil jet and install an oil jet into each crankcase half (**Figure 203**).

5. Lightly oil the right-hand main bearing and the right-hand end of the crankshaft (primary drive gear splines).

6. Position the crankshaft so the connecting rods are toward the top of the crankcase. Position the front cylinder connecting rod so it fits into the cylinder relief in the crankcase (**Figure 214**) and lower the crankshaft straight into the right crankcase half (**Figure 215**).

7. Hold onto the connecting rods and turn the crankshaft slowly to make sure it spins freely. If not, repeat Step 6 and position the crankshaft correctly.

8. If removed, install the locating dowel and O-ring seal (**Figure 216**) into the left-hand crankcase.

9. Refer to Chapter Five and reinstall the transmission shaft assemblies and the internal shift mechanism.

10. Apply a coat of cold grease to the thrust washer and place it on the output gear case final drive bearing in the right-hand crankcase (**Figure 217**).

11. Place the output gear case final drive gear (A, **Figure 218**) and bushing (B, **Figure 218**) into place in the right-hand crankcase.

12. Temporarily insert the final drive gear assembly into the output gear case final drive gear and thrust washer (**Figure 219**). This will align the holes in the gear and washer with the inside diameter of the bearing in the crankcase.

13. Carefully pull the output gear case final drive gear assembly (**Figure 220**) straight up and out of the gear and thrust washer. Do not disturb their alignment during removal of the gear assembly.

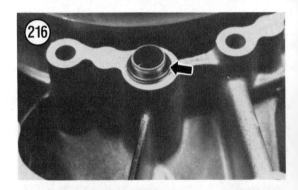

14. Install the oil pump assembly into the left-hand crankcase as described in this chapter.

15. Install the alignment dowels (**Figure 221**) into one of the crankcase halves.

16. Spray the sealing surface of both crankcase halves with aerosol electrical contact cleaner. This will remove any traces of oil from the surfaces to achieve a better seal.

17. Apply a light even coat of liquid gasket sealer to the sealing surface of one crankcase half.

NOTE
On 1985-1986 models, since the external finish of the engine is black, use a black colored sealer such as Permatex RTV Black Silicone Adhesive Sealer (part No. 16B) or equivalent.

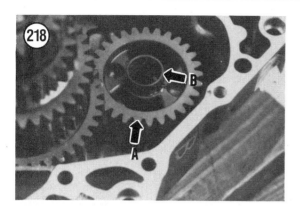

18. Set the left-hand case in place over the right crankcase assembly. Push it down squarely into place until it reaches the crankshaft bearing. There is usually about 13 mm (1/2 in.) to go.

19. Lightly tap the case halves together with a plastic or rubber mallet until they seat.

CAUTION
Crankcase halves should fit together without force. If the crankcase halves do not fit together completely, do not attempt to pull them together with the crankcase screws. Separate the crankcase halves and investigate the cause of the interference. If the transmission shafts were disassembled, recheck to make sure that a gear is not installed backwards. Do not risk damage by trying to force the cases together.

20. Install the output gear case as described in this chapter.

21. Rotate the crankshaft and transmission shafts by hand to make sure they rotate freely.

NOTE
Be sure to install the washer under the correct bolt as indicated in W, Figure 202.

22. Install and tighten the right-hand crankcase 6 mm and 8 mm bolts (**Figure 202**) in the indicated torque pattern in 2-3 steps. Tighten the bolts to the torque specifications listed in **Table 2**.

23. Install the left-hand crankcase bolts:
   a. 8 mm flange bolt (**Figure 199**).
   b. 8 mm Allen bolt (**Figure 200**).
   c. 6 mm flange bolt (**Figure 201**).
Tighten the bolts in 2-3 steps to the torque specifications listed in **Table 2**.

NOTE
The crankshaft has so much end float and it is so heavy that it may not want to rotate with the crankcase assembly on its side. Therefore, it is necessary for the crankcase to be upright.

24. After the crankcase halves are completely assembled, turn the crankcase assembly upright. Once again rotate the crankshaft and transmission shafts by hand to make sure they rotate freely and that there is no binding. If any is present, disassemble the crankcase and correct the problem.

25. Slide the rear cylinder timing sprocket (**Figure 198**) onto the crankshaft.

26. Install and properly mesh the rear cylinder cam chain onto the timing sprocket (**Figure 197**).

27. Install the front cylinder cam chain (**Figure 196**) onto the timing gear on the crankshaft.

NOTE
Use the same tool set-up used during removal to prevent the gears from moving while you tighten the bolt on the output gear shaft.

28. Install the bolt and washer (**Figure 195**) securing the output gear shaft. Tighten the bolt to the torque specification listed in **Table 2**.

29. Install the clutch as described in Chapter Five.

NOTE
Wedge a soft copper washer between the primary drive gear and the gear on the clutch outer housing to keep the primary drive gear from rotating during installation of the bolt.

30. Tighten the bolt (**Figure 193**) securing the primary drive gear to the end of the crankshaft. Tighten to the torque specification listed in **Table 2**.

31. Install all exterior engine assemblies as described in this chapter and other related chapters:

    a. Cylinder heads (this chapter).

    b. Cylinders (this chapter).

    c. Pistons and piston pins (this chapter).

    d. Alternator (this chapter).

    e. External shift mechanism (Chapter Six).

    f. Water pump (Chapter Nine).

    g. Starter gears (this chapter).

    h. Starter motor (Chapter Eight).

32. Install the engine as described in this chapter.

33. Fill the engine with the recommended viscosity and quantity of engine oil. Refer to Chapter Three.

CRANKSHAFT

The left-hand end of the crankshaft, where the alternator rotor is attached, is different between the 1985-1986 and the 1987-on models. On 1985-1986 models, the alternator rotor is splined onto the crankshaft end while the 1987-on models there is a locking taper and Woodruff key to secure the rotor.

Inspection

1. Remove the connecting rods from the crankshaft as described in this chapter.

2. Clean crankshaft thoroughly with solvent. Clean oil holes (**Figure 222**) with rifle cleaning brushes; flush thoroughly with new solvent and dry with compressed air. Lightly oil all bearing journal surfaces immediately to prevent rust.

3. Carefully inspect each journal for scratches, ridges, scoring, nicks, etc. Refer to **Figure 223** for 1985-1986 models or **Figure 224** for 1987-on mod-

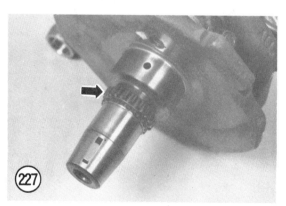

els. Very small nicks and scratches may be removed with fine emery cloth. More serious damage must be removed by grinding—a job for a machine shop or dealer.

4. If the surface on all journals is satisfactory, take the crankshaft to a dealer or machine shop to be checked for out-of-roundness, taper and wear on the bearing journals (**Figure 225**). Also check crankshaft runout. The service limit is listed in **Table 1**.

5. Inspect the sprocket teeth (front cylinder) for the cam chain. Refer to A, **Figure 226** for 1985-1986 models or **Figure 227** for 1987-on models. If damaged, the crankshaft must be replaced.

6. Inspect the splines for the timing sprocket. Refer to **Figure 228** for 1985-1986 models or **Figure 229** for 1987-on models. If damaged, the crankshaft must be replaced.

7. On 1985-1986 models, inspect the splines for the alternator rotor (B, **Figure 226**). If damaged, the crankshaft must be replaced.

**Crankshaft Main
Bearing Inspection**

The crankshaft main bearing inserts in the crankcase *cannot* be replaced. If worn or damaged, the crankcase half must be replaced. The crankcase halves can be replaced individually. It is not necessary to replace them as a matched pair.

1. Check the inside surface of the bearing inserts (A, **Figure 230**) for wear, bluish tint (burned), flaking, abrasion and scoring. If the insert is questionable, replace the crankcase half.

2. Clean the bearing surfaces of the crankshaft and the main bearing inserts. Measure the main bearing clearance by performing the following steps:

a. Measure the inside diameter of the bearing insert (B, **Figure 230**) with an inside micrometer.

b. Measure the outside diameter of the crankshaft main bearing journal with a micrometer (**Figure 225**).

c. Subtract the main bearing journal OD from the bearing insert ID. This will give you the clearance between the 2 parts. The service limit dimension is listed in **Table 1**.

3. If the bearing clearance is greater than specified, use the following steps for selecting a new crankcase half:

a. The crankshaft main journals are marked with numbers "1" or "2" (**Figure 231**).

NOTE
The number on the left-hand end (end with the cam chain sprocket) relates to the bearing insert in the left-hand crankcase and the number on the right-hand end (primary drive gear splines) relates to the bearing insert in the right-hand crankcase. Remember the left-hand side relates to the engine as it sits in the bike's frame, not as it sits on your workbench.

b. The crankcase main bearing insert is marked adjacent to the insert (**Figure 232**) and is sometimes marked with paint on the backside of the crankcase halves (**Figure 233**).

c. If the crankshaft main journal dimension is within the tolerances stated in **Table 1**, the new crankcase can be selected by referring to **Table 4**. Cross-reference the main journal number (**Figure 231**) in the horizontal column of **Table 4** to the crankcase insert letter (**Figure 232**) in the vertical column. Where the 2 columns intersect, the new crankcase letter is indicated.

d. If any main bearing journal measurements taken during inspection do not fall within the tolerance range listed in **Table 4**, the crankshaft must be replaced. Honda recommends the crankshaft be replaced whenever a main bearing journal dimension is beyond the specified range in **Table 1**.

4. After a new crankcase has been purchased, recheck clearance by repeating this procedure.

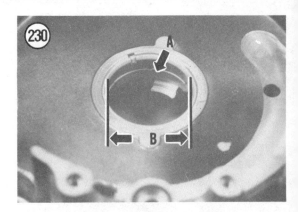

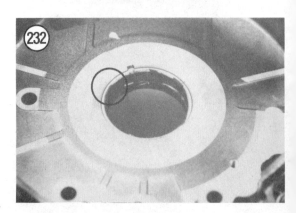

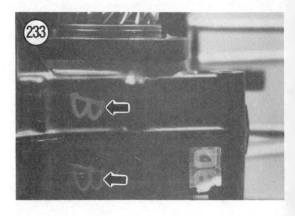

CONNECTING RODS

Removal/Installation

1. Remove the engine as described in this chapter.

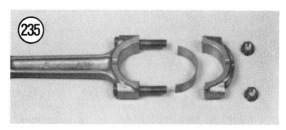

2. Split the crankcase and remove the crankshaft assembly as described under *Crankcase Disassembly* in this chapter.

NOTE
Prior to disassembly, mark the rods and caps. Mark them with an "L" for lefthand end (end with the cam chain sprocket) or "R" for the right-hand end (primary drive gear splines). Remember the left-hand side relates to the engine as it sits in the bike's frame, not as it sits on your workbench.

3. Measure the connecting rod side clearance as described under *Connecting Rod Inspection* in this chapter.

4. Remove the nuts securing the connecting rod caps and remove the caps (**Figure 234**).

5. Carefully remove the connecting rods from the crankshaft.

6. Remove and mark the back of each bearing insert (**Figure 235**) with the cylinder "R" (right) or "L" (left) location and "U" (upper) or "L" (lower).

7. Install by reversing these removal steps while noting the following.

8. Install the bearing inserts into each connecting rod and cap. Make sure they are locked into place correctly (**Figure 236**).

NOTE
If the old bearing inserts are reused, be sure they are installed into their original positions; refer to Step 6.

9. Apply molybdenum disulfide grease to the bearing inserts, crank pins and connecting rod bolt threads. Install the connecting rods and rod caps. Tighten the cap nuts evenly in 2-3 steps to the torque specifications listed in **Table 2**.

10. After all rod caps have been installed, rotate the crankshaft several times and check that the bearings are not too tight. Make sure there is no binding.

Connecting Rod Inspection

1. Prior to removing the connecting rods from the crankshaft, measure the side clearance as follows:

    a. Insert a flat feeler gauge between the side of the connecting rod and the crankshaft as shown in **Figure 237**.

b. Refer to the service limit dimension listed in **Table 1**.

c. Replace the connecting rod(s) if it is worn to the service limit dimension or less.

2. Remove the connecting rods from the crankshaft as described in this chapter.

3. Clean the connecting rods and inserts in solvent and dry with compressed air.

4. Carefully inspect each rod journal (**Figure 238**) on the crankshaft for scratches, ridges, scoring, nicks, etc. Very small nicks and scratches may be removed with fine emery cloth. More serious damage must be removed by grinding—a job for a machine shop or dealer.

5. If the surface on all journals is satisfactory, take the crankshaft to a dealer or machine shop to be checked for out-of-roundness, taper and wear on the rod bearing journals (**Figure 239**).

Connecting Rod Bearing Selection

1. Check the inside and outside surfaces of the bearing inserts for wear, bluish tint (burned), flaking, abrasion and scoring. If the bearings are good, they may be reused. If any insert is questionable, replace the entire set.

2. Measure the inside diameter of the small end of the connecting rod (**Figure 240**) with an inside dial gauge. Check against the dimension listed in **Table 1**; replace the rod if necessary.

3. Clean the rod bearing surfaces of the crankshaft and the rod bearing inserts. Measure the rod bearing clearance by performing the following steps:

a. Place a strip of Plastigage over each rod bearing journal parallel to the crankshaft (**Figure 241**). Do not place the Plastigage material over an oil hole in the crankshaft.

NOTE
Do not rotate connecting rod on the crankshaft while the Plastigage strips are in place.

b. Install the rod cap onto one rod and tighten the nuts to the torque specification listed in **Table 2**.

c. Remove the rod cap and measure the width of the flattened Plastigage (**Figure 242**) following the manufacturer's instructions. Measure both ends of the Plastigage strip. A difference

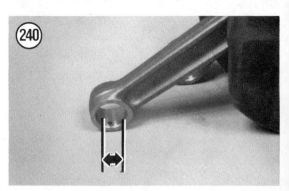

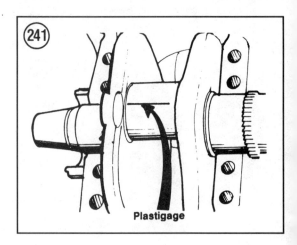

Plastigage

of 0.025 mm (0.001 in.) or more indicates a tapered journal. Confirm with a micrometer.

d. New bearing clearance and the service limit are listed in **Table 1**. Remove all of the Plastigage material from the crankshaft journals and the connecting rods.

4. If the rod bearing clearance is greater than specified, use the following steps for new bearing selection:

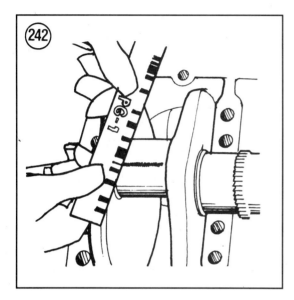

a. The crankshaft connecting rod journals are marked with letters "A" or "B" (**Figure 243**).

NOTE
The letter on the counterbalance weight refers to the rod journal to the right of the weight. The left-hand end of the crankshaft is the end with the cam chain sprocket and the right-hand end is the end with the primary drive gear splines. Remember the left-hand side relates to the engine as it sits in the bike's frame, not as it sits on your workbench.

b. The connecting rod and cap are marked with numbers "1" or "2" (**Figure 244**).

c. Measure the rod journal with a micrometer (**Figure 239**). If the rod journal dimension is within the tolerances stated for each letter code in **Table 5**, the bearing can be selected by color code.

d. Select new bearings by cross-referencing the rod journal letters (**Figure 243**) in the horizontal column of **Table 5** to the rod bearing number (**Figure 244**) in the vertical column. Where the 2 columns intersect, the new bearing color is indicated. **Table 6** gives the bearing insert color and thickness.

5. If any rod bearing journal measurements taken during inspection do not fall within the tolerance range for the letter codes, the serviceability of the crankshaft must be carefully examined. If the rod bearing journal in question is not tapered, out-of-round or scored, the crankshaft may still be used. However, the bearing selection will have to be made based on the measured diameter of the bearing journal and not by the letter code. Honda recommends the crankshaft be replaced whenever a rod bearing journal dimension is beyond the specified range of the stamped letter code.

6. When replacing connecting rods, the front and rear rods must be matched in weight. Use the following steps for new connecting rod selection.

a. A weight code is stamped on the connecting rod (**Figure 245**).

b. Cross-reference the front and rear connecting rods with the listings in **Table 7**. Where the 2 columns intersect with an "X" mark, the connecting rods are matched and can be used together.

7. After new bearings have been installed, recheck clearance by repeating this procedure.

8. Repeat Steps 1-7 for the other cylinder.

OUTPUT GEAR UNIT

Gear Case
Removal/Installation

1. Remove the engine as described in this chapter.

2. Remove the flange bolts (**Figure 246**) securing the output gear case to the left-hand crankcase half.

3. Remove the output gear case (**Figure 247**).

4. Remove the shim (**Figure 248**).

5. Remove the oil control orifice (**Figure 249**) from the crankcase where the oil pickup line is located.

6. Clean the orifice in solvent and dry with compressed air. Make sure the orifice (**Figure 250**) is clean to ensure maximum oil flow to the output gear assembly.

7. Inspect the splines (**Figure 251**) on the cross shaft for wear or damage. Replace if necessary.

8. Install by reversing these removal steps while noting the following.

> *CAUTION*
> *The following shim has an effect on gear backlash. The correct shim thickness must be installed or the output gear unit may be damaged.*

9. If the shim requires replacement, replace with a shim of the *same* thickness. There are 5 different shims available from 0.40-0.60 mm (0.016-0.024 in.) in 0.05 mm (0.002 in.) increments. Take the old shim to your dealer and get a replacement shim of the same thickness.

10. Install a new O-ring seal on the oil control orifice. Install the oil control orifice in the crankcase.

11. Install the flange bolts (**Figure 246**) and tighten to the torque specification listed in **Table 2**.

Output Gear Assembly
Removal

1. Remove the engine as described in this chapter.

2. Remove the clutch assembly as described in Chapter Five.

> *NOTE*
> *Install the drive shaft universal joint onto the splined end of the output gear shaft (**Figure 252**). Place a large screwdriver or drift between the 2 sections of the universal joint. Hold onto the screwdriver or large drift to prevent the gears from moving while you remove the bolt and washer on the output gear shaft.*

3. Remove the bolt and washer (**Figure 253**) securing the output gear shaft.

4. Remove the flange bolts (**Figure 246**) securing the output gear case to the left-hand crankcase half.

5. Remove the output gear case (**Figure 247**).

6. Remove the shim (**Figure 248**).

7. Remove the oil control orifice (**Figure 249**) from the crankcase where the oil pickup line is located.

8. Withdraw the output gear assembly (**Figure 254**) from the crankcase.

Output Gear Assembly
Installation

1. Apply clean engine oil to the O-ring seal (**Figure 255**).

2. Install the output gear assembly (**Figure 256**) into the crankcase and through the output gear within the crankcase.

3. There will be a slight gap (**Figure 257**) between the mounting flange and the crankcase surface. This is normal due to the internal spring pressure on the damper spring.

4. Install a new O-ring seal on the oil control orifice. Install the oil control orifice in the crankcase (**Figure 258**). If the inner diameter of the orifice is chamfered, install the orifice with the chamfer facing the oil pressure side of the crankcase.

CAUTION
The following shim has an effect on gear backlash. The correct thickness shim must be installed or the output gear unit may be damaged.

5. If the shim requires replacement, replace with a shim of the *same* thickness. There are 5 different shims available from 0.40-0.60 mm (0.016-0.024 in.) in 0.05 mm (0.002 in.) increments. Take the old shim to your dealer and get a replacement shim of the same thickness.

6. Install the shim (**Figure 248**).

7. Install the output gear case (**Figure 247**).

8. Install the output gear case flange bolts (**Figure 246**) and tighten to the torque specification listed in **Table 2**.

NOTE
Use the same tool set-up used during removal to prevent the gears from moving while you tighten the bolt on the output gear shaft.

9. Install the bolt and washer (**Figure 253**) securing the output gear shaft. Tighten the bolt to the torque specification listed in **Table 2**.

10. Install the clutch assembly as described in Chapter Five.

11. Install the engine as described in this chapter.

Inspection

1. Inspect the O-ring seal (**Figure 255**) for wear, deterioration or if it is starting to harden. Replace if necessary.

2. Inspect the damper spring (**Figure 259**) for damage or fatigue. If damaged, have it replaced.

3. Inspect the damper lifter ramps (**Figure 260**) for wear or damage. If damaged, have it replaced.

4. Inspect the cross shaft gear teeth (**Figure 261**) for chipped or missing teeth. If damaged, have it replaced.

Disassembly/Assembly

Output gear case disassembly and assembly requires a considerable number of special Honda tools. The price of all of these tools could be more than the cost of most repairs done by a dealer.

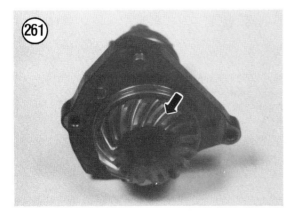

Figure 262 shows the internal components of the output gear case.

CAUTION
Do not try to disassemble the gear case with make-shift tools. Approximately 13 special tools and a hydraulic press are required to disassemble and assemble the unit. If assembled incorrectly, the gear tooth contact pattern and set-up tolerance will be incorrect and the unit will be damaged.

ALTERNATOR ROTOR, STARTER CLUTCH ASSEMBLY AND STARTER GEARS

The alternator rotor, starter clutch assembly and starter gears can be removed with the engine in the frame. The starter motor can be left in place, if desired.

Refer to the following illustrations for this procedure:

    a. **Figure 263**: starter gears.

    b. **Figure 264**: alternator assembly (1985-1986 models).

    c. **Figure 265**: alternator assembly (1987-on models).

Removal

1. Place the bike on the centerstand.

2. Remove both side covers and the seat.

3. Disconnect the battery negative lead (**Figure 266**).

4. Remove the clutch slave cylinder as described in Chapter Five. It is not necessary to remove the slave cylinder completely, just move it out of the way.

5. Remove the bolts securing the starter gear cover (**Figure 267**) and remove the cover and gasket. Don't lose the locating dowels.

6. Remove the starter drive gear (**Figure 268**) and the starter torque limiter (**Figure 269**).

7A. On 1985-1986 models, perform the following:

    a. Remove the bolt securing the gearshift pedal arm and remove the arm from the shift shaft.

    b. Remove the bolts securing the gearshift pedal and left-hand footpeg assembly as described in Chapter Thirteen.

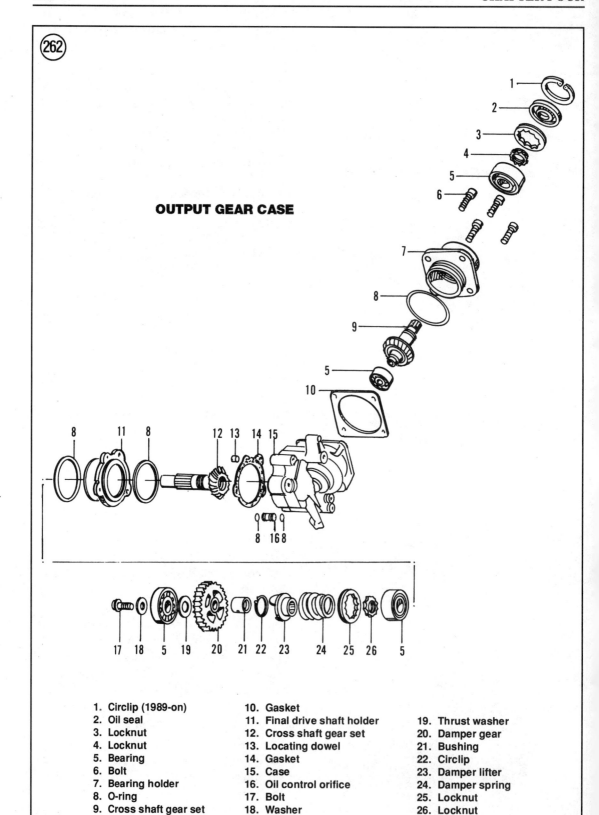

(262)

OUTPUT GEAR CASE

1. Circlip (1989-on)
2. Oil seal
3. Locknut
4. Locknut
5. Bearing
6. Bolt
7. Bearing holder
8. O-ring
9. Cross shaft gear set
10. Gasket
11. Final drive shaft holder
12. Cross shaft gear set
13. Locating dowel
14. Gasket
15. Case
16. Oil control orifice
17. Bolt
18. Washer
19. Thrust washer
20. Damper gear
21. Bushing
22. Circlip
23. Damper lifter
24. Damper spring
25. Locknut
26. Locknut

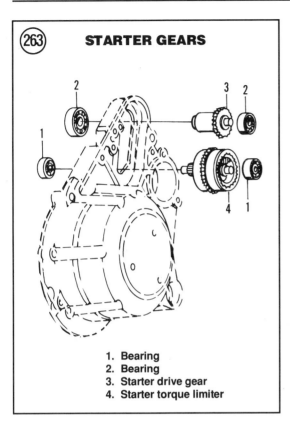

STARTER GEARS

1. Bearing
2. Bearing
3. Starter drive gear
4. Starter torque limiter

7B. On 1987-on models, remove the bolts securing the gearshift pedal and left-hand footpeg assembly as described in Chapter Thirteen.

8. Disconnect the electrical connectors going to the alternator stator assembly.

9. Remove the bolt securing the oil pipe clamp (A, **Figure 270**) and remove the clamp.

10. Remove the bolts securing the alternator cover (B, **Figure 270**) and remove the cover, gasket and the electrical harness from the frame. Note the path of the wire harness as it must be routed the same during installation.

11A. On 1985-1986 models, perform the following:

NOTE
To keep the rotor from turning while removing the bolt, shift the transmission into gear and have an assistant hold the rear brake on.

CAUTION
*The bolt securing the alternator rotor has **left-hand** threads. The bolt must be turned **clockwise** for removal.*

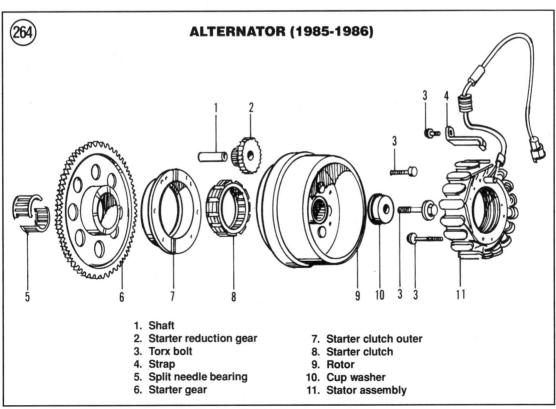

ALTERNATOR (1985-1986)

1. Shaft
2. Starter reduction gear
3. Torx bolt
4. Strap
5. Split needle bearing
6. Starter gear
7. Starter clutch outer
8. Starter clutch
9. Rotor
10. Cup washer
11. Stator assembly

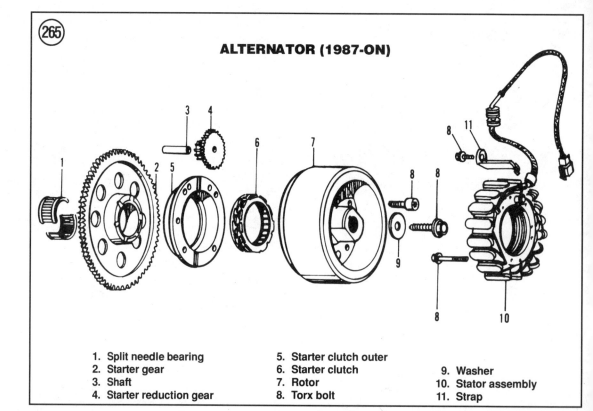

ALTERNATOR (1987-ON)

1. Split needle bearing
2. Starter gear
3. Shaft
4. Starter reduction gear
5. Starter clutch outer
6. Starter clutch
7. Rotor
8. Torx bolt
9. Washer
10. Stator assembly
11. Strap

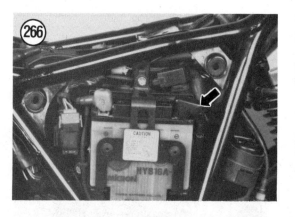

a. Loosen the bolt (**Figure 271**) securing the alternator rotor. Turning a socket *clockwise*, remove the bolt and cup washer securing the alternator rotor.

NOTE
The rotor should slide off of the crankshaft splines. If it will come off easily, use a gear puller and remove the rotor.

b. Remove the rotor (**Figure 272**) from the splines on the crankshaft.

11B. On 1987-on models, perform the following:

NOTE
To keep the rotor from turning while removing the bolt, shift the transmission into gear and have an assistant hold the rear brake on.

CAUTION
*The bolt securing the alternator rotor has **left-hand** threads. The bolt must be turned **clockwise** for removal.*

a. Remove the bolt (**Figure 273**) securing the alternator rotor. Turning a socket *clockwise*, remove the bolt securing the alternator rotor.

b. Screw in the rotor puller (**Figure 274**) until it stops. Use the Honda rotor puller (part No. 07933-3950000), K & N rotor puller (part No. 82-0190) or equivalent.

CAUTION
Don't try to remove the rotor without a puller; any attempt to do so will ultimately lead to some form of damage to the engine and/or rotor. Many aftermarket pullers are available from motorcycle dealers or mail order houses. The

cost of one of these pullers is low and it makes an excellent addition to any mechanic's tool box. If you can't buy or borrow one, have the dealer remove the rotor.

c. Turn the rotor puller with a wrench until the rotor is free.

NOTE
If the rotor is difficult to remove, strike the puller with a hammer a few times. This will usually break it loose.

CAUTION
If normal rotor removal attempts fail, do not force the puller as the threads may be stripped out of the rotor causing expensive damage. Take the bike to a dealer and have the rotor removed.

d. Remove the rotor (**Figure 275**) and remove the puller from the rotor.

12. Remove the starter reduction gear and shaft (**Figure 276**).

13. Remove the shift spindle guide plug (**Figure 277**) from the crankcase. Be careful not to damage the O-ring seal on the plug.

14. Carefully pull the gearshift spindle "A" (A, **Figure 278**) part way out and let it pivot down slightly. It is not necessary to remove the gearshift spindle "A."

15. Remove the starter gear (B, **Figure 278**).

16. Remove the split roller bearing (**Figure 279**) from the crankshaft.

Disassembly/Inspection/ Assembly

1. Carefully inspect the inside of the rotor (**Figure 280**) for small bolts, washers or other metal "trash" that may have been picked up by the magnets. These small metal bits can cause severe damage to the alternator stator assembly.

2. On 1985-1986 models, inspect the inner splines (**Figure 281**) of the rotor for wear or damage. Replace the rotor if necessary.

3. Place the alternator rotor with the starter clutch assembly facing down.

4. Remove the Torx screws (**Figure 282**) securing the starter clutch and starter clutch outer.

5. Turn the alternator rotor over and remove the starter clutch outer (A, **Figure 283**) and the starter clutch (B, **Figure 283**).

6. Check the rollers (B, **Figure 283**) in the starter clutch for uneven or excessive wear; replace if necessary.

7. Measure the inside diameter of the starter clutch outer and compare to dimensions listed in **Table 1**. Replace if necessary.

8. Measure the outside diameter of the starter driven gear where the starter clutch rides (**Figure 284**) and compare to dimensions listed in **Table 1**. Replace if necessary.

9. Inspect the teeth on the starter driven gear (**Figure 285**). Check for chipped or missing teeth. Replace if necessary.

10. Check the split needle bearing (**Figure 286**) for wear or damage. It must rotate freely. Replace if necessary.

11. Inspect the surface of the starter drive gear (**Figure 287**) where it rides in the ball bearing. If worn or damaged, replace the gear if necessary.

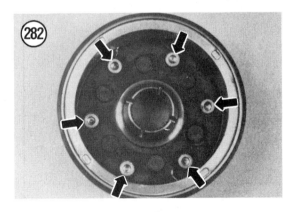

12. Inspect the teeth on the starter drive gear (**Figure 288**). Check for chipped or missing teeth. Look for uneven or excessive wear on the gear face. Replace if necessary.

13. Inspect the teeth on the starter reduction gears (**Figure 289**). Check for chipped or missing teeth. Look for uneven or excessive wear on the gear faces. Replace if necessary.

14. Install the shaft (A, **Figure 290**) into the starter reduction gear (B, **Figure 290**). Rotate the shaft, it must rotate freely with no binding. Replace the worn part(s) if necessary.

15. Inspect the teeth on the starter torque limiter (**Figure 291**). Check for chipped or missing teeth. Look for uneven or excessive wear on the gear faces. Replace if necessary.

16. Make sure the internal circlip is seated correctly within the starter torque limiter at each end. Refer to **Figure 292** and **Figure 293**.

17. Check the ball bearings (**Figure 294**) in the starter gear cover for wear or damage. They must rotate freely. Replace if necessary.

18. Assemble by reversing these disassembly steps while noting the following.

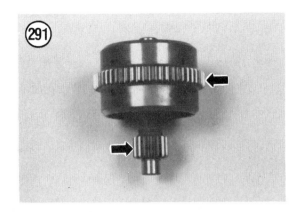

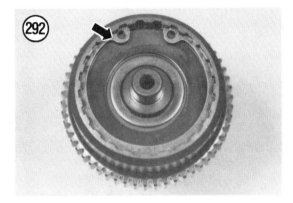

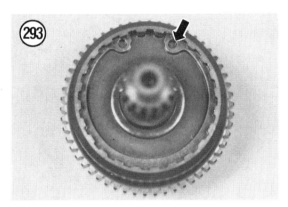

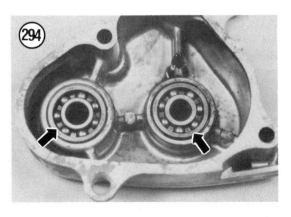

19. Apply red Loctite (No. 271) to the threads of the Torx bolts prior to installing them and tighten to the torque specifications listed in **Table 2**.

Installation

1. Apply cold grease to the split roller bearings and install them onto the crankshaft (**Figure 295**).

2. Install the starter gear (B, **Figure 278**) onto the split roller bearings. Make sure the split bearings stay in place on the crankshaft while installing the starter gear.

3. Move the gearshift spindle "A" up and into position and align the gearshift spindles sector gears of both arms as shown in **Figure 296**. Push the gearshift spindle "A" in all the way (**Figure 297**).

4. Install the starter reduction gear and shaft (**Figure 276**).

5A. On 1985-1986 models, perform the following:

    a. With your fingers, rotate the starter gear *clockwise* and push the rotor assembly onto the crankshaft splines. Push it on all the way.

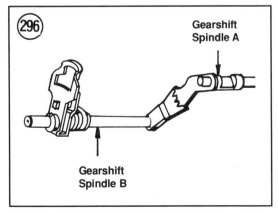

Gearshift Spindle A

Gearshift Spindle B

b. Install the cup washer and the bolt (**Figure 271**).

CAUTION
*Remember, the bolt securing the alternator rotor has **left-hand** threads. The bolt must be turned **counterclockwise** for installation.*

c. Use the same tool set-up used for removal and tighten the bolt *counterclockwise* to the torque specification listed in **Table 2**

5B. On 1987-on models, perform the following:

a. Make sure the Woodruff key is in place on the crankshaft taper.

b. With your fingers, rotate the starter gear *clockwise* and push the rotor assembly onto the crankshaft taper. Push it on all the way (**Figure 275**).

c. Install the washer and bolt (**Figure 273**).

CAUTION
*Remember, the bolt securing the alternator rotor has **left-hand** threads. The bolt must be turned **counterclockwise** for installation.*

d. Use the same tool set-up used for removal and tighten the bolt *counterclockwise* to the torque specification listed in **Table 2**.

6. Inspect the O-ring seal (**Figure 298**) on the guide plug and carefully install the gearshift spindle guide plug (**Figure 277**). Do not damage the O-ring seal during installation.

7. Make sure the locating dowels (A, **Figure 299**) are in place and install a new gasket (B, **Figure 299**).

8. Install the alternator cover (B, **Figure 270**) and bolts. Tighten the bolts securely. Route the electrical harness through the frame in the same path noted prior to removal.

9. Install the bolt and clamp securing the oil pipe clamp (A, **Figure 270**). Tighten the bolt securely.

10. Connect the electrical connectors going to the alternator stator assembly.

11A. On 1985-1986 models, perform the following:

a. Install the gearshift pedal and left-hand footpeg assembly as described in Chapter Thirteen.

b. Install the gearshift pedal arm onto the shift shaft. Tighten the bolt securely.

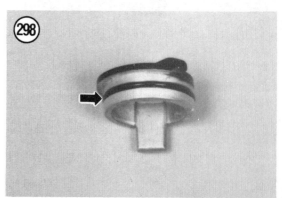

11B. On 1987-on models, install the gearshift pedal and left-hand footpeg assembly as described in Chapter Thirteen.

12. Install the starter torque limiter (**Figure 269**) and the starter drive gear (**Figure 268**).

13. Make sure the locating dowels (A, **Figure 300**) are in place and install a new gasket (B, **Figure 300**).

14. Install the starter gear cover (**Figure 267**). Install the bolts and tighten securely.

15. Install the clutch slave cylinder as described in Chapter Five.

16. Connect the battery negative lead.

17. Install both side covers and the seat.

BREAK-IN PROCEDURE

If the rings were replaced, new pistons installed, the cylinders rebored or honed or major lower-end work performed, the engine should be broken in just as though it were new. The performance and service life of the engine depend greatly on a careful and sensible break-in.

For the first 800 km (500 miles), no more than one-third throttle should be used and speed should be varied as much as possible within the one-third throttle limit. Prolonged steady running at one speed, no matter how moderate, is to be avoided as well as hard acceleration.

Following the *800 km (500 Mile) Service* described in this chapter, full throttle should not be used until the motorcycle has covered at least 1,600 km (1,000 miles) and then it should be limited to short bursts of speed until 2,500 km (1,500 miles) have been logged.

The mono-grade oils recommended for break-in and normal use provide a better bedding pattern for rings and cylinders than do multi-grade oils. As a result, piston ring and cylinder bore life are greatly increased. During this period, oil consumption will be higher than normal. It is therefore important to check and correct oil level frequently. At no time during the break-in or later should the oil level be below the bottom line on the dipstick; if the oil level is low, the oil will become overheated resulting in insufficient lubrication and increased wear.

800 km (500 Mile) Service

It is essential that the oil and filter be changed after the first 800 km (500 miles). In addition, it is a good idea to change the oil and filter at the completion of the break-in (about 2,500 km/1,500 miles) to ensure that all of the particles produced during break-in are removed from the lubrication system. The small added expense may be considered a smart investment that will pay off in increased engine life.

Table 1 ENGINE SPECIFICATIONS

	Specification	Wear limit
General		
Engine type	Water-cooled, 4-stroke, SOHC, V-Twin	
Bore and stroke	87.5 × 91.4 mm (3.44 × 3.60 in.)	
Displacement	1099 cc (67.0 cid)	
Compression ratio		
1985-1986	9.0 to 1	
1987-on	8.5 to 1	
Valve train	Hi-vo multi-link drive chain, OHC with rocker arms and hydraulic valve tappets	
Maximum horsepower		
1985-1986	78.4 BHP @ 6,500 rpm	
1987-on	68 BHP @ 5,500 rpm	
Maximum torque		
1985-1986	10.1 kg/m (73.0 ft.-lb.) @ 4,500 rpm	
1987-on	10.2 kg/m (73.8 ft.-lb.) @ 3,000 rpm	
Lubrication	Wet sump	
Air filtration	Paper element type	
Engine weight (dry)		
1985-1986	92.3 kg (203 lb.)	
1987-on	91.5 kg (201.7 lb.)	
Cylinders		
Bore	87.500-87.515 mm (3.4449-3.4455 in.)	87.545 mm (3.4466 in.)
Out of round	—	0.05 mm (0.002 in.)
Taper	—	0.05 mm (0.002 in.)
Warpage	—	0.05 mm (0.002 in.)
Piston/cylinder clearance	0.01-0.045 mm (0.0004-0.0018 in.)	0.32 mm (0.0126 in.)
Pistons		
Diameter	87.46-87.49 mm (3.443-3.444 in.)	87.41 mm (3.441 in.)
Clearance in bore	0.01-0.045 mm (0.0004-0.0018 in.)	0.32 mm (0.0126 in.)
Piston pin bore	22.002-22.008 mm (0.8662-0.8665 in.)	22.018 mm (0.8668 in.)
Piston pin outer diameter	21.994-22.000 mm (0.8659-0.8661 in.)	21.984 mm (0.8655 in.)
Piston-to-pin clearance	0.002-0.014 mm (0.0001-0.0005 in.)	0.34 mm (0.013 in.)
Piston rings		
Number per piston		
Compression	2	
Oil control	1	
Ring end gap		
Top and second	0.20-0.35 mm (0.008-0.0138 in.)	0.50 mm (0.02 in.)
Oil (side rail)	0.30-0.90 mm (0.012-0.035 in.)	1.10 mm (0.04 in.)
Ring side clearance		
Top and second	0.015-0.045 mm (0.0006-0.0018 in.)	0.25 mm (0.010 in.)
Oil (side rail)	0.030-0.035 mm (0.0012-0.0014 in.)	0.1 mm (0.004 in.)
Connecting rod		
Small end inner diameter	20.020-20.041 mm (0.8669-0.8678 in.)	20.051 mm (0.8681 in.)

(continued)

Table 1 ENGINE SPECIFICATIONS (continued)

	Specification	Wear limit
Crankshaft		
Runout	—	0.05 mm (0.002 in.)
Main bearing oil clearance	0.030-0.046 mm (0.0012-0.0018 in.)	0.060 mm (0.0025 in.)
Connecting rod oil clearance	0.038-0.062 mm (0.0015-0.0024 in.)	0.070 mm (0.0028 in.)
Connecting rod big end clearance	0.10-0.25 mm (0.004-0.010 in.)	0.28 mm (0.011 in.)
Camshaft		
Cam lobe height (1985-1986)		
Intake and exhaust	36.690 mm (1.4445 in.)	36.670 mm (1.4437 in.)
Cam lobe height (1987-on)		
Front IN and rear EX	36.041 mm (1.4189 in.)	36.022 mm (1.4182 in.)
Rear IN and front EX	36.237 mm (1.4267 in.)	36.219 mm (1.4259 in.)
Runout	0.03 mm (0.0010 in.)	0.05 mm (0.002 in.)
Oil clearance		
Location A and B	0.020-0.062 mm (0.0008-0.0024 in.)	0.07 mm (0.0028 in.)
Location C	0.045-0.087 mm (0.0018-0.0034 in.)	0.097 mm (0.0038 in.)
Rocker arm bore	13.750-13.768 mm (0.5413-0.5420 in.)	13.778 mm (0.5424 in.)
Rocker arm shaft		
Intake	13.716-13.734 mm (0.5400-0.5407 in.)	13.706 mm (0.5396 in.)
Exhaust	13.716-13.737 mm (0.5400-0.5408 in.)	13.706 mm (0.5396 in.)
Tappet assist spring free length	18.57 mm (0.731 in.)	17.80 mm (0.701 in.)
Tappet compression stroke in kerosene	—	0.20 mm (0.0079 in.)
Valves		
Valve stem outer diameter		
Intake	6.570-6.595 mm (0.2587-0.2596 in.)	6.56 mm (0.258 in.)
Exhaust	6.550-6.575 mm (0.2579-0.2589 in.)	6.54 mm (0.257 in.)
Valve guide inner diameter		
Intake	6.600-6.615 mm (0.2598-0.2604 in.)	6.635 mm (0.2612 in.)
Exhaust	6.600-6.615 mm (0.2598-0.2604 in.)	6.655 mm (0.2620 in.)
Stem to guide clearance		
Intake	0.005-0.045 mm (0.0002-0.0018 in.)	0.075 mm (0.0030 in.)
Exhaust	0.025-0.065 mm (0.0010-0.0026 in.)	0.115 mm (0.0045 in.)
Valve seat width		
Intake and exhaust	0.9-1.10 mm (0.035-0.043 in.)	1.50 mm (0.059 in.)

(continued)

4

Table 1 ENGINE SPECIFICATIONS (continued)

	Specification	Wear limit
Valve springs free length		
Intake		
Outer	45.7 mm (1.79 in.)	43.9 mm (1.73 in.)
Inner	37.9 mm (1.49 in.)	36.40 mm (1.433 in.)
Exhaust		
Outer	43.5 mm (1.71 in.)	41.8 mm (1.64 in.)
Inner	37.9 mm (1.49 in.)	36.40 mm (1.433 in.)
Cylinder head warpage	—	0.05 mm (0.002 in.)
Oil pump		
Inner rotor tip to outer clearance	0.15 mm (0.006 in.)	0.20 mm (0.008 in.)
Outer rotor to body clearance	0.15-0.22 mm (0.006-0.009 in.)	0.35 mm (0.014 in.)
End clearance to body	0.02-0.07 mm (0.001-0.003 in.)	0.10 mm (0.004 in.)
Oil pump pressure (at switch) @ 6,000 rpm		
1985-1986	470-610 kPa (67-87 psi)	
1987-on	441 kPa (64 psi)	
Starter gears		
Driven gear outer diameter	57.749-57.768 mm (2.2735-2.2743 in.)	57.639 mm (2.2692 in.)
Clutch inner diameter	74.414-74.440 mm (2.9297-2.9307 in.)	74.50 mm (2.933 in.)

Table 2 ENGINE TORQUE SPECIFICATIONS

Item	N·m	ft.-lb.
Engine mounting bolts		
Front through bolt	45-60	33-43
Rear upper through bolt	45-60	33-43
Rear lower through bolt	60-70	43-51
Cylinder head-to-frame		
bolts (1987-on)	27	20
Sub-frame bolts		
Upper	60-70	43-51
Lower	35-45	25-33
Cylinder head cover, cam sprocket cover		
and camshaft holder		
8 mm	25-29	18-21
10 mm	38-42	27-30
Cam chain cover	25-29	18-21
Cam sprocket bolts	16-20	12-14
Spark plug sleeve*	10-15	7-11
External oil pipe		
6 mm oil bolt	10-14	7-10
10 mm oil bolt	20-25	14-18
Oil pump driven sprocket bolt	15-20	11-14
Oil pump mounting bolts	8-12	6-9
Crankcase bolts		
6 mm	10-15	7-11
8 mm	25-29	18-21
Connecting rod cap nuts	58-62	42-45
Output drive shaft bolt	45-55	33-40
Output gear case bolts	30-34	22-25
	(continued)	

Table 2 ENGINE TORQUE SPECIFICATIONS (continued)

Item	N·m	ft.-lb.
Primary drive gear bolt	95-105	69-76
Oil pipe bolts		
6 mm	10-14	7-10
10 mm	20-25	14-18
Alternator rotor bolt	130-150	94-108
Oil pressure switch**	10-14	7-10
Starter clutch Torx bolts***	21-25	15-18
Timing hole cap*	15-20	11-14

* Apply molybdenum disulfide grease to the threads before installation.
** Apply Three-Bond No. 1211, or equivalent, liquid sealant to threads before installation.
*** Apply Loctite Lock N' Seal #200 to the threads before installation.

Table 3 HYDRAULIC TAPPET SHIM SELECTION

Assist shaft stroke	Number of shims required
0.00-1.20 mm (0-0.047 in.)	0
1.20-1.50 mm (0.047-0.059 in.)	1
1.50-1.80 mm (0.059-0.070 in.)	2
1.80-2.10 mm (0.070-0.083 in.)	3
2.10-2.40 mm (0.083-0.094 in.)	4
2.40-2.70 mm (0.094-01.069 in.)	5

Table 4 CRANKCASE REPLACEMENT CODES

	Crankcase main bearing ID code letter	
	A	B
Crankshaft main journal OD code number		
No. 1	X	—
No. 2	—	X

Table 5 CONNECTING ROD BEARING SELECTION

	Crankpin journal OD size code letter and dimension	
	Letter A 47.982-47.990 mm (1.8891-1.8894 in.)	**Letter B** 47.974-47.982 mm (1.8887-1.8891 in.)
Connecting rod ID code number and dimension		
Number 1 51.000-51.008 mm (2.0079-2.0082 in.)	Pink	Yellow

(continued)

Table 5 CONNECTING ROD BEARING SELECTION (continued)

| | Crankpin journal OD size code letter and dimension | |
	Letter A 47.982-47.990 mm (1.8891-1.8894 in.)	Letter B 47.974-47.982 mm (1.8887-1.8891 in.)
Connecting rod ID code number and dimension		
Number 2 51.008-51.016 mm (2.0082-2.0085 in.)	Yellow	Green

Table 6 CONNECTING ROD BEARING INSERT THICKNESS

Color	mm	in.
Green	1.495-1.499	0.0589-0.0590
Yellow	1.491-1.495	0.0587-0.0589
Pink	1.487-1.491	0.0585-0.0587

Table 7 CONNECTING ROD WEIGHT SELECTION

| | Rear rod code marking | | | | |
	A	B	C	D	E
Front rod code marking					
A	X	X			
B	X	X	X		
C		X	X	X	
D			X	X	X
E				X	X

CLUTCH

This chapter describes complete clutch service procedures. **Table 1** and **Table 2** are at the end of this chapter.

CLUTCH

The clutch is a wet, multiplate type which operates immersed in engine oil. It is mounted on the right-hand end of the transmission mainshaft. The outside clutch center is splined to the mainshaft. The outer clutch housing can rotate freely on the mainshaft and is geared to the primary driven gear splined to the end of the crankshaft.

The clutch release mechanism is hydraulic and requires no routine adjustment. The mechanism consists of a clutch master cylinder on the left-hand handlebar, a slave cylinder on the left-hand side of the engine just behind the alternator and a pushrod that rides within the channel in the transmission mainshaft.

The clutch is activated by hydraulic fluid pressure and is controlled by the clutch master cylinder. The hydraulic pressure generated by the master cylinder activates the clutch slave cylinder that in turn pushes the clutch pushrod. The clutch pushrod pushes on the joint piece, thus moving the lifter plate and pressure plate which disengages the clutch mechanism.

Clutch Center Assembly Removal/Disassembly

All clutch components except the clutch outer housing can be removed by simply removing the clutch cover on the right-hand crankcase cover. It is only necessary to remove the right-hand crankcase cover if the clutch outer housing is going to be removed.

Refer to **Figure 1** when performing this procedure.

1. Place the bike on the centerstand.

2. Drain the engine oil as described in Chapter Three.

NOTE
Do not operate the clutch lever after the clutch assembly or slave cylinder is removed from the engine. If the lever is applied, it will force the slave cylinder piston out of the body and make slave cylinder installation difficult.

3. Shift the transmission into 4th gear.

4. Place a block of wood between the clutch lever and the hand grip to hold the lever in the released position. Secure the wood with a rubber band, tape or tie wrap. This will prevent the clutch lever from being applied accidentally after the clutch slave cylinder is removed from the crankcase.

5. On 1985-1986 models, remove the bolts securing the right-hand front footpeg assembly (**Figure 2**).

6. Remove the Allen bolts securing the clutch cover (**Figure 3**) and remove the cover and gasket.

7. Remove the snap ring (**Figure 4**) securing the clutch lifter plate "A" and remove the clutch lifter plate assembly (**Figure 5**).

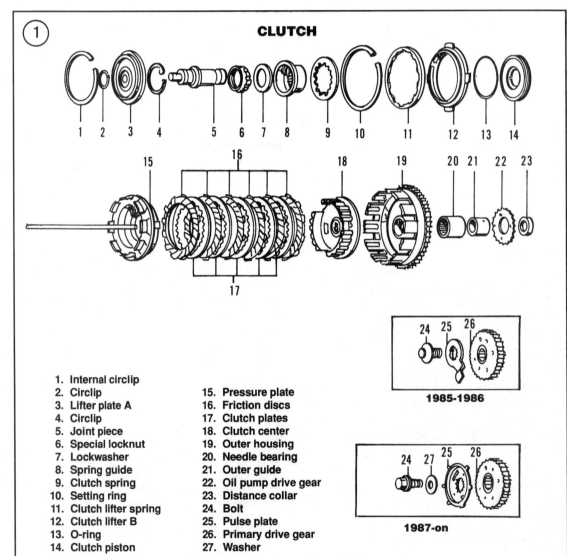

CLUTCH

1. Internal circlip
2. Circlip
3. Lifter plate A
4. Circlip
5. Joint piece
6. Special locknut
7. Lockwasher
8. Spring guide
9. Clutch spring
10. Setting ring
11. Clutch lifter spring
12. Clutch lifter B
13. O-ring
14. Clutch piston
15. Pressure plate
16. Friction discs
17. Clutch plates
18. Clutch center
19. Outer housing
20. Needle bearing
21. Outer guide
22. Oil pump drive gear
23. Distance collar
24. Bolt
25. Pulse plate
26. Primary drive gear
27. Washer

1985-1986

1987-on

8. Have an assistant apply the rear brake. This will keep the clutch assembly from rotating when loosening the clutch nut in Step 9.

> *NOTE*
> *A special tool is required to loosen and remove the special clutch locknut. The special tool is Honda part No.07916-4220000.*

> *CAUTION*
> *Do not try to remove the clutch nut without the use of the special tool as the clutch will be damaged.*

9. Using the Honda special tool (**Figure 6**), remove the clutch nut (**Figure 7**) and the lockwasher (**Figure 8**).

10. Remove the clutch spring guide (**Figure 9**) and the clutch spring (**Figure 10**).

11. Remove the clutch center assembly (**Figure 11**) from the clutch outer housing.

12. Disassemble the clutch center assembly as follows:

   a. Remove the setting ring (**Figure 12**).

4

b. Remove the clutch lifter "B" spring (**Figure 13**) and clutch lifter "B" (**Figure 14**).

c. Remove the clutch piston and O-ring seal (**Figure 15**).

d. Remove the pressure plate (**Figure 16**).

e. Remove the clutch plates and friction discs.

13. Disassemble the lifter plate "A" as follows:

a. Remove the circlip (**Figure 17**) securing the joint piece (**Figure 18**) and remove the joint piece.

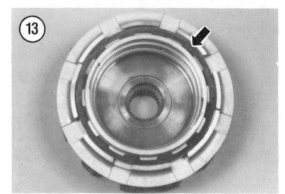

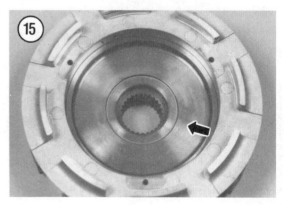

b. If necessary, remove the circlip securing the bearing and remove the bearing.

14. Inspect all components as described in this chapter.

Clutch Center Assembly
Assembly/Installation

Refer to **Figure 1** when performing this procedure.

1. If the lifter plate "A" was disassembled, perform the following:

a. Install the bearing and install the circlip.

b. Install the joint piece and install the circlip (**Figure 17**).

> *CAUTION*
> *If either or both friction discs and clutch plates have been replaced with new ones, apply new engine oil to all surfaces to avoid having the clutch lock up when used for the first time.*

> *NOTE*
> *The friction discs must be installed in their correct location and with their grooves facing in the correct direction as shown in **Figure 19** and **Figure 20**.*

> *NOTE*
> *On 1985-1986 models, there are two different friction discs. The friction discs "B" have a notch cutout of their tabs while the friction discs "A" are not notched as shown in **Figure 21**.*

2A. On 1985-1986 models, position a friction disc "B" (**Figure 22**) with the grooves facing in the

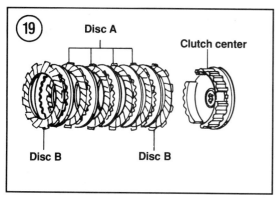

Disc A — Clutch center

Disc B — Disc B

correct direction and install the friction disc onto the clutch center.

2B. On 1987-on models, position a friction disc with the grooves facing in the correct direction and install the friction disc onto the clutch center.

3. On 1985-1986 models, install a clutch plate (**Figure 23**) and a friction disc "A" that has a notch cut out of the tabs.

4A. On 1985-1986 models, install a clutch plate and another friction disc "A" (**Figure 24**).

4B. On 1987-on models, install a clutch plate and another friction disc.

5. Continue to install a clutch plate and then a friction disc. Alternate them until all discs are installed.

6. Install the last clutch plate.

7A. On 1985-1986 models, install the other friction disc "B" (**Figure 25**).

7B. On 1987-on models, install the last friction disc.

8. Align the raised tabs on the clutch friction discs (**Figure 26**). This will make installation of this assembly into the clutch center much easier.

9. Align the raised bars (A, **Figure 27**) in the pressure plate with the reliefs (B, **Figure 27**) in the clutch center.

10. Install the clutch pressure plate (**Figure 16**).

11. Apply clean engine oil to the O-ring seal in the clutch piston and install the clutch piston (**Figure 28**) into the pressure plate. Push the clutch center all the way down into the pressure plate until it bottoms out (**Figure 15**).

12. Install the clutch lifter "B" (**Figure 14**).

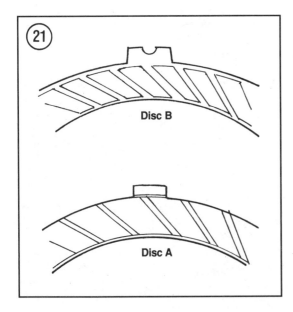

26

27

28

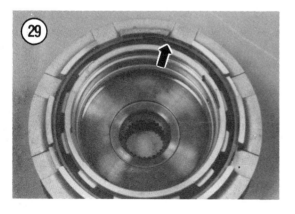

29

13. Position the clutch lifter "B" spring with the dished side facing toward the inside and install the spring (**Figure 13**).

14. Compress the clutch lifter "B" spring and install the setting ring (**Figure 29**). Make sure it is properly seated in the groove in the clutch lifter "B" (**Figure 30**).

15. Align the splines in the clutch center with the splines on the transmission shaft.

16. Align the raised tabs on the clutch friction discs with the grooves in the clutch center (**Figure 31**) and install the clutch center assembly into the clutch outer housing. Push the assembly in until it bottoms out (**Figure 32**).

17. Position the clutch spring with the dished side facing toward the outside and install the clutch spring (**Figure 33**).

18. Install the clutch spring guide into the clutch lifter "B" (**Figure 34**).

5

30

31

19. Install the lockwasher (**Figure 35**) and locknut (**Figure 36**).

20. Make sure the transmission is still in 4th gear.

21. Have an assistant apply the rear brake. This will keep the clutch assembly from rotating when tightening the clutch nut in Step 22.

22. Using the same Honda special tool used during disassembly, tighten the clutch nut to the torque specification listed in **Table 2**.

23. Install clutch lifter plate "A" assembly (**Figure 37**).

24. Because of the slight internal hydraulic pressure within the clutch release mechanism, you must push on the clutch lifter plate "A" with a soft-ended tool while installing the snap ring.

25. Install the snap ring (**Figure 38**) securing the clutch lifter plate "A" assembly and make sure the snap ring is completely seated in the groove in the clutch pressure plate (**Figure 39**).

26. Install the lower locating dowel and O-ring seal (**Figure 40**).

27. Make sure the other two locating dowels (A, **Figure 41**) are in place in the crankcase cover.

28. Install a new clutch cover gasket (B, **Figure 41**).

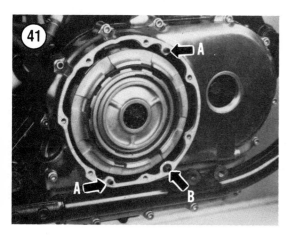

29. Install the clutch cover (**Figure 42**) and Allen bolts. Tighten the Allen bolts securely and in a criss-cross pattern.

30. On 1985-1986 models, install the right-hand front footpeg assembly and tighten the bolts securely.

31. Fill the crankcase with the recommended type and quantity of engine oil. Refer to Chapter Three.

Clutch Outer Housing
Removal

It is only necessary to remove the right-hand crankcase cover if the clutch outer housing requires removal.

Refer to **Figure 43** when performing this procedure.

1. Remove the clutch center assembly as described under *Clutch Center Removal/Disassembly* in this chapter.

2. On 1985-1986 models, remove the exhaust system as described under *Exhaust System Removal/Installation (1985-1986)* in Chapter Seven.

3. Remove the radiator as described under *Radiator Removal/Installation* in Chapter Nine.

4. On 1987-on models, perform the following:

    a. Remove the rear brake pedal assembly as described under *Rear Brake Pedal Removal/Installation (1987-on)* in Chapter Twelve.

    b. Remove the right-hand foot peg assembly as described under *Foot Peg Removal/Installation* in Chapter Thirteen.

5. Place a jack underneath the engine. Place wood blocks on top of the jack and raise the jack support so that it just rests against the bottom of the engine.

6. Remove the right-hand sub-frame as follows:

a. Remove the front engine mount bolt and spacers (**Figure 44**). Reinstall the spacers and nut onto the bolt to avoid misplacing them.

b. Remove the upper and lower Allen bolts (**Figure 45**) and pull the sub-frame away from the engine.

c. Remove the sub-frame (**Figure 46**).

NOTE
The following steps are shown with the engine removed from the frame for clarity. It is not necessary to remove the engine for this part of the procedure.

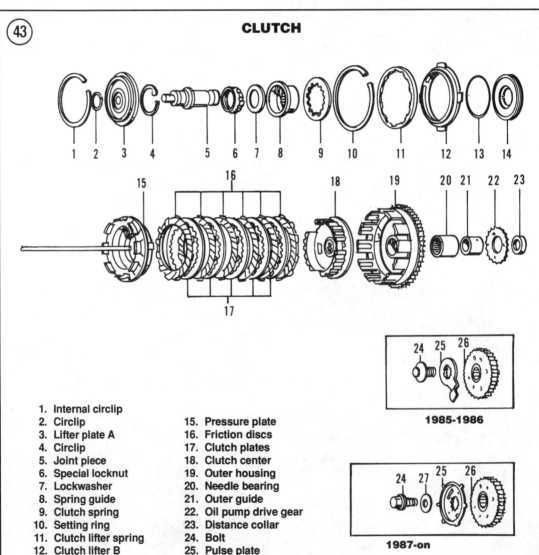

CLUTCH

1985-1986

1987-on

1. Internal circlip
2. Circlip
3. Lifter plate A
4. Circlip
5. Joint piece
6. Special locknut
7. Lockwasher
8. Spring guide
9. Clutch spring
10. Setting ring
11. Clutch lifter spring
12. Clutch lifter B
13. O-ring
14. Clutch piston
15. Pressure plate
16. Friction discs
17. Clutch plates
18. Clutch center
19. Outer housing
20. Needle bearing
21. Outer guide
22. Oil pump drive gear
23. Distance collar
24. Bolt
25. Pulse plate
26. Primary drive gear
27. Washer

45

46

47

48

7. Remove the screws securing the right-hand crank-case cover (**Figure 47**), gasket, dowel pins and O-ring seal.

8. Insert a screwdriver into the primary drive gear and align its sub-gear teeth (**Figure 48**). Then slide the clutch outer housing (A, **Figure 49**) off the transmission mainshaft.

9. Slide the clutch outer housing needle bearing and bushing (**Figure 50**) off the transmission mainshaft.

10. Inspect all components as described in this chapter.

Clutch Outer Housing
Installation

5

1. Install the clutch outer housing bushing (**Figure 50**) onto the transmission mainshaft.

2. Oil the needle bearing pins. Then slide the needle bearing into the clutch outer housing.

3. Rotate the oil pump drive sprocket so the pins are lined up at the 12, 3, 6 and 9 o'clock positions.

49

50

4. Align the index holes in the backside of the clutch outer housing with the sprocket pins and install the clutch outer housing partway onto the transmission mainshaft.

5. Align the primary drive gear with the sub-gear teeth with a screwdriver (**Figure 51**). Then push the housing (A, **Figure 49**) on all the way and make sure that the pins and holes are indexed properly.

6. Slowly rotate the oil pump driven gear and drive chain (B, **Figure 49**) until the pins and index holes align properly.

CAUTION
The oil pump sprocket and the clutch outer housing must index properly so that the housing will go on all the way. Otherwise, the clutch will not function properly nor will the oil pump rotate. If alignment is incorrect, severe engine damage will result.

7. Install the dowel pins (C, **Figure 49**) and a new crankcase gasket (D, **Figure 49**).

8. Install a new O-ring seal on the inner dowel pin (**Figure 52**).

9. Install the right-hand crankcase cover (**Figure 47**). Tighten the bolts securely.

10. Install the right-hand sub-frame as follows:
    a. Move the sub-frame into position.
    b. Install the upper and lower Allen bolts (**Figure 45**).
    c. Install the front engine mount bolt and spacers (**Figure 44**).
    d. Tighten the mounting bolt and Allen bolts to the torque specification listed in **Table 2**.

11. Release the jack pressure and remove it from underneath the engine.

12. Install the radiator as described in Chapter Nine.

13. On 1987-on models, perform the following:
    a. Install the right-hand foot peg assembly as described under *Foot Peg Removal/Installation* in Chapter Thirteen.
    b. Install the rear brake pedal assembly as described under *Rear Brake Pedal Removal/Installation (1987-on)* in Chapter Twelve.

14. On 1985-1986 models, install the exhaust system as described under *Exhaust System Removal/Installation (1985-1986)* in Chapter Seven.

15. Install the clutch center assembly as described under *Clutch Center Assembly/Installation* in this chapter.

Clutch Component Inspection

1. Clean all clutch parts in petroleum-based solvent such as kerosene and thoroughly dry with compressed air.

2. Measure the thickness of each friction disc at several places around the disc as shown in **Figure 53**. Compare to the specifications listed in **Table 1**. Replace any disc that is worn to the service limit or less. For optimum performance, replace all friction discs as a set even if only a few require replacement.

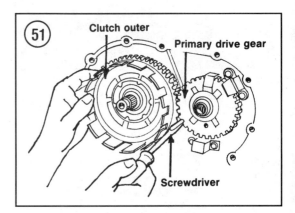

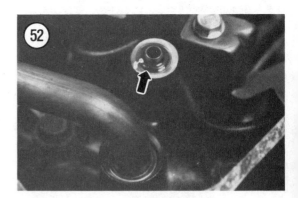

3. Check the clutch plates for warpage on a surface plate such as a piece of plate glass (**Figure 54**). Compare to the specifications listed in **Table 1**. Replace any plate that is warped to the service limit or more. For optimum performance, replace all clutch plates as a set even if only a few require replacement.

4. Inspect the teeth of the outer housing (**Figure 55**) for wear or damage. Remove any small nicks on the gear teeth with an oilstone. If damage is severe, the housing must be replaced. Also check the teeth and inner splines on the driven gear; it may also need replacing.

5. Inspect the slots in the clutch outer housing (**Figure 56**) for cracks, nicks or galling where they come in contact with the friction disc tabs. If any severe damage is evident, the housing must be replaced.

6. Inspect the damper springs (**Figure 57**) in the backside clutch outer housing for wear or sagging. If worn or sagged, the housing must be replaced.

7. Inspect the inner surface of the clutch outer housing (**Figure 58**) where the needle bearing rides for damage or galling. If any severe damage is evident, the housing must be replaced.

8. Inspect the needle bearing (**Figure 59**) in the clutch outer housing. Make sure it rotates smoothly with no signs of wear; replace if necessary.

9. Measure the inside diameter of the outer guide (**Figure 60**). If it is worn to the service limit listed in **Table 1**, or greater, it must be replaced.

10. Install the outer guide into the needle bearing (**Figure 61**) and rotate the 2 parts. Make sure they rotate smoothly with no signs of wear; replace the defective part if necessary.

11. Inspect the inner splines (**Figure 62**) of the clutch center; replace if necessary.

12. Inspect the outer grooves (**Figure 63**) of clutch center; replace if necessary.

13. Inspect the clutch pressure plate (**Figure 64**) for wear or damage; replace if necessary.

14. Inspect the surface of the clutch pressure plate where the friction disc makes contact (A, **Figure 65**) and the grooves for the clutch plate (B, **Figure 65**). Check for wear or damage; replace if necessary.

15. Inspect the oil flow holes (**Figure 66**) in the clutch pressure plate. These holes must be open for

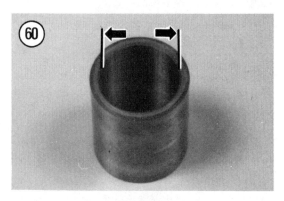

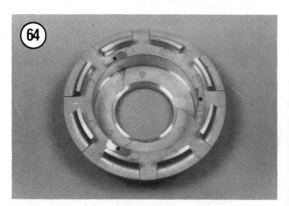

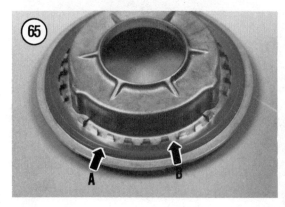

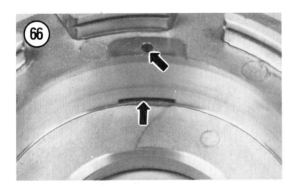

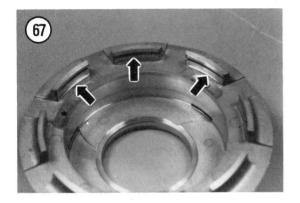

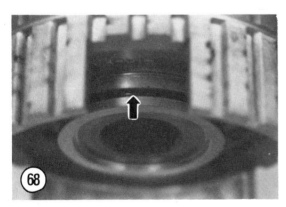

the clutch to operate properly. Blow out with compressed air if necessary.

16. Inspect the setting ring grooves (**Figure 67**) in the clutch pressure plate for wear or damage. If any are damaged, replace the clutch pressure plate.

17. Inspect the O-ring (**Figure 68**) on the clutch center for hardness, wear or damage; replace if necessary.

18. Inspect the surface of the joint piece where it makes contact with the clutch push rod (A, **Figure 69**). Check for wear or damage; replace if necessary.

19. Make sure the oil hole (B, **Figure 69**) in the joint piece is clean and open. Blow out with compressed air if necessary. It must be clear and open for the clutch to operate properly.

20. Inspect the O-ring (**Figure 70**) on the clutch piston for hardness, wear or damage; replace if necessary.

21. Inspect the clutch piston (**Figure 71**) for wear or damage; replace if necessary.

22. Measure the height of the clutch spring (**Figure 72**) with a vernier caliper. Replace the spring if it has sagged to the service limit listed in **Table 1**.

23. Make sure the bearing in the lifter plate "A" rotates smoothly with no signs of wear or damage; replace if necessary.

24. Inspect the internal circlip and the setting ring (**Figure 73**) for wear, distortion or damage; replace if necessary.

25. Inspect clutch lifter "B" (**Figure 74**) for wear or damage; replace if necessary.

26. Make sure the oil flow path in the clutch cover is clear and open. Apply compressed air to the side opening (A, **Figure 75**) and make sure it exits the oil seal opening (B, **Figure 75**). It must be clear and open for the clutch to operate properly.

27. Make sure the oil seal (A, **Figure 76**) in the clutch cover is in good condition. If replacement is necessary, remove the circlip (B, **Figure 76**) and carefully pry the oil seal out of the cover. Install a new oil seal and install the circlip.

28. Inspect the outer grooves (A, **Figure 77**) and the threads (B, **Figure 77**) for wear or damage; replace if necessary.

29. Inspect the inner splines (**Figure 78**) of the spring guide for wear or damage; replace if necessary.

30. Remove the oil control bolt (**Figure 79**) in the clutch cover. Apply compressed air to the opening and make sure it exits the oil seal opening (A, **Figure 80**) on the inner surface of the clutch cover. Clean out with solvent and compressed air if necessary.

CLUTCH OIL RELIEF VALVE

The right-hand crankcase cover is equipped with the clutch oil relief valve.

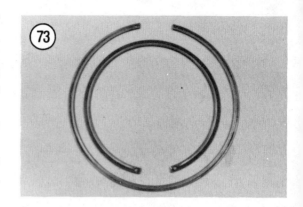

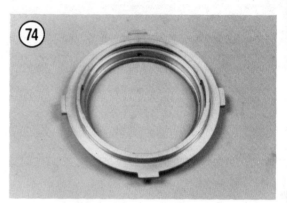

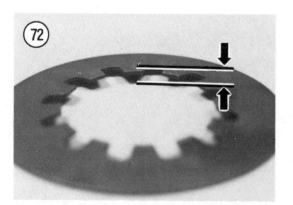

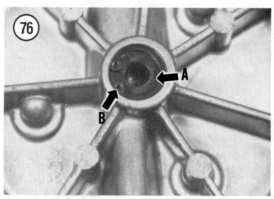

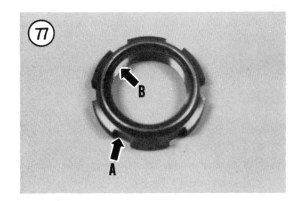

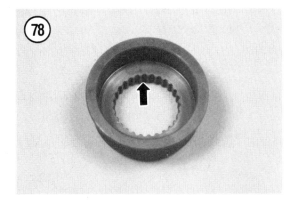

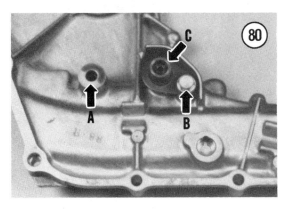

Removal/Disassembly

1. Remove the right-hand crankcase cover as described under *Clutch Outer Housing Removal* for your specific model as described in this chapter.

2. Remove the bolt (B, **Figure 80**) securing the clutch oil relief valve (C, **Figure 80**) to the right-hand crankcase cover.

3. Remove the clutch oil relief valve from the cover.

4. If disassembly is necessary, perform the following:

    a. Remove the circlip from the body.

    b. Remove the spring seat, spring and piston from the body.

5. Inspect all parts for wear or damage. Replace any damaged parts.

Assembly/Installation

1. If disassembled, perform the following:

    a. Install the piston with the open end going in last.

    b. Install the spring and the spring seat.

    c. Install the circlip into the groove in the body.

2. Inspect the O-ring seal in the body. Replace if worn, damaged or starting to harden.

3. Apply engine oil to the O-ring seal and install the clutch oil relief valve into the cover.

4. Install the bolt (B, **Figure 80**) securing the clutch oil relief valve (C, **Figure 80**) to the right-hand crankcase cover and tighten securely.

5. Install the right-hand crankcase cover as described under *Clutch Outer Housing Installation* for your specific model as described in this chapter.

CLUTCH HYDRAULIC SYSTEM

The clutch is actuated by hydraulic fluid pressure and is controlled by the hand lever on the clutch master cylinder. As clutch components wear, the fluid level drops in the reservoir and automatically adjusts for wear. There is no routine adjustment necessary or possible.

When working on the clutch hydraulic system, it is necessary that the work area and all tools be absolutely clean. Any tiny particles of foreign matter and grit in the clutch slave cylinder or the clutch master cylinder can damage the components. Also, sharp tools must not be used inside the slave cylinder or on the piston. If there is any doubt about your ability to correctly and safely carry out major service on the clutch hydraulic components, take the job to a dealer.

> *CAUTION*
> *Throughout the text, reference is made to hydraulic fluid. Hydraulic fluid is the same as DOT 4 brake fluid. Use only DOT 4 brake fluid; do **not** use other types of fluids as they are not compatible. Do not intermix silicone based (DOT 5) brake fluid as it can cause clutch component damage leading to clutch system failure.*

CLUTCH MASTER CYLINDER

Removal/Installation

1. Remove the rear view mirror (A, **Figure 81**) from the clutch master cylinder.

> *CAUTION*
> *Cover the fuel tank and instrument cluster with a heavy cloth or plastic tarp to protect them from accidental hydraulic fluid spills. Wash fluid off any painted or plated surfaces immediately, as it will destroy the finish. Use soapy water and rinse completely.*

2. Pull back the rubber boot (B, **Figure 81**) and remove the union bolt securing the clutch hose to the clutch master cylinder. Remove the clutch hose; tie the hose up and cover the end to prevent entry of foreign matter.

3. Disconnect the electrical connector to the clutch switch (C, **Figure 81**).

4. Remove the clamping bolts and clamp securing the clutch master cylinder to the handlebar and remove the clutch master cylinder (D, **Figure 81**).

5. Install by reversing these removal steps while noting the following.

6. Install the clamp (**Figure 82**), aligning the end of the clamp with the punch mark on the handlebar. Tighten the upper bolt first, then the lower. Tighten the bolts securely.

7. Install the clutch hose onto the clutch master cylinder. Be sure to place a sealing washer on each side of the fitting and install the union bolt. Tighten the union bolt to the torque specifications listed in **Table 2**.

8. Attach the electrical connector to the clutch switch.

9. Bleed the clutch as described in this chapter.

Disassembly

Refer to **Figure 83** for this procedure.

1. Remove the clutch master cylinder as described in this chapter.

2. Remove the screws securing the top cover (**Figure 84**).

3. Remove the top cover, set plate (**Figure 85**) and diaphragm (**Figure 86**).

4. Pour out the hydraulic fluid and discard it. *Never reuse hydraulic fluid.*

5. Remove the pushrod and end piece.

6. Remove the rubber boot (**Figure 87**) from the area where the hand lever pushrod actuates the internal piston.

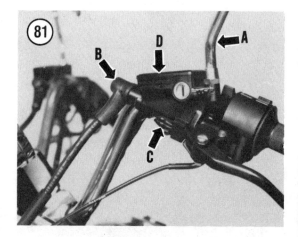

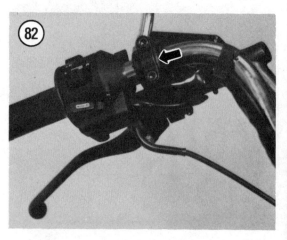

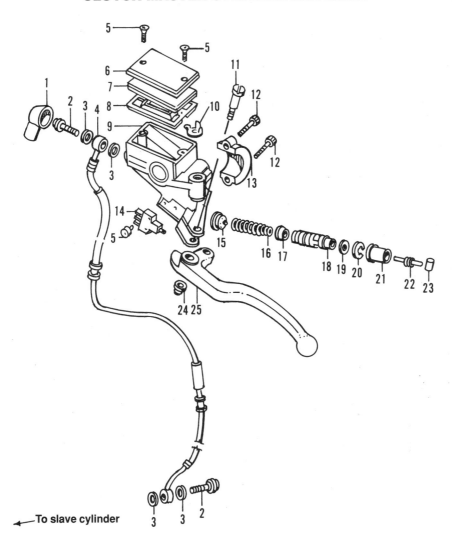

83

CLUTCH MASTER CYLINDER AND HOSE

To slave cylinder

1. Rubber boot
2. Union bolt
3. Sealing washer
4. Hose
5. Screw
6. Top cover
7. Set plate
8. Diaphragm
9. Housing
10. Protector
11. Bolt
12. Bolt
13. Clamp
14. Switch
15. Primary cup
16. Spring
17. Secondary cup
18. Piston assembly
19. Washer
20. Circlip
21. Rubber boot
22. Pushrod
23. End piece
24. Nut
25. Lever

5

7. Using circlip pliers, remove the internal circlip and washer (**Figure 88**) from the body.

8. Remove the secondary cup and the piston assembly.

9. Remove the primary cup and spring.

10. If necessary, remove the screw and remove the clutch switch (**Figure 89**).

11. Remove the pivot bolt and nut securing the clutch lever and remove the lever (**Figure 90**).

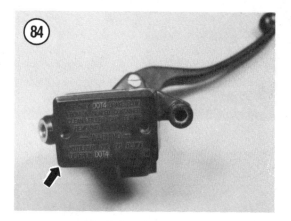

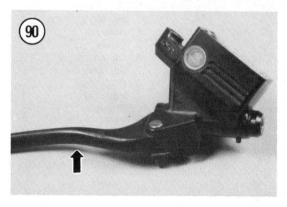

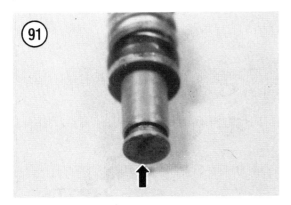

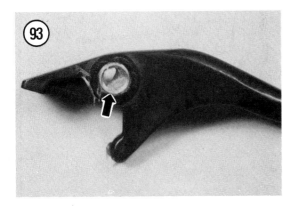

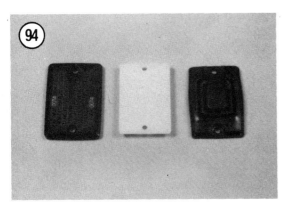

Inspection

1. Clean all parts in denatured alcohol or fresh hydraulic fluid. Inspect the cylinder bore and piston contact surfaces for signs of wear and damage. If either part is less than perfect, replace it.

2. Check the end of the piston (**Figure 91**) for wear caused by the hand lever pushrod. Replace the piston if necessary.

3. Check both the primary and secondary cup for damage. Replace as necessary. Replace the piston if the secondary cup requires replacement.

4. Check the hand lever pivot bore (**Figure 92**) in the clutch master cylinder. If worn or elongated, the master cylinder must be replaced.

5. Inspect the pivot bore (**Figure 93**) in the hand lever. If worn or elongated it must be replaced.

6. Make sure the passages in the bottom of the fluid reservoir are clear.

7. Check the reservoir top cover, set plate and diaphragm (**Figure 94**) for damage and deterioration and replace as necessary.

8. Inspect the threads in the bore for the fluid line (**Figure 95**).

9. Inspect the cylinder bore (**Figure 96**) for scratches or damage. Replace the master cylinder if necessary.

10. Measure the cylinder bore (**Figure 97**). Replace the clutch master cylinder if the bore exceeds the specifications given in **Table 1**.

11. Measure the outside diameter of the piston as shown in **Figure 98** with a micrometer. Replace the piston assembly if it is less than the specifications given in **Table 1**.

Assembly

1. Soak the new cups in fresh hydraulic fluid for at least 15 minutes to make them pliable. Coat the inside of the cylinder with fresh fluid prior to assembly of parts.

> *CAUTION*
> *When installing the piston assembly, do not allow the cups to turn inside out as they will be damaged and allow clutch fluid leakage within the cylinder bore.*

2. Install the spring, primary cup and piston assembly into the cylinder together (**Figure 99**).

> *NOTE*
> *Be sure to install the primary cup with the open end in first, toward the spring.*

3. Push the piston assembly down as far as it will go (**Figure 100**).

4. Install the washer and the circlip (**Figure 88**); make sure the circlip seats firmly in the groove (**Figure 101**).

5. Slide in the rubber boot (**Figure 87**), the pushrod and the pushrod end piece.

6. Install the diaphragm, set plate and top cover. Do not tighten the cover screws at this time as fluid will have to be added later.

7. Install the lever onto the master cylinder body. Install and tighten the pivot bolt and nut securely.

8. If removed, install the clutch switch (**Figure 89**) and tighten the screw securely.

9. Install the clutch master cylinder and bleed the clutch system as described in this chapter.

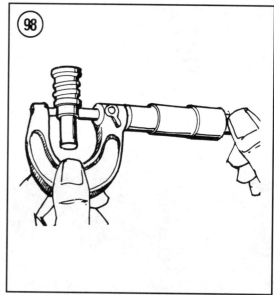

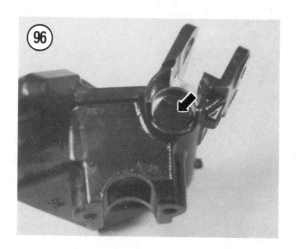

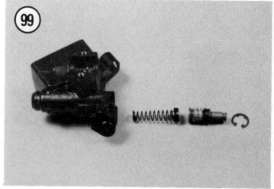

HOSE REPLACEMENT

There is no factory-recommended replacement interval but it is a good idea to replace the clutch hose assembly every four years or when it shows signs of cracking or damage. The hydraulic hose assembly consists of 2 flexible hoses that are permanently attached to each end of the section of metal tubing. The entire hose assembly must be replaced as a unit as it cannot be separated.

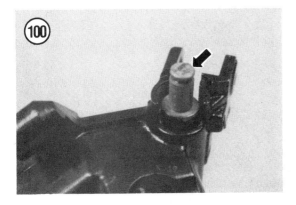

CAUTION
Cover the front wheel, fender and frame with a heavy cloth or plastic tarp to protect them from accidental spilling of hydraulic fluid. Wash the fluid off of any painted or plated surface immediately, as it will destroy the finish. Use soapy water and rinse completely.

1. Remove the seat and both side covers.

2A. On 1985-1986 models, remove the main fuel tank as described in Chapter Seven.

2B. On 1987-on models, remove the fuel tank as described in Chapter Seven.

3. Pull back the rubber boot (B, **Figure 81**) and remove the union bolt securing the clutch hose to the clutch master cylinder.

4. Remove the clutch hose; tie the hose up and cover the end to prevent entry of foreign matter.

5. Remove the bolt securing the left-hand rear crankcase cover and remove the cover.

6. Attach a hose to the bleed valve (A, **Figure 102**) on the clutch slave cylinder.

7. Place the loose end of the hose into a container and open the bleed valve. Operate the clutch lever until all fluid is pumped out of the system. Close the bleed valve and remove the hose.

WARNING
Dispose of this fluid according to local EPA regulations—never reuse hydraulic fluid. Contaminated fluid can cause clutch failure.

8. Place a container under the clutch hose at the clutch slave cylinder to catch any remaining fluid. Remove the union bolt and sealing washers (B, **Figure 102**) securing the clutch hose to the clutch slave cylinder. Remove the clutch hose and let any remaining fluid drain out into the container.

9. Remove the metal clamp bands securing the clutch metal hose and other hoses to the frame.

10. Withdraw the flexible clutch hose from between the steering stem and the left-hand fork leg.

11. Remove the hose assembly from the frame.

CAUTION
After removing the hose assembly, wash any hydraulic fluid off of any painted or plated surface immediately, as it will destroy the finish.

12. Install the hose assembly, sealing washers and union bolts in the reverse order of removal. Be sure to install new sealing washers in the correct position on each side of each union bolt.

13. Tighten all union bolts to torque specifications listed in **Table 2**.

14. Refill the clutch master cylinder to the upper line (**Figure 103**) with fresh hydraulic fluid clearly marked DOT 4 only. Bleed the clutch system as described in this chapter.

15. Install the left-hand rear crankcase cover.

SLAVE CYLINDER

Removal and installation are covered in 2 different ways. The first procedure is for removing the slave cylinder from the crankcase intact when no service procedures are going to be performed. The second procedure is used when the slave cylinder is going to be disassembled, inspected and serviced. Follow the correct procedure for your specific needs.

Refer to **Figure 104** for both procedures.

Removal/Installation (Intact)

This procedure is for removal and installation only—not for disassembly, inspection and service.

1. Place a piece of wood between the clutch lever and the hand grip to hold the lever in the released position. Secure the piece of wood with a rubber band or tape. This will prevent the clutch lever from being applied accidentally after the clutch slave cylinder is removed from the crankcase.

NOTE
Do not operate the clutch lever after the slave cylinder is removed from the crankcase. If the clutch lever is applied, it will force the piston out of the slave cylinder body and make installation difficult.

2. Remove the bolts securing the left-hand rear crankcase cover and remove the cover (**Figure 105**).

3. Remove the bolts (**Figure 106**) securing the clutch slave cylinder and bracket to the crankcase and

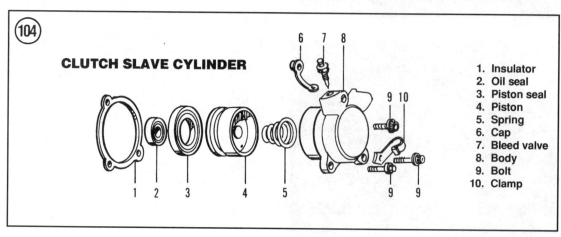

CLUTCH SLAVE CYLINDER

1. Insulator
2. Oil seal
3. Piston seal
4. Piston
5. Spring
6. Cap
7. Bleed valve
8. Body
9. Bolt
10. Clamp

withdraw the unit from the crankcase. Don't lose the thick black insulator between the slave cylinder and the crankcase.

4. Tie the clutch slave cylinder up and out of the way.

5. Apply a light coat of high-temperature silicone grease (or hydraulic fluid) to the piston seal and the oil seal prior to installing the assembly.

NOTE
Inspect the piston seal and the oil seal.
Replace if their condition is doubtful. If

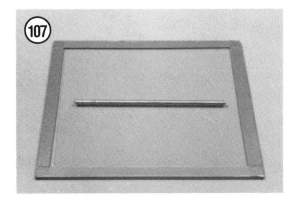

either seal is removed from the piston,
it must be replaced with a new seal.

6. Make sure the piston seal is still correctly seated in the groove in the piston. If not seated correctly, fluid will leak past the seal and render the clutch useless.

NOTE
Sometimes the piston will move out
slightly from the slave cylinder body
when the body is withdrawn from the
crankcase during removal.

7. Withdraw the clutch pushrod from the transmission main shaft and use it to push the piston as far back in as possible into the slave cylinder body.

8. While the pushrod is out, inspect it for bending. Place the pushrod on a flat surface like a piece of plate glass (**Figure 107**) and roll it back and forth. It should roll smoothly and should not make any "clicking" noise indicating that the pushrod is bent slightly. If the pushrod clicks, replace it.

9. Reinstall the clutch pushrod (**Figure 108**) into the transmission main shaft.

10. Install the insulator onto the slave cylinder and install the slave cylinder onto the crankcase.

11. Make sure the pushrod is inserted correctly into the receptacle in the slave cylinder piston.

NOTE
After being positioned correctly in the
crankcase, the slave cylinder assembly
may stick out by about 3/8 in. from the
mating surface of the crankcase. This is
due to the pressure within the hydraulic
system.

12. Install the bracket and then the bolts securing the slave cylinder. Gradually tighten the bolts in a criss-cross pattern. Continue to tighten until the slave cylinder has bottomed out on the mating surface of the crankcase. Tighten the bolts securely.

13. Install the left-hand rear crankcase cover.

Removal

This procedure is for a complete service procedure of removal, disassembly, inspection, assembly and installation of the slave cylinder.

1. Remove the bolts securing the left-hand rear crankcase cover and remove the cover (**Figure 105**).

2. Attach a hose to the bleed valve on the clutch slave cylinder (A, **Figure 102**).

3. Place the loose end of the hose into a container and open the bleed valve. Operate the clutch lever until all fluid is pumped out of the system. Close the bleed valve and remove the hose.

WARNING
Dispose of this fluid according to local EPA regulations—never reuse hydraulic fluid. Contaminated fluid can cause clutch failure.

4. Place a container under the clutch hose at the clutch slave cylinder to catch any remaining fluid. Remove the union bolt and sealing washers (B, **Figure 102**) securing the clutch hose to the clutch slave cylinder. Remove the clutch hose and let any remaining fluid drain out into the container.

5. Remove the bolts securing the clutch slave cylinder and bracket to the crankcase and withdraw the unit from the crankcase. Don't lose the thick black insulator between the slave cylinder and the crankcase.

Disassembly/Inspection

1. To remove the piston, perform the following:
   a. Remove the union bolt (A, **Figure 109**) from the slave cylinder.
   b. Hold the slave cylinder body in your hand with the piston facing away from you. Place a clean shop cloth behind the piston (B, **Figure 109**).
   c. Carefully apply a *small* amount of compressed air in short spurts into the hole where the union bolt was attached (**Figure 110**). The air pressure will force the piston out of the body.

CAUTION
Be sure to catch the piston when it is pushed out of the body. Failure to do so will result in damage to the piston.

2. Remove the spring from the piston.

3. Check the spring for damage or sagging. Honda does not provide service limit dimensions for this spring. Replace the spring if its condition is doubtful.

4. Remove the oil seal and the piston seal from the piston; discard both seals.

5. Use a vernier caliper and measure the outside diameter of the piston as shown in **Figure 111**. Replace the piston if it is worn to the service limit listed in **Table 1**.

6. Use a vernier caliper and measure the inside diameter of the slave cylinder body as shown in **Figure 112**. Replace the body if it is worn to the service limit listed in **Table 1**.

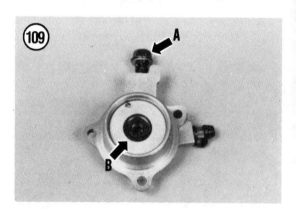

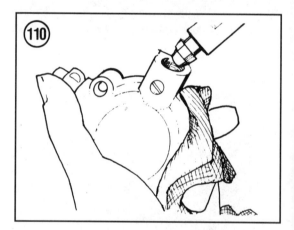

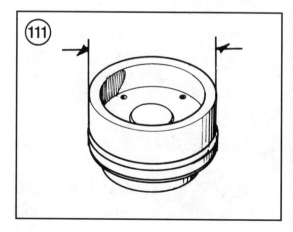

Assembly/Installation

1. Apply a light coat of high-temperature silicone grease (or hydraulic fluid) to the new piston seal and the oil seal prior to installation.

2. Install both seals onto the piston. Make sure the piston seal is correctly seated in the groove in the piston. If not seated correctly, fluid will leak past the seal and render the clutch useless.

NOTE
A new piston seal and oil seal must be installed every time the slave cylinder is removed.

3. Withdraw the clutch pushrod from the transmission main shaft and use it to push the piston all the way into the slave cylinder body. Reinstall the clutch pushrod (**Figure 108**).

4. Install the insulator onto the slave cylinder and install the slave cylinder onto the crankcase.

5. Install the bracket and then the bolts. Tighten in a crisscross pattern in 2-3 stages. Tighten the bolts securely.

6. Install the union bolt and sealing washers to the slave cylinder. Tighten the union bolts to the torque specification listed in **Table 2**.

7. Clean the top of the clutch master cylinder of all dirt and foreign matter.

8. Remove the top cover, set plate and diaphragm. Fill the reservoir almost to the top line (**Figure 103**);

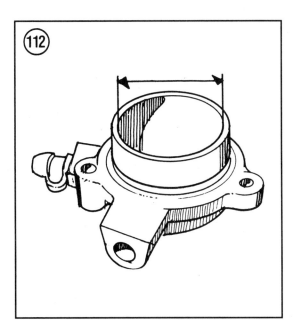

insert the diaphragm, set plate and install the top cover loosely.

9. Bleed the clutch as described in this chapter.

BLEEDING THE CLUTCH

This procedure is not necessary unless the clutch feels spongy (air in the line), there has been a leak in the system, a component has been replaced or the hydraulic fluid is being replaced. If the clutch operates correctly when the engine is cold or in cool weather but operates erratically (or not at all) after the engine warms up or in hot weather, there is air in the hydraulic line and the clutch must be bled.

CAUTION
Throughout the text reference is made to hydraulic fluid. Hydraulic fluid is the same as DOT 4 brake fluid. Use only DOT 4 fluid; do not use other fluids as they are not compatible. Do not intermix silicone based (DOT 5) brake fluid as it can cause clutch component damage leading to clutch system failure.

1. Remove the bolts securing the left-hand rear crankcase cover and remove the cover (**Figure 105**).

2. Remove the dust cap (A, **Figure 102**) from the bleed valve on the clutch slave cylinder.

3. Connect a length of clear tubing to the bleed valve.

4. Place the other end of the tube into a clean container. Fill the container with enough fresh hydraulic fluid to keep the end submerged. The tube should be long enough so that a loop can be made higher than the bleed valve to prevent air from being drawn into the clutch slave cylinder during bleeding.

CAUTION
Cover the clutch slave cylinder and lower frame with a heavy cloth or plastic tarp to protect them from accidental fluid spilling. Wash any fluid off of any painted or plated surface immediately, as it will destroy the finish. Use soapy water and rinse completely.

5. Clean the top of the clutch master cylinder of all dirt and foreign matter.

6. Remove the top cover, set plate and diaphragm. Fill the reservoir almost to the top line (**Figure 103**), insert the diaphragm, set plate and install the top cover loosely.

CAUTION
Failure to install the diaphragm on the master cylinder will allow fluid to spurt out when the clutch lever is applied.

CAUTION
Use hydraulic fluid clearly marked DOT 4 only. Others may vaporize and cause clutch failure. Always use the same brand name; do not intermix as many brands are not compatible. Do not intermix silicone based (DOT 5) brake fluid as it can cause clutch component damage leading to clutch system failure.

7. Insert a 20 mm (3/4 in.) spacer between the handlebar grip and the clutch lever. This will prevent over-travel of the piston within the clutch master cylinder.

8. Slowly apply the clutch lever several times. Hold the lever in the applied position. Open the bleed valve about one-half turn. Allow the lever to travel to its limit against the installed spacer. When this limit is reached, tighten the bleed valve. Occasionally tap or jiggle the clutch flexible hoses to loosen any trapped air bubbles that won't come out the normal way. As the fluid enters the system, the level will drop in the reservoir. Maintain the level at the top of the reservoir to prevent air from being drawn into the system.

9. Repeat Step 8 until the fluid emerging from the hose is completely free of bubbles.

NOTE
Do not allow the reservoir to empty during the bleeding operation or air will enter the system. If this occurs, the entire procedure must be repeated.

10. Hold the lever in, tighten the bleed valve, remove the bleed tube and install the bleed valve dust cap.

11. If necessary, add fluid to correct the level in the reservoir. It should be to the upper level line.

12. Install the reservoir cap.

13. Test the feel of the clutch lever. It should be firm and should offer the same resistance each time it's operated. If it feels spongy, it is likely that there still is air in the system and it must be bled again. When all air has been bled from the system and the fluid level is correct in the reservoir, double-check for leaks and tighten all the fittings and connections.

CLUTCH OIL PRESSURE CHECK

This test requires two Honda special tools. They are as follows:

 a. Oil pressure gauge: Honda part No. 07756-3000000.

 b. Oil pressure gauge attachment: Honda part No. 07710-4220100.

1. Warm the engine to normal operating temperature. Usually 10-15 minutes of stop-and-go riding is sufficient. Shut the engine off.

2. Place the bike on the centerstand.

3. Remove the cover cap (**Figure 113**) from the clutch cover.

4. Remove the oil passage plug (**Figure 114**).

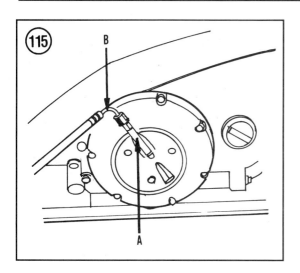

5. Install the attachment (A, **Figure 115**) into the oil passage.

6. Attach the oil pressure gauge hose (B, **Figure 115**) to the attachment.

7. Connect a portable tachometer following the manufacturer's instructions.

8. Start the engine and let it idle and then increase to the indicated rpm.

9. At the indicated engine speed, the oil pressure should be as follows:

    a. 900 rpm: 100 kPa (14 psi).

    b. 3,000 rpm: 250 kPa (36 psi).

10. Shut the engine off.

11. Remove the special tools from the engine.

12. Apply 3-Bond sealant to the threads of the oil passage plug and install the plug. Tighten the plug securely.

13. Install the cover cap onto the clutch cover.

14. If the oil pressure is not as specified, the passageway in the joint piece may be clogged. Remove the joint piece as described in this chapter and clean out with solvent and compressed air.

Tables are on the following page.

Table 1 CLUTCH SPECIFICATIONS

Item	Standard	Wear limit
Friction disc thickness		
1985-1986		
Disc "A"	3.72-3.88 mm	3.1 mm (0.12 in.)
	(0.147-0.153 in.)	
Disc "B"	3.52-3.68 mm	3.1 mm (0.12 in.)
	(0.139-0.145 in.)	
1987-on	3.72-3.88 mm	3.1 mm (0.12 in.)
	(0.147-0.153 in.)	
Clutch plate warpage	—	0.30 mm (0.012 in.)
Clutch spring height	4.9 mm (0.19 in.)	4.5 mm (0.18 in.)
Outer guide ID	24.995-25.012 mm	25.08 mm (0.987 in.)
	(0.9841-0.9847 in.)	
Clutch slave cylinder		
Cylinder ID	38.100-38.162 mm	38.18 mm (1.503 in.)
	(1.5000-1.5024 in.)	
Piston OD	38.036-38.075 mm	38.02 mm (1.497 in.)
	(1.4975-1.4990 in.)	
Clutch master cylinder		
Cylinder bore ID	14.000-14.043 mm	14.06 mm (0.553 in.)
	(0.5512-0.5524 in.)	
Piston OD	13.957-13.984 mm	13.94 mm (0.549 in.)
	(0.5495-0.5506 in.)	

Table 2 CLUTCH MECHANISM TORQUE SPECIFICATIONS

Item	N·m	ft.-lb.
Clutch locknut	95-105	69-76
Engine mounting bolts		
Front bolt	45-60	33-43
Rear upper bolt	45-60	33-43
Rear lower bolt	60-70	43-51
Sub-frame bolts		
Upper	60-70	43-51
Lower	35-45	25-33
Clutch hose union bolts	25-35	18-25
Clutch master cylinder		
cover screws	1-2	9-17 in.-lb.
Clutch slave cylinder		
bleed valve	4-7	3-5

CHAPTER SIX

TRANSMISSION AND GEARSHIFT MECHANISM

EXTERNAL SHIFT MECHANISM

The external shift mechanism is located on the same side of the engine as the clutch assembly and can be removed with the engine in the frame. To remove the shift drum and shift forks it is necessary to remove the engine and split the crankcase. That procedure is covered under *Internal Shift Mechanism* in this chapter.

Refer to **Figure 1** for 1985-1986 models or **Figure 2** for 1987-on models for this procedure.

Removal

NOTE
This procedure is shown with the engine removed from the frame for clarity. It is not necessary to remove the engine to perform this procedure.

1. Remove the clutch outer housing as described in Chapter Five.
2. Remove the oil pipe (**Figure 3**). Discard the O-rings at each end of the oil pipe. They must be replaced with new ones every time the oil pipe is removed.

3. Remove the bolt and washer (**Figure 4**) securing the oil pump driven gear.

4. Remove the oil pump driven gear (A, **Figure 5**) and the drive chain (B, **Figure 5**).

5. Remove gearshift spindle assembly "B" (**Figure 6**) from the crankcase. If the spindle assembly will not come out, shift the transmission to another gear and align the cutout in the gearshift spindle with the ramps on the shift drum cam.

6. Remove the bolt, washer, return spring and the shift drum stopper arm (**Figure 7**).

7. Remove the bolt (**Figure 8**) securing the shift drum cam plate and remove the cam plate (**Figure 9**).

8. Remove the shift drum positive stopper (A, **Figure 10**) from the shift drum. Don't lose the dowel pin in the end of the shift drum (B, **Figure 10**).

9. Remove the shift spindle guide plug (**Figure 11**) from the crankcase. Be careful not to damage the O-ring seal on the plug.

10. Remove the alternator rotor as described in Chapter Four.

11. Remove the starter reduction gear and shaft (**Figure 12**).

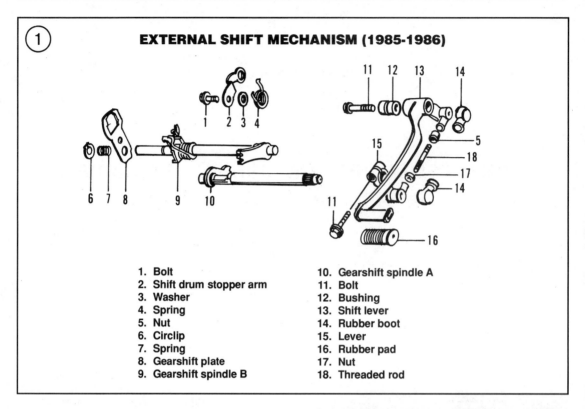

EXTERNAL SHIFT MECHANISM (1985-1986)

1. Bolt
2. Shift drum stopper arm
3. Washer
4. Spring
5. Nut
6. Circlip
7. Spring
8. Gearshift plate
9. Gearshift spindle B
10. Gearshift spindle A
11. Bolt
12. Bushing
13. Shift lever
14. Rubber boot
15. Lever
16. Rubber pad
17. Nut
18. Threaded rod

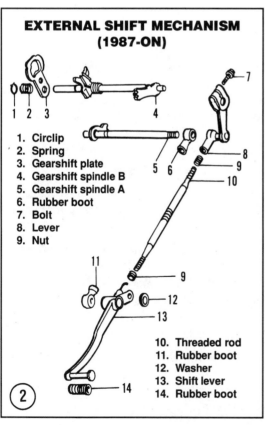

EXTERNAL SHIFT MECHANISM (1987-ON)

1. Circlip
2. Spring
3. Gearshift plate
4. Gearshift spindle B
5. Gearshift spindle A
6. Rubber boot
7. Bolt
8. Lever
9. Nut
10. Threaded rod
11. Rubber boot
12. Washer
13. Shift lever
14. Rubber boot

6

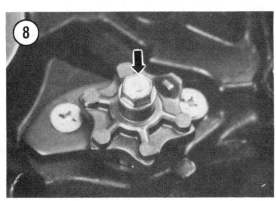

12. Carefully pull the gearshift spindle "A" (A, **Figure 13**) part way out and let it pivot down slightly.

13. Remove the starter gear (B, **Figure 13**).

14. Remove the gearshift spindle "A" (**Figure 14**) from the crankcase. It is necessary to move the spindle around slightly in order to remove the end of the spindle from the hole in the crankcase.

Inspection

1. Inspect the spring (**Figure 15**) on the shift spindle plate. If broken or weak it must be replaced.

2. Inspect the return spring on the gearshift spindle "B" (A, **Figure 16**). If broken or weak it must be replaced.

3. Inspect the gearshift spindle "B" shaft (B, **Figure 16**) for bending, wear or other damage; replace if necessary.

4. Inspect the teeth on gearshift spindle "B" (**Figure 17**). If worn or damaged, it must be replaced.

5. Inspect the gearshift spindle "A" shaft (A, **Figure 18**) for bending, wear or other damage; replace if necessary.

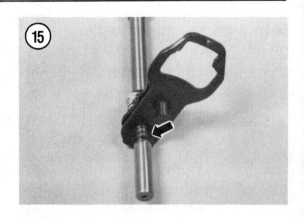

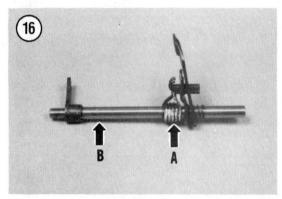

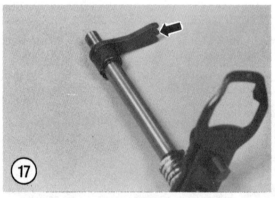

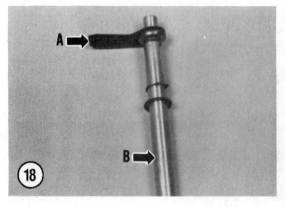

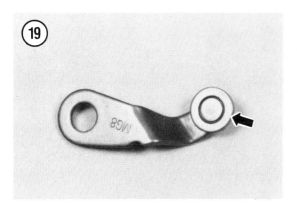

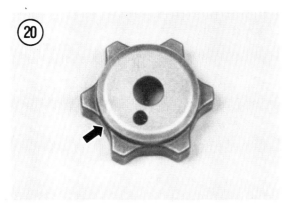

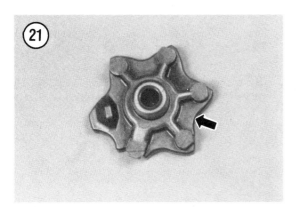

6. Inspect the teeth on gearshift spindle "A" (B, **Figure 18**). If worn or damaged, it must be replaced.

7. Inspect the roller (**Figure 19**) on the shift drum stopper arm. It must rotate freely; replace if necessary.

8. Inspect the detents (**Figure 20**) on the gearshift positive stopper for wear or damage. Replace if necessary.

9. Inspect the ramps (**Figure 21**) on the gearshift cam plate for wear or damage. Replace if necessary.

Installation

1. Make sure the dowel pin is installed in the end of the shift drum.

2. Align the hole in the gearshift drum positive stopper with the dowel pin (B, **Figure 10**) in the shift drum and install the positive stopper (A, **Figure 10**).

3. Align the hole in the backside of the shift drum cam plate (A, **Figure 22**) with the pin on the shift drum (B, **Figure 22**) and install the cam plate (**Figure 9**).

4. Install the bolt (**Figure 8**) securing the cam plate and tighten to the torque specification listed in **Table 1**.

5. Install the shift drum stopper arm, return spring, washer and bolt (**Figure 23**). Do not index it into the shift drum cam plate at this time.

6. Partially screw in the bolt and then index the stopper arm into the shift drum cam plate. Tighten the bolt to the torque specification listed in **Table 1**.

7. Install the gearshift spindle "B" (**Figure 6**) and push it in all the way. Position it correctly onto the gearshift cam plate.

8. The "IN" mark on the oil pump driven gear must face in toward the engine.

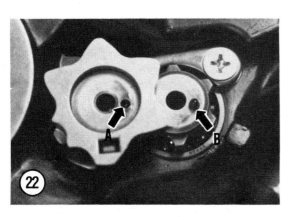

9. Assemble the oil pump driven gear and the drive chain as an assembly. Install this assembly onto the driven gear and the oil pump drive shaft.

10. Install the bolt and washer (**Figure 4**) securing the oil pump driven gear.

11. Make sure the O-ring seal (**Figure 24**) is in place on each end of the oil pipe. Install the oil pipe (**Figure 3**) and push it in until it completely seats at each end.

12. Install the clutch as described in Chapter Five.

13. From the other side, partially install the gearshift spindle "A" (**Figure 14**).

14. Install the starter gear (B, **Figure 13**).

15. Move the gearshift spindle "A" up and into position and align the gearshift spindles sector gears of both arms as shown in **Figure 25**. Push the gearshift spindle "A" in all the way (**Figure 26**).

16. Install the starter reduction gear and shaft (**Figure 12**).

17. Install the alternator rotor as described in Chapter Four.

18. Inspect the O-ring seal (**Figure 27**) on the guide plug and carefully install the gearshift spindle guide plug (**Figure 11**). Do not damage the O-ring seal during installation.

19. Install the clutch outer housing as described in Chapter Five.

TRANSMISSION

The transmission is located within the engine crankcase. To gain access to the transmission and internal shift mechanism it is necessary to remove the engine and disassemble the crankcase. The transmission in the 1985-1986 models is a 5-speed unit while the 1987-on models is equipped with a 4-speed unit. Transmission assembly removal and installation is the same for all models but disassembly and assembly is different and is covered in two separate procedures.

Specifications for the transmission components are listed in **Table 2**.

Transmission and Internal Shift Mechanism Removal/Installation (All Models)

1. Disassemble the crankcase as described in Chapter Four.

2. Withdraw the shift fork shaft (**Figure 28**).

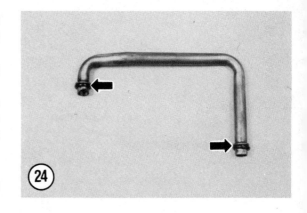

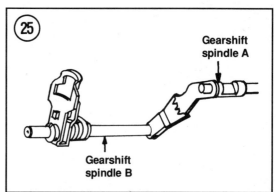

Gearshift spindle A

Gearshift spindle B

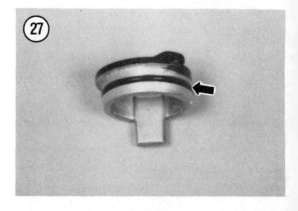

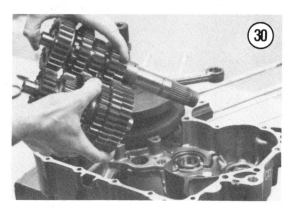

3. Disengage the shift forks from the shift drum and remove the shift drum (**Figure 29**).

4. Remove the shift forks.

5. Remove the main shaft assembly and countershaft assembly as an assembly.

NOTE
Prior to installing any components, coat all bearing surfaces with assembly oil.

6. Mesh the transmission assemblies together and install them into the right-hand crankcase half (**Figure 30**).

7. After both shaft assemblies are installed, tap on the end of both shafts (**Figure 31**) with a plastic or rubber mallet to make sure they are completely seated.

8. When both shafts are installed correctly, the top gear on the countershaft (A, **Figure 32**) will be slightly lower than the mating gear on the mainshaft (B, **Figure 32**). This is correct as the gear on the countershaft will be raised up when the shift fork is installed.

9A. On 1985-1986 models, perform the following:

    a. Install the right-hand shift fork with the "R" mark facing down (A, **Figure 33**).

    b. Install the center shift fork with the "C" mark facing up (B, **Figure 33**).

    c. Install the left-hand shift fork with the "L" mark facing down (C, **Figure 33**).

    d. Install the shift drum (**Figure 29**) and mesh the pin follower of each shift fork into their respective groove of the shift drum.

    e. Position the shift fork shaft with the oil hole end going in last and install the shift fork shaft (**Figure 28**).

9B. On 1987-on models, perform the following:

a. Install the right-hand shift fork with the "R" mark facing down.

b. Install the center shift fork with the "C" mark facing up.

c. Mesh the pin follower of each shift fork into their respective groove of the shift drum.

d. Position the shift fork shaft with the oil hole end going in last and install the shift fork shaft.

10. Spin the transmission shafts and shift through the gears using the shift drum. Make sure you can shift into all gears. This is the time to find that something may be installed incorrectly—not after the crankcase is completely assembled.

NOTE
This procedure is best done with the aid of a helper as the assemblies are loose and won't spin very easily. Have the helper spin the transmission shafts while you turn the shift drum through all the gears.

11. Make sure the thrust washer (D, **Figure 33**) is in place on the transmission main shaft assembly.

12. Assemble the crankcase as described in Chapter Four.

Preliminary Inspection (All Models)

After the transmission shaft assemblies have been removed from the crankcase halves, clean and inspect the assemblies prior to disassembling them. Place the assembled shaft into a large can or plastic bucket and thoroughly clean with a petroleum based solvent such as kerosene and a stiff brush. Dry with compressed air or let it sit on rags to drip dry. Repeat for the other shaft assembly.

1. After they have been cleaned, visually inspect the components of the assemblies for excessive wear. Any burrs, pitting or roughness on the teeth of a gear will cause wear on the mating gear. Minor roughness can be cleaned up with an oilstone but there's little point in attempting to remove deep scars.

NOTE
Defective gears should be replaced. It's a good idea to replace the mating gear on the other shaft even though it may not show as much wear or damage.

2. Carefully check the engagement dogs. If any are chipped, worn, rounded or missing, the affected gear must be replaced.

3. Rotate the transmission and shift drum bearings in the crankcases by hand. Refer to **Figure 34**. Check for roughness, noise and radial play. Any bearing that is suspect should be replaced as described in Chapter Four.

4. If the transmission shafts are satisfactory and are not going to be disassembled, apply assembly oil or engine oil to all components and reinstall them in the crankcase as described in this chapter.

NOTE
If disassembling a used, well run-in transmission for the first time by your-

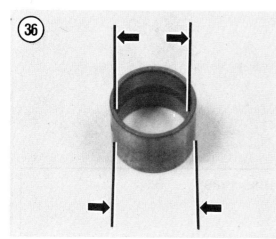

self, pay particular attention to any additional shims that may have been added by a previous owner. These may have been added to take up the tolerance of worn components and must be reinstalled in the same position since the shims have developed a wear pattern. If new parts are going to be installed, these shims may be eliminated. This is something you will have to determine upon reassembly.

Final Drive Output Gear Inspection

1. Measure the inside diameter of the final drive output gear (**Figure 35**). Refer to dimensions listed in **Table 2**. If the gear is worn to the service limit, the gear must be replaced.

2. Measure the inside and outside diameter of the final drive damper gear bushing (**Figure 36**). Refer to dimensions listed in **Table 2**. If the bushing is worn to the service limit, the bushing must be replaced.

3. Make sure the oil hole (**Figure 37**) in the bushing is clear. Clean out with solvent if necessary.

4. Inspect the ramps (**Figure 38**) for wear or damage, replace the gear if necessary.

5. Check the gear for excessive wear, burrs, pitting or chipped or missing teeth (**Figure 39**). Replace the gear if necessary.

Main Shaft Disassembly/ Inspection/Assembly (1985-1986)

Refer to **Figure 40** for this procedure.

NOTE
A helpful "tool" that should be used for transmission disassembly is a large egg flat (the type restaurants get their eggs in) (**Figure 41**). *As you remove a part from the shaft, set it in one of the depressions in the same position from which it was removed. This is an easy way to remember the correct relationship of all parts.*

1. Clean the shaft as described under *Preliminary Inspection* in this chapter.

2. Slide off the thrust washer.

3. Slide off the 5th gear, the 5th gear bushing and the splined washer.

4. Remove the circlip.

5. Slide off the 2nd/4th combination gear.

6. Remove the circlip and slide off the splined washer.

7. Slide off the 3rd gear and the 3rd gear bushing.

8. Check each gear for excessive wear, burrs, pitting or chipped or missing teeth (A, **Figure 42**). Make sure the gear's dogs (B, **Figure 42**) are in good condition.

9. Inspect the inner splines (**Figure 43**) of the 3rd/4th gear for wear or damage. Replace the combination gear if necessary.

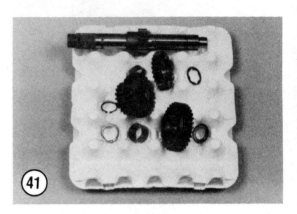

(41)

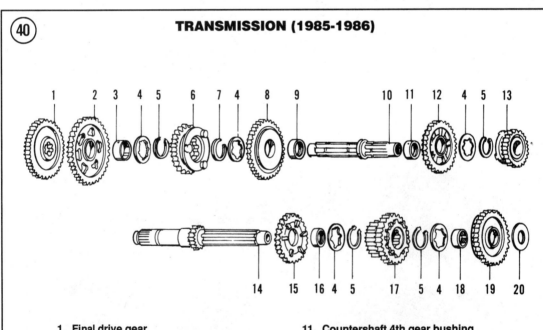

(40) **TRANSMISSION (1985-1986)**

1. Final drive gear
2. Countershaft 1st gear
3. Countershaft 1st gear bushing
4. Splined washer
5. Circlip
6. Countershaft 3rd gear
7. Circlip
8. Countershaft 2nd gear
9. Countershaft 2nd gear bushing
10. Countershaft

11. Countershaft 4th gear bushing
12. Countershaft 4th gear
13. Countershaft 5th gear
14. Mainshaft/1st gear
15. Mainshaft 3rd gear
16. Mainshaft 3rd gear bushing
17. Mainshaft 2nd/4th combination gear
18. Mainshaft 5th gear bushing
19. Mainshaft 5th gear
20. Washer

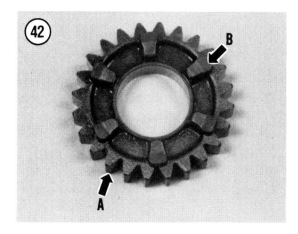

10. Inspect the gearshift fork groove (**Figure 44**) in the respective gears for wear or damage. Replace the gear(s) if necessary.

> *NOTE*
> *Defective gears should be replaced. It is a good idea to replace the mating gear on the countershaft even though it may not show as much wear or damage.*

> *NOTE*
> *The 1st gear is part of the main shaft. If the gear is defective, the shaft must be replaced.*

11. Make sure that all gears and bushings slide smoothly on the main shaft splines.

12. Measure the outside diameter of the main shaft where the 3rd gear bushing rides (**Figure 45**). Refer to dimensions listed in **Table 2**. If the shaft is worn to the service limit, the shaft must be replaced.

13. Measure the inside diameter of the main shaft 3rd and 5th gears (**Figure 46**). Refer to dimensions listed in **Table 2**. If the gear(s) is worn to the service limit, the gear(s) must be replaced.

14. Measure the outside diameter of the main shaft 3rd and 5th gear bushings (**Figure 47**) and the inside diameter of the 3rd gear bushing. Refer to dimensions listed in **Table 2**. If the bushing(s) is worn to the service limit, the bushing(s) must be replaced.

> *NOTE*
> *It is a good idea to replace all circlips every other time the transmission shaft is disassembled to ensure proper gear alignment.*

15. Align the oil hole in the 3rd gear bushing with the oil hole in the main shaft (**Figure 48**) and slide the bushing into place. This alignment is necessary for proper oil flow.

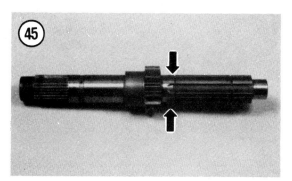

16. Slide on the 3rd gear (flush side first) (**Figure 49**) and splined washer (**Figure 50**).

17. Install the circlip (**Figure 51**).

18. Position the 2nd/4th combination gear with the smaller diameter 2nd gear going on first (**Figure 52**). Slide on the 2nd/4th combination gear (**Figure 53**) and install the circlip (**Figure 54**).

19. Install the splined washer (**Figure 55**).

20. Align the oil hole in the 5th gear bushing with the oil hole in the main shaft (**Figure 56**) and slide

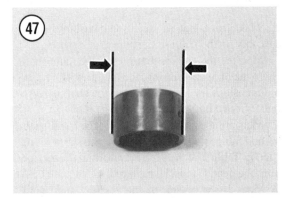

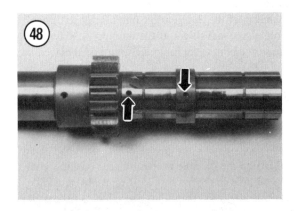

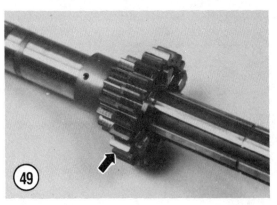

(54)

the bushing into place. This alignment is necessary for proper oil flow.

21. Install the 5th gear (**Figure 57**) and thrust washer (**Figure 58**).

22. Before installation, double-check the placement of all gears (**Figure 59**). Make sure all circlips are seated in the main shaft grooves.

23. Make sure each gear engages properly with the adjoining gears where applicable.

Countershaft Disassembly/ Inspection/Assembly (1985-1986)

Refer to **Figure 40** for this procedure.

NOTE
Use the same large egg flat (used on the main shaft disassembly) **Figure 60** *during the countershaft disassembly. This is an easy way to remember the correct relationship of all parts.*

1. Slide off the 5th gear.

2. Remove the circlip and slide off the splined washer.

(55)

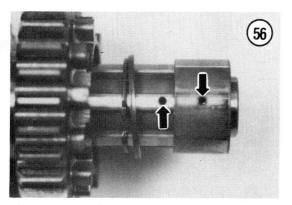

(56)

(58)

(57)

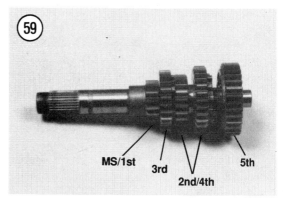

(59)

MS/1st   3rd   5th
           2nd/4th

3. Slide off the 4th gear and the 4th gear bushing.

4. From the other end of the shaft, slide off the final drive gear.

5. Slide off the 1st gear and the 1st gear bushing.

6. Slide off the splined washer and remove the circlip.

7. Slide off the 3rd gear.

8. Remove the circlip and slide off the splined washer.

9. Slide off the 2nd gear and the 2nd gear bushing.

10. Check each gear for excessive wear, burrs, pitting or chipped or missing teeth (**Figure 61**). Make sure the lugs (**Figure 62**) are in good condition.

NOTE
Defective gears should be replaced. It is a good idea to replace the mating gear on the main shaft even though it may not show signs of wear or damage.

11. Make sure all gears and gear bushings slide smoothly on the countershaft splines.

12. Measure the inside diameter of the 1st, 2nd and 4th gears (**Figure 46**). Compare with the dimensions listed in **Table 2**.

13. Measure the outside diameter of the 1st, 2nd and 4th gear bushings (**Figure 47**). Compare with the dimensions listed in **Table 2**.

14. Inspect the gearshift fork groove (**Figure 44**) in the respective gears for wear or damage. Replace the gear(s) if necessary.

NOTE
It is a good idea to replace all circlips every other time the shaft is disassembled to ensure proper gear alignment.

15. Install the 4th gear bushing (**Figure 63**). The alignment of the oil hole to the shaft is *not* necessary as this bushing rotates freely on the shaft.

16. Install the 4th gear and splined washer (**Figure 64**).

17. Install the circlip (**Figure 65**).

18. Position the 5th gear with the shift fork groove going on first and slide on the 5th gear (**Figure 66**).

19. Onto the other end of the shaft, install the 2nd gear bushing (**Figure 67**). The alignment of the oil hole to the shaft is *not* necessary as this bushing rotates freely on the shaft.

20. Slide on the 2nd gear (flush side first) (**Figure 68**) and the splined washer (ground surface toward 2nd gear) (**Figure 69**).

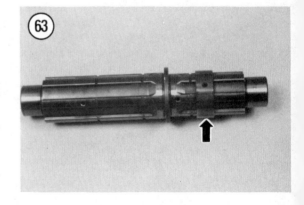

64

21. Install the circlip (**Figure 70**).

22. Position the 3rd gear with the shift fork groove going on first and slide on the 3rd gear (**Figure 71**).

23. Install the circlip (**Figure 72**).

24. Slide on the splined washer (**Figure 73**).

25. Align the oil hole in the 1st gear bushing with the oil hole in the shaft (**Figure 74**) and slide on the bushing. This alignment is necessary for proper oil flow.

26. Position the 1st gear with the flush side going on last and slide on the 1st gear (**Figure 75**).

65

68

66

69

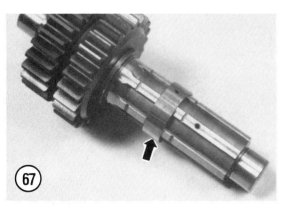

67

70

27. Position the final drive gear with the raised shoulder side on last and slide on the gear (**Figure 76**).

28. Before installation, double-check the placement of all gears (**Figure 77**). Make sure all circlips are correctly seated in the countershaft grooves.

29. After both transmission shafts have been assembled, mesh the 2 assemblies together in the correct position (**Figure 78**). Check that all gears meet correctly. This is your last check prior to installing the assemblies into the crankcase; make sure they are correctly assembled.

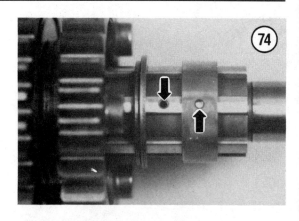

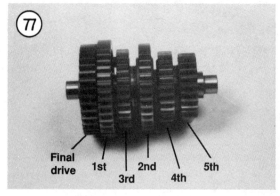

Main Shaft Disassembly/ Inspection/Assembly (1987-on)

Refer to **Figure 79** for this procedure.

NOTE
A helpful "tool" that should be used for transmission disassembly is a large egg

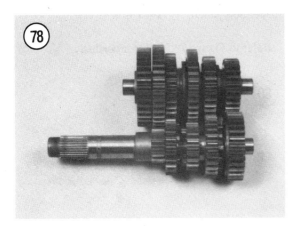

flat (the type restaurants get their eggs in). As you remove a part from the shaft, set it in one of the depressions in the same position from which it was removed. This is an easy way to remember the correct relationship of all parts.

1. Clean the shaft as described under *Preliminary Inspection* in this chapter.

2. Slide off the thrust washer.

3. Slide off the 4th gear, the 4th gear bushing and the splined washer.

4. Remove the circlip.

5. Slide off the 2nd gear.

6. Remove the circlip and slide off the splined washer.

7. Slide off the 3rd gear and the 3rd gear bushing.

8. Check each gear for excessive wear, burrs, pitting or chipped or missing teeth. Make sure the gear's dogs are in good condition.

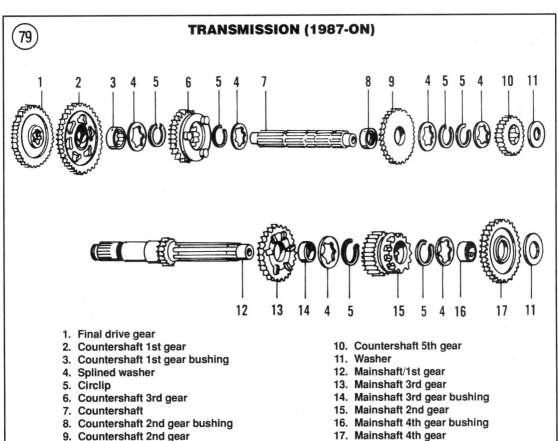

TRANSMISSION (1987-ON)

1. Final drive gear
2. Countershaft 1st gear
3. Countershaft 1st gear bushing
4. Splined washer
5. Circlip
6. Countershaft 3rd gear
7. Countershaft
8. Countershaft 2nd gear bushing
9. Countershaft 2nd gear
10. Countershaft 5th gear
11. Washer
12. Mainshaft/1st gear
13. Mainshaft 3rd gear
14. Mainshaft 3rd gear bushing
15. Mainshaft 2nd gear
16. Mainshaft 4th gear bushing
17. Mainshaft 4th gear

NOTE
Defective gears should be replaced. It is a good idea to replace the mating gear on the countershaft even though it may not show as much wear or damage.

NOTE
The 1st gear is part of the main shaft. If the gear is defective, the shaft must be replaced.

9. Make sure that all gears and bushings slide smoothly on the main shaft splines.

10. Measure the outside diameter of the main shaft at the location where the 3rd gear bushing rides (**Figure 80**). Refer to dimensions listed in **Table 2**. If the shaft is worn to the service limit, the shaft must be replaced.

11. Measure the inside diameter of the main shaft 3rd and 4th gears (**Figure 81**). Refer to dimensions listed in **Table 3**. If the gear(s) is worn to the service limit, the gear(s) must be replaced.

12. Measure the outside diameter of the main shaft 3rd and 4th gear bushings (**Figure 82**) and the inside diameter of the 3rd gear bushing. Refer to dimensions listed in **Table 3**. If the bushing(s) is worn to the service limit, the bushing(s) must be replaced.

NOTE
It is a good idea to replace all circlips every other time the transmission shaft is disassembled to ensure proper gear alignment.

13. Align the oil hole in the 3rd gear bushing with the oil hole in the main shaft and slide the bushing into place. This alignment is necessary for proper oil flow.

14. Slide on the 3rd gear (flush side on first) and splined washer.

15. Install the circlip.

16. Position the 2nd gear with the shift fork groove side going on last and slide on the 2nd gear.

17. Install the circlip.

18. Install the splined washer.

19. Align the oil hole in the 4th gear bushing with the oil hole in the main shaft and slide the bushing into place. This alignment is necessary for proper oil flow.

20. Install the 4th gear and thrust washer.

21. Before installation, double-check the placement of all gears. Make sure all circlips are seated in the main shaft grooves.

22. Make sure each gear engages properly with the adjoining gears where applicable.

Countershaft Disassembly/ Inspection/Assembly (1987-on)

Refer to **Figure 79** for this procedure.

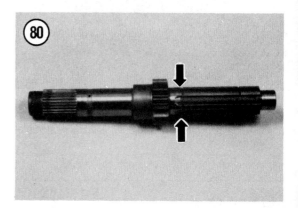

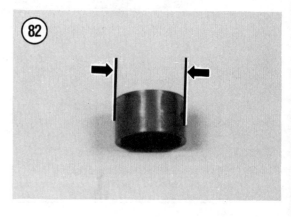

NOTE
Use the same large egg flat (used on the main shaft disassembly) during the countershaft disassembly. This is an easy way to remember the correct relationship of all parts.

1. Slide off the thrust washer and the 4th gear.
2. Slide off the splined washer and remove the circlip.
3. Remove the circlip and slide off the splined washer.
4. Slide off the 2nd gear, the 2nd gear bushing and splined washer.
5. From the other end of the shaft, slide off the final drive gear.
6. Slide off the 1st gear and the 1st gear bushing.
7. Slide off the splined washer and remove the circlip.
8. Slide off the 3rd gear.
9. Check each gear for excessive wear, burrs, pitting or chipped or missing teeth (**Figure 83**). Make sure the lugs (**Figure 84**) are in good condition.

NOTE
Defective gears should be replaced. It is a good idea to replace the mating gear on the main shaft even though it may not show signs of wear or damage.

10. Make sure all gears and gear bushings slide smoothly on the countershaft splines.
11. Measure the inside diameter of the 1st, 2nd and 4th gears (**Figure 81**). Refer to dimensions listed in **Table 3**. If the gear(s) is worn to the service limit, the gear(s) must be replaced.
12. Measure the outside diameter of the 1st, 2nd and 4th gear bushings. Compare with the dimensions listed in **Table 3**.

NOTE
It is a good idea to replace all circlips every other time the shaft is disassembled to ensure proper gear alignment.

13. Align the oil hole in the 2nd gear bushing with the oil hole in the shaft and slide on the bushing. This alignment is necessary for proper oil flow.
14. Slide on the 2nd gear (flush side on last), splined washer (ground surface toward the 2nd gear).
15. Install the circlip.
16. Install the circlip and splined washer.
17. Slide on the 4th gear (flush side on last).
18. Slide on the thrust washer.
19. Onto the other end of the shaft, install the 3rd gear with the shift fork groove end going on first.
20. Install the circlip and splined washer.
21. Align the oil hole in the 1st gear bushing with the oil hole in the shaft and slide on the bushing. This alignment is necessary for proper oil flow.
22. Slide on the 1st gear.
23. Position the final drive gear with the raised shoulder side on last and slide on the gear.
24. Before installation, double-check the placement of all gears. Make sure all circlips are correctly seated in the countershaft grooves.
25. After both transmission shafts have been assembled, mesh the 2 assemblies together in the correct position. Check that all gears meet correctly. This is your last check prior to installing the assemblies into the crankcase; make sure they are correctly assembled.

INTERNAL SHIFT MECHANISM

The internal shift mechanism is removed during transmission removal as described in this chapter.

Inspection

Refer to **Figure 85** for 1985-1986 models or **Figure 86** for 1987-on models for this procedure.

Refer to **Table 4** for shift fork, shift fork shaft and shift drum specifications.

1. Inspect each shift fork (**Figure 87**) for signs of wear or cracking. Check for bending and make sure each fork slides smoothly on the shaft (**Figure 88**). Replace any worn or damaged forks.

2. Check for any arc-shaped wear or burn marks on the shift forks (**Figure 89**). This indicates that the shift fork has come in contact with the gear as a result of excessively worn fork fingers. The shift fork must be replaced.

3. Measure the width of the gearshift fork fingers with a micrometer (**Figure 90**). Replace any that are worn to the service limit listed in **Table 4**.

4. Check the shift drum dowel pin (**Figure 91**) on each shift fork for wear or damage; replace the shift fork as necessary.

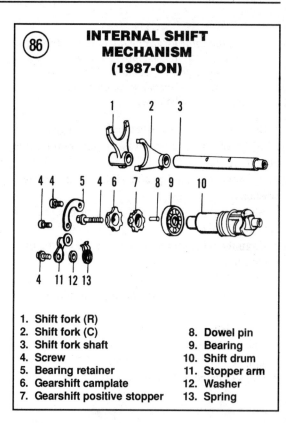

86 INTERNAL SHIFT MECHANISM (1987-ON)

1. Shift fork (R)
2. Shift fork (C)
3. Shift fork shaft
4. Screw
5. Bearing retainer
6. Gearshift camplate
7. Gearshift positive stopper
8. Dowel pin
9. Bearing
10. Shift drum
11. Stopper arm
12. Washer
13. Spring

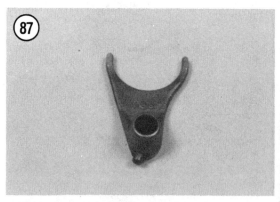

87

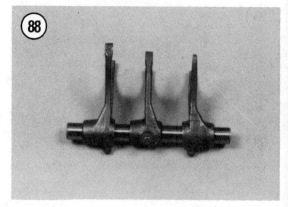

88

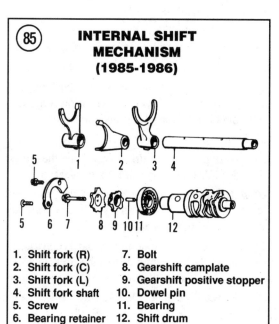

85 INTERNAL SHIFT MECHANISM (1985-1986)

1. Shift fork (R)
2. Shift fork (C)
3. Shift fork (L)
4. Shift fork shaft
5. Screw
6. Bearing retainer
7. Bolt
8. Gearshift camplate
9. Gearshift positive stopper
10. Dowel pin
11. Bearing
12. Shift drum

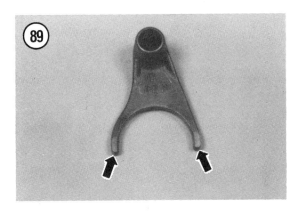

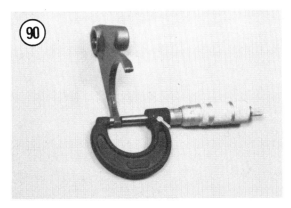

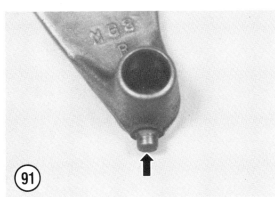

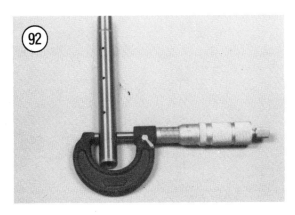

5. Roll the shift fork shaft on a flat surface such as a piece of plate glass and check for any bends. If the shaft is bent, it must be replaced.

6. Measure the outside diameter of the shift fork shaft at each end with a micrometer. Refer to **Figure 92** for the right-hand end and **Figure 93** for the left-hand end. Replace if worn to either service limit listed in **Table 4**.

7. Make sure the oil holes (**Figure 94**) in the shift fork shaft are clear. If necessary, clean out the hole with a piece of wire and then with solvent and compressed air.

8. Check the grooves (**Figure 95**) in the shift drum for wear or roughness. If any of the groove profiles have excessive wear or damage; replace the shift drum.

9. Make sure the oil holes (**Figure 96**) in the shift drum are open and sludge free. If necessary, clean out with solvent and compressed air.

10. Inspect the shift drum bearing in the crankcase. It must rotate smoothly with no roughness or noise. If damaged, the bearing must be replaced.

11. Measure the outside diameter of the shift drum (**Figure 97**) with a micrometer. Replace if worn to either service limit listed in **Table 4**.

6

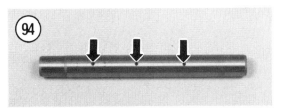

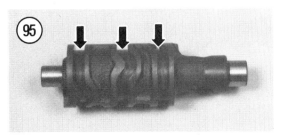

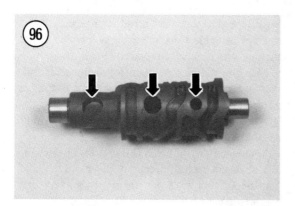

Table 1 GEARSHIFT MECHANISM TORQUE SPECIFICATIONS

Item	N•m	ft.-lb.
Camplate bolt	8-12	6-9
Stopper arm bolt	8-12	6-9

Table 2 TRANSMISSION SPECIFICATIONS (1985-1986)

Item	Specification	Wear limit
Gear backlash		
1st	0.044-0.133 mm (0.0017-0.0052 in.)	0.18 mm (0.007 in.)
2nd	0.046-0.140 mm (0.0018-0.0055 in.)	0.18 mm (0.007 in.)
3rd, 4th and 5th	0.068-0.136 mm (0.0027-0.0054 in.)	0.18 mm (0.007 in.)
Gear ID main shaft		
3rd, 5th gear	31.000-31.025 mm (1.2205-1.2215 in.)	31.035 mm (1.2218 in.)
Gear ID countershaft		
1st and 2nd	33.000-33.025 mm (1.2992-1.3002 in.)	33.035 mm (1.3006 in.)
4th	31.000-31.025 mm (1.2205-1.2215 in.)	31.035 mm (1.2218 in.)
Gear bushing OD		
Main shaft		
3rd and 5th	30.950-30.975 mm (1.2185-1.2195 in.)	30.94 mm (1.2181 in.)
Countershaft		
1st and 2nd	32.950-32.975 mm (1.2972-1.2982 in.)	32.94 mm (1.2968 in.)
4th	30.950-30.975 mm (1.2185-1.2195 in.)	30.94 mm (1.2181 in.)
Gear bushing ID		
Main shaft 3rd	27.995-28.016 mm (1.1022-1.1030 in.)	28.026 mm (1.1043 in.)
Main shaft OD		
@ 3rd gear bushing	27.997-27.990 mm (1.1022-1.1020 in.)	27.967 mm (1.1011 in.)
Gear-to-bushing clearance		
Mainshaft		
3rd and 5th	0.025-0.065 mm (0.0010-0.0030 in.)	0.095 mm (0.0037 in.)
Countershaft		
1st, 2nd and 4th	0.025-0.065 mm (0.0010-0.0030 in.)	0.095 mm (0.0037 in.)
Gear bushing-to-shaft clearance		
Mainshaft 3rd	0.005-0.039 mm (0.0002-0.0015 in.)	0.059 mm (0.0023 in.)
Damper gear backlash	0.034-0.102 mm (0.0013-0.0040 in.)	0.18 mm (0.007 in.)
Final driven gear ID	25.000-25.021 mm (0.9843-0.9851 in.)	25.031 mm (0.9855 in.)

(continued)

6

Table 2 TRANSMISSION SPECIFICATIONS (1985-1986) (continued)

Item	Specification	Wear limit
Final driven gear bushing		
OD	24.959-24.980 mm (0.9826-0.9835 in.)	24.949 mm (0.9822 in.)
ID	22.020-22.041 mm (0.8669-0.8678 in.)	22.051 mm (0.8681 in.)
Output drive shaft OD	21.979-22.000 mm (0.8653-0.8661 in.)	21.969 mm (0.8649 in.)
Damper spring free length	58.5 mm (2.30 in.)	57.3 mm (2.26 in.)

Table 3 TRANSMISSION SPECIFICATIONS (1987-ON)

Item	Specification	Wear limit
Gear backlash		
1st	0.044-0.133 mm (0.0017-0.0052 in.)	0.18 mm (0.007 in.)
2nd	0.046-0.140 mm (0.0018-0.0055 in.)	0.18 mm (0.007 in.)
3rd and 4th	0.068-0.136 mm (0.0027-0.0054 in.)	0.18 mm (0.007 in.)
Gear ID main shaft		
3rd and 4th	31.000-31.025 mm (1.2205-1.2215 in.)	31.035 mm (1.2218 in.)
Gear ID countershaft		
1st and 2nd	33.000-33.025 mm (1.2992-1.3002 in.)	33.035 mm (1.3006 in.)
Gear bushing OD		
Main shaft		
3rd and 4th	30.950-30.975 mm (1.2185-1.2195 in.)	30.94 mm (1.2181 in.)
Countershaft		
1st and 2nd	32.950-32.975 mm (1.2972-1.2982 in.)	32.94 mm (1.2968 in.)
Gear bushing ID		
Main shaft 3rd	27.995-28.016 mm (1.1022-1.1030 in.)	28.026 mm (1.1043 in.)
Main shaft OD		
@ 3rd gear bushing	27.997-27.990 mm (1.1022-1.1019 in.)	27.967 mm (1.1011 in.)
Gear-to-bushing clearance		
Mainshaft		
3rd	0.025-0.065 mm (0.0010-0.0030 in.)	0.095 mm (0.0037 in.)
Countershaft		
1st and 2nd	0.025-0.065 mm (0.0010-0.0030 in.)	0.095 mm (0.0037 in.)
Gear bushing-to-shaft clearance		
Mainshaft 3rd	0.005-0.039 mm (0.0002-0.0015 in.)	0.059 mm (0.0023 in.)
Damper gear backlash	0.034-0.102 mm (0.0013-0.0040 in.)	0.18 mm (0.007 in.)
Final driven gear ID	25.000-25.021 mm (0.9843-0.9851 in.)	25.031 mm (0.9855 in.)

(continued)

Table 3 TRANSMISSION SPECIFICATIONS (1987-ON) (continued)

Item	Specification	Wear limit
Final driven gear bushing		
OD	24.959-24.980 mm (0.9826-0.9835 in.)	24.949 mm (0.9822 in.)
ID	22.020-22.041 mm (0.8669-0.8678 in.)	22.051 mm (0.8681 in.)
Output drive shaft OD	21.979-22.000 mm (0.8653-0.8661 in.)	21.969 mm (0.8649 in.)
Damper spring free length	68.5 mm (2.70 in.)	67.3 mm (2.65 in.)

Table 4 SHIFT FORK, SHIFT SHAFT AND SHIFT DRUM SPECIFICATIONS

Item	Specification	Wear limit
Shift fork fingers		
Left (1985-1986 only)	5.93-6.00 mm (0.233-0.236 in.)	5.83 mm (0.230 in.)
Right and center	6.43-6.50 mm (0.253-0.256 in.)	6.33 mm (0.249 in.)
Shift fork shaft OD		
Left end	13.466-13.484 mm (0.5302-0.5309 in.)	13.456 mm (0.5298 in.)
Right end	13.966-13.984 mm (0.5498-0.5506 in.)	13.956 mm (0.5494 in.)
Shift drum end OD		
Left end	13.966-13.984 mm (0.5498-0.5506 in.)	13.956 mm (0.5494 in.)

6

FUEL, EMISSION CONTROL AND EXHAUST SYSTEMS

The fuel system consists of the fuel tanks, shutoff valve, fuel pump and filter, 2 Keihin constant velocity carburetors and the air filter.

The exhaust system consists of 2 exhaust pipes and 2 mufflers.

This chapter includes service procedures for all parts of the fuel and exhaust systems except the air filter which is covered in Chapter Three. Carburetor specifications are listed in **Table 1**. **Table 1** and **Table 2** are at the end of this chapter.

The carburetors on all U.S. models are engineered to meet stringent EPA (Environmental Protection Agency) regulations. The carburetors are flow tested and preset at the factory for maximum performance and efficiency within EPA regulations. Altering preset carburetor jet needle and pilot screw adjustments is forbidden by law. Failure to comply with EPA regulations may result in heavy fines.

CARBURETOR OPERATION

An understanding of the function of each of the carburetor components and their relation to one another is a valuable aid for pinpointing a source of carburetor trouble.

The carburetor's purpose is to supply and atomize fuel and mix it in correct proportions with air that is drawn in through the air intake. At the primary throttle opening (idle), a small amount of fuel is siphoned through the pilot jet by the incoming air. As the throttle is opened further, the air stream begins to siphon fuel through the main jet and needle jet. The tapered needle increases the effective flow capacity of the needle jet as it is lifted, in that it occupies progressively less of the area of the jet.

At full throttle, the carburetor venturi is fully open and the needle is lifted far enough to permit the main jet to flow at full capacity.

The choke circuit is a "bystarter" system in which the choke lever opens a valve rather than closing a butterfly in the venturi area as on many carburetors. In the open position, the slow jet discharges a stream of fuel into the carburetor venturi, to enrich the mixture when the engine is cold.

CARBURETOR SERVICE

Carburetor service (removal and cleaning) should be performed when poor engine performance or hesitation is observed. If, after servicing the carburetors and making the adjustments described in this

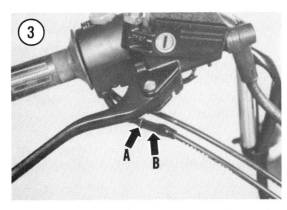

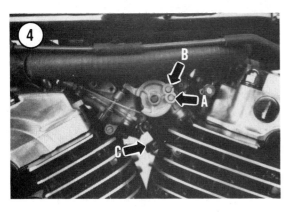

chapter, the motorcycle does not perform correctly and assuming that other factors affecting performance, such as ignition timing and condition, etc., are correct, the motorcycle should be checked by a dealer or a qualified performance tuning specialist.

Removal/Installation
(1985-1986)

1. Place the bike on the centerstand.
2. Remove the right-hand side cover (**Figure 1**).
3. Disconnect the battery negative lead (**Figure 2**).
4. Remove the main fuel tank as described in this chapter.
5. Remove the air filter case as described in this chapter.
6. Remove the screws securing the throttle linkage cover and remove the cover.
7. At the hand throttle, loosen the throttle cable locknut (A, **Figure 3**) and turn the adjusting barrel (B, **Figure 3**) all the way in. This provides the necessary slack for ease of cable removal at the carburetor assembly.
8. Loosen the locknuts securing the throttle cables to the cable bracket.
9. Disconnect the "pull" throttle cable from the lower portion of the bracket and from the lower slot (A, **Figure 4**) in the throttle wheel.
10. Disconnect the "push" throttle cable from the upper portion of the bracket and from the upper slot (B, **Figure 4**) in the throttle wheel.
11. Tie the loose ends of the throttle cables to the frame at a location that will not restrict carburetor removal.
12. Pull back the rubber boots at the end of each choke cable.
13. Loosen the choke valve nut on each cable.
14. Remove the choke valve, spring and nut from each cable on each carburetor.
15. Disconnect the fuel line at the T-fitting. Plug the end of the fuel line with a golf tee to prevent the spillage of fuel.
16. On models so equipped, disconnect the lines from the carburetors that go to the PCV valve.
17. Label and disconnect all hoses at the carburetor.
18. Loosen the clamping bands on the carburetors (C, **Figure 4**).
19. Pull the carburetors and the rubber intake tubes from the intake parts on the cylinder heads.

7

20. Slowly and carefully pull the carburetor assembly out of the frame (**Figure 5**). Be careful not to damage any of the carburetor components.

21. Remove the carburetor assembly.

22. Install by reversing these removal steps while noting the following.

23. Before installing the carburetor assembly, coat the inside surface of both rubber intake tubes with Armor-All or rubber lube. This will make it easier to install the carburetor throats into the intake tubes.

NOTE
The rear cylinder intake tube band ends and screw must be positioned at a right angle to the front cylinder to prevent interference with the throttle drum.

24. Be sure the throttle cables and choke cable are correctly positioned in the frame—not twisted or kinked and without any sharp bends. Tighten the locknuts securely.

25. Attach the "pull" throttle cable into the lower portion of the bracket and into the lower slot (A, **Figure 4**) in the throttle wheel.

26. Attach the "push" throttle cable into the upper portion of the bracket and into the upper slot (B, **Figure 4**) in the throttle wheel.

27. Adjust the throttle cable as described in Chapter Three.

28. Adjust the choke as described in this chapter.

Removal/Installation
(1987-on)

1. Place the bike on the centerstand.

2. Remove the right-hand side cover.

3. Disconnect the battery negative lead.

4. Remove the fuel tank as described in this chapter.

5. Remove the bolt securing the crankcase breather system oil catch tank. Disconnect the hoses and remove the oil catch tank.

6. Loosen the clamping screws on the inlet air connecting tube. Remove the air connecting tube from the carburetors and the frame.

7. Remove the screws securing the throttle linkage cover and remove the cover.

8. At the hand throttle, loosen the throttle cable locknut and turn the adjusting barrel all the way in. This provides the necessary slack for ease of cable removal at the carburetor assembly.

9. Loosen the locknuts securing the throttle cables to the cable bracket.

10. Disconnect the "pull" throttle cable from the lower portion of the bracket and from the lower slot in the throttle wheel.

11. Disconnect the "push" throttle cable from the upper portion of the bracket and from the upper slot in the throttle wheel.

12. Tie the loose ends of the throttle cables to the frame at a location that will not restrict carburetor removal.

13. Pull back the rubber boots at the end of each choke cable.

14. Loosen the choke valve nut on each cable and remove the cable end (choke valve) from each carburetor.

15. Disconnect the vacuum hoses from the air vent control valve body.

16. Label and disconnect all hoses at the carburetor.

17. Disconnect the fuel line at the T-fitting. Plug the end of the fuel line with a golf tee to prevent spillage of fuel.

18. On models so equipped, disconnect the lines from the carburetors that go to the PCV valve.

19. Label and disconnect all hoses at the carburetor.

20. Loosen the clamping bands on the carburetors.

21. Pull the carburetors and the rubber intake tubes from the intake parts on the cylinder heads.

22. Slowly and carefully pull the carburetor assembly out of the frame. Be careful not to damage any of the carburetor components.

23. Remove the carburetor assembly.

24. Install by reversing these removal steps while noting the following.

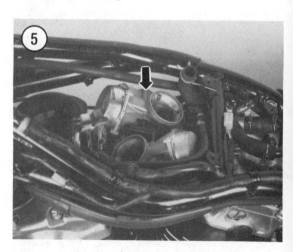

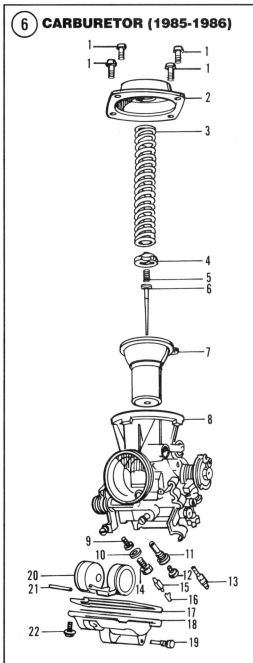

CARBURETOR (1985-1986)

1. Screw
2. Top cover
3. Vacuum cylinder spring
4. Needle holder
5. Spring
6. Jet needle
7. Vacuum cylinder
8. Carburetor body
9. Filter
10. Washer
11. Main jet holder
12. Main jet
13. Slow jet
14. Float valve seat
15. Float valve
16. Float valve clip
17. Gasket
18. Float bowl
19. Drain screw
20. Float
21. Float pin
22. Screw

25. Before installing the carburetor assembly, coat the inside surface of both rubber intake tubes with Armor-All or rubber lube. This will make it easier to install the carburetor throats into the intake tubes.

NOTE
The rear cylinder intake tube band ends and screw must be positioned at a right angle to the front cylinder to prevent interference with the throttle drum.

26. Be sure the throttle cables and choke cable are correctly positioned in the frame—not twisted or kinked and without any sharp bends. Tighten the locknuts securely.

27. Attach the "pull" throttle cable into the lower portion of the bracket and into the lower slot in the throttle wheel.

28. Attach the "push" throttle cable into the upper portion of the bracket and into the upper slot in the throttle wheel.

29. Adjust the throttle cable as described in Chapter Three.

30. Adjust the choke as described in this chapter.

Disassembly

Refer to **Figure 6** for 1985-1986 models or **Figure 7** for 1987-on models for this procedure.

It is recommended that only one carburetor be disassembled and cleaned at a time. This will prevent an accidental interchange of parts.

1. On 1985-1986 models, remove the screws securing the air cut-off valve (**Figure 8**) and remove the valve and its related hoses.

2. Remove the screws (**Figure 9**) securing the carburetor top cover to the main body and remove the cover (A, **Figure 10**).

3. Remove the vacuum cylinder spring (B, **Figure 10**).

4. Remove the vacuum cylinder (**Figure 11**). Carefully work the diaphragm away from the main body and lift the vacuum cylinder out of the carburetor.

5. Remove the jet needle as follows.

   a. Put a Phillips screwdriver down into the vacuum cylinder cavity (**Figure 12**).

   b. Place the screwdriver on the needle jet holder and turn the holder 60° in either direction to unlock it from the tangs within the vacuum cylinder. Remove the needle jet holder and spring (**Figure 13**).

7

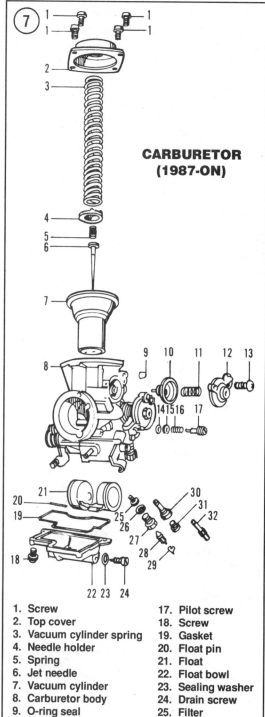

**CARBURETOR
(1987-ON)**

1. Screw
2. Top cover
3. Vacuum cylinder spring
4. Needle holder
5. Spring
6. Jet needle
7. Vacuum cylinder
8. Carburetor body
9. O-ring seal
10. Diaphragm
11. Spring
12. Air cutoff valve cover
13. Screw
14. O-ring
15. Washer
16. Spring

17. Pilot screw
18. Screw
19. Gasket
20. Float pin
21. Float
22. Float bowl
23. Sealing washer
24. Drain screw
25. Filter
26. Washer
27. Float valve seat
28. Float valve
29. Float valve clip
30. Main jet holder
31. Main jet
32. Slow jet

c. Remove the jet needle (**Figure 14**).

6. Remove the screws securing the float bowl (**Figure 15**) to the main body and lift the float bowl off.

7. Carefully push out the float pin (**Figure 16**).

8. Lift the float and needle valve (**Figure 17**) out of the main body.

9. Inspect the float valve seat (**Figure 18**) for grooves and nicks. If damaged, it must be replaced.

10. If necessary, remove the float valve seat and filter (**Figure 18**).

11. Remove the main jet (**Figure 19**).

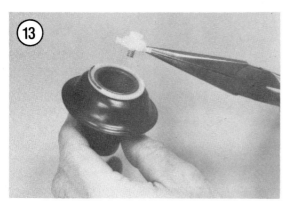

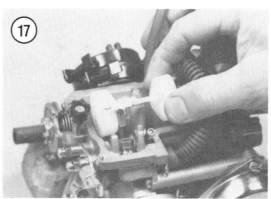

12. Remove the main jet holder (**Figure 20**).

13. Remove the slow jet (A, **Figure 21**).

14. The starter jet (B, **Figure 21**) is pressed into place and cannot be removed.

15. The needle jet (**Figure 22**) is not removable.

> *NOTE*
> *The pilot screws are covered by a metal plug (**Figure 23**) that has to be drilled out in order to remove the screw. If removal is necessary, refer to **Pilot Screw and Plug Removal Installation** in this chapter.*

16. On 1987-on models, remove the air cut-off valve from the main body as described in this chapter.

17. Remove the drain screw (**Figure 24**) from the float bowl. If necessary, clean out the drain tube outlet and reinstall the drain screw.

> *NOTE*
> *Further disassembly is neither necessary nor recommended. If throttle shafts or butterflies are damaged, take the carburetor body to a dealer for replacement.*

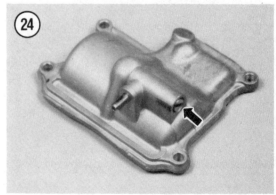

Cleaning and Inspection

1. Clean the carburetor assembly and all parts in solvent.

NOTE
It is recommended that one carburetor be cleaned at a time to avoid inter-changing parts.

2. Clean all parts, except rubber or plastic parts in a good grade of carburetor cleaner. This solution is

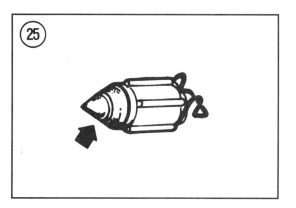

available at most automotive supply stores in a re-sealable tank with a dip basket. If it is tightly sealed when not in use, the solution will last for several cleanings. Follow the manufacturer's instructions for correct soak time—usually about 1/2 hour.

WARNING
Wear goggles and a respirator when blowing carburetor cleaner off the parts.

3. Remove the parts from the cleaner and wash thoroughly with soap and water. Rinse with clean water and thoroughly dry with compressed air.

4. Blow out the jets with compressed air. Do *not* use a piece of wire to clean them as minor gouges in a jet can alter flow rate and upset the fuel/air mixture.

5. Inspect the end of the float valve needle (**Figure 25**) and seat for wear or damage. Replace either or both parts if necessary.

6. Inspect the filter (A, **Figure 26**) on the float valve seat. If damaged, the float valve must be replaced.

7. If removed, inspect the pilot screw for wear or damage that may have occurred during removal. Replace both pilot screws even if only one requires replacement. This is necessary for correct pilot screw adjustment as described in this chapter.

8. Check the float bowl O-ring (**Figure 27**) for flat spots, hardness or other damage; replace if necessary.

9. Check the float assembly for leaks. Place the float in a container of water and push it down. There should be no bubbles. Replace the float assembly if necessary.

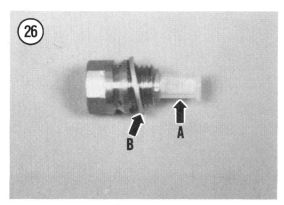

Assembly

1. If removed, screw the pilot screw into the exact same position (same number of turns) as recorded during disassembly.

NOTE
If new pilot screws were installed, turn them out the number of turns indicated in ***Table 1*** *from the* ***lightly*** *seated position.*

2. To assemble the vacuum cylinder (**Figure 28**), perform the following.

   a. Insert the jet needle (**Figure 14**) into the vacuum cylinder.

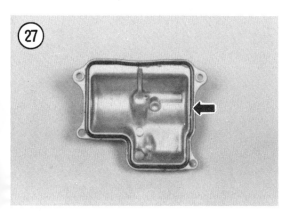

7

b. Insert the spring in the end of the needle holder (**Figure 13**).

c. Secure the end of the needle jet holder with a Phillips screwdriver (**Figure 12**) and insert the holder into the vacuum cylinder. Turn the needle jet holder 60° in either direction to lock the holder in place within the vacuum holder.

3. Install the vacuum cylinder into the carburetor body. Align the tab on the diaphragm with the hole (**Figure 29**) in the carburetor body.

4. Install the vacuum cylinder compression spring (B, **Figure 10**) into the vacuum cylinder and index it onto the boss on the top cover (A, **Figure 10**).

5. Align the hole in the vacuum cylinder with the raised boss on the top cover. Install the top cover and tighten the screws securely.

6. On 1987-on models, install the air cut-off valve as described in this chapter.

7. Install the slow jet (**Figure 30**).

8. Install the main jet holder (**Figure 31**) and the main jet (**Figure 32**).

9. Make sure the gasket (B, **Figure 26**) is in place on the float valve and install the float valve seat and filter (**Figure 33**).

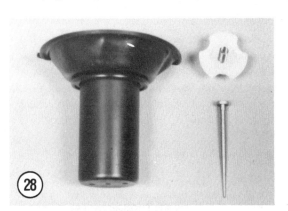

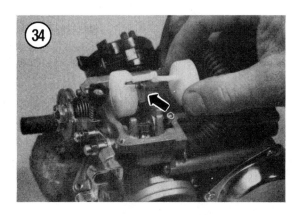

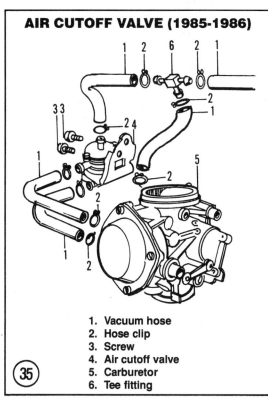

AIR CUTOFF VALVE (1985-1986)

1. Vacuum hose
2. Hose clip
3. Screw
4. Air cutoff valve
5. Carburetor
6. Tee fitting

10. Install the needle valve (**Figure 34**) onto the float.

11. Install the float and needle valve and install the float pin (**Figure 16**).

12. Inspect the float height and adjust if necessary as described in this chapter.

13. Install the gasket into the float bowl (**Figure 27**).

14. Install the float bowl (**Figure 15**) and tighten the screws securely.

15. On 1985-1986 models, install the air cut-off valve and hoses. Tighten the screws securely.

16. After assembly and installation are completed, adjust the carburetors as described in this chapter.

**Air Cut-off Valve
Removal/Installation
(1985-1986)**

Refer to **Figure 35** for this procedure.

1. Remove the seats as described in Chapter Thirteen.

2. Remove the bolts securing the fuel tank and raise the rear of the fuel tank up off of the frame. It is not necessary to remove the fuel tank—just raise it up.

3. Tag all hoses (A, **Figure 36**) prior to disconnecting them from the air cut-off valve fittings.

4. Remove the screws (B, **Figure 36**) securing the air cut-off valve to the carburetor assembly and remove the valve.

5. Install by reversing these removal steps while noting the following.

6. Be sure to connect the hoses to the correct fittings on the air cut-off valve.

**Air Cut-off Valve
Removal/Installation
(1987-on)**

1. Remove the carburetors as described in this chapter.

2. Remove the air cut-off valve cover.

3. Remove the spring, O-ring seal and diaphragm.

4. Check the diaphragm for wear or damage. Also check the diaphragm plunger for wear or damage. Replace the diaphragm if necessary.

5. Check the O-ring for wear or flat spots; replace if necessary.

6. Install by reversing these steps.

7

Carburetor
Separation/Assembly

1. Remove the carburetor assembly as described in this chapter.

2. Disconnect the fuel lines and T-fitting (**Figure 37**).

3. Loosen the synchronizing screw (A, **Figure 38**) and remove the spring (B, **Figure 38**).

4. Remove the screw on each side securing the carburetors together. Refer to **Figure 39** and **Figure 40**.

5. Don't lose the throttle link thrust spring (C, **Figure 38**) where the carburetors are held together.

6. Loosen the throttle adjust screw (A, **Figure 41**).

7. Remove the nut (B, **Figure 41**) securing the throttle drum and remove the throttle drum (C, **Figure 41**) and return spring (D, **Figure 41**).

8. Carefully pull the carburetors apart.

9. Assemble by reversing these disassembly steps while noting the following.

10. Install new O-ring seals onto the air joint pipe and coat them with oil.

11. Tighten the throttle adjust screw until the throttle valve on the left-hand carburetor aligns with the *small* bypass hole in the venturi (A, **Figure 42**).

12. Turn the synchronizing screw until the throttle valve on the right-hand carburetor aligns with the *small* bypass hole in the venturi (B, **Figure 42**).

13. Using the throttle linkage, open the throttle a little then release it. The throttle should return smoothly with no drag.

14. If there is drag or the throttle does not move smoothly, recheck all previous steps until the problem is solved.

NOTE
If the carburetors have been assembled
correctly and the throttle still does not

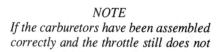

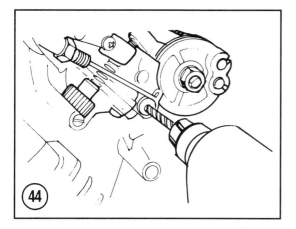

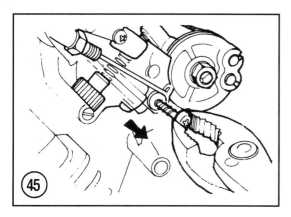

operate correctly, there may be internal damage to the throttle shafts or butterfly valves. Take the assembly to a dealer for inspection and replacement.

Pilot Screw and Plug
Removal/Installation

The pilot screws are covered by a metal plug (**Figure 43**) that has to be drilled out in order to remove the screw. The screws can be removed with the carburetor assembly either installed on the bike or removed. It is easier to perform this operation with the carburetor assembly installed on the bike. Do not remove these plugs and screws unless you suspect they are not functioning properly.

> *CAUTION*
> *If the carburetor assembly is removed from the engine, put tape over all openings in the carburetor bodies to keep out metal shavings during the drilling operation.*

1. Use a small center punch and hammer to center punch the middle of the plug (**Figure 43**) for a drill guide.

> *CAUTION*
> *Be careful not to drill too far into the plug. You could damage the pilot screw.*

2. Drill through the plug (**Figure 44**) with a 4 mm (5/32 in.) drill bit. If available, attach a drill stop to the drill bit 3 mm (1/8 in.) from the end of the drill bit to prevent the accidental drilling of the pilot screw.

> *NOTE*
> *If you do not have a drill stop, wrap 8-10 layers of masking tape on the drill bit at the prescribed distance from the end. This can be used as a guide for the distance the drill bit has traveled. The tape will not stop the drill from traveling further in—it is only a visual guide.*

3. Force a 4 mm self-tapping screw into the drilled hole. Continue to turn the screw until the plug starts to rotate with the screw.

4. Withdraw the plug and screw with a pair of pliers (**Figure 45**) and blow away all metal shavings from the area.

NOTE
Before removing the pilot screw, record the number of turns necessary until the screw lightly seats. Record the number of turns for each individual carburetor as the screws must be reinstalled into the exact same setting.

5. While noting the number of turns, lightly seat the pilot screw.

6. Remove and clean and inspect the pilot screw as outlined in this chapter.

7. Install the pilot screw as outlined under *Assembly* in this section.

8. Perform *Pilot Screw Adjustment and Plug Installation* in this chapter.

CARBURETOR ADJUSTMENTS

Float Adjustment

The carburetor assembly must be removed and partially disassembled for this adjustment.

1. Remove the carburetors as described in this chapter.

2. Remove the screws securing the float bowl to the main bodies and remove them.

3. Hold the carburetor assembly with the carburetor inclined 15-45° from vertical so that the float arm is just touching the float needle. Use a float level gauge (Honda part No. 07401-0010000 or equivalent) and measure the distance from the carburetor body to the float arm (**Figure 46**). The correct height is listed in **Table 1**.

4. Adjust by carefully bending the tang on the float arm (**Figure 47**).

5. If the float level is too high, the result will be a rich fuel/air mixture. If it is too low, the mixture will be too lean.

NOTE
The floats on both carburetors must be adjusted at the same height to maintain the same fuel/air mixture to both cylinders.

6. Reassemble and install the carburetors.

Needle Jet Adjustment

The needle jet is *non-adjustable* on all models.

Choke Adjustment

First make sure the choke operates smoothly with no binding. The choke cable starts as a single cable at the lever on the handlebar lever and about halfway down it branches out into 2 cables, one cable for each carburetor. If the cable binds, lubricate it as described in Chapter Three. If the cable still does not operate smoothly, it must be replaced as described in this chapter.

NOTE
The choke circuit is a "bystarter" system in which the choke lever opens a valve rather than closing a butterfly in the venturi area as on many carburetors. In the open position, the slow jet discharges a stream of fuel into the carburetor venturi to enrich the mixture when the engine is cold.

1. Operate the choke lever (**Figure 48**) and check for smooth operation of the cable and choke mechanism.

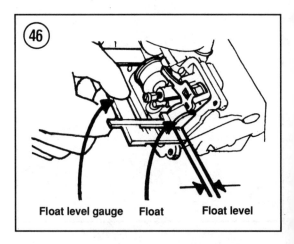

46

Float level gauge   Float   Float level

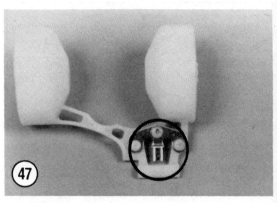

47

2. At the carburetor assembly, slide back the rubber boot on the choke cable.

3. Unscrew the choke valve nut and remove the choke cable, valve and spring from the carburetor.

4. Move the choke lever all the way *down* to the fully closed position.

5. Using vernier calipers, measure the distance between the end of the threads of the choke valve nut and the choke valve. It should be 10-11 mm (0.39-0.43 in.). Refer to **Figure 49**.

6. To adjust, perform the following.

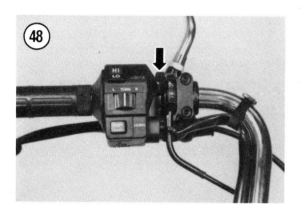

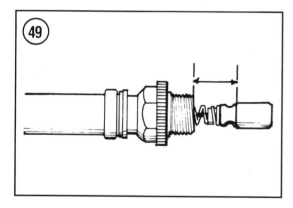

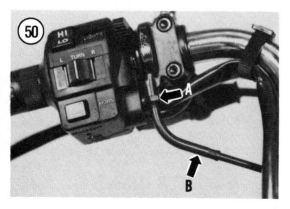

a. Loosen the locknut (A, **Figure 50**) on the choke cable at the lever.

b. Turn the elbow (B, **Figure 50**) in either direction until the dimension at the cable end is correct.

c. Tighten the locknut and recheck the dimension in Step 7.

7. Repeat Steps 2-6 for the other carburetor. The dimension in Step 5 must be the same for both carburetors.

8. Install the choke valve into the carburetor body.

9. Tighten the choke valve nut by hand then turn it an additional 1/4 turn with a 14 mm wrench.

10. Reinstall the fuel tank, seat and side covers.

Pilot Screw Adjustment and Plug Installation

> *NOTE*
> *The pilot screws are pre-set at the factory. Adjustment is not necessary unless the carburetors have been overhauled or someone has misadjusted them.*

The air filter element must be cleaned before starting this procedure or the results will be inaccurate.

The plugs have to be removed from the carburetor bodies as described in this chapter.

1. For the preliminary adjustment, carefully turn the pilot screw on each carburetor in until it *lightly* seats and then back it out the number of turns listed in **Table 1**.

2. Start the engine and let it reach normal operating temperature. Stop-and-go riding for approximately 10-15 minutes is sufficient.

3. Shut the engine off and place the bike on the centerstand.

4. Connect a portable tachometer following the manufacturer's instructions. Use a tachometer that can register a change of 50 rpm. The bike's tachometer is not accurate enough at low rpm.

> *NOTE*
> ***Figure 51*** *is shown with the carburetor assembly removed for clarity.*

5. Start the engine and turn the large black plastic idle adjust screw (**Figure 51**) in or out to achieve the idle speed listed in **Table 1**.

6. Turn each pilot screw *out* 1/2 turn from the initial setting in Step 1. If the engine speed increases by 50 rpm or more, turn each pilot screw out by an additional 1/2 turn at a time until engine speed drops by 50 rpm or less.

7. Turn the idle adjust screw in or out again to achieve the idle speed listed in **Table 1**.

8. Turn the pilot screw on the left-hand carburetor *in* 1/2 turn at a time until engine speed drops by 50 rpm.

9. Turn the pilot screw on the left-hand carburetor *out* 1 turn from the position obtained in Step 8.

10. Turn the idle adjust screw in or out again to achieve the desired idle speed listed in **Table 1**.

11. Repeat Steps 8-10 on the right-hand carburetor pilot screw.

12. Turn the engine off and disconnect the portable tachometer.

13. After this adjustment is completed, test ride the bike. Throttle response from idle should be rapid and without any hesitation.

14. Use a suitable size drift and carefully drive a new plug (**Figure 43**) into each pilot screw bore in the carburetor body. The plug is fully seated when it is recessed into the hole by 1 mm.

High Elevation Adjustment

If the bike is going to be ridden for any sustained period of time at high elevation (2,000 m/6,500 ft.), the carburetors must be readjusted to improve performance and decrease exhaust emissions.

1. Remove each pilot screw plug as described in this chapter.

2. Start the engine and let it reach normal operating temperature. Stop-and-go riding for approximately 10 minutes is sufficient. Turn off the engine.

3. Connect a portable tachometer following the manufacturer's instructions. The bike's tachometer is not accurate enough at low rpm.

4. Turn each pilot screw *clockwise* 1/2 turn (1986-on), as viewed from the side of the carburetor.

5. Restart the engine and turn the large idle screw (**Figure 51**) to achieve an idle speed listed in **Table 1**.

6. Turn the engine off and disconnect the portable tachometer.

7. Install new pilot screw plugs as described in this chapter.

8. When the bike is returned to elevations near sea level, the pilot screws must be returned to their original position and the idle speed readjusted to the rpm listed in **Table 1**.

Rejetting the Carburetors

Do not try to solve a poor running engine problem by rejetting the carburetors if all of the following conditions hold true.

a. The engine has held a good tune in the past with the standard jetting.

b. The engine has not been modified.

c. The motorcycle is being operated in the same geographical region under the same general climatic conditions as in the past.

d. The motorcycle was and is being ridden at average highway speeds.

If those conditions all hold true, the chances are that the problem is due to a malfunction in the carburetor or in another component that needs to be adjusted or repaired. Changing carburetor jet size probably won't solve the problem. Rejetting the carburetors may be necessary if any of the following conditions hold true.

a. A non-standard type of air filter element is being used.

b. A non-standard exhaust system is installed on the motorcycle.

c. Any of the top end components in the engine (pistons, cams, valves, compression ratio, etc.) have been modified.

d. The motorcycle is in use at considerably higher or lower elevations or in a considerably hotter or colder climate than in the past.

e. The motorcycle is being operated at considerably higher speeds than before and changing

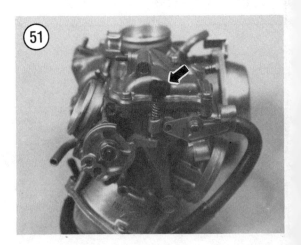

to colder spark plugs does not solve the problem.

    f. Someone has previously changed the carburetor jetting.

    g. The motorcycle has never held a satisfactory engine tune.

If it is necessary to rejet the carburetors, check with a dealer or motorcycle performance tuner for recommendations as to the size of jets to install for your specific situation.

If you do change the jets, do so only one size at a time. After rejetting, test ride the bike and perform a spark plug test. Refer to *Reading Spark Plugs* in Chapter Three.

AIR FILTER CASE

Removal/Installation
(1985-1986)

1. Remove the main fuel tank as described in this chapter.

2. Unhook the rubber cover from the rear of the air filter case.

3. Release the fuel and temperature gauges' electrical harness (A, **Figure 52**) from the clip on the top of the air filter case. Move the harness out of the way.

4. Remove the bolts securing the air filter case to the frame.

5. Loosen all clamping bands securing the hoses to the air filter case.

6. Disconnect the crankcase breather tube and drain tube from the air filter case.

7. Remove the air filter case (B, **Figure 52**) from the frame.

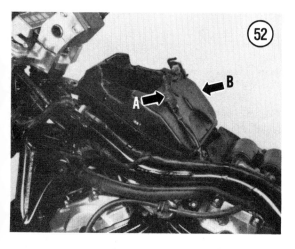

8. Insert clean shop cloths into the carburetor air intake tubes to prevent the entry of foreign matter.

9. Install by reversing these removal steps.

Removal/Installation
(1987-on)

1. Remove the seats as described in Chapter Thirteen.

2. Remove the right- and left-hand frame side covers.

3. Remove the battery as described in Chapter Three.

4. Remove the spark unit and starter solenoid along with their rubber mounts from the battery case.

5. Remove the bolts securing the battery case and remove the case from the frame.

6. Disconnect the rear turn signal and taillight/license plate electrical connectors from the main wiring harness.

7. Remove the rear fender as described in Chapter Thirteen.

8. Remove the radiator coolant reserve tank from the air filter case.

9. Disconnect the crankcase breather tube and drain tube from the air filter case.

10. Remove the electrical connector box and disconnect all electrical wires from the box.

11. Remove the bolts securing the air filter case to the frame.

12. Loosen all clamping bands securing the hoses to the air filter case.

13. Partially remove the air filter case from the frame and remove the nuts securing the fuel pump and fuel filter. Remove the fuel pump and fuel filter.

14. Remove the air filter case from the left-hand side of the frame.

15. Insert clean shop cloths into the carburetor air intake tubes to prevent the entry of foreign matter.

16. Install by reversing these removal steps while noting the following.

17. Make sure all electrical connectors are free of corrosion and are tight.

THROTTLE CABLE REPLACEMENT

1. Place the bike on the centerstand and remove the right- and left-hand side covers.

2. Remove the screws securing the throttle linkage cover and remove the cover.

3. Disconnect the front brake light switch electrical connectors (A, **Figure 53**).

4. Remove the screws securing the right-hand switch/throttle housing halves together (B, **Figure 53**).

5. Remove the housing from the handlebar and disengage the throttle cables (C, **Figure 53**) from the throttle grip.

6. At the carburetor assembly, loosen the locknuts securing the throttle cables to the cable bracket.

7. Disconnect the throttle cables from the throttle wheel.

NOTE
The string attached in the next step will be used to pull the new throttle cables back through the frame so they will be routed in exactly the same position as the old ones.

8. Tie a piece of heavy string or cord (approximately 7 ft./2 m long) to the carburetor end of the throttle cables. Wrap this end with masking or duct tape. Do not use an excessive amount of tape as it must be pulled though the frame loop during removal. Tie the other end of the string to the frame or air box.

9. At the throttle grip end of the cables, carefully pull the cables and attached string out through the frame, past the electrical harness and from behind the headlight housing. Make sure the attached string follows the same path as the cable through the frame.

10. Remove the tape and untie the string from the old cables.

11. Lubricate the new cables as described in Chapter Three.

12. Tie the string to the carburetor end of the new throttle cables and wrap it with tape.

13. Carefully pull the string back through the frame, routing the new cables through the same path as the old cables.

14. Remove the tape and untie the string from the cables and the frame.

CAUTION
*The throttle cables are the push/pull type and must be installed as described and shown in Step 15 and Step 16. Do **not** interchange the 2 cables.*

15. Attach the throttle "pull" cable to the bottom portion of the bracket and into the lower hole in the throttle wheel (A, **Figure 54**). The other end is

attached to the front receptacle of the throttle/switch housing.

16. Attach the throttle "push" cable to the upper portion of the bracket and into the upper hole in the throttle wheel (B, **Figure 54**). The other end is attached to the rear receptacle of the throttle/switch housing.

17. Install the throttle/switch housing and tighten the screws securely.

18. Attach the front brake light switch connectors.

19. Operate the throttle grip and make sure the carburetor throttle linkage is operating correctly with no binding. If operation is incorrect or there is binding, carefully check that the cables are attached correctly and there are no tight bends in the cables.

20. Adjust the throttle cables as described in Chapter Three.

21. Test ride the bike slowly at first and make sure the throttle is operating correctly.

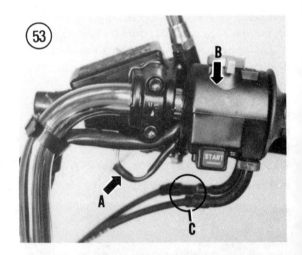

CHOKE CABLE REPLACEMENT

The choke cable starts as a single cable at the lever on the handlebar and about half way down the cable branches out into 2 cables, one for each carburetor.

1. Remove both side covers and the seat.

2A. On 1985-1986 models, remove the main fuel tank as described in this chapter.

2B. On 1987-on models, remove the fuel tank as described in this chapter.

3. At the carburetor assembly, slide back the rubber boot on the choke cable.

4. Unscrew the choke valve nut and remove the choke cable, valve and spring from the carburetor.

5. Repeat Step 3 and Step 4 for the other carburetor.

6. Remove the clutch switch wires at the clutch lever.

CAUTION
Cover the frame and front wheels with a heavy cloth or plastic tarp to protect it from accidental spilling of hydraulic fluid. Wash any spilled hydraulic fluid off any painted or plated surface immediately, as it will destroy the finish. Use soapy water and rinse thoroughly.

7. Remove the bolts (A, **Figure 55**) and clamp securing the clutch master cylinder to the handlebar.

8. Remove the clutch master cylinder and lay it over the front fender. Keep the reservoir in an upright position to minimize loss of hydraulic fluid and to keep air from entering the clutch system.

9. Remove the screw securing the switch assembly together (B, **Figure 55**).

10. Remove the choke cable (C, **Figure 55**) from the switch and choke lever assembly on the handlebar.

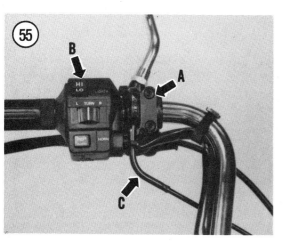

11. Remove the plastic trim panels on each side of the steering head.

NOTE
The piece of string attached in the next step will be used to pull the new choke cable back through the frame so it will be routed in the same position as the old cable.

12. Tie a piece of heavy string or cord (approximately 7 ft./2 m long) to the carburetor end of *each* choke cable. Wrap the end with masking or duct tape. Do not use an excessive amount of tape as it must be pulled through the frame loop during removal. Tie the other end of the string to the frame or air box.

13. Unhook the choke cable from any clips on the frame.

14. At the choke lever end of the cable, carefully pull the cable assembly and attached string out through the frame and from behind the headlight housing. Make sure the attached string follows the same path that the cable does through the frame.

15. Remove the tape and untie the string from the old cable assembly.

16. Lubricate the new cable assembly as described in Chapter Three.

17. Tie the string to the carburetor end of the new choke cable assembly and wrap it with tape.

18. Carefully pull the string back through the frame, routing the new cables through the same path as the old cables.

19. Remove the tape and untie the string from the cable and the frame.

20. Attach the choke cable onto the choke lever assembly.

21. Install the choke valve onto the carburetor body.

22. Tighten the choke valve nut by hand and then turn it an additional 1/4 turn with a 14 mm wrench.

23. Repeat Steps 20-22 for the other carburetor.

24. Install the switch/choke assembly on the handlebar and tighten the screws securely.

25. Install the clutch master cylinder as described in Chapter Five.

26. Attach the clutch switch wires to the clutch lever.

27. Operate the choke lever and make sure the carburetor choke linkage is operating correctly, with no binding. If operation is incorrect or there is binding, carefully check that the cable is attached correctly and there are no tight bends in the cable.

28A. On 1985-1986 models, install the main fuel tank as described in this chapter.

28B. On 1987-on models, install the fuel tank as described in this chapter.

29. Install the seat and side covers.

30. Adjust the choke cables as described in this chapter.

FUEL SHUTOFF VALVE

Removal/Installation (1985-1986)

The fuel shutoff valve is not equipped with an integral fuel filter. There is a separate fuel filter as described in this chapter.

The fuel from both the main and sub-tank must be completely drained prior to removing the fuel shutoff valve. Have a fire extinguisher, rated for gasoline fires, close by just in case it is needed.

1. Remove the frame left-hand side cover.

2. Disconnect the battery negative (–) lead (**Figure 56**).

3. Turn the fuel shutoff valve on the sub-fuel tank to the OFF position.

4. Disconnect the fuel inlet hose (**Figure 57**) from the fuel pump.

5. Place the loose end of the fuel inlet hose into a funnel or larger diameter hose and into a clean, metal sealable container. If the fuel is kept clean, it can be returned to the fuel tank at the end of this procedure.

6. Open the fuel filler cap. This will allow the fuel to flow out quicker.

7. Turn the fuel shutoff valve to the ON position and completely drain the fuel from both tanks.

8. Plug the end of the inlet hose with a golf tee to prevent any fuel drainage.

9. Remove the screw (A, **Figure 58**) securing the handle to the fuel shutoff valve and remove the handle.

10. Remove the bolts (B, **Figure 58**) securing the fuel shutoff valve to the fuel sub-tank and remove the valve and the gasket. Discard the gasket, it cannot be reused with the possibility of fuel leakage.

11. Install by reversing these removal steps while noting the following.

12. Install a new gasket between the fuel tank and the fuel shutoff valve and tighten the screws securely.

13. Refill the fuel system, turn the valve to the ON position.

14. Carefully check for any fuel leaks. Repair any fuel leaks prior to riding the bike.

Removal/Installation (1987-on)

1. Remove the fuel tank as described in this chapter.

2. Place a blanket or some clean shop cloths on the workbench to protect the fuel tank finish.

3. Lay the fuel tank on its right-hand side.

4. Unscrew the shutoff valve from the fuel tank and remove the valve and the gasket. Discard the gasket,

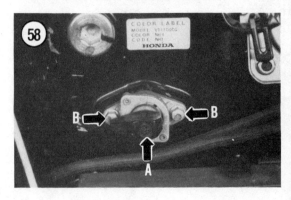

it cannot be reused with the possibility of fuel leak-age.

5. Install a new gasket between the fuel tank and the fuel shutoff valve and tighten the screws securely.

6. Refill the fuel system, turn the valve to the ON position.

7. Carefully check for any fuel leaks. Repair any fuel leaks prior to riding the bike.

FUEL FILTER

These models have a separate fuel filter that can-not be cleaned. If dirty, a new filter must be installed.

It should be replaced at the interval indicated in Chapter Three.

Replacement (1985-1986)

Refer to **Figure 59** for this procedure.

1. Remove the frame left-hand side cover.

2. Disconnect the battery negative (–) lead (**Figure 56**).

3. Turn the fuel shutoff valve to the OFF position.

4. Disconnect the fuel inlet hose (**Figure 57**) from the fuel pump.

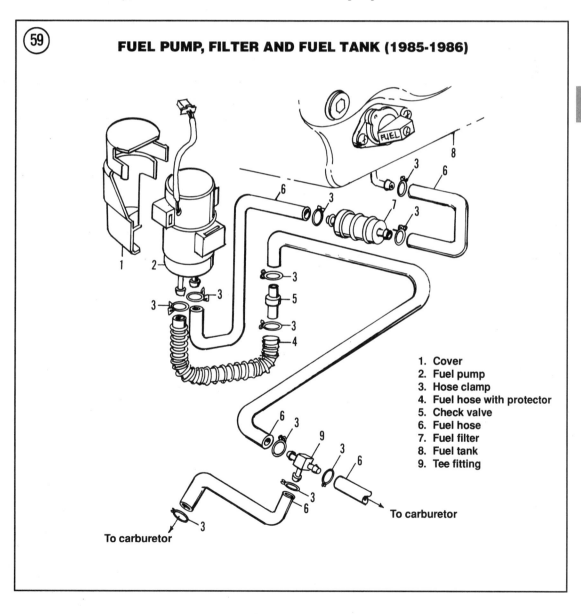

FUEL PUMP, FILTER AND FUEL TANK (1985-1986)

1. Cover
2. Fuel pump
3. Hose clamp
4. Fuel hose with protector
5. Check valve
6. Fuel hose
7. Fuel filter
8. Fuel tank
9. Tee fitting

To carburetor

To carburetor

7

5. Remove the nuts (**Figure 60**) securing the voltage regulator/rectifier to the mounting bracket and move the voltage regulator/rectifier out of the way.

6. Remove the nut securing the fuel filter holder to the fuel sub-tank.

7. Remove the holder and the fuel filter from the fuel sub-tank.

8. Disconnect the flexible fuel lines from the fuel filter and plug the ends of the fuel lines with golf tees.

9. Install a new filter with the arrow on the filter pointing toward the outlet side or toward the fuel pump.

10. Turn the valve to the ON position.

11. Carefully check for any fuel leaks. Repair any fuel leaks prior to riding the bike.

Replacement (1987-on)

Refer to **Figure 61** for this procedure.

1. Disconnect the battery negative (–) lead (**Figure 56**).

2. Turn the fuel shutoff valve to the OFF position.

3. Remove the exhaust pipe from the rear cylinder as described in this chapter.

4. Remove the holder and the fuel filter from the frame mount.

5. Disconnect the flexible fuel lines from the fuel filter and plug the ends of the fuel lines with golf tees.

6. Install a new filter with the larger end of the filter facing toward the fuel pump.

7. Turn the valve to the ON position.

8. Carefully check for any fuel leaks. Repair any fuel leaks prior to riding the bike.

FUEL PUMP

Fuel pump performance testing is covered in Chapter Eight.

Removal/Installation (1985-1986)

Refer to **Figure 59** for this procedure.

1. Remove the frame left-hand side cover.

2. Disconnect the battery negative (–) lead (**Figure 56**).

3. Turn the fuel shutoff valve to the OFF position.

4. Disconnect the electrical connector from the fuel pump.

5. Remove the holder and the fuel pump from the mounting tab on the frame (A, **Figure 62**).

6. Place a clean container under the fuel pump to catch any spilled fuel when the fuel hoses are disconnected.

7. Disconnect the fuel hoses (B, **Figure 62**) from the fuel pump and plug the ends of the fuel lines with golf tees to prevent fuel leakage.

8. Install by reversing these removal steps while noting the following.

9. Turn the valve to the ON position.

10. Carefully check for any fuel leaks. Repair any fuel leaks prior to riding the bike.

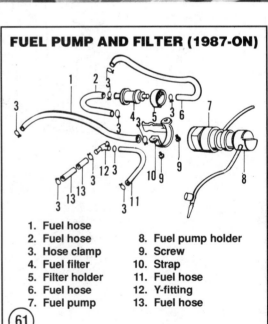

FUEL PUMP AND FILTER (1987-ON)

1. Fuel hose
2. Fuel hose
3. Hose clamp
4. Fuel filter
5. Filter holder
6. Fuel hose
7. Fuel pump
8. Fuel pump holder
9. Screw
10. Strap
11. Fuel hose
12. Y-fitting
13. Fuel hose

Removal/Installation
(1987-on)

Refer to **Figure 61** for this procedure.

1. Remove the frame left-hand side cover.

2. Disconnect the battery negative (–) lead.

3. Remove the air filer case as described in this chapter.

4. Place a clean container under the fuel pump to catch any spilled fuel when the fuel hoses are disconnected.

5. Disconnect the electrical connector from the fuel pump.

6. Remove the holder and the fuel pump from the mounting tab on the frame.

7. Disconnect the fuel hoses from the fuel pump and plug the ends of the fuel lines with golf tees to prevent fuel leakage.

8. Install by reversing these removal steps while noting the following.

9. Turn the valve to the ON position.

10. Carefully check for any fuel leaks. Repair any fuel leaks prior to riding the bike.

FUEL TANKS (1985-1986)

Main Fuel Tank
Removal/Installation

Refer to **Figure 63** for this procedure.

1. Place the bike on the centerstand.

2. Remove the seats as described in Chapter Thirteen.

3. Remove the frame left-hand side cover.

4. Remove the bolts securing the fuel tank cover.

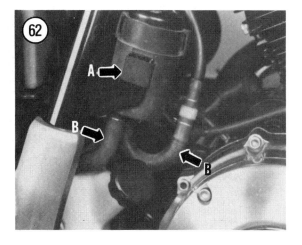

5. Partially lift the cover and disconnect the fuel and temperature gauges' electrical connectors.

6. Remove the fuel tank cover.

7. Remove the bolt at the rear (**Figure 64**) and the bolt on each side (**Figure 65**) securing the fuel tank to the frame.

8. Turn the fuel shutoff valve on the sub-fuel tank to the OFF position.

9. Disconnect the fuel inlet hose from the fuel pump.

10. Place the loose end of the fuel inlet hose into a funnel or larger diameter hose and into a clean, metal sealable container. If the fuel is kept clean, it can be returned to the fuel tank at the end of this procedure.

11. Open the fuel filler cap. This will allow the fuel to flow out quicker.

12. Turn the fuel shutoff valve to the ON position and completely drain the fuel from both tanks.

13. Plug the end of the inlet hose with a golf tee to prevent any fuel drainage.

14. Disconnect the main fuel tank fuel hose from the sub-fuel tank. Cover the end of the sub-fuel tank fitting with duct tape or plastic tape to keep out foreign matter.

15. Partially lift the fuel tank and disconnect the breather tubes from the tank.

16. Remove the main fuel tank.

17. Inspect the rubber mounting cushion (**Figure 66**) for damage or deterioration. Replace if necessary.

18. Install by reversing these removal steps while noting the following.

19. Spray a small amount of WD-40 (or equivalent) onto the inside ends of the fuel and breather hoses. This will make installation of the lines a little easier. Make sure they are completely installed onto the fittings on the sub-fuel tank. Tighten the clamps securely.

20. Turn the valve to the ON position.

21. Carefully check for any fuel leaks. Repair any fuel leaks prior to riding the bike.

Sub-Fuel Tank
Removal/Installation

Refer to **Figure 67** for this procedure.

1. Place the bike on the centerstand.

2. Remove the main fuel tank as described in this chapter.

3. Remove the rear wheel as described under *Rear Wheel Removal/Installation* in Chapter Eleven.

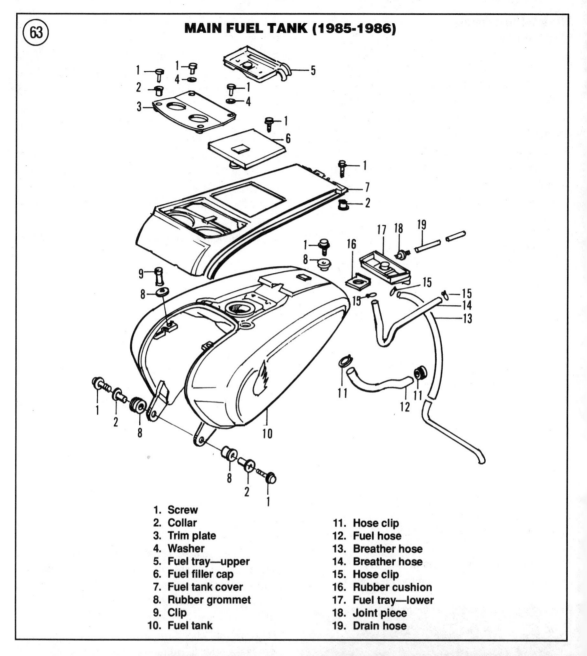

MAIN FUEL TANK (1985-1986)

63

1. Screw
2. Collar
3. Trim plate
4. Washer
5. Fuel tray—upper
6. Fuel filler cap
7. Fuel tank cover
8. Rubber grommet
9. Clip
10. Fuel tank
11. Hose clip
12. Fuel hose
13. Breather hose
14. Breather hose
15. Hose clip
16. Rubber cushion
17. Fuel tray—lower
18. Joint piece
19. Drain hose

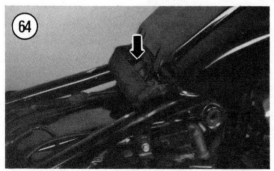

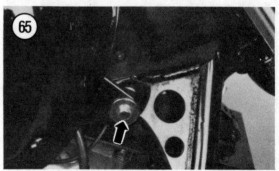

(66)

4. Remove the rear fender as described in Chapter Thirteen.

5. Remove the nuts (**Figure 60**) securing the voltage regulator/rectifier to the mounting bracket and move the voltage regulator/rectifier out of the way.

6. Disconnect the electrical connectors from the fuel gauge sending unit (A, **Figure 68**) on the side of the sub-fuel tank. Move the electrical harness out of the way.

7. Remove the screw securing the handle on the fuel shutoff valve and remove the handle.

8. Disconnect the fuel inlet hose (**Figure 57**) from the fuel pump and plug the end of the hose with a golf tee to prevent any fuel drainage.

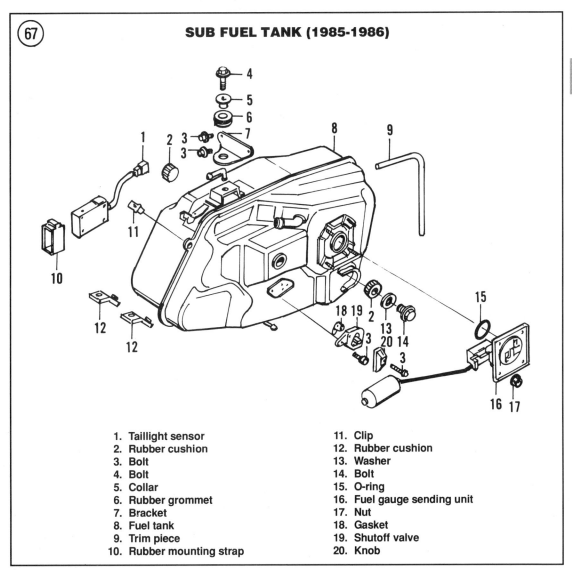

(67)

SUB FUEL TANK (1985-1986)

7

1. Taillight sensor
2. Rubber cushion
3. Bolt
4. Bolt
5. Collar
6. Rubber grommet
7. Bracket
8. Fuel tank
9. Trim piece
10. Rubber mounting strap
11. Clip
12. Rubber cushion
13. Washer
14. Bolt
15. O-ring
16. Fuel gauge sending unit
17. Nut
18. Gasket
19. Shutoff valve
20. Knob

9. Remove the battery (A, **Figure 69**) as described in Chapter Three.

10. Remove the nut securing the fuel filter holder to the sub-fuel tank and move the holder off of the mounting tab.

11. Disconnect the fuel outlet hose from the fuel pump and plug the end of the hose with a golf tee to prevent any fuel drainage.

12. Remove the bolts securing the battery holder (B, **Figure 69**) and the spark unit.

13. Remove the battery holder and move the spark unit out of the way.

14. Remove the mounting bolt and washer (C, **Figure 69**) securing the sub-fuel tank to the frame.

15. Carefully move the tank (B, **Figure 68**) toward the rear and remove it from the frame.

16. Install by reversing these removal steps while noting the following.

17. Spray a small amount of WD-40 (or equivalent) onto the inside ends of the fuel hoses. This will make installation of the hoses a little easier. Make sure they are completely installed onto the fittings on the sub-fuel tank. Tighten the clamps securely.

18. Turn the valve to the ON position.

19. Carefully check for any fuel leaks. Repair any fuel leaks prior to riding the bike.

FUEL TANK (1987-ON)

Removal/Installation

Refer to **Figure 70** for this procedure.

1. Place the bike on the centerstand.

2. Remove the seats as described in Chapter Thirteen.

3. Remove the frame left-hand side cover.

4. Disconnect the battery negative (–) lead.

5. Turn the fuel shutoff valve to the OFF position.

6. Disconnect the fuel hose from the shutoff valve and plug the end of the hose with a golf tee to prevent any fuel drainage.

7. Remove the bolt at the front and at the rear securing the fuel tank to the frame.

8. Partially lift the fuel tank and disconnect the breather tubes from the tank.

9. Remove the main fuel tank.

10. Install by reversing these removal steps while noting the following.

11. Turn the valve to the ON position.

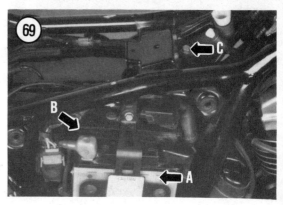

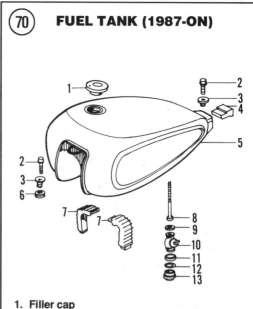

FUEL TANK (1987-ON)

1. Filler cap
2. Bolt
3. Metal collar
4. Rubber cushion
5. Fuel tank
6. Rubber grommet
7. Rubber mount
8. Fuel filter
9. Gasket
10. Fuel shutoff valve
11. Filter
12. O-ring
13. Cup

12. Carefully check for any fuel leaks. Repair any fuel leaks prior to riding the bike.

CRANKCASE BREATHER SYSTEM

To comply with air pollution standards, all Honda 1100 cc Shadows are equipped with a crankcase breather system. This system draws blow-by gases from the crankcase and recirculates them into the fuel/air mixture and thus into the engine to be re-burned. Refer to **Figure 71** for 1985-1986 models or **Figure 72** for 1987-on models.

Inspection/Cleaning

Make sure all hose clamps are tight. Check all hoses for deterioration and replace as necessary.

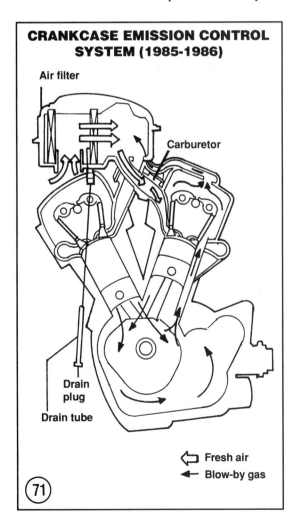

CRANKCASE EMISSION CONTROL SYSTEM (1985-1986)

Air filter

Carburetor

Drain plug

Drain tube

⇦ Fresh air
◀ Blow-by gas

71

Slide the drain tube out of the bracket on the battery holder. Remove the drain plug from the drain hose and drain out all residue. This cleaning procedure should be done more frequently if a considerable amount of riding is done at full throttle or in the rain.

Install the drain plug and clamp.

EVAPORATIVE EMISSION CONTROL SYSTEM

Fuel vapor from the fuel tank is routed into a charcoal canister. This vapor is stored when the engine is not running. When the engine is running, these vapors are drawn through a purge control valve and into the carburetor to be burned. Refer to **Figure 73** for 1985-1986 models or **Figure 74** for 1987-on models.

Make sure all hose clamps are tight and are not kinked. Check all hoses for deterioration or any possible clogs; replace as necessary.

Refer to the vacuum hose routing label mounted on the backside of one of the side covers for correct hose routing for your model.

Testing

If the engine becomes difficult to start after it is warm or hot, have the purge control valve (PCV) or air control valve (AVCV) tested by a Honda dealer.

Charcoal Canister
Removal/Installation

When removing the hoses on any emission control component, mark the hose and the fitting with a piece of masking tape and identify where the hose goes. There are so many vacuum hoses on these models that re-connection can be very confusing.

1. Disconnect the hoses attached to the charcoal canister.

2. Remove the bolts securing the charcoal canister to the frame and remove the canister assembly.

3. Check the canister for damage; replace if necessary.

4. Install by reversing these removal steps. Be sure to install the hoses to their correct fittings on the canister.

7

EXHAUST SYSTEM

The exhaust system consists of 2 exhaust pipes and 2 mufflers. The 1985-1986 models have a common collector between the 2 mufflers.

Removal/Installation (1985-1986)

Refer to **Figure 75** for this procedure.

1. Place the bike on the centerstand.

2. To remove the exhaust pipe from the front cylinder, perform the following.

    a. Remove the nuts (**Figure 76**) securing the right-hand exhaust pipe flange to the cylinder head.

    b. Slide the flange down.

    c. Loosen the clamping bolt (**Figure 77**) securing the exhaust pipe to the muffler.

    d. Remove the right-hand exhaust pipe.

3. To remove the exhaust pipe from the rear cylinder, perform the following.

    a. Remove the nuts (**Figure 78**) securing the left-hand exhaust pipe flange to the cylinder head.

    b. Slide the flange down.

    c. Loosen the clamping bolt (**Figure 79**) securing the exhaust pipe to the muffler.

    d. Remove the left-hand exhaust pipe.

4. Remove the rear footpeg bracket assembly from each side as described in Chapter Thirteen. The same bolts that secure the bracket also hold the common collector/muffler assembly to the frame.

5. Move the assembly down and out from the frame.

6. Inspect the gaskets at all joints; replace as necessary.

7. Be sure to install a new gasket in each exhaust port in both cylinder heads.

8. Apply a light coat of multipurpose grease to the inside surface of the gaskets in the common collector. This will make insertion of the exhaust pipes into the common collector easier.

9. Install the assembly into position and install all bolts and nuts only finger-tight until the exhaust

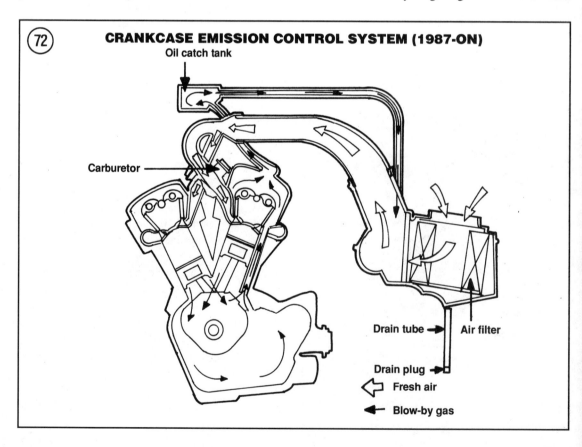

(72) **CRANKCASE EMISSION CONTROL SYSTEM (1987-ON)**

Oil catch tank

Carburetor

Drain tube → Air filter

Drain plug →

⬅ Fresh air

◄ Blow-by gas

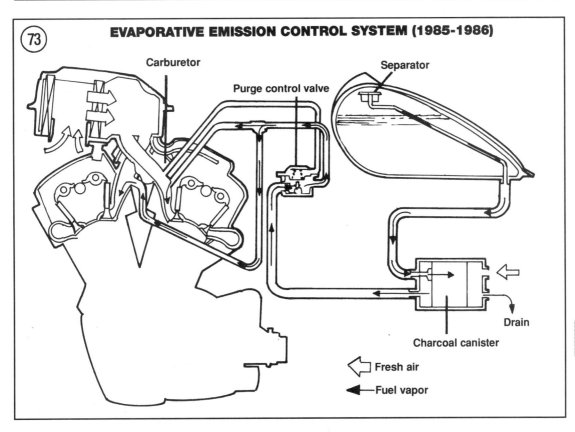

EVAPORATIVE EMISSION CONTROL SYSTEM (1985-1986)

Carburetor

Separator

Purge control valve

Drain

Charcoal canister

⟵ Fresh air

◄— Fuel vapor

7

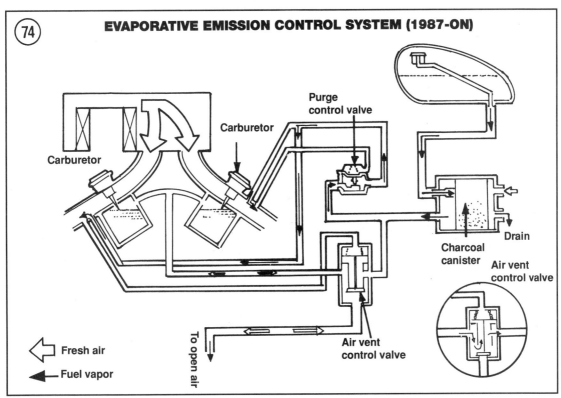

EVAPORATIVE EMISSION CONTROL SYSTEM (1987-ON)

Purge
control valve

Carburetor

Carburetor

Drain

Charcoal
canister

Air vent
control valve

To open air

Air vent
control valve

⟵ Fresh air

◄— Fuel vapor

(75)

EXHAUST SYSTEM (1985-1986)

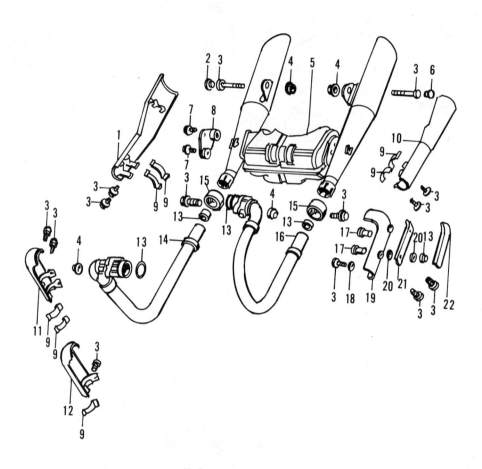

1. Protector
2. Trim cap
3. Bolt
4. Nut
5. Mufflers/common collector
6. Trim cap
7. Screw
8. Mounting bracket
9. Mounting strap
10. Protector
11. Protector
12. Protector
13. Gasket
14. Front cylinder exhaust pipe
15. Clamp
16. Rear cylinder exhaust pipe
17. Spacer
18. Washer
19. Protector
20. Washer
21. Spacer
22. Heat shield

flange nuts are installed and securely tightened. This will minimize an exhaust leak at the cylinder heads.

10. Tighten all bolts and nuts to the torque specifications listed in **Table 2**. Tighten the common collector/muffler mounting bolts securely.

11. After installation is complete, make sure there are no exhaust leaks.

**Removal/Installation
(1987-on)**

Refer to **Figure 80** for this procedure.

*NOTE
It is suggested that the exhaust system be removed as an assembly since the mufflers are connected into a single unit.*

1. Place the bike on the centerstand.

2. Remove the nuts securing the exhaust pipe flange to the front cylinder head and to the rear cylinder head.

3. Have an assistant hold onto the exhaust system.

4. Remove the nuts securing the muffler assembly to the mounting bracket.

5. Carefully remove the exhaust system from the engine and frame.

5. Inspect the gaskets at all joints; replace as necessary.

6. Be sure to install a new gasket in each exhaust port in both cylinder heads.

7. Install the assembly into position and install all nuts only finger-tight until the exhaust flange nuts are installed and securely tightened. This will minimize an exhaust leak at the cylinder heads.

8. Tighten all nuts to the torque specifications listed in **Table 2**.

9. After installation is complete, make sure there are no exhaust leaks.

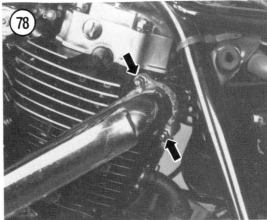

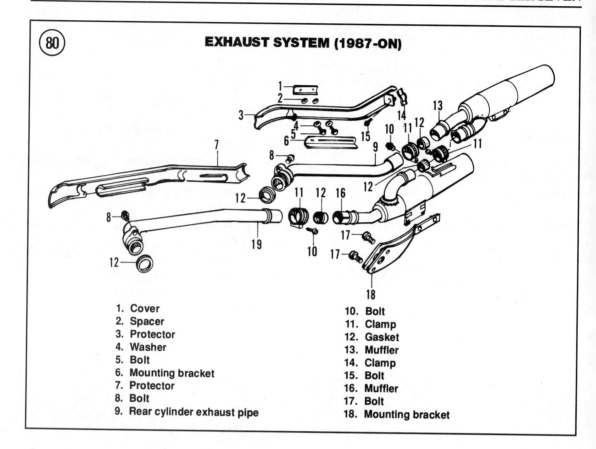

EXHAUST SYSTEM (1987-ON)

1. Cover
2. Spacer
3. Protector
4. Washer
5. Bolt
6. Mounting bracket
7. Protector
8. Bolt
9. Rear cylinder exhaust pipe
10. Bolt
11. Clamp
12. Gasket
13. Muffler
14. Clamp
15. Bolt
16. Muffler
17. Bolt
18. Mounting bracket

Table 1 CARBURETOR SPECIFICATIONS

	1985	1986
Carburetor model No.		
49-state	VD7DA	VD7DC
California	VD7EA	VD7FA
Main jet number		
Front cylinder	148	140
Rear cylinder	145	140
Slow jet number	42	42
Jet needle clip setting	Non-adjustable	Non-adjustable
Float level	9.0 mm (0.35 in.)	9.2 mm (0.36 in.)
Idle speed	1,000 ±100 rpm	1,000 ±100 rpm
Pilot screw initial setting	3 turns out	2 1/4 turns out
	1987	**1988-ON**
Carburetor model No.		
49-state	VDGAA	VDGAB
California	VDGAB	VDGABB
Main jet number		
Front cylinder	158	165
Rear cylinder	158	165
Slow jet number	42	42
Jet needle clip setting	Non-adjustable	Non-adjustable
Float level	9.2 mm (0.36 in.)	9.2 mm (0.36 in.)
Idle speed	1,000 ±100 rpm	1,000 ±100 rpm
Pilot screw initial setting		
Front cylinder	3 turns out	2 3/4 turns out
Rear cylinder	3 turns out	2 3/4 turns out

Table 2 EXHAUST SYSTEM TORQUE SPECIFICATIONS

Item	N·m	ft.-lb.
Exhaust pipe flange nut	20-23	14-22
Exhaust pipe-to-muffler clamp bolt	15-25	11-18
Muffler mounting bolt (1987-on)	23	17

CHAPTER EIGHT

ELECTRICAL SYSTEM

The electrical system consists of the following:

a. Charging system.

b. Ignition system.

c. Lighting system.

d. Directional signal system.

e. Switches.

f. Electrical components.

Tables 1-3 are located at the end of this chapter. Wiring diagrams are at the end of the book.

For complete spark plug and battery information, refer to Chapter Three.

CHARGING SYSTEM

The charging system consists of the battery, alternator and a voltage regulator/rectifier (**Figure 1**).

Alternating current generated by the alternator is rectified to direct current. The voltage regulator maintains the voltage to the battery and additional electrical loads (lights, ignition, etc.) at a constant voltage regardless of variations in engine speed and load.

Output Test (1985-1986)

Whenever charging system trouble is suspected, make sure the battery is fully charged and in good condition before going any further. Clean and test the battery as described in Chapter Three.

Before starting this test, start the bike and let it reach normal operating temperature. Shut off the engine.

1. Remove the right-hand side cover and the seats.

2. Remove the headlight and disconnect the electrical wires going to the bulb.

3. Disconnect the regulator/rectifier 6-pin connector (**Figure 2**). Use a narrow-blade screwdriver and carefully push the male end of the black wire out of the connector. Reconnect the connector with the black wire left out in the open, not connected.

> *NOTE*
> *Do not disconnect either the positive or negative battery cables. They are to remain in the circuit.*

4. Connect a 0-10 DC ammeter in line with the main fuse connectors. Remove the rubber cover (**Figure 3**) and remove the main fuse.

NOTE
During the test, if the needle of the ammeter reads in the opposite direction on the scale, reverse the polarity of the test leads.

5. Start the engine and gradually increase engine speed. Charging amperage should start at 1,000 rpm and should be a minimum of 8.5 amperes. At 5,000 rpm it should be a minimum of 23.5 amperes. If the charging amperage is not within specifications, first check the alternator stator and then the voltage regulator/rectifier as described in this chapter.

6. Disconnect the ammeter and reinstall the fusible link.

7. Reinstall the headlight and reconnect the black wire to the voltage regulator/rectifier connector.

Output Test (1987-on)

Whenever charging system trouble is suspected, make sure the battery is fully charged and in good

8

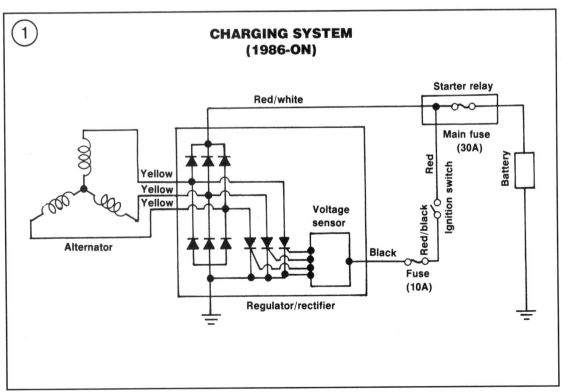

CHARGING SYSTEM
(1986-ON)

condition before going any further. Clean and test the battery as described in Chapter Three.

1. Remove the left-hand side cover.

2. Start the engine and let it reach normal operating temperature. Turn the engine off.

3. Leave the battery wires connected to the battery and connect a 0-15 volt DC voltmeter between the battery terminals (**Figure 4**).

CAUTION
Make sure the positive voltmeter cable does not touch any component on the frame.

4. Start the engine and let it idle. Gradually increase engine speed to 5,000 rpm. At 5,000 rpm, the voltmeter should read 14-15 volts. If the output voltage is not within specifications, first check the alternator-to-battery wire harness for loose or damaged connectors. If the wire harness connectors are in good condition, check the alternator stator and then the voltage regulator/rectifier as described in this chapter.

5. Disconnect the voltmeter and reinstall the left-hand side cover.

ALTERNATOR

An alternator is a form of electrical generator in which a magnetized field called a rotor revolves within a set of stationary coils called a stator. As the rotor revolves, alternating current is induced into the stator. The current is then rectified to direct current and used to operate the electrical accessories on the motorcycle and to charge the battery. The rotor is permanently magnetized.

Rotor removal and installation procedures are covered in Chapter Four.

Rotor Testing

The rotor is permanently magnetized and cannot be tested except by replacement with a rotor known to be good. A rotor can lose magnetism from old age or a sharp blow. If defective, the rotor must be replaced; it cannot be remagnetized.

Stator Removal/Installation

1. Place the bike on the centerstand.

2. Remove both side covers and the seats.

3. Disconnect the battery negative lead (**Figure 5**).

4. Remove the clutch slave cylinder as described in Chapter Five. It is not necessary to remove the slave cylinder completely, just move it out of the way.

5. Remove the starter gears as described in Chapter Four.

6A. On 1985-1986 models, perform the following:
   a. Remove the bolt securing the gearshift pedal arm and remove the arm from the shift shaft.
   b. Remove the bolts securing the gearshift pedal and left-hand footpeg assembly as described in Chapter Thirteen.

6B. On 1987-on models, remove the bolts securing the gearshift pedal and left-hand footpeg assembly as described in Chapter Thirteen.

7. Disconnect the electrical connectors going to the alternator stator assembly.

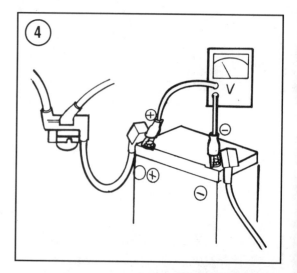

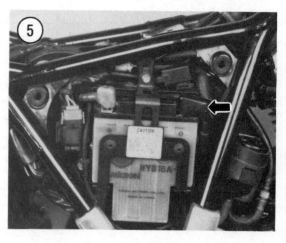

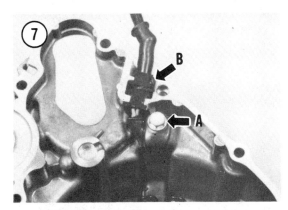

8. Remove the bolt securing the oil pipe clamp (A, **Figure 6**) and remove the clamp.

9. Remove the bolts securing the alternator cover (B, **Figure 6**) and remove the cover, gasket and the electrical harness from the frame. Note the path of the wire harness as it must be routed the same during installation.

10. Remove the electrical harness from the clips on the frame.

11. Remove the bolt and wire clamp (A, **Figure 7**) securing the wire to the housing.

12. Remove the bolts (**Figure 8**) securing the alternator stator to the alternator cover.

13. Carefully pull the rubber grommet (B, **Figure 7**) and electrical wire harness from the alternator cover.

14. While the cover is removed from the engine, inspect the gearshift shaft oil seal (**Figure 9**). If the oil seal is worn or damaged; replace it.

15. Install by reversing these removal steps while noting the following.

16. Be sure to install the wire clamp. If the clamp is left off, the rotor may rub against the wires, wear off the insulation and cause a short in the circuit.

Stator Testing

1. Remove both side covers and the seats.

2. Disconnect the 3-pin alternator electrical connector (**Figure 10**).

3. Use an ohmmeter set at R × 1 and check continuity between each yellow terminal. Replace the stator if any yellow terminal shows *no* continuity to any other. This would indicate an open in the winding.

4. Use an ohmmeter and check for continuity between each yellow terminal and ground. Replace the stator if any of the terminals show continuity to

ground. This would indicate a short within a winding.

> *NOTE*
> *Prior to replacing the stator with a new one, check the electrical wires to and within the terminal connector for any open or poor connections.*

VOLTAGE REGULATOR/
RECTIFIER

Removal/Installation

1. Remove both side covers and the seats.
2. Disconnect the battery negative lead (**Figure 5**).
3A. On 1985-1986 models, disconnect the 2 electrical connectors. Both connectors contain 3 wires (**Figure 2**).
3B. On 1987-on models, disconnect the 3 electrical connectors. One connector contains 3 wires and the other 2 contain 2 wires.
4A. On 1985-1986 models, remove the nuts (**Figure 11**) securing the voltage regulator/rectifier to the bracket on the left-hand side and remove the voltage regulator/rectifier.
4B. On 1987-on models, remove the bolts securing the voltage regulator/rectifier to the frame just below the right-hand side of the radiator.
5. Carefully pull the voltage regulator/rectifier and all electrical connectors and wires out from the frame.
6. Install by reversing these removal steps. Make sure all electrical connections are tight.

Testing

To test the voltage regulator/rectifier, disconnect the 2 or 3 electrical connectors from the harness.

Make the following measurements using an ohmmeter and referring to **Figure 12**. These are the only measurements Honda specifies.

> *NOTE*
> *The following tests are set up for a positive ground ohmmeter. If a negative ground ohmmeter is used, the test results will be the opposite.*

1. Connect the positive (+) ohmmeter lead to the yellow lead and the negative (–) ohmmeter lead to

the green lead. There should be continuity (low resistance).
2. Reverse the ohmmeter leads and repeat Step 1. This time there should be no continuity (infinite resistance).
3. Connect the positive (+) ohmmeter lead to the red/white lead and the negative (–) ohmmeter lead to the yellow lead. There should be continuity (low resistance).
4. Reverse the ohmmeter leads and repeat Step 3. This time there should be no continuity (infinite resistance).
5. If the voltage regulator/rectifier fails to pass any of these tests, the unit is defective and must be replaced.

Voltage Regulator
Performance Test

Connect a voltmeter to the battery negative and positive terminals (**Figure 13**). Leave the battery

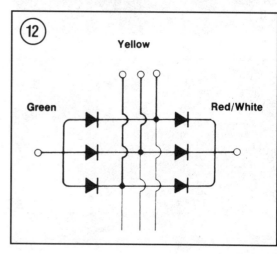

cables attached. Start the engine and let it idle; increase engine speed until the voltage going to the battery reaches 14.0-15.0 volts. At this point, the voltage regulator/rectifier should prevent any further increase in voltage. If this does not happen and voltage increases above specifications, the voltage regulator/rectifier is faulty and must be replaced.

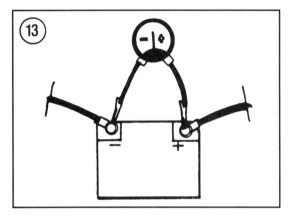

IGNITION SYSTEM

On 1985-1986 models, the ignition system consists of 2 ignition coils, 2 spark units, 3 ignition pulse generators and 4 spark plugs (2 spark plugs per cylinder). Refer to **Figure 14** for a diagram of the ignition circuit.

On 1987-on models, the ignition system consists of 2 ignition coils, 1 spark unit, 2 ignition pulse generators and 4 spark plugs (2 spark plugs per cylinder). Refer to **Figure 15** for 1987-1988 models or **Figure 16** for 1989-on models for a diagram of the ignition circuit.

The V-Twins are equipped with a solid state ignition system that uses no breaker points. This system provides a longer life for components and delivers a more efficient spark throughout the entire speed range of the engine. Ignition timing is fixed with no means of adjustment. If ignition timing is incorrect, it is due to a faulty unit within the ignition system.

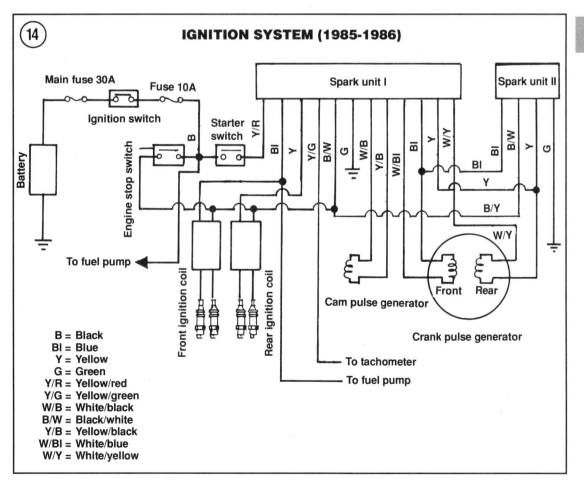

Direct current charges the capacitor. As the piston approaches the firing position, a pulse from the pulse generator coil triggers the silicone controlled rectifier. The rectifier in turn allows the capacitor to discharge quickly into the primary circuit of the ignition coil, where the voltage is stepped up in the secondary circuit to a value sufficient to fire the spark plugs. Both spark plugs in the same cylinder will fire at the same time. The distribution of the pulses from the pulse generators is controlled by the rotation of the pulse generator plate that is attached to the primary drive gear.

Ignition System Precautions

Certain measures must be taken to protect the ignition system. Instantaneous damage to the semiconductors in the system will occur if the following precautions are not observed.

1. Never connect the battery backwards. If the connected battery polarity is wrong, damage will occur to the voltage regulator/rectifier, the alternator and the spark units.

2. Do not disconnect the battery when the engine is running. A voltage surge will occur which will damage the voltage regulator/rectifier and possibly burn out the lights.

3. Keep all connections between the various units clean and tight. Be sure that the wiring connections are pushed together firmly to help keep out moisture.

4. Do not substitute another type of ignition coil.

5. Each component is mounted within a rubber vibration isolator. Always be sure that the isolator is in place when installing any units in the system.

Ignition System Troubleshooting

Problems with the ignition system are usually the production of a weak spark or no spark at all.

1. Check all connections to make sure they are tight and free of corrosion.

2. Check the ignition coils as described in this chapter.

3A. On 1985-1986 models, check the cylinder ignition pulse generator coils with an ohmmeter:

   a. Remove the seats and both side covers.

   b. Disconnect the 2-pin and the 2 individual cylinder ignition pulse generator electrical connectors (**Figure 2**).

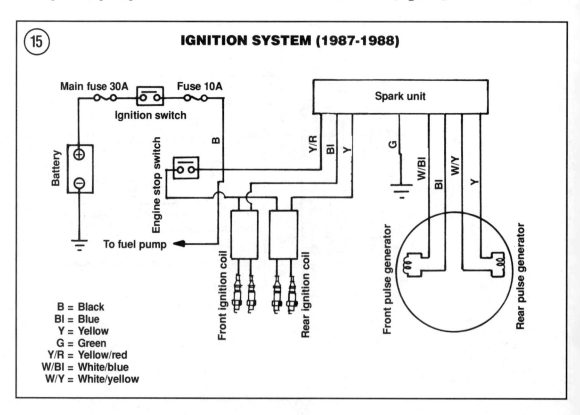

(15)   **IGNITION SYSTEM (1987-1988)**

B = Black
BI = Blue
Y = Yellow
G = Green
Y/R = Yellow/red
W/BI = White/blue
W/Y = White/yellow

c. Connect the ohmmeter leads between the white/blue and the blue leads (front cylinder) and then between the white/yellow and the yellow leads (front cylinder).

d. The resistance for each coil should be 450-550 ohms at 68° F (20° C). If the pulse generator coils do not meet these specifications, the ignition pulse generator assembly must be replaced as described in this chapter. It cannot be serviced.

3B. On 1985-1986 models, check the camshaft ignition pulse generator coil with an ohmmeter:

a. Remove the fuel tank as described in Chapter Seven.

b. Disconnect the 2-pin camshaft ignition pulse generator electrical connector.

c. Connect the ohmmeter leads between the white/blue and the yellow/black leads.

d. The resistance for the coil should be 570-690 ohms at 68° F (20° C). If the camshaft pulse generator coil does not meet these specifications, the camshaft pulse generator assembly must be replaced as described in this chapter. It cannot be serviced.

3C. On 1987-on models, check the cylinder ignition pulse generator coils with an ohmmeter:

a. Remove the seats.

b. Disconnect the 4-pin ignition pulse generator electrical connector.

c. Connect the ohmmeter leads between the white/yellow and the yellow leads (rear cylinder) and then between the white/blue and the blue leads (front cylinder).

d. The resistance for each coil should be 450-550 ohms on 1987-1990 models and 400-500 ohms on 1992-on models at 68° F (20° C). If the pulse generator coils do not meet these

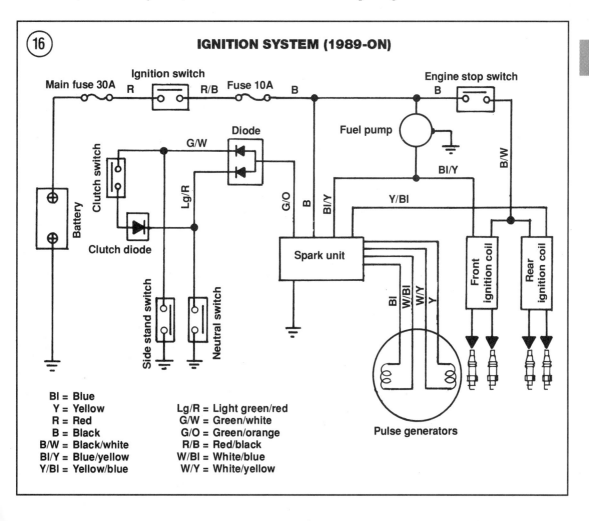

IGNITION SYSTEM (1989-ON)

Bl = Blue
Y = Yellow
R = Red
B = Black
B/W = Black/white
Bl/Y = Blue/yellow
Y/Bl = Yellow/blue

Lg/R = Light green/red
G/W = Green/white
G/O = Green/orange
R/B = Red/black
W/Bl = White/blue
W/Y = White/yellow

specifications, the ignition pulse generator assembly must be replaced as described in this chapter. It cannot be serviced.

4. If the ignition coils and ignition pulse generator assembly check out okay, the spark units are at fault and must be replaced.

SPARK UNIT

Replacement

1. Remove the seats and both side covers.

2A. On 1985-1986 models, disconnect the electrical connectors going to spark unit I located behind the battery (**Figure 17**) and to spark unit II below the battery.

2B. On 1987-on models, disconnect the electrical connectors going to the spark unit located behind the battery.

3. Remove the spark units from their rubber mounts.

4. Install by reversing these removal steps while noting the following.

5. Make sure all electrical connections are tight and free of corrosion.

Testing

Honda does not provide test procedures nor specifications for the spark units. If the ignition coils, the pulse generator assembly and the wiring harness are good and the ignition timing is not within specifications, replace the spark units with known good units.

IGNITION COIL

There are 2 ignition coils: one fires the plugs for the front cylinder and the other fires the plugs for the rear cylinder.

The ignition coil is a form of transformer which develops the high voltage required to jump the spark plug gap. The only maintenance required is that of keeping the electrical connections clean and tight and occasionally checking to see that the coils are mounted securely.

Removal/Installation

1. Remove both side covers and the seats.

2. Disconnect the battery negative lead (**Figure 5**).

3. On 1987-on models, perform the following:

a. Remove the fuel tank as described in Chapter Seven.

b. Remove the screws securing the electrical wiring connector box and move the box out of the way.

4. Remove the bolts (**Figure 18**) securing the ignition coils and bracket to the frame. Partially pull the coil assembly up to gain access to the wires attached to the coils.

5. Disconnect the spark plug leads.

6. Disconnect the primary wire connectors for both coils. The wire colors are as follows:

a. 1985-1986:
   front cylinder—black/white and blue.
   rear cylinder—yellow and black/white.

b. 1987-1988:
   front cylinder—black/white and blue/yellow.
   rear cylinder—yellow and black/white.

c. 1989-on:
   front cylinder—black/white and blue/yellow.
   rear cylinder—yellow/blue and black/white.

7. Remove the ignition coils and bracket assembly.

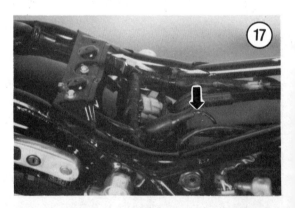

8. Install by reversing these removal steps while noting the following.

9. Make sure all electrical connections are tight and free of corrosion.

10. Route the spark plug wires to the correct cylinder. Each spark plug wire is numbered adjacent to the spark plug rubber boot.

Dynamic Test

Disconnect the high voltage lead from one of the spark plugs. Remove the spark plug from the cylinder head. Connect a new or known good spark plug to the high voltage lead and place the spark plug base on a good ground like the engine cylinder head. Position the spark plug so you can see the electrodes.

> *WARNING*
> *If it is necessary to hold the high voltage lead, do so with an insulated pair of pliers. The high voltage generated could produce serious or fatal shocks.*

Push the starter button to turn the engine over a couple of times. If a fat blue spark occurs, the coil is in good condition: if not, it must be replaced. Make sure that you are using a known good spark plug for this test. If the spark plug used is defective, the test results will be incorrect.

Reinstall the spark plug in the cylinder head.

Continuity Test

1. Use an ohmmeter set at R × 10 and measure between the 2 primary connector lugs on the coil. The specified resistance is listed in **Table 1**.

2. Use an ohmmeter set at R × 1,000 and measure between the 2 secondary leads (spark plug leads) with the spark plug caps in place. The specified resistance is listed in **Table 1**.

3. Use an ohmmeter set at R × 10 and measure between the 2 secondary leads terminals of the coil with the spark plug leads removed. The specified resistance is listed in **Table 1**.

> *NOTE*
> *Honda provides resistance values for spark plug leads for the 1987-on models only.*

4. If the coil(s) pass the test in Step 3 but fail Step 2, the spark plug caps may be faulty. On 1987-on models only, disconnect the spark plug leads from the ignition coil. Use an ohmmeter and check for continuity through the spark plug cap. The specified resistance is listed in **Table 1**. If there is no continuity, the spark plug cap is faulty and must be replaced.

5. If the coil(s) fail to pass any of these tests, the coil should be replaced.

PULSE GENERATOR

All models have 2 pulse generators that are triggered by the pulse generator rotor tip attached to the right-hand end of the crankshaft. The 1985-1986 models also have a pulse generator adjacent to the right-hand end of the rear cylinder's camshaft.

Crankshaft Mounted
Removal/Installation

1. Drain the engine oil as described in Chapter Three.

2. Remove the seats and both side covers.

3. Remove the complete clutch assembly including the clutch outer housing as described in Chapter Five.

4. Disconnect the ignition pulse generator electrical connector (**Figure 2**).

> *NOTE*
> *The following steps are shown with the engine removed and disassembled for clarity. The pulse generators can be removed with the engine in the frame.*

5. Remove the bolt and wiring harness clip securing the harness adjacent to the rubber grommet.

6. Remove the bolts securing the upper pulse generator (A, **Figure 19**) to the crankcase.

7. Remove the bolts (B, **Figure 19**) securing the lower pulse generator and wiring harness clips and remove the clips.

8. Carefully remove the rubber grommet (C, **Figure 19**) and electrical wires from the crankcase and remove the assembly from the frame.

9. Install by reversing these removal steps while noting the following.

10. Make sure the bolts securing the pulse generators are tight and that the wires are routed correctly in the frame.

11. Refill the engine with the recommended viscosity and quantity of engine oil as described in Chapter Three.

**Camshaft Mounted
Removal/Installation
(1985-1986)**

1. Remove the engine from the frame as described in Chapter Four.
2. Remove the bolts securing the rear cylinder's cam chain cover (**Figure 20**) and remove the cover and gasket.
3. Remove the bolts securing the camshaft pulse generator to the cylinder head.
4. Remove the assembly from the cylinder head.
5. Install by reversing these removal steps while noting the following.
6. Make sure the bolts securing the pulse generators are tight.

STARTING SYSTEM

The starting system consists of the starter motor, starter gears, solenoid and the starter button.

The layout of the starting system is shown in **Figure 21** for 1985-1988 models or **Figure 22** for

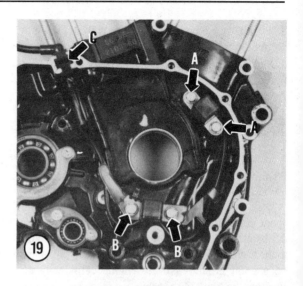

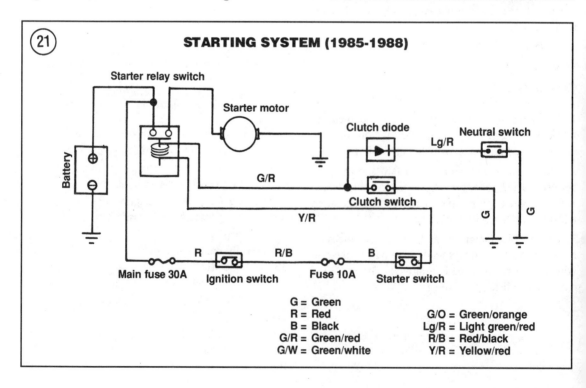

STARTING SYSTEM (1985-1988)

Starter relay switch

Starter motor

Clutch diode

Neutral switch

Lg/R

Battery

G/R

Clutch switch

Y/R

R   R/B   B

Main fuse 30A   Ignition switch   Fuse 10A   Starter switch

G = Green
R = Red
B = Black
G/R = Green/red
G/W = Green/white

G/O = Green/orange
Lg/R = Light green/red
R/B = Red/black
Y/R = Yellow/red

1989-on models. When the starter button is pressed, it allows current flow through the solenoid coil. The coil contacts close, allowing electricity to flow from the battery to the starter motor.

> *CAUTION*
> *Do not operate the starter for more than 5 seconds at a time. Let it rest approximately 10 seconds, then use it again.*

The starter gears and starter clutch assembly are covered in Chapter Four.

Table 2 lists possible starter problems, probable causes and most common remedies.

STARTER

Removal/Installation

1. Place the bike on the centerstand.

2. Remove the seats and both side covers.

3. Disconnect the battery negative lead (**Figure 5**).

4. Remove the starter gears as described in Chapter Four.

5A. On 1985-1986 models, remove the fuel pump as described in Chapter Seven.

5B. On 1987-on models, remove the exhaust system as described in Chapter Seven.

6. Disconnect the electric starter cable from the starter (A, **Figure 23**).

7. Remove the bolts securing the starter to the crank-case.

8. Pull the starter (B, **Figure 23**) to the right and remove the starter from the crankcase.

9. Install by reversing these removal steps. Make sure the electrical wire connection is tight and free of corrosion.

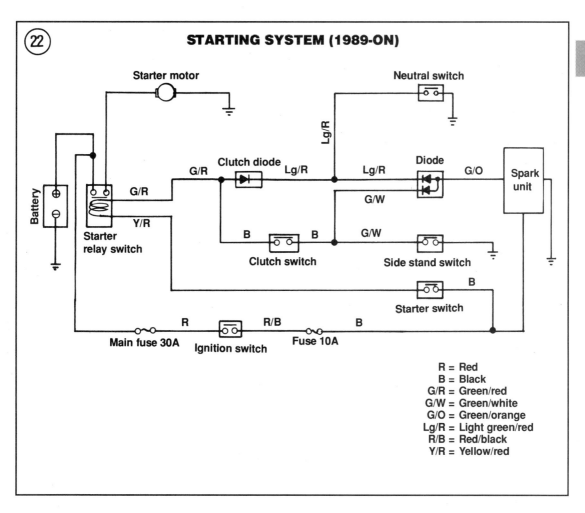

STARTING SYSTEM (1989-ON)

R = Red
B = Black
G/R = Green/red
G/W = Green/white
G/O = Green/orange
Lg/R = Light green/red
R/B = Red/black
Y/R = Yellow/red

Preliminary Inspection

The overhaul of a starter motor is best left to an expert. This procedure shows how to detect a defective starter.

Inspect the O-ring seal (A, **Figure 24**). O-rings tend to harden after prolonged use and heat and therefore lose their ability to seal properly. Replace as necessary.

Inspect the gear teeth (B, **Figure 24**) for chipped or missing teeth. If damaged, the starter assembly must be replaced.

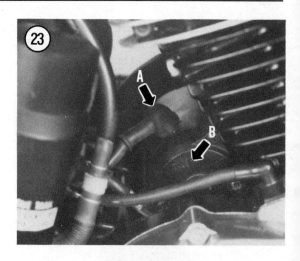

Disassembly/Inspection/Assembly

Refer to **Figure 25** for this procedure.

NOTE
Figure 26 shows only 2 case screws, there are 3 screws. The lower one is not visible.

1. Remove the case screws (A, **Figure 26**) and separate the case and covers.

NOTE
Write down the number of shims used on the shaft next to the commutator. Be sure to install the same number when reassembling the starter.

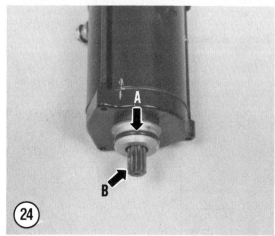

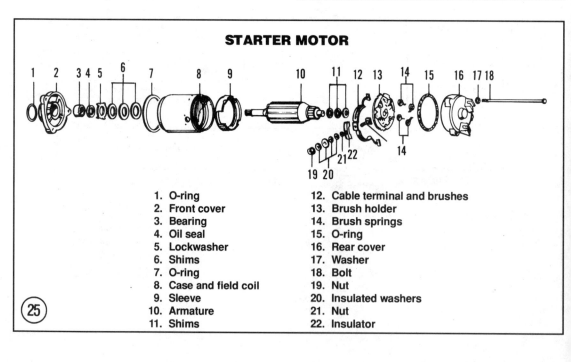

STARTER MOTOR

1. O-ring
2. Front cover
3. Bearing
4. Oil seal
5. Lockwasher
6. Shims
7. O-ring
8. Case and field coil
9. Sleeve
10. Armature
11. Shims
12. Cable terminal and brushes
13. Brush holder
14. Brush springs
15. O-ring
16. Rear cover
17. Washer
18. Bolt
19. Nut
20. Insulated washers
21. Nut
22. Insulator

2. Clean all grease, dirt and carbon from the armature, case and end covers.

CAUTION
Do not immerse brushes or the wire windings in solvent as the insulation

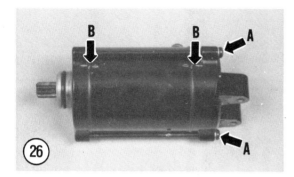

may be damaged. Wipe the windings with a cloth lightly moistened with solvent and dry thoroughly.

3. Measure the length of each brush (**Figure 27**) with a vernier caliper. If the length is 6.5 mm (0.26 in.) or less for any one of the brushes, the brush holder assembly and cable terminal and brush assembly must be replaced. The brushes cannot be replaced individually.

4. To replace the brushes, perform the following:

NOTE
Prior to removing the nuts and washers, write down their description and order. They must be reinstalled in the same order to insulate this set of brushes from the case.

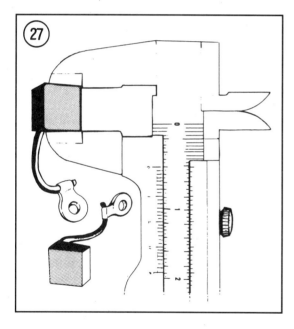

a. Remove the nuts, washers and O-ring (A, **Figure 28**) securing the cable terminal and brush assembly.

b. Slide the armature and brush holder assemblies partially out of the case.

c. Remove the old brush holders and install new brush holders.

d. Slide the armature and brush holder assemblies back into the case.

e. Install the nuts and washers in the original order to secure the cable terminal and brush assembly.

5. Inspect the commutator. The mica in a good commutator is below the surface of the copper bars as shown in **Figure 29**. On a worn commutator, the mica and copper bars may be worn to the same level (**Figure 30**). If necessary, have the commutator serviced by a dealer or electrical repair shop.

6. Inspect the commutator copper bars for discoloration. If a pair of bars are discolored, grounded armature coils are indicated.

7. Use an ohmmeter and check for continuity between the commutator bars (**Figure 31**); there should be continuity between pairs of bars. Also check for continuity between the commutator bars and the shaft (**Figure 32**); there should be no continuity. If the unit fails either of these tests, the armature is faulty and must be replaced.

8. Use an ohmmeter and check for continuity between the starter cable terminal and the starter case; there should be no continuity (infinite resistance). Also check for continuity between the starter cable terminal and each brush wire terminal; there should

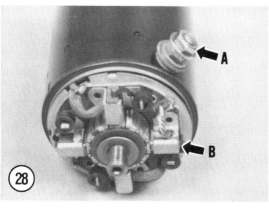

8

be continuity (low resistance). If the unit fails either of these tests, the case/field coil assembly must be replaced.

9. Inspect the oil seal and bushing in the rear cover. If either is damaged, replace the starter assembly as these parts are not available separately.

10. Inspect the bushing (A, **Figure 33**) in the front cover. If either is damaged, replace the starter assembly as these parts are not available separately.

11. Inspect the case/field coil assembly for wear or damage. If it is damaged, replace the starter assembly as this part is not available separately.

12. Inspect the brush holder for wear or damage. Replace if necessary.

13. Inspect the cable/brush terminal set (B, **Figure 28**) for wear or damage. Replace as necessary.

14. Assemble the case as follows:

   a. Align the pin in the brush holder with the notch in the case (**Figure 34**).

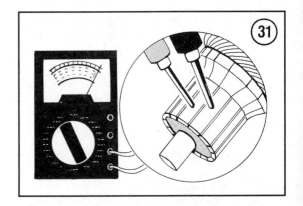

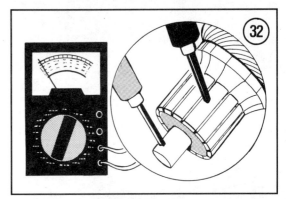

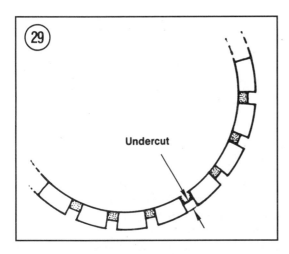

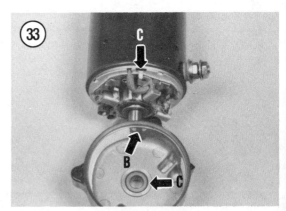

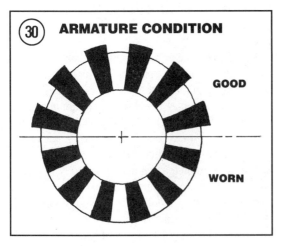

ARMATURE CONDITION

GOOD

WORN

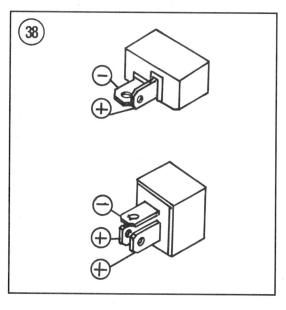

b. Align the slot in the rear cover (B, **Figure 33**) with the pin on the brush holder (C, **Figure 33**).

c. Align the marks on the case and end covers (**Figure 26**) and install the case screws.

STARTER SOLENOID

Removal/Installation

1. Remove the frame left-hand side cover.

2. Disconnect the negative battery lead (**Figure 35**).

3. Slide off the rubber protective boot (A, **Figure 36**) and disconnect the electrical wires from the top terminals.

4. Remove the solenoid from the rubber mounting receptacle on the frame (B, **Figure 36**).

5. Install by reversing these removal steps while noting the following.

6. If installing a new solenoid, transfer the fuse holder from the old solenoid to the new solenoid.

CLUTCH DIODE

Testing

1. Remove the seats and both side covers.

2A. On 1985-1986 models, remove the main fuel tank as described in Chapter Seven.

2B. On 1987-on models, remove the fuel tank as described in Chapter Seven.

3. Disconnect the clutch diode (**Figure 37**) from the wire harness.

4. Use an ohmmeter and check for continuity between the 2 terminals on the clutch diode as shown in **Figure 38**. Connect the negative (–) test lead to the negative (–) terminal and the positive (+) test lead to the positive (+) terminal. There should be continuity (low resistance) in the normal direction and no continuity (infinite resistance) in the reverse direction.

5. Replace the diode if it fails this test.

LIGHTING SYSTEM

The lighting system consists of a headlight, taillight/brake light combination, turn signals, indicator lights and meter illumination lights. **Table 3** lists replacement bulbs for these components.

Always use the correct wattage bulb as indicated in this section. The use of a larger wattage bulb will give a dim light and a smaller wattage bulb will burn out prematurely.

Headlight Bulb Replacement

The headlight is equipped with a quartz halogen bulb. Special handling of the quartz halogen bulb is required as specified in this procedure.

Refer to **Figure 39** for 1985-1986 models or **Figure 40** for 1987-on models for this procedure.

1. Remove the screw (**Figure 41**) on each side of the headlight case securing the headlight assembly.

2. Pull out on the bottom of the headlight assembly and disengage it from the locating tab on top of the headlight housing.

3. Disconnect the electrical connector (**Figure 42**) from the headlight lens unit.

CAUTION
Carefully read all instructions shipped with the replacement quartz halogen bulb. Do not touch the bulb glass with your fingers. Any traces of oil on the glass will drastically reduce the life of the bulb. Clean any traces of oil from the bulb with a cloth moistened in alcohol or lacquer thinner.

4. Remove the rubber cover (**Figure 43**).

5. Remove the set spring and bulb assembly (**Figure 44**).

6. Replace with a new bulb assembly (**Figure 45**)— do not touch the bulb with your fingers. Assemble by reversing this sequence.

6. Install by reversing these removal steps.

7. Adjust the headlight as described in this chapter.

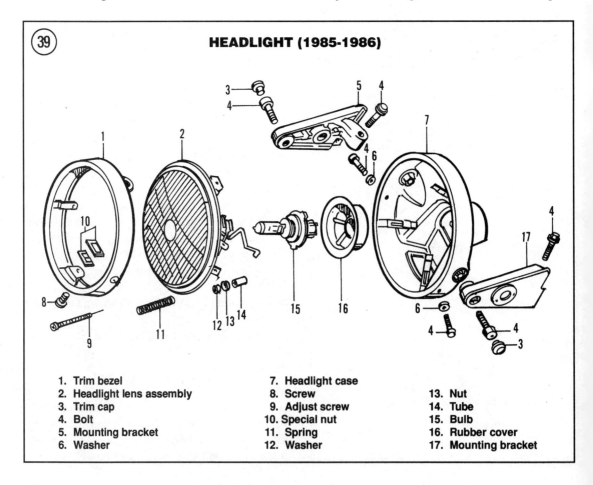

(39) HEADLIGHT (1985-1986)

1. Trim bezel
2. Headlight lens assembly
3. Trim cap
4. Bolt
5. Mounting bracket
6. Washer
7. Headlight case
8. Screw
9. Adjust screw
10. Special nut
11. Spring
12. Washer
13. Nut
14. Tube
15. Bulb
16. Rubber cover
17. Mounting bracket

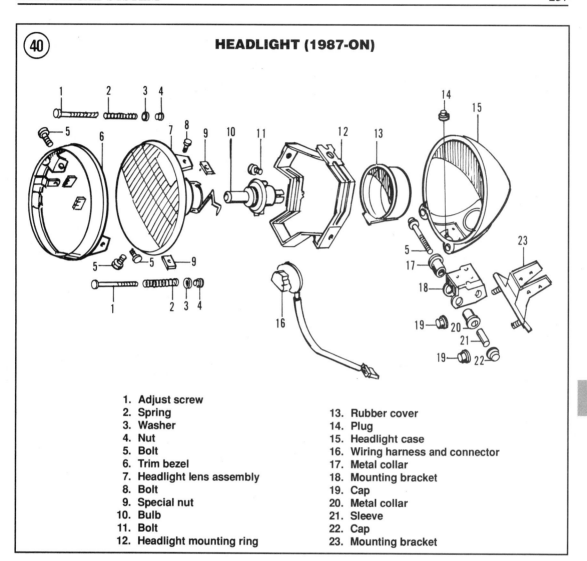

HEADLIGHT (1987-ON)

1. Adjust screw
2. Spring
3. Washer
4. Nut
5. Bolt
6. Trim bezel
7. Headlight lens assembly
8. Bolt
9. Special nut
10. Bulb
11. Bolt
12. Headlight mounting ring
13. Rubber cover
14. Plug
15. Headlight case
16. Wiring harness and connector
17. Metal collar
18. Mounting bracket
19. Cap
20. Metal collar
21. Sleeve
22. Cap
23. Mounting bracket

8

Headlight Housing
Removal/Installation

Refer to **Figure 39** for 1985-1986 models or **Figure 40** for 1987-on models for this procedure.

1. Remove the headlight (A, **Figure 46**) as described in this chapter.

2. Disconnect all electrical connectors within the headlight housing (B, **Figure 46**).

3. Carefully withdraw the electrical connectors through the headlight housing.

4A. On 1985-1986 models, perform the following:

    a. Remove the trim plug from the Allen bolt on each side.

    b. Remove the Allen bolt on each side securing the headlight case assembly to the case mounting brackets on the forks. Remove the housing.

    c. To remove the assembly mounting brackets, disconnect all electrical connectors to the front turn signals. Remove the cap nut securing each headlight bracket/turn signal assembly and remove each assembly from the upper fork bridge.

4B. On 1987-on models, remove the bolt and nut securing the headlight case to the mounting bracket on the steering stem pipe and remove the housing.

5. Install by reversing these removal steps while noting the following.

6. On 1985-1986 models, install the headlight bracket/turn signal bracket and align the index mark on the bracket with the index mark on the upper fork bridge.

7. Prior to installing the headlight lens assembly, check out the operation of the following items controlled by the electrical connections in the headlight housing:

    a. Headlight.

    b. Right and left turn signals.

8. On 1985-1986 models, for a preliminary adjustment, locate the headlight case so the index marks on the case and the bracket align.

9. Adjust the headlight as described in this chapter.

Headlight Adjustment
(1985-1986)

Adjust the headlight horizontally and vertically according to Department of Motor Vehicle regulations in your area.

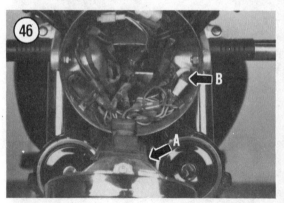

To adjust the headlight horizontally, turn the screw (A, **Figure 47**) on the left-hand side of the headlight trim bezel. Turning the screw clockwise turns the light toward the right-hand side of the rider and counterclockwise will direct the light to the left-hand side of the rider.

To adjust the headlight vertically, loosen the Allen bolts (B, **Figure 47**) on each side of the headlight assembly. Position the headlight correctly. Retighten the Allen bolts.

Headlight Adjustment (1987-on)

Adjust the headlight horizontally and vertically according to Department of Motor Vehicle regulations in your area.

To adjust the headlight horizontally, turn the screw on the left-hand side of the headlight trim bezel. Turning the screw clockwise turns the light toward the right-hand side of the rider and counterclockwise will direct the light to the left-hand side of the rider.

To adjust the headlight vertically, turn the screw on the right-hand side of the headlight trim bezel. Turning the screw clockwise turns the light lower and counterclockwise will direct the light upward.

Taillight/Brake Light Replacement

Refer to **Figure 48** for 1985-1986 models or **Figure 49** for 1987-on models for this procedure.

1. Remove the screws securing the lens and remove the lens.

2. Wash the inside and outside of the lens with a mild detergent and wipe dry. Wipe off the reflective base surrounding the bulbs with a soft cloth.

3. Inspect the lens gasket and replace if it is damaged or deteriorated.

4. Replace the bulb and install the lens; do not overtighten the screws as the lens may crack.

Turn Signal Light Replacement

1. Remove the screws securing the lens and remove the lens (**Figure 50**).

2. Wash the inside and outside of the lens with a mild detergent and wipe dry.

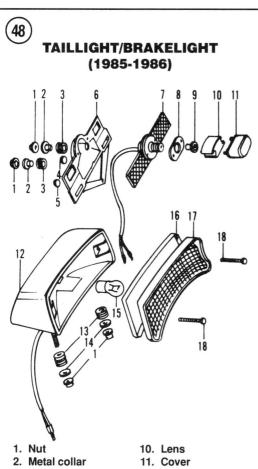

TAILLIGHT/BRAKELIGHT (1985-1986)

1. Nut
2. Metal collar
3. Rubber grommet
4. Nut
5. Nut
6. Bracket
7. Base
8. Gasket
9. Bulb
10. Lens
11. Cover
12. Housing
13. Rubber grommet
14. Washer
15. Bulb
16. Gasket
17. Lens
18. Screw

3. Inspect the lens gasket and replace if it is damaged or deteriorated.

4. Replace the bulb and install the lens; do not overtighten the screws as the lens may crack.

Indicator Light Replacement (1985-1986)

Refer to **Figure 51** for this procedure.

1. Remove the screw on each side of the indicator panel and remove the panel.

2. Remove the defective bulb(s) and replace with new ones.

3. Install the indicator panel and screws.

Indicator Light Replacement (1987-on)

Refer to **Figure 52** for this procedure.

1. Remove the speedometer as described in this chapter.

2. Remove the screw on each side of the indicator panel and remove the panel.

3. Remove the defective bulb(s) and replace with new ones.

4. Install the indicator panel and screws.

5. Install the speedometer as described in this chapter.

Meter Illumination Light Replacement

Refer to **Figure 51** for 1985-1986 models or **Figure 52** for 1987-on models for this procedure.

(50)

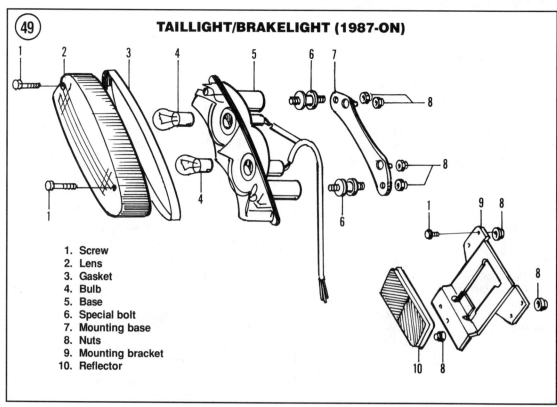

(49) **TAILLIGHT/BRAKELIGHT (1987-ON)**

1. Screw
2. Lens
3. Gasket
4. Bulb
5. Base
6. Special bolt
7. Mounting base
8. Nuts
9. Mounting bracket
10. Reflector

1A. On 1985-1986 models, remove the bolt securing the meter to the mounting bracket and remove the meter.

1B. On 1987-on models, remove the cap nuts securing the meter to the mounting bracket and remove the meter.

WARNING
In the next step do not allow the instruments to remain upside-down any longer than necessary as the needle damping fluid will leak out onto the instrument face and lens.

2. Turn the instrument cluster upside-down on the workbench.

3. Remove the screws securing the cover to the backside of the meter and remove the cover.

4. Carefully pull the socket/bulb assembly out of the backside of the housing.

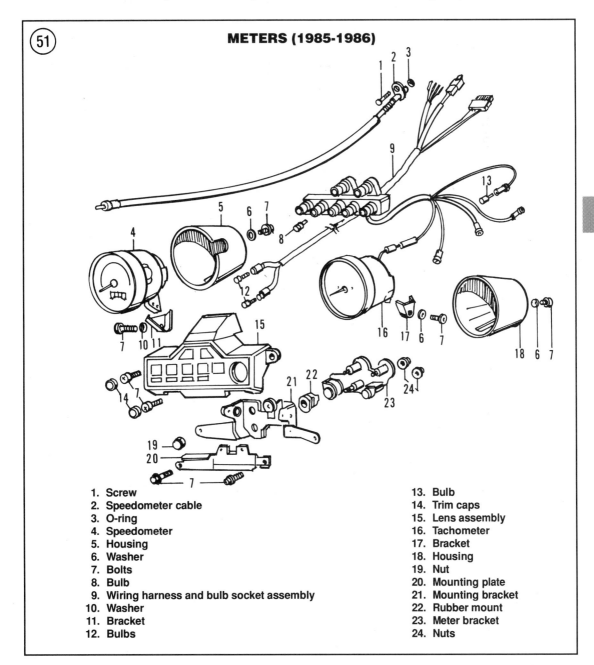

METERS (1985-1986)

1. Screw
2. Speedometer cable
3. O-ring
4. Speedometer
5. Housing
6. Washer
7. Bolts
8. Bulb
9. Wiring harness and bulb socket assembly
10. Washer
11. Bracket
12. Bulbs
13. Bulb
14. Trim caps
15. Lens assembly
16. Tachometer
17. Bracket
18. Housing
19. Nut
20. Mounting plate
21. Mounting bracket
22. Rubber mount
23. Meter bracket
24. Nuts

8

METERS (1987-ON)

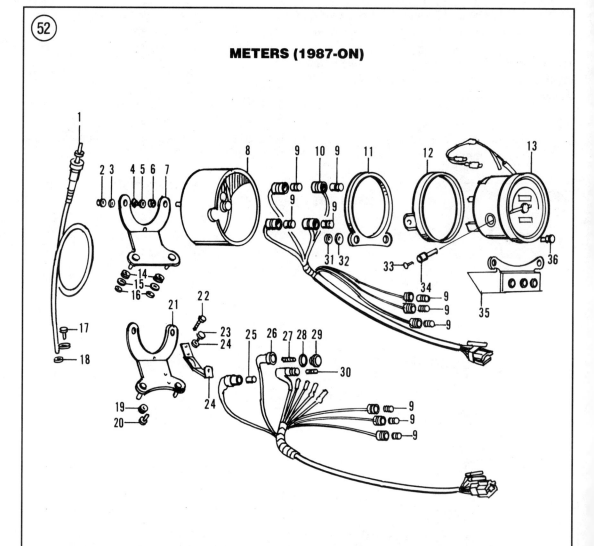

1. Speedometer cable
2. Nut
3. Washer
4. Washer
5. Nut
6. Washer
7. Mounting bracket
8. Housing
9. Bulb
10. Wiring harness and bulb socket assembly
11. Mounting ring
12. Trim ring
13. Speedometer
14. Rubber grommets
15. Washers
16. Nuts
17. Bolt
18. O-ring
19. Washer
20. Bolt
21. Mounting bracket
22. Bolt
23. Trim cap
24. Washer
25. Bulb
26. Wiring harness and bulb socket assembly
27. Bulb
28. O-ring
29. Lens
30. Bulb
31. Nut
32. Washer
33. Screw
34. Knob
35. Lens bracket
36. Bolt

5. Replace the defective bulb(s).

6. Assemble and install by reversing these disassembly steps.

SWITCHES

Ignition Switch
Removal/Installation
(1985-1986)

1. Remove the left-hand side cover.

2. Disconnect the battery negative lead.

3. Remove the headlight and case as described in this chapter.

4. Remove the bolts securing the ignition switch to the upper fork bridge.

5. Install by reversing these removal steps.

Ignition Switch
Removal/Installation
(1987-on)

1. Remove the left-hand side cover.

2. Disconnect the battery negative lead.

3A. On 1987-1990 models, remove the bolts securing the ignition switch to the frame tube ahead of the battery.

3B. On 1992-on models, remove the bolts and collars securing the ignition switch to the frame tube ahead of the battery.

4. Install by reversing these removal steps.

Ignition Switch
Continuity Test (All Models)

To check continuity of the switch, use an ohmmeter and perform the following:

1. Connect the ohmmeter leads to the electrical connector attached to the electrical contact portion of the ignition switch.

2. Refer to **Figure 53** and connect the ohmmeter test leads to the indicated color wires with the ignition switch in the indicated positions.

3. If the ignition switch fails any one of the tests, the electrical contact portion of the switch, must be replaced.

Engine Stop Switch and Starter Button
Removal/Continuity Test/Installation

The engine stop switch and starter button are an integral part of the right-hand switch assembly. If either of these switches are faulty, the entire switch assembly must be replaced.

1A. On 1985-1986 models, perform the following:

    a. Remove the headlight as described in this chapter.

    b. Remove the screws securing the electrical junction box cover (**Figure 54**) and remove the cover.

1B. On 1987-on models, perform the following:

    a. Remove the fuel tank as described in Chapter Seven.

    b. Remove the fuel tank rubber protective straps from the frame.

    c. Remove the electrical junction box cover.

2. Disconnect the electrical connectors (going to the right switch assembly) from the junction box and/or in the headlight case.

3A. To check continuity of the engine stop switch, use an ohmmeter and perform the following:

    a. Connect the ohmmeter leads to the electrical connector attached to the electrical contact portion of the engine stop switch.

53

IGNITION SWITCH

	BAT	IG	FAN	TL$_1$	TL$_2$	P
ON	•———•———•			•———•		
OFF						
P	•———————					———•
Color Code	R	R/Bl	Bu/O	Br/W	Br	Y/Bl

8

b. Refer to **Figure 55** and connect the ohmmeter test leads to the indicated color wires with the engine stop switch in the indicated positions.

c. If the engine stop switch fails this test, the right-hand switch assembly must be replaced.

3B. To check continuity of the starter button, use an ohmmeter and perform the following:

a. Connect the ohmmeter leads to the electrical connector attached to the electrical contact portion of the engine stop switch.

b. Refer to **Figure 56** and connect the ohmmeter test leads to the indicated color wires with the starter button in the indicated positions.

c. If the starter button fails any one of the tests, the right-hand switch assembly must be replaced.

4. Remove the screws clamping the right-hand switch assembly together (A, **Figure 57**).

5. Unhook any straps (B, **Figure 57**) securing the electrical wires to the handlebar.

6. Remove the right-hand switch assembly and electrical wires from the frame.

7. Install a new switch by reversing these removal steps. Make sure all electrical connections are tight and free of corrosion.

Headlight Dimmer Switch,
Horn Button and Turn Signal Switch
Removal/Continuity Test/Installation

The headlight dimmer switch, horn button and turn signal switch are an integral part of the left-hand switch assembly. If any are faulty, the entire switch assembly must be replaced.

1A. On 1985-1986 models, perform the following:

a. Remove the headlight as described in this chapter.

b. Remove the screws securing the electrical junction box cover (**Figure 54**) and remove the cover.

1B. On 1987-on models, perform the following:

a. Remove the fuel tank as described in Chapter Seven.

b. Remove the fuel tank rubber protective straps from the frame.

c. Remove the electrical junction box cover.

2. Disconnect the electrical connectors (going to the left-hand switch assembly) from the junction box and/or in the headlight case.

3A. To check continuity of the headlight dimmer switch, use an ohmmeter and perform the following:

a. Connect the ohmmeter leads to the electrical connector attached to the electrical contact portion of the headlight dimmer switch.

b. Refer to **Figure 58** and connect the ohmmeter test leads to the indicated color wires with the headlight dimmer switch in the indicated positions.

55

ENGINE STOP SWITCH

	IG$_1$	BAT$_2$
ON		
RUN	•———•	
Color Code	Bl/W	Bl

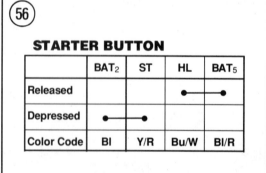

56

STARTER BUTTON

	BAT$_2$	ST	HL	BAT$_5$
Released			•———•	
Depressed	•———•			
Color Code	Bl	Y/R	Bu/W	Bl/R

57

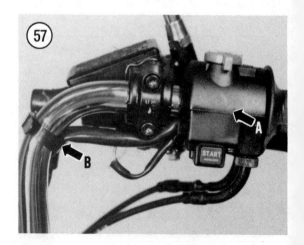

c. If the headlight dimmer switch fails any one of the tests, the left-hand switch assembly must be replaced.

3B. To check continuity of the horn button, use an ohmmeter and perform the following:

a. Connect the ohmmeter leads to the electrical connector attached to the electrical contact portion of the horn button.

b. Refer to **Figure 59** and connect the ohmmeter test leads to the indicated color wires with the horn button in the indicated positions.

DIMMER SWITCH

	HL	Hi	Lo
Hi	•—•		
(N)	•—•—•		
Lo	•——•—•		
Color Code	Bu/W	Bu	W

HORN BUTTON

	Ho$_2$	Ho$_1$
Depressed	•—•	
Released		
Color Code	Lg	W/G

TURN SIGNAL SWITCH

	W	L	R	P	PR	PL
Left	•—•			•—•		
Off				•—•—•		
Right	•——•—		•	•——•—		•
Color Code	Gr	O	Lb	Br/W	Lb/W	O/W

c. If the horn button fails any one of the tests, the left-hand switch assembly must be replaced.

3C. To check continuity of the turn signal switch, use an ohmmeter and perform the following:

a. Connect the ohmmeter leads to the electrical connector attached to the electrical contact portion of the turn signal switch.

b. Refer to **Figure 60** and connect the ohmmeter test leads to the indicated color wires with the turn signal switch in the indicated positions.

c. If the turn signal switch fails any one of the tests, the left-hand switch assembly must be replaced.

4. Remove the screws clamping the left-hand switch assembly together (A, **Figure 61**).

5. Unhook any straps (B, **Figure 61**) securing the electrical wires to the handlebar.

6. Remove the left-hand switch assembly and electrical wires from the frame.

7. Install a new switch by reversing these removal steps. Make sure all electrical connections are tight and free of corrosion.

Clutch Switch Testing/Replacement

1. Disconnect the electrical wires (**Figure 62**) from the clutch switch.

2. Use an ohmmeter and check for continuity between the 2 terminals on the clutch switch. There should be no continuity (infinite resistance) with the clutch lever released. With the clutch lever applied, there should be continuity (low resistance). If the switch fails either of these tests, the switch must be replaced.

3. Remove the screw securing the clutch switch and remove the clutch switch from the clutch master cylinder.

4. Install a new switch by reversing these removal steps. Make sure all electrical connections are tight and free of corrosion.

Oil Pressure Switch Testing/Replacement

The oil pressure switch is located on the lower left side of the crankcase just in front of the oil filter.

1. Pull back the rubber boot and remove the screw securing the electrical connector to the switch. Remove the electrical connector.

2. Use an ohmmeter and check for continuity between the electrical connector and the base of the switch.

3. There should be no continuity (infinite resistance) with no pressure applied or up to 0.1-0.2 kg/cm^2 (1.4-2.8 psi) of pressure.

4. With pressure applied above 0.1-0.2 kg/cm^2 (1.4-2.8 psi) there should be continuity (low resistance).

5. If the switch fails either test in Step 3 and/or Step 4, the switch must be replaced.

6. Replace the switch as follows:

    a. Drain the engine oil as described in Chapter Three.

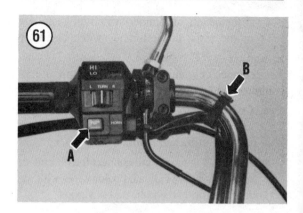

> *NOTE*
> *Figure 63 is shown with some components removed from the engine for clarity. It is not necessary to remove these components for this procedure.*

    b. Unscrew the switch (**Figure 63**) from the crankcase.

    c. Apply Three-Bond liquid sealant, or equivalent, to the switch threads.

    d. Install the switch and screw it in. Then tighten to 10-14 N•m (7-10 ft.-lb.).

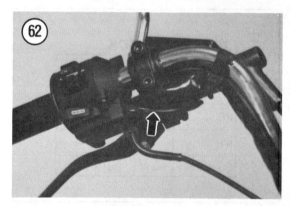

7. Attach the electrical wire. Make sure the connection is tight and free from oil.

8. Slide the rubber boot back into position.

9. Refill the engine with the correct type and quantity of engine oil; refer to Chapter Three.

Thermostatic Switch Testing/Replacement

The thermostatic switch controls the radiator fan according to engine coolant temperature.

> *NOTE*
> *If the cooling fan is not operating correctly, make sure that the fan motor fuse has not blown prior to starting this test. Also clean off any rust or corrosion from the electrical terminals on the thermostatic switch.*

1. Place the bike on the centerstand.

2. Pull back the rubber boot from the switch located on the lower right-hand side of the radiator.

3. Disconnect the electrical wire connector (A, **Figure 64**) from the back of the thermostatic switch.

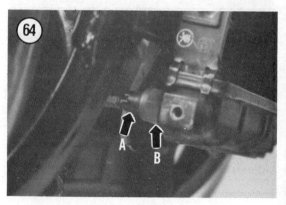

4. Place a jumper wire between the black/blue and green electrical wires within the electrical connector.

5. Turn the ignition switch ON; the cooling fan should start running.

6. If the fan now runs, the thermostatic switch is defective and must be replaced.

7. If the fan does not run under any circumstances, either the fan or the wiring to the fan is faulty. Replace the fan if the wiring checks out okay.

8. Turn the ignition switch OFF.

9. Drain the cooling system as described in Chapter Three.

10. Carefully unscrew the switch (B, **Figure 64**) from the radiator.

11. Install a new O-ring seal on the switch and install the switch into the radiator.

12. Install all items removed.

13. Refill the cooling system with the recommended type and quantity of coolant. Refer to Chapter Three.

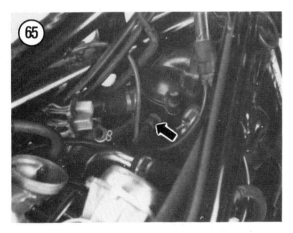

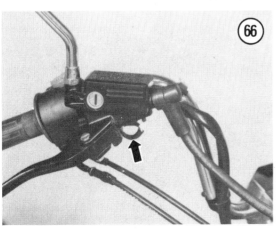

Temperature Sensor Testing/Replacement

The engine must be cold for this test, preferably not operated for 12 hours.

1. Remove the seats and side covers.

2A. On 1985-1986 models, perform the following:

   a. Remove the main fuel tank as described in Chapter Seven.

   b. Remove the air filter case as described in Chapter Seven.

2B. On 1987-on models, remove the fuel tank as described in Chapter Seven.

3. Disconnect the green/blue electrical wire from the temperature sensor located on the thermostat housing (**Figure 65**).

4. Use an ohmmeter and check for continuity between the electrical connector and the thermostat housing (ground).

5. There should be continuity (low resistance). If there is no continuity (infinite resistance), the switch is faulty and must be replaced.

6. If faulty, remove the temperature sensor from the thermostat housing.

7. Apply a non-hardening sealer to the threads and install the temperature sensor.

8. Connect the electrical wires to the temperature sensor.

9. Install all items removed.

Front Brake Light Switch Testing/Replacement

1. Disconnect the electrical wires to the brake light switch (**Figure 66**).

2. Use an ohmmeter and check for continuity between the 2 terminals on the brake light switch. There should be no continuity (infinite resistance) with the brake lever released. With the brake lever applied, there should be continuity (low resistance). If the switch fails either of these tests, the switch must be replaced.

3. Remove the screw securing the brake switch and remove the brake switch from the brake master cylinder.

4. Install a new switch by reversing these removal steps. Make sure all electrical connections are tight and free of corrosion.

8

Rear Brake Light Switch
Testing/Replacement

> *NOTE*
> *Figure 67 is shown on a 1986 model with the right-hand footpeg bracket removed in order to show the brake light switch. It is not necessary to remove the bracket for this test.*

1. Disconnect the electrical wires (A, **Figure 67**) to the rear brake light switch.

2. Use an ohmmeter and check for continuity between the 2 terminals on the brake light switch. There should be no continuity (infinite resistance) with the brake pedal released. With the brake pedal down or applied, there should be continuity (low resistance). If the switch fails either of these tests, the switch must be replaced.

3. Unhook the return spring and unscrew the locknut securing the rear brake light switch to the frame. Remove the switch from the frame.

4. Install a new switch by reversing these removal steps while noting the following.

5. Make sure all electrical connections are tight and free of corrosion.

6. Adjust the switch as described in this chapter.

Rear Brake Light
Switch Adjustment

1. Turn the ignition switch ON.

2. Depress the brake pedal. The light should come on just as the brake begins to work.

> *NOTE*
> *Figure 67 is shown on a 1986 model with the right-hand footpeg bracket removed in order to show the brake light switch. It is not necessary to remove the bracket for this test.*

3. To make the light come on earlier, hold the switch body and turn the adjusting nut (B, **Figure 67**) *clockwise* as viewed from the top. Turn *counterclockwise* to delay the light from coming on.

> *NOTE*
> *Some riders prefer the light to come on a little early. This way, they can tap the pedal without braking to warn drivers who are following too closely.*

ELECTRICAL COMPONENTS

This section contains information on electrical components other than switches.

Turn Signal Relay Replacement
(1985-1986)

1. Remove the right-hand side cover.

2. Pull the turn signal relay (**Figure 68**) out of the rubber mount above the battery.

3. Transfer the electrical wires to the new relay and install the relay in the rubber mount. Install all parts removed.

Turn Signal Relay Replacement
(1987-on)

1. Remove the fuel tank as described in Chapter Seven.

2. Remove the frame left-hand front cover.

3. Pull the turn signal relay out of the rubber mount on the left-hand side of the frame tube.

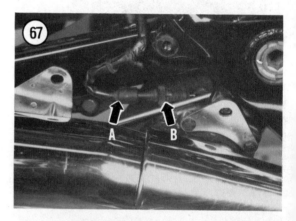

4. Transfer the electrical wires to the new relay and install the relay in the rubber mount. Install all parts removed.

Instrument Cluster
Removal/Installation
(1985-1986)

1. Remove the left side cover.

2. Disconnect the battery negative lead (**Figure 35**).

3. Remove the cover (**Figure 54**) from the electrical junction box.

4. Disconnect the speedometer cable (A, **Figure 69**) from the meter.

5. Remove the headlight and case (B, **Figure 69**) as described in this chapter.

6. Disconnect all electrical connectors going to the instrument cluster from the junction box.

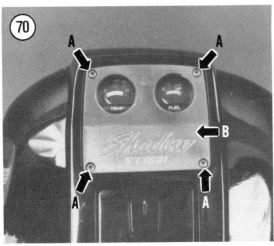

7. Remove the cap nuts securing the instrument cluster.

> *WARNING*
> *After the instrument cluster has been removed, set the cluster down with the meter face and needles facing upward. If the cluster is set face-down, the needle damping fluid will leak out onto the instrument face and lens.*

8. Remove the instrument cluster (C, **Figure 69**).

9. Install by reversing these removal steps.

Speedometer
Removal/Installation
(1987-on)

1. Remove the left side cover.

2. Disconnect the battery negative lead.

3. Disconnect the speedometer cable from the meter.

4. Disconnect all electrical connectors going to the speedometer from the junction box.

5. Remove the cap nuts securing the speedometer.

> *WARNING*
> *After the speedometer has been removed, set the speedometer down with the meter face and needle facing upward. If the speedometer is set face-down, the needle damping fluid will leak out onto the instrument face and lens.*

6. Remove the speedometer assembly.

7. Install by reversing these removal steps.

Fuel Tank Gauges
Removal/Installation
(1985-1986)

1. Remove the fuel tank as described in Chapter Seven.

2. Remove the Allen bolts and collars (A, **Figure 70**) securing the trim plate.

3. Remove the trim plate (B, **Figure 70**).

4. Push the gauges and rubber mounts (**Figure 71**) up and out of the fuel tank and remove them.

5. Install by reversing these removal steps.

8

Horn Removal/Installation

1. Disconnect the electrical connections (A, **Figure 72**) from the horn(s).

2A. On 1985-1986 models, remove the nuts and washers securing each horn to the mounting bracket and remove the horn (B, **Figure 72**) .

2B. On 1987-on models, remove the bolt and washer securing each horn to the rear cylinder head and remove the horns.

3. Install by reversing these removal steps. Make sure the electrical connections are tight and free of corrosion.

Horn Testing

Remove the horn as described in this chapter. Connect a 12-volt battery to the horn. If the horn is good, it will sound. If not, replace it.

Fuel Pump Flow Test

1. Turn the ignition switch to the OFF position.

2A. On 1985-1986 models, perform the following:

  a. Disconnect the electrical connector from the fuel pump relay.

  b. Connect a jumper wire between the black and the black/blue terminals at the main harness coupler.

  c. Disconnect the fuel line from the fuel pump.

2B. On 1987-on models, perform the following:

  a. Disconnect the electrical connector from the fuel pump.

  b. Connect a jumper wire between the black and the black/yellow terminals at the main harness coupler.

  c. Disconnect the fuel line from the "T" joint near the carburetor.

3. Place the loose end of the fuel line into a graduated beaker (**Figure 73**).

4. Turn the ignition switch ON and allow the fuel to run out of the fuel line (into the graduated beaker) for 5 seconds.

5. Turn the ignition OFF.

6. Multiply the amount of fuel in the beaker by 12 ($12 \times 5 = 60$ seconds). This will give the fuel pump flow capacity for one minute.

7. The fuel pump flow capacity for one minute should be as follows:

  a. 1985-1986 models: 650 cc (22 oz.) per minute.

  b. 1987-on models: 700 cc (23.7 oz.) per minute.

8. If the fuel pump does not flow to the specified capacity, it must be replaced. Refer to Chapter Seven.

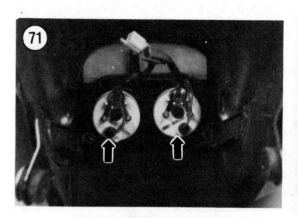

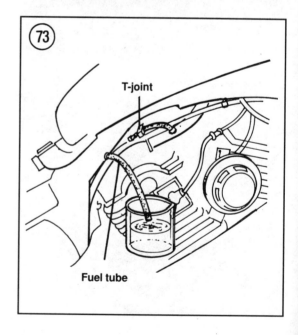

T-joint

Fuel tube

9. Reconnect the fuel line to the carburetors and the electrical connector to the fuel pump or relay.

Fuses

There are 7 fuses. On 1985-1986 models, the main fuse (**Figure 74**) is located adjacent to the starter relay. On 1987-on models, there is a 30 amp main fuse adjacent to the battery.

CAUTION
When replacing a fuse, make sure the ignition switch is OFF. This will lessen the chance of a short circuit.

The remaining fuses are located in the fuse panel. On 1985-1986 models, they are located under the cover on the handlebar holder. On 1987-on models, they are located on the left-hand side on the frame rear down tube.

NOTE
These fuses are not the typical glass tube with metal ends. Carry extra fuses in your tool box as this fuse type may not be available everywhere.

Whenever a fuse blows, find out why before replacing the fuse. Usually the trouble is a short circuit in the wiring. This may be caused by worn-through insulation or a disconnected wire shorted to ground.

CAUTION
Never substitute aluminum foil or wire for a fuse. Never use a higher amperage fuse than specified. An overload could cause a fire and complete loss of the motorcycle.

8

Tables are on the following page.

Table 1 IGNITION COIL RESISTANCE SPECIFICATIONS

Year	Resistance Value
1985-1986	
Primary coil resistance	Approx. 2 ohms
Secondary coil resistance	
With spark plug caps attached	21,000-39,900 ohms
With spark plug caps removed	20,600-27,400 ohms
Spark plug cap wire resistance	3,750-6,250 ohms
1987-on	
Primary coil resistance	2.0-2.6 ohms
Secondary coil resistance	
With spark plug caps attached	29,000-37,000 ohms
With spark plug caps removed	20,000-26,000 ohms
Spark plug cap wire resistance	NA

NA = Information not available from Honda.

Table 2 STARTER TROUBLESHOOTING

Symptom	Probable Cause	Remedy
Starter does not work	Low battery	Recharge battery
	Worn brushes	Replace brushes
	Defective relay	Repair or replace
	Defective switch	Repair or replace
	Defective wiring connection	Repair wire or clean connection
	Internal short circuit	Repair or replace defective component
Starter action is weak	Low battery	Recharge battery
	Pitted relay contacts	Clean or replace
	Worn brushes	Replace brushes
	Defective connection	Clean and tighten
	Short circuit in commutator	Replace armature
Starter runs continuously	Stuck relay	Replace relay
Starter turns; does not turn engine	Defective starter clutch	Replace starter clutch

Table 3 REPLACEMENT BULBS

Item	Wattage	Number
Headlight (quartz bulb)	12V 60/55	H4
Tail/brakelight	12V 3/32 cp	SAE No. 1157
Front turn signal and running light	12V 32 cp	SAE No. 1034
Rear turn signal	12V 32 cp	SAE No. 1073
Instrument lights		
1985-1986	12V 3W	—
1987-on	12V 1.7W	—
Indicator lights	12V 3W	—
High beam indicator	12V 3W	—
Turn signal indicator	12V 3W	—
Neutral indicator	12V 3W	—
Overdrive indicator (1985-1986)	12V 3W	—
Oil pressure warning	12V 3W	—

CHAPTER NINE

COOLING SYSTEM

The pressurized cooling system consists of the radiator, water pump, thermostat, electric cooling fan and a coolant reserve tank. The system uses a 73.5-103.0 kPa (10.7-14.9 psi) radiator fill cap and is designed to operate with a 180° F (82° C) thermostat, which is located on the right-hand side of the engine.

The water pump requires no routine maintenance and is replaced as a complete unit if defective.

It is important to keep the coolant level between the 2 marks on the coolant reserve tank (**Figure 1**). Always add coolant to the reserve tank, not to the radiator. If the cooling system requires repeated refilling, there is probably a leak somewhere in the system. Perform the *Cooling System Inspection* in Chapter Three.

> *CAUTION*
> *Drain and flush the cooling system at least every 2 years. Refill with a mixture of ethylene glycol antifreeze (formulated for aluminum engines) and distilled water. Do not reuse the old coolant as it deteriorates with use. Do **not** operate the cooling system with only distilled water (even in climates where antifreeze protection is not required). This is important because the engine is all aluminum; it will not rust but it will oxidize internally and have to be replaced. Refer to **Coolant Change** in Chapter Three.*

This chapter describes repair and replacement of cooling system components. **Table 1** at the end of this chapter lists all of the cooling system specifications. For routine maintenance of the cooling system, refer to Chapter Three.

> *WARNING*
> *Do not remove the radiator filler cap (**Figure 2**) when the engine is hot. The coolant is very hot and is under pressure. Severe scalding could result if the coolant comes in contact with your skin. If it is necessary to add coolant to the system, it should be added to the coolant recovery tank (**Figure 3**).*

The cooling system must be cool prior to removing any component of the system.

Major components of the cooling system are shown in **Figure 4** for 1985-1986 models or **Figure 5** for 1987-on models.

COOLING SYSTEM CHECK

Two checks should be made before disassembly, if a cooling system fault is suspected.

1. Run the engine until it reaches normal operating temperature. While the engine is running, a pressure surge should be felt when the upper radiator hose is squeezed.

2. If a substantial coolant loss is noted, one of the head gaskets may be blown. In extreme cases, sufficient coolant will leak into a cylinder(s) when the bike is left standing for several hours so the engine cannot be turned over with the starter. White smoke (steam) might also be observed at the muffler(s) when the engine is running. Coolant may also find its way into the oil. Unscrew the dipstick and look at the oil residue on it. If the oil looks like a "green chocolate malt" there is coolant in the oil system. If so, correct the cooling system problem immediately.

> *CAUTION*
> *After the cooling system problem is corrected, drain and thoroughly flush out the engine oil system to eliminate all coolant residue. Refill with fresh engine oil; refer to Chapter Three.*

RADIATOR

Removal/Installation

1. Remove the seat and both side covers.

2. Drain the cooling system as described in Chapter Three.

3. Disconnect the overflow tube from the radiator filler neck.

4A. On 1985-1986 models, remove the main fuel tank as described in Chapter Seven.

4B. On 1987-on models, remove the fuel tank as described in Chapter Seven.

5. Remove the screw securing the black radiator cover (**Figure 6**) and remove the radiator cover.

6. Disconnect the cooling fan 2-pin electrical connector.

7. Pull back the rubber boot and disconnect the electrical wires (**Figure 7**) from the thermostatic switch coupler at the base of the radiator.

8. Loosen the clamping screws on the upper (**Figure 8**) and lower (**Figure 9**) radiator hose bands.

9. Remove the radiator upper mounting bolt (**Figure 10**).

10. Pull the radiator slightly forward while working both radiator hoses loose from the radiator. Pull the radiator forward, up and out of the lower receptacles on the frame (**Figure 11**).

11. Install by reversing these removal steps while noting the following.

12. Replace both radiator hoses if either is starting to harden, deteriorate or is damaged.

13. Refill the cooling system with the recommended type and quantity of coolant as described in Chapter Three.

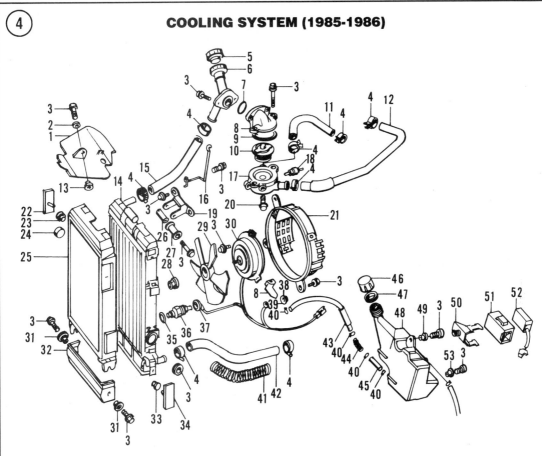

④

COOLING SYSTEM (1985-1986)

1. Cylinder head heat shield
2. Washer
3. Bolt
4. Hose clamp
5. Radiator cap
6. Filler neck
7. O-ring
8. Thermostat housing cover
9. O-ring
10. Thermostat
11. Hose
12. Hose
13. Nut
14. Radiator
15. Upper hose
16. Stay
17. Thermostat housing
18. Coolant temperature sending unit
19. Radiator mounting bracket
20. Bolt
21. Fan shroud
22. Reflector
23. Nut
24. Cap
25. Radiator cover
26. Collar
27. Spacer

28. Nut
29. Fan blade
30. Fan motor
31. Collar
32. Lower cover
33. Nut
34. Reflector
35. O-ring
36. Thermostatic switch
37. Connector
38. Nut
39. Connector
40. Hose clamp
41. Hose guard
42. Lower hose
43. Hose
44. Spring
45. Connector
46. Cap
47. Gasket
48. Coolant recovery tank
49. Metal collar
50. Mounting bracket
51. Rubber holder
52. Fuel cutoff relay
53. Metal collar

9

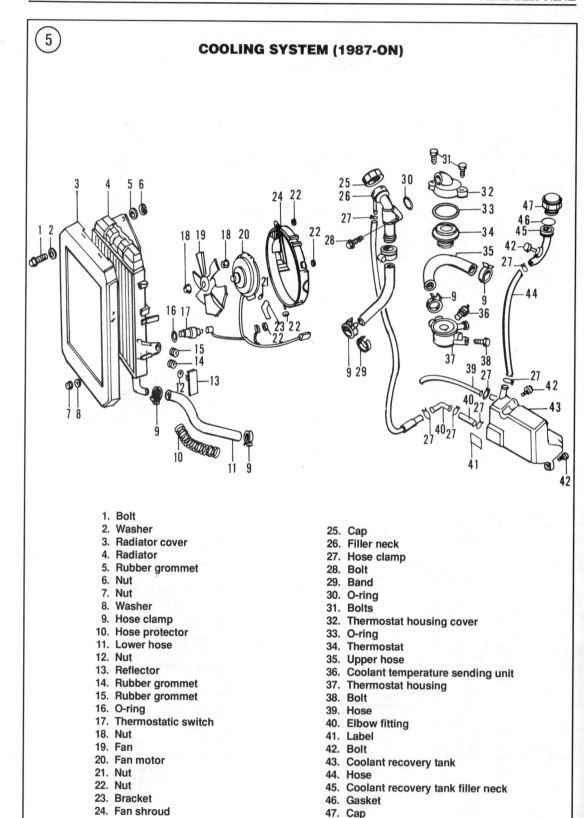

COOLING SYSTEM (1987-ON)

1. Bolt
2. Washer
3. Radiator cover
4. Radiator
5. Rubber grommet
6. Nut
7. Nut
8. Washer
9. Hose clamp
10. Hose protector
11. Lower hose
12. Nut
13. Reflector
14. Rubber grommet
15. Rubber grommet
16. O-ring
17. Thermostatic switch
18. Nut
19. Fan
20. Fan motor
21. Nut
22. Nut
23. Bracket
24. Fan shroud
25. Cap
26. Filler neck
27. Hose clamp
28. Bolt
29. Band
30. O-ring
31. Bolts
32. Thermostat housing cover
33. O-ring
34. Thermostat
35. Upper hose
36. Coolant temperature sending unit
37. Thermostat housing
38. Bolt
39. Hose
40. Elbow fitting
41. Label
42. Bolt
43. Coolant recovery tank
44. Hose
45. Coolant recovery tank filler neck
46. Gasket
47. Cap

Inspection

1. Flush off the exterior of the radiator with a garden hose on low pressure. Spray both the front and the back to remove all road dirt and bugs. Carefully use a whisk broom or stiff paint brush to remove any stubborn dirt.

> *CAUTION*
> *Do not press too hard or the cooling fins and tubes may be damaged.*

2. Carefully straighten out any bent cooling fins with a broad tipped screwdriver or putty knife.

3. Check for cracks or leakage (usually a moss-green colored residue) at the inlet (**Figure 12**) and outlet hose fittings and the upper and lower tank seams (**Figure 13**).

4. If the condition of the radiator is doubtful, have it pressure-checked as described in Chapter Three. The radiator can be pressure-checked while removed or installed on the bike.

COOLING FAN

Removal/Installation

1. Remove the radiator as described in this chapter.
2. Remove the ground nut and wire (**Figure 14**).
3. Remove the bolts securing the fan shroud and fan assembly and remove the assembly from the radiator (**Figure 15**).
4. To remove the fan blade from the motor, remove the nut and washers securing the fan blade to the motor and remove the fan blade.
5. To remove the fan motor, remove the screws securing the fan assembly to the fan shroud and remove the fan motor.
6. Install by reversing these removal steps while noting the following.
7. Apply red Loctite No. 271 to the threads on the fan motor shaft prior to installing the fan blade nut. Install the washer, lockwasher and nut and tighten the nut securely.
8. Refill the cooling system with the recommended type and quantity of coolant as described in Chapter Three.

THERMOSTAT

Removal/Installation
(1985-1986)

1. Remove the seat and both side covers.
2. Drain the cooling system as described in Chapter Three.
3. Disconnect the overflow tube from the radiator filler neck.
4. Remove the main fuel tank as described in Chapter Seven.
5. Remove the air filter case as described in Chapter Seven.
6. Remove the screw securing the black radiator cover (**Figure 6**) and remove the radiator cover.
7. Loosen the clamping screws on the upper (**Figure 8**) radiator hose band.
8. Remove the radiator upper mounting bolt (**Figure 10**).
9. Pull the upper portion of the radiator slightly forward while working the upper radiator hose loose from the radiator.
10. Remove the bolt securing the thermostat housing and the engine heat shield to the frame.

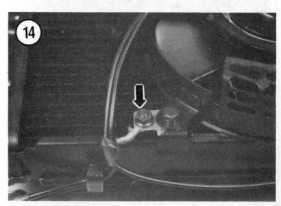

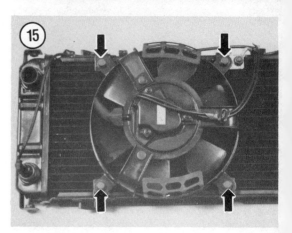

11. Pull the thermostat housing toward the rear and disconnect the coolant filler neck (A, **Figure 16**) from the housing.

12. Remove the bolts securing the thermostat housing cover (B, **Figure 16**) and remove the cover and gasket.

13. Remove the thermostat from the housing.

14. To remove the thermostat housing, perform the following:

    a. Disconnect the electrical connector to the temperature sensor (C, **Figure 16**).

    b. Remove the cooling hoses (D, **Figure 16**) from the housing.

    c. Remove the housing.

15. Install by reversing these removal steps while noting the following.

16. Make sure the O-ring seal in the thermostat housing cover is in good condition. If it is starting to deteriorate or has become brittle with age, it should be replaced as it will no longer seal properly.

17. Replace any coolant hoses that are starting to harden, deteriorate or are damaged.

18. Refill the cooling system with the recommended type and quantity of coolant as described in Chapter Three.

Removal/Installation (1987-on)

1. Remove the seat and both side covers.

2. Remove the fuel tank as described in Chapter Seven.

3. Drain the cooling system as described in Chapter Three.

4. Remove the bolts securing the steering stem side covers on each side and remove both covers.

5. Remove the fuel tank rubber protective straps from the frame.

6. Remove the screws securing the electrical wiring connector box and move the box out of the way.

7. Remove the bolts securing the ignition coils and bracket to the frame and move both coils toward the rear.

8. Remove the bolt securing the thermostat housing to the frame.

9. Remove the bolts securing the thermostat housing cover.

10. Remove the thermostat housing cover and O-ring seal.

11. Remove the thermostat from the housing.

12. To remove the thermostat housing, perform the following:

    a. Disconnect the electrical connector to the temperature sensor.

    b. Remove the cooling hoses from the housing.

    c. Remove the housing.

13. Install by reversing these removal steps while noting the following.

14. Make sure the O-ring seal in the thermostat housing cover is in good condition. If it is starting to deteriorate or has become brittle with age, it should be replaced as it will no longer seal properly.

15. Replace any coolant hoses that are starting to harden, deteriorate or are damaged.

16. Refill the cooling system with the recommended type and quantity of coolant as described in Chapter Three.

9

Thermostat Testing

Test the thermostat to ensure proper operation. The thermostat should be replaced if it remains open at normal room temperature or stays closed after the specified temperature has been reached during the test procedure.

Place the thermostat on a small piece of wood in a pan of water (**Figure 17**). Place a thermometer in the pan of water (use a cooking or candy thermometer that is rated higher than the test temperature). Gradually heat the water and continue to stir the water gently until it reaches 176-183° F (80-84° C). At this temperature, the thermostat valve should open.

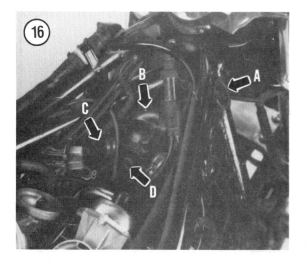

NOTE
Valve operation is sometimes sluggish; it usually takes 3-5 minutes for the valve to operate properly.

If the valve fails to open, the thermostat should be replaced (it cannot be serviced). Be sure to replace it with one of the same temperature rating.

WATER PUMP

Mechanical Seal Inspection

Check the lower area of the water pump for signs of coolant leakage (usually a moss-green colored residue).

If the mechanical seal is leaking, the coolant will drip out of the weep hole in the bottom of the water pump. If the seal is leaking, the water pump assembly must be replaced. It cannot be serviced.

Removal

Refer to **Figure 18** for this procedure.

1. Remove the engine from the frame as described in Chapter Four.

2. Remove the coolant pipes from the engine and water pump as described in this chapter.

3. If still attached, remove the radiator lower hose from the water pump.

4. Remove the bolts (**Figure 19**) securing the water pump cover and remove the cover. Don't lose the locating dowels.

5. Withdraw the water pump from the crankcase.

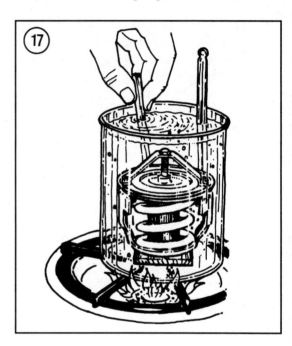

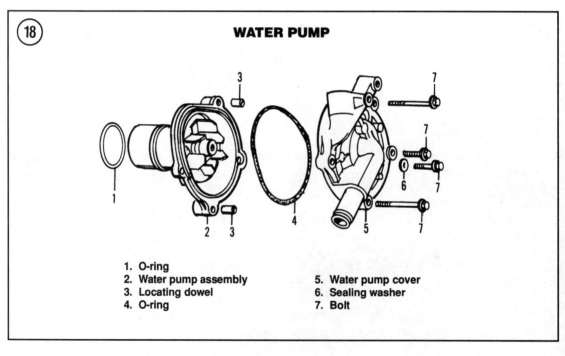

WATER PUMP

1. O-ring
2. Water pump assembly
3. Locating dowel
4. O-ring
5. Water pump cover
6. Sealing washer
7. Bolt

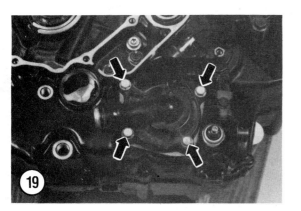

Inspection

1. Inspect the water pump assembly for wear or damage.

2. Rotate the impeller to make sure the bearings are not worn or damaged. If the bearings are damaged, the assembly must be replaced, as it cannot be serviced.

3. Check the impeller blades (**Figure 20**) for wear or damage.

4. Rotate the water pump shaft (**Figure 21**). It should rotate smoothly with no binding.

5. Remove the O-ring seal (**Figure 22**) in the water pump assembly. Replace with a new one.

6. Inspect the cover and inlet and outlet pipes for cracks or damage (**Figure 23**). If damaged, the assembly must be replaced—it cannot be serviced.

Installation

1. If removed, install the locating dowels into the water pump assembly.

2. Within the crankcase, rotate the oil pump shaft so the tab on the end of the shaft is vertical (**Figure 24**).

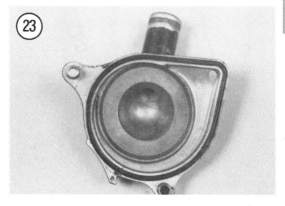

9

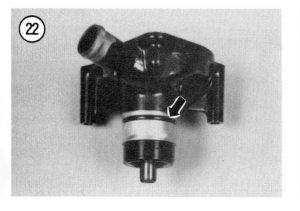

3. Apply a coat of clean engine oil to the new O-ring seal (**Figure 22**) on the water pump housing.

4. Position the groove on the water pump shaft vertically so it will align with the tab on the oil pump shaft.

5. Install the water pump into the crankcase and slightly wiggle the water pump impeller to assure proper alignment of the tab and groove. Push the water pump assembly all the way on until it is properly seated against the crankcase. The assembly should fit snugly without using any force. If it will not fit properly, withdraw the assembly and realign the tab of the oil pump shaft and the groove on the water pump.

CAUTION
Do not install the cover nor any bolts until the assembly is completely seated against the crankcase. Do not try to force the assembly into place with the mounting screws.

6. Make sure the dowel pins are installed in the water pump assembly.

7. Make sure the O-ring seal is installed in the water pump assembly.

8. Install the water pump cover and the bolts and tighten the bolts securely.

9. Connect the electrical connector onto the oil pressure switch.

10. Install the coolant pipes onto the engine and water pump as described in this chapter.

11. Install the engine into the frame as described in Chapter Four.

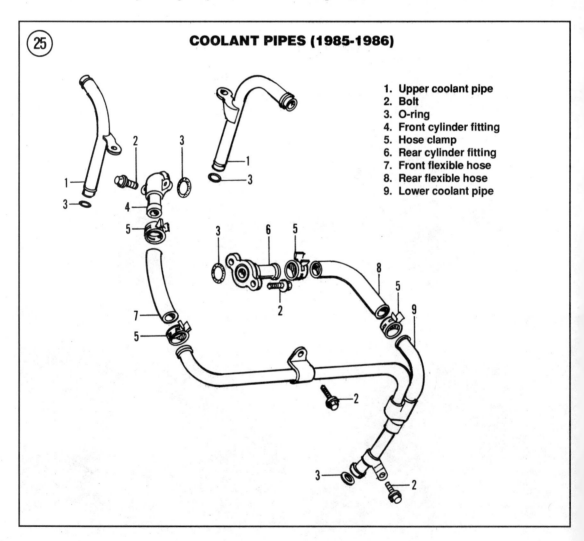

COOLANT PIPES (1985-1986)

1. Upper coolant pipe
2. Bolt
3. O-ring
4. Front cylinder fitting
5. Hose clamp
6. Rear cylinder fitting
7. Front flexible hose
8. Rear flexible hose
9. Lower coolant pipe

12. Refill the cooling system with the recommended type and quantity of coolant as described in Chapter Three.

13. Start the bike and check for leaks.

COOLANT PIPES

Removal/Installation

Refer to **Figure 25** for 1985-1986 models or **Figure 26** for 1987-on models for this procedure.

1. Remove the engine from the frame as described in Chapter Four.

2. Remove the front cylinder upper coolant pipe from the front cylinder (A, **Figure 27**) and rear cylinder (B, **Figure 27**).

3. Remove the bolts securing the lower coolant pipe to the front cylinder (**Figure 28**) and rear cylinder (**Figure 29**).

4. Remove the bolts (A, **Figure 30**) securing the lower coolant pipe to the crankcase and remove the coolant pipe assembly (B, **Figure 30**).

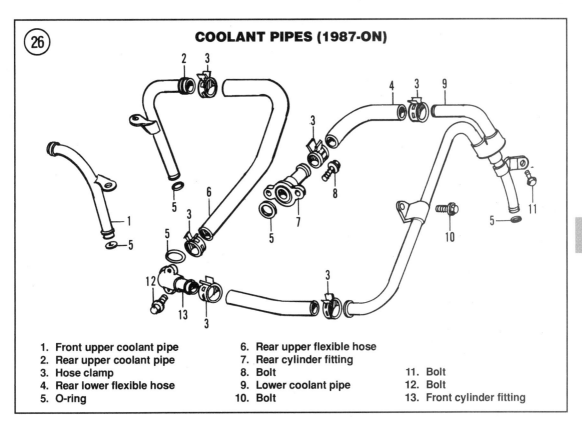

COOLANT PIPES (1987-ON)

1. Front upper coolant pipe	6. Rear upper flexible hose
2. Rear upper coolant pipe	7. Rear cylinder fitting
3. Hose clamp	8. Bolt
4. Rear lower flexible hose	9. Lower coolant pipe
5. O-ring	10. Bolt

11. Bolt	
12. Bolt	
13. Front cylinder fitting	

5. Inspect the flexible hoses (**Figure 31**) on the coolant pipe assembly. If they are starting to harden or deteriorate, they should be replaced.

6. Install by reversing these removal steps while noting the following.

7. Install new O-ring seals (**Figure 32**) on all coolant pipes.

8. Refill the cooling system with the recommended type and quantity of coolant as described in Chapter Three.

COOLANT HOSES

Hoses deteriorate with age and should be replaced periodically or whenever they show signs of cracking or leakage. To be safe, replace the hoses every 2 years. The spray of hot coolant from a cracked hose can injure the rider and passenger. Loss of coolant can also cause engine damage.

Whenever any component of the cooling system is removed, inspect the hose(s) and determine if replacement is necessary.

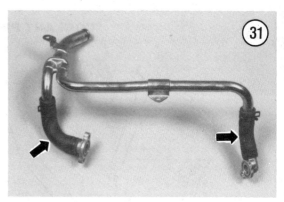

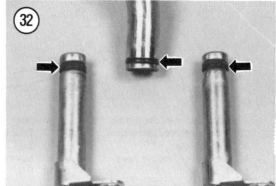

Table 1 COOLING SYSTEM SPECIFICATIONS

Coolant capacity	
Total system	2.20 liters (2.31 US qt., 1.94 Imp. qt.)
Radiator and engine	1.86 liters (1.95 US qt., 1.64 Imp. qt.)
Reserve tank	0.34 liters (0.36 US qt., 0.30 Imp. qt.)
Radiator cap relief pressure	73.5-103.0 kPa (10.7-14.9 psi)
Thermostat	
Begins to open	80-84° C (176-183° F)
Valve lift	Minimum of 8 mm @ 95° C (203° F)
Boiling point (50:50 mixture)	
Unpressurized	107.7° C (226° F)
Pressurized (cap on)	125.6° C (258° F)
Freezing point (hydrometer test)	
55:45 water/antifreeze ratio	-32° C (-25° F)
50:50 water/antifreeze ratio	-37° C (-34° F)
45:55 water/antifreeze ratio	-45° C (-48° F)

9

FRONT SUSPENSION AND STEERING

This chapter describes repair and maintenance procedures for the front wheel, forks and steering components.

Front suspension torque specifications are covered in **Table 1**. **Tables 1-4** are at the end of this chapter.

FRONT WHEEL

Removal

1. Place the bike on the centerstand or place wood blocks under the engine or frame to support it securely with the front wheel off the ground.

2. Remove the speedometer cable set screw (A, **Figure 1**). Pull the speedometer cable (B, **Figure 1**) free from the speedometer gear box.

3. On 1985-1986 models, remove the left-hand brake caliper as described in Chapter Twelve.

NOTE
Insert a piece of vinyl tubing or wood into the caliper(s) in place of the brake disc(s). That way if the brake lever is inadvertently squeezed, the pistons will

not be forced out of the cylinder. If this does happen, the caliper may have to be disassembled to reseat the pistons and the system will have to be bled. By using the wood, bleeding the brake is not necessary when installing the wheel.

4A. On 1985-1986 models, perform the following:

   a. Remove the nuts (**Figure 2**) securing the axle holder on each side and remove both holders.

   b. Pull the wheel and front axle assembly down and forward and remove it.

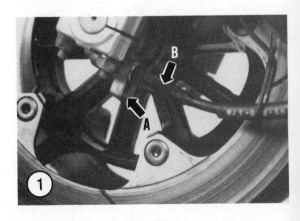

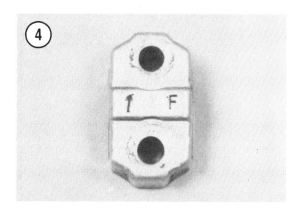

4B. On 1987-on models, perform the following:

   a. Loosen the axle pinch bolts on the right-hand side and remove the axle pinch bolts.

   b. Unscrew the front axle from the right-hand fork leg.

   c. Pull the wheel forward and remove it.

CAUTION
*Do not set the wheel down on the disc surface as it may get scratched or warped. Set the sidewalls on 2 wood blocks (**Figure 3**).*

Installation

1. Make sure the axle bearing surfaces of the fork slider and axle are free from burrs and nicks.

2. Remove the vinyl tubing or piece(s) of wood from the brake caliper(s).

3. Make sure the side collar is in place on the right-hand side and the speedometer gear box is in place on the left-hand side.

4. Position the wheel into place.

5. Position the speedometer housing tang *behind* the raised boss on the left-hand fork.

6A. On 1985-1986 models, perform the following:

   a. Move the wheel and front axle assembly into position.

   b. Install the axle holders so that the arrow (**Figure 4**) on the bottom of the holders faces to the front.

   c. Install the axle holder nuts (**Figure 2**). Tighten the front nuts and then the rear nuts to the torque specifications in **Table 1**. After the nuts have been tightened, there must be a gap at the rear (**Figure 5**).

6B. On 1987-on models, perform the following:

   a. Insert the front axle from the left-hand side and screw it into the right-hand fork leg.

   b. Tighten the front axle to the torque specification listed in **Table 1**.

   c. Install and tighten the axle pinch bolts on the right-hand side.

   d. Tighten the axle pinch bolts to the torque specifications in **Table 1**.

7. On 1985-1986 models, install the left-hand brake caliper as described in Chapter Twelve. Be careful not to damage the brake pads.

10

8. Slowly rotate the wheel and install the speedometer cable into the speedometer housing. Install the cable set screw and tighten securely.

9. After the wheel is completely installed, rotate it several times and apply the front brake a couple of times to make sure that it rotates freely and that the brake pads are against the disc(s) correctly.

Inspection

Measure the axial and radial runout of the wheel with a dial indicator as shown in **Figure 6**. The maximum axial and radial runout is 2.0 mm (0.08 in.). If the runout exceeds this dimension, check the wheel bearing condition.

If the wheel bearings are okay, the alloy wheel will have to be replaced as it cannot be serviced. Inspect the wheel for signs of cracks, fractures, dents or bends. If it is damaged in any way, it must be replaced.

> *WARNING*
> *Do not try to repair any damage to an alloy wheel as it will result in an unsafe riding condition.*

Check axle runout as described under *Front Hub Inspection* in this chapter.

FRONT HUB

Inspection

Inspect each wheel bearing prior to removing it from the wheel hub.

> *CAUTION*
> *Do not remove the wheel bearings for inspection as they will be damaged during removal. Remove wheel bearings only if they are to be replaced.*

1. Perform Steps 1-4 of *Front Hub Disassembly* in this chapter.

2. Turn each bearing by hand (**Figure 7**). Make sure the bearings turn smoothly.

3. On non-sealed bearings, check the balls for evidence of wear, pitting or excessive heat (bluish tint). Replace the bearings if necessary; always replace as a complete set. When replacing the bearings, be sure to take your old bearings along to ensure a perfect match.

> *NOTE*
> *Fully sealed bearings are available from many bearing specialty shops. Fully sealed bearings provide better protection from dirt and moisture that may get into the hub.*

4. Check the axle for wear and straightness. Use V-blocks and a dial indicator as shown in **Figure 8**.

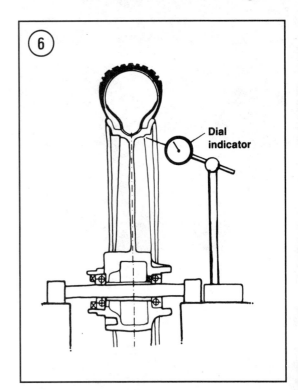

Dial indicator

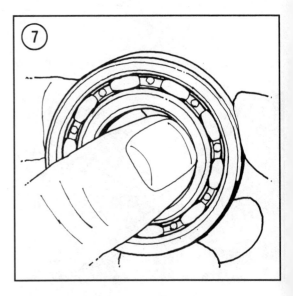

If the runout is 0.2 mm (0.01 in.) or greater, the axle should be replaced.

Disassembly

Refer to **Figure 9** for 1985-1986 models or **Figure 10** for 1987-on models for this procedure.

1. Remove the front wheel as described in this chapter.

2A. On 1985-1986 models, perform the following:

  a. Hold the left side of the axle with a wrench.

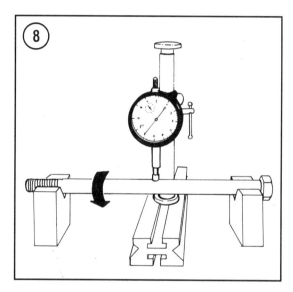

  b. Loosen and remove the right-hand axle nut (A, **Figure 11**).

  c. Remove the axle (A, **Figure 12**) from the left-hand side.

  d. Remove the speedometer gear box (B, **Figure 12**) from the left-hand side.

  e. Remove the side collar (B, **Figure 11**) from the right-hand side.

2B. On 1987-on models, perform the following:

  a. Remove the side collar from the right-hand side.

  b. Remove the speedometer housing from the left-hand side.

3. Remove the grease seal (**Figure 13**) from the right-hand side.

4. Remove the grease seal (A, **Figure 14**) and speedometer drive dog (B, **Figure 14**) from the left-hand side.

5. Before proceeding further, inspect the wheel bearings as described in this chapter. If they must be replaced, proceed as follows.

NOTE
*On 1985-1986 models, the brake discs are marked with a "R" (right-hand side) and "L" (left-hand side) (**Figure 15**). The brake discs must be reinstalled on the correct side for proper brake operation.*

10

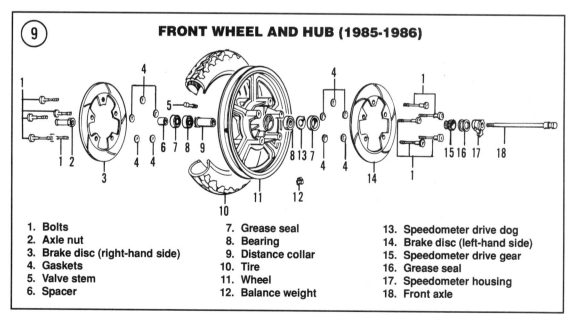

FRONT WHEEL AND HUB (1985-1986)

1. Bolts
2. Axle nut
3. Brake disc (right-hand side)
4. Gaskets
5. Valve stem
6. Spacer
7. Grease seal
8. Bearing
9. Distance collar
10. Tire
11. Wheel
12. Balance weight
13. Speedometer drive dog
14. Brake disc (left-hand side)
15. Speedometer drive gear
16. Grease seal
17. Speedometer housing
18. Front axle

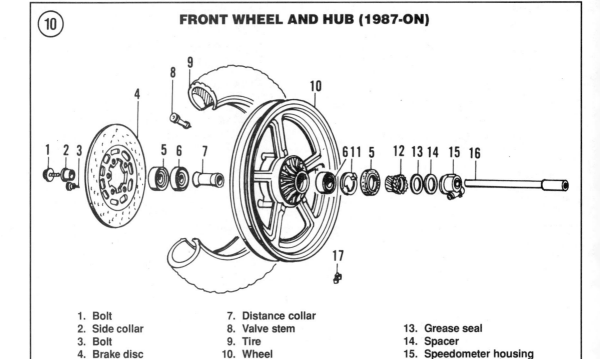

FRONT WHEEL AND HUB (1987-ON)

1. Bolt
2. Side collar
3. Bolt
4. Brake disc
5. Grease seal
6. Bearing
7. Distance collar
8. Valve stem
9. Tire
10. Wheel
11. Speedometer drive dog
12. Speedometer drive gear
13. Grease seal
14. Spacer
15. Speedometer housing
16. Front axle
17. Balance weight

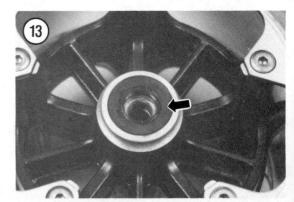

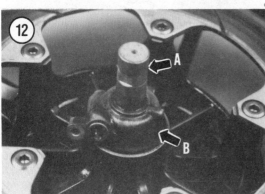

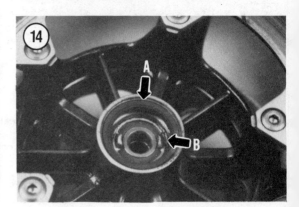

6. Remove the bolts (**Figure 16**) securing the brake disc(s) and remove the discs.

7A. A special Honda tool set-up can be used to remove the wheel bearings as follows:

    a. On 1985-1986 models, install the 15 mm bearing remover (Honda part No. 07746-0050400) into the right-hand bearing.

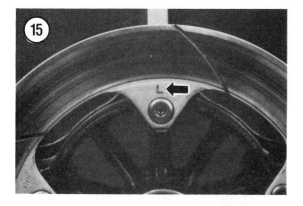

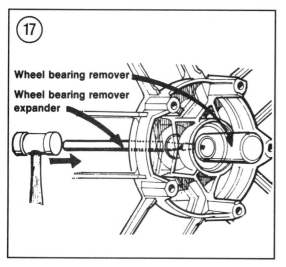

Wheel bearing remover

Wheel bearing remover expander

    b. On 1987-on models, install the 20 mm bearing remover (Honda part No. 07746-0050600) into the right-hand bearing.

    c. Turn the wheel over (left-hand side up) on the workbench so the bearing remover is touching the workbench surface.

    d. From the left-hand side of the hub, install the bearing remover expander (Honda part No. 07746-050100) into the bearing remover. Using a hammer, tap the expander into the bearing remover with a hammer.

    e. Stand the wheel up to a vertical position.

    f. Tap on the end of the expander (**Figure 17**) and drive the right bearing out of the hub. Remove the bearing and the distance collar.

    g. Repeat for the left bearing.

7B. If special tools are not available, perform the following:

    a. To remove the right- and left-hand bearings and distance collar, insert a soft aluminum or brass drift into one side of the hub.

    b. Push the distance collar over to one side and place the drift on the inner race of the lower bearing.

    c. Tap the bearing out of the hub with a hammer, working around the perimeter of the inner race.

    d. Repeat for the other bearing.

8. Clean the inside and the outside of the hub with solvent. Dry with compressed air.

Assembly

1. On non-sealed bearings, pack the bearings with a good-quality bearing grease. Work the grease in between the balls thoroughly; turn the bearing by hand a couple of times to make sure the grease is distributed evenly inside the bearing.

2. Blow any dirt or foreign matter out of the hub prior to installing the bearings.

> *CAUTION*
> *Install non-sealed bearings with the single sealed side facing outward. Tap the bearings squarely into place and tap on the outer race only. Use a socket (**Figure 18**) that matches the outer race diameter. Do not tap on the inner race or the bearing might be damaged. Be sure that the bearings are completely seated.*

10

3. Install the right-hand bearing and press the distance collar into place.

4. Install the left-hand bearing.

5. Install the brake disc(s).

> *NOTE*
> *On 1985-1986 models, the brake discs must be reinstalled on the correct side for proper brake operation. Refer to the marks on the brake discs: "R" (right-hand side) or "L" (left-hand side) (**Figure 15**).*

6. On 1985-1990 models, apply a light coat of grease or oil to the brake disc bolts. On all models, install the bolts (**Figure 16**) and tighten to the torque specification listed in **Table 1**. On 1985-1986 models, repeat for the other disc.

7. Install the grease seal (**Figure 13**) on the right-hand side.

8. Install the speedometer drive dog (B, **Figure 14**) and the grease seal (A, **Figure 14**) into the left-hand side.

9. Align the tangs of the speedometer drive gear with the drive dog in the hub and install the speedometer gear box (B, **Figure 12**).

10. Install the side collar (B, **Figure 11**) on the right-hand side.

11. On 1985-1986 models, perform the following:

    a. Insert the axle (A, **Figure 12**) in from the left-hand side.

    b. Install the axle nut (A, **Figure 11**) and tighten it to the torque specifications in **Table 1**.

12. Install the front wheel as described in this chapter.

WHEEL BALANCE

An unbalanced wheel is unsafe. Depending on the degree of unbalance and the speed of the motorcycle, the rider may experience anything from a mild vibration to a violent shimmy which may even result in loss of control.

On alloy wheels, weights are attached to the rim. A kit of Tape-A-Weight or equivalent may be purchased from most motorcycle supply stores. This kit contains test weights and strips of adhesive-backed weights that can be cut to the desired weight and attached directly to the rim.

Before you attempt to balance the wheel, check to be sure that the wheel bearings are in good condition and properly lubricated and that the brakes do not drag. The wheel must rotate freely.

1. Remove the wheel as described in this chapter or Chapter Eleven.

2. Mount the wheel on a fixture such as the one shown in **Figure 19** so it can rotate freely.

3. Give the wheel a spin and let it coast to a stop. Mark the tire at the lowest point.

4. Spin the wheel several more times. If the wheel keeps coming to rest at the same point, it is out of balance.

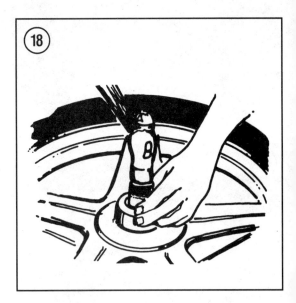

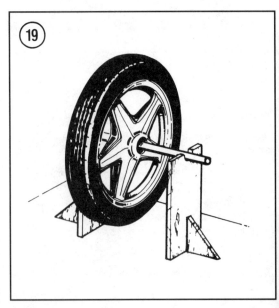

5. Tape a test weight to the upper (or light) side of the wheel.

6. Experiment with different weights until the wheel, when spun, comes to a rest at a different position each time.

7. Remove the test weight and install the correct size adhesive-backed or clamp-on weight (**Figure 20**).

TIRE CHANGING

The rim of the alloy wheel is aluminum and the exterior appearance can easily be damaged. Special care must be taken with tire irons when changing a tire to avoid scratches and gouges to the outer rim surface. Insert scraps of leather between the tire iron and the rim to protect the rim from gouges. Honda offers rim protectors (part No. 07772-0020200) for this purpose that are very handy to use. All models are factory-equipped with tubeless tires and wheels designed specifically for use with tubeless tires.

> *WARNING*
> *Do not install tubeless tires on wheels designed for use only with tube-type tires. Personal injury and tire failure may result from rapid tire deflation while riding. Wheels for use with tubeless tires are so marked.*

Removal

1. Remove the valve core to deflate the tire.

2. Press the entire bead on both sides of the tire into the center of the rim. Lubricate the beads with soapy water.

3. Insert the tire iron under the bead next to the valve (**Figure 21**). Force the bead on the opposite side of the tire into the center of the rim and pry the bead over the rim with the tire iron.

4. Insert a second tire iron next to the first to hold the bead over the rim. Then work around the tire with the first tire iron, prying the bead over the rim (**Figure 22**).

5. Stand the tire upright. Insert the tire iron between the second bead and the side of the rim that the first bead was pried over (**Figure 23**). Force the bead on the opposite side from the tire iron into the center of the rim. Pry the second bead off the rim, working around as with the first.

6. Honda recommends that the tire valve stem be replaced whenever the tire is removed from the wheel.

Installation

1. Carefully inspect the tire for any damage, especially inside.

2. A new tire may have balancing rubbers inside. These are not patches and should not be disturbed. A colored spot near the bead indicates a lighter point on the tire. This spot (**Figure 24**) should be placed next to the valve stem.

3. Install the tire so that it revolves in the proper direction. The tire is marked with an arrow and "Direction" on the sidewall (**Figure 25**).

4. Lubricate both beads of the tire with soapy water.

5. Place the backside of the tire into the center of the rim. The lower bead should go into the center of the rim and the upper bead outside. Work around the tire in both directions (**Figure 26**). Use a tire iron for the last few inches of bead (**Figure 27**).

6. Press the upper bead into the rim opposite the valve (**Figure 28**). Pry the bead into the rim on both sides of the initial point with a tire iron, working around the rim to the valve (**Figure 29**).

7. Check the bead on both sides of the tire for even fit around the rim.

8. Bounce the wheel several times, rotating it each time. This will force the tire beads against the rim flanges. After the tire beads are in contact with the rim evenly, inflate the tire to seat the beads.

> *NOTE*
> *If you are unable to get an airtight seal this way, install an inflatable band around the circumference of the tire.*

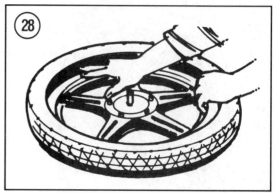

*Slowly inflate the band until the beads
are seated against the rim flanges, then
inflate the tire. If you still encounter
trouble, deflate the inflation band and
the tire. Apply additional lubricant to
the beads and repeat the inflation procedure. Also try rolling the tire back and
forth while inflating it.*

9. Inflate the tire to more than the recommended
inflation pressure for the initial seating of the rim
flanges. Once the beads are seated correctly, deflate
the tire to the correct pressure. Refer to **Table 2**.

WARNING
*Never exceed 4.0 kg/cm^2 (56 psi) infla-
tion pressure as the tire could burst
causing severe injury. Never stand directly over the tire while inflating it.*

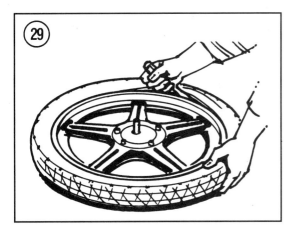

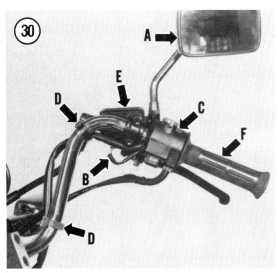

TIRE REPAIRS

Patching a tubeless tire on the road is very difficult. If both beads are still in place against the rim,
a can of pressurized tire sealant may inflate the tire
and seal the hole. The beads must be against the
wheel for this method to work. Another solution is
to carry a spare inner tube that could be temporarily
installed and inflated. This will enable you to get to
a service station where the tire can be correctly
repaired. Be sure that the tube is designed for use
with a tubeless tire.

Honda (and the tire industry) recommends that the
tubeless tire be patched from the inside. Therefore,
do not patch the tire with an external type plug. If
you find an external patch on a tire, it is recommended that it be patch-reinforced from the inside.

Due to the variations of material supplied with
different tubeless tire repair kits, follow the instructions and recommendations supplied with the repair
kit.

Honda recommends that the valve stem be replaced each time the tire is removed from the wheel.

HANDLEBAR

Removal

1. Remove the left-hand side cover.
2. Disconnect the battery negative lead.
3. Remove the right-hand rear view mirror (A, **Figure 30**).
4. Disconnect the brake light switch electrical connector (B, **Figure 30**).
5. Remove the screws securing the right handlebar
switch assembly (C, **Figure 30**) and remove the
electrical wires from the clips (D, **Figure 30**) on the
handlebar.

CAUTION
*Cover the frame with a heavy cloth or
plastic tarp to protect it from accidental
spilling of brake fluid. Wash any spilled
brake fluid off any painted or plated
surface immediately, as it will destroy
the finish. Use soapy water and rinse
thoroughly.*

6. Remove the 2 bolts securing the brake master
cylinder (E, **Figure 30**) and lay it over the frame.
Keep the reservoir in the upright position to minimize loss of brake fluid and to keep air from entering

10

into the brake system. It is not necessary to remove the hydraulic brake line.

7. Remove the throttle assembly (F, **Figure 30**) and carefully lay the throttle assembly and cables over the fender or back over the frame. Be careful that the cables do not get crimped or damaged.

8. Remove the left-hand rear view mirror (A, **Figure 31**).

9. Disconnect the clutch switch wires.

10. Remove the 2 bolts securing the clutch master cylinder (B, **Figure 31**) and lay it over the frame. Keep the reservoir in the upright position to minimize loss of hydraulic fluid and to keep air from entering the clutch system. It is not necessary to remove the hydraulic line.

11. Disconnect the choke cable from the choke lever.

12. Remove the screws securing the left-hand handlebar switch assembly (C, **Figure 31**) and remove the electrical wires from the clips on the handlebar (D, **Figure 31**).

13A. On 1985-1986 models, perform the following:

 a. Remove the handlebar center cover.

 b. Remove the plastic plugs and remove the Allen bolts securing the handlebar upper holder in place.

 c. Remove the handlebar upper holder then remove the handlebar.

13B. On 1987-on models, perform the following:

 a. Remove the plastic plugs and remove the Allen bolts securing the handlebar upper holders in place.

 b. Remove the handlebar upper holders then remove the handlebar.

14. To maintain a good grip on the handlebar and to prevent it from slipping down, clean the knurled section of the handlebar with a wire brush. It should be kept rough so it will be held securely by the holders. The handlebar holder and the holders on the upper fork bridge should also be kept clean and free of any metal that may have been gouged loose by handlebar slippage.

Installation

1. Position the handlebar on the upper fork bridge so the punch mark on the handlebar is aligned with the top surface of the raised portion of the upper fork bridge.

2A. On 1985-1986 models, perform the following:

 a. Install the handlebar upper holder over the handlebar.

 b. Install the Allen bolts securing the handlebar upper holder in place.

 c. Tighten the forward bolts first and then the rear bolts. Tighten all bolts to the torque specification listed in **Table 1**.

 d. Install the plastic plugs.

 e. Install the handlebar center cover.

2B. On 1987-on models, perform the following:

 a. Install the handlebar upper holders over the handlebar.

 b. Install the Allen bolts securing the handlebar upper holders in place.

 c. Tighten the forward bolts first and then the rear bolts. Tighten all bolts to the torque specification listed in **Table 1**.

 d. Install the plastic plugs.

3. After installation is complete, recheck the alignment of the handlebar punch mark.

4. Apply a light coat of multipurpose grease to the throttle grip area on the handlebar prior to installing the throttle grip assembly.

NOTE
When installing all assemblies, align the punch mark on the handlebar with the slit on the mounting bracket.

5. Install the throttle grip assembly and right-hand switch assembly.

6. Install the brake master cylinder onto the handlebar. Install the clamp with the punch mark facing down or with the "UP" arrow (**Figure 32**) facing up

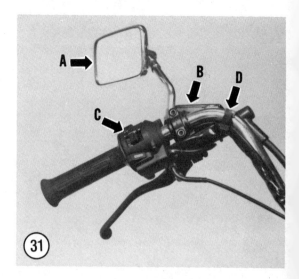

and align the clamp mating surface with the punch mark on the handlebar. Tighten the upper bolt first and then the lower bolt.

WARNING
After installation is completed, make sure the brake lever does not come in contact with the throttle grip assembly when it is pulled on fully. If it does, the brake fluid may be low in the reservoir; refill as necessary. Refer to Chapter Twelve.

7. Install the clutch master cylinder onto the handlebar. Install the clamp and tighten the upper bolt first and then the lower bolt.

WARNING
After installation is completed, make sure the clutch lever does not come in contact with the hand grip assembly when it is pulled on fully. If it does, the hydraulic fluid may be low in the reservoir; refill as necessary. Refer to Clutch Master Cylinder in Chapter Five.

8. Connect the choke cable to the choke lever.

9. Install the left-hand handlebar switch assembly and tighten the bolts securely.

10. Install the clips onto the electrical wires on the handlebar.

11. Connect the battery negative lead to the battery.

12. Install the rear view mirrors.

13. Adjust the throttle operation as described in Chapter Three.

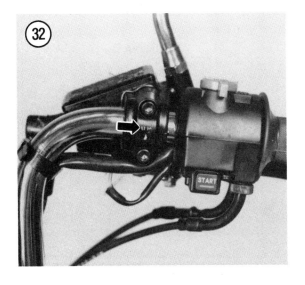

STEERING HEAD AND STEM

Disassembly

Refer to **Figure 33** for 1985-1986 models or **Figure 34** for 1987-on models for this procedure.

1. Remove the front wheel as described in this chapter.

2. Remove the handlebar (A, **Figure 35**) as described in this chapter.

3. Remove the headlight assembly (B, **Figure 35**) as described in Chapter Eight.

4A. On 1985-1986 models, remove the instrument cluster (C, **Figure 35**) as described in Chapter Eight.

4B. On 1987-on models, remove the speedometer as described in Chapter Eight.

5. Remove the ignition switch as described in Chapter Eight.

6. On 1985-1986 models, remove the front brake 3-way fitting from the base of the steering stem as described in Chapter Twelve. It is not necessary to disconnect any of the hydraulic lines. If any of the lines are disconnected or loosened, the brake system will have to be bled as described in Chapter Twelve.

7. Remove the steering stem nut.

8. Remove the front forks as described in this chapter.

9. Remove the upper fork bridge.

10. On 1985-1986 models, remove the horns as described in Chapter Eight.

NOTE
When removing the bearing adjustment nut in Step 12, loosen the nut with a large drift and hammer or use the easily improvised tool as shown in Figure 36.

11. Pry the lockwasher tab(s) away from the bearing adjustment nut (**Figure 37**).

12. Lift the bearing adjustment nut lockwasher (**Figure 37**) off of the steering stem.

13. Loosen and remove the bearing adjustment nut (**Figure 38**) and remove the upper bearing inner race (**Figure 39**).

14. Lower the steering stem assembly down and out of the steering head.

Inspection

1. Clean the bearing races in the steering head and the bearings with solvent.

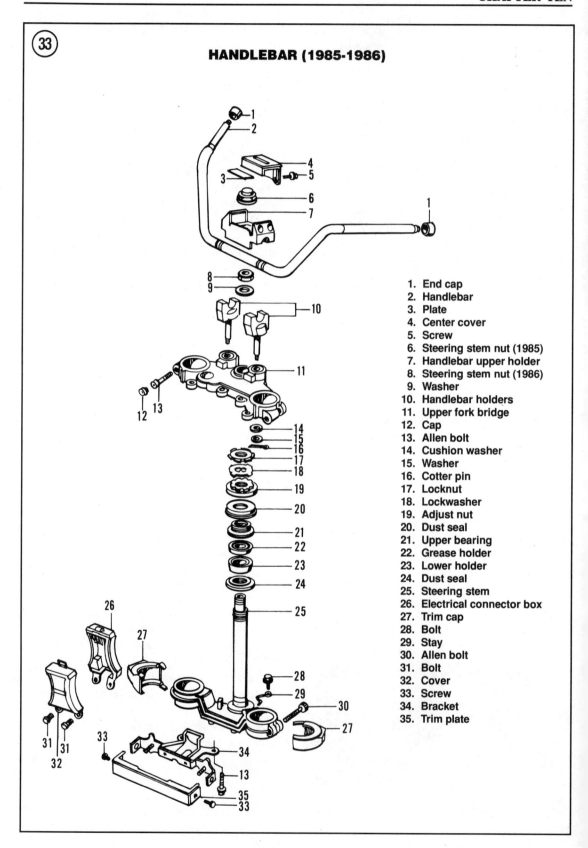

HANDLEBAR (1985-1986)

1. End cap
2. Handlebar
3. Plate
4. Center cover
5. Screw
6. Steering stem nut (1985)
7. Handlebar upper holder
8. Steering stem nut (1986)
9. Washer
10. Handlebar holders
11. Upper fork bridge
12. Cap
13. Allen bolt
14. Cushion washer
15. Washer
16. Cotter pin
17. Locknut
18. Lockwasher
19. Adjust nut
20. Dust seal
21. Upper bearing
22. Grease holder
23. Lower holder
24. Dust seal
25. Steering stem
26. Electrical connector box
27. Trim cap
28. Bolt
29. Stay
30. Allen bolt
31. Bolt
32. Cover
33. Screw
34. Bracket
35. Trim plate

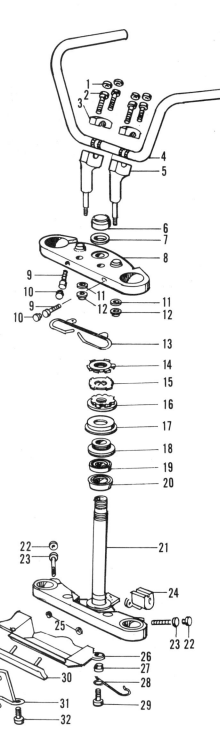

(34)

HANDLEBAR (1987-ON)

1. Trim cap
2. Bolt
3. Handlebar upper holder
4. Handlebar
5. Handlebar upper holder
6. Steering stem nut
7. Washer
8. Upper fork bridge
9. Allen bolt
10. Cap
11. Cushion washer
12. Washer
13. Stay
14. Locknut
15. Lockwasher
16. Adjust nut
17. Dust seal
18. Upper bearing
19. Grease holder
20. Lower holder
21. Steering stem
22. Cap
23. Allen bolt
24. Lock
25. Nuts
26. Bracket
27. Collar
28. Stay
29. Bolt
30. Trim plate
31. Stay
32. Bolt

10

2. Check the welds around the steering head for cracks and fractures. If any are found, have them repaired by a competent frame shop or welding service.

3. Check the bearings for pitting, scratches or discoloration indicating wear or corrosion.

4. Turn the bearings by hand and check for excessive noise, looseness or roughness. After cleaning the bearings, dip them in clean engine oil and cover them with a clean rag to prevent contamination.

5. Check the races for pitting, galling and corrosion. If any of these conditions exist, replace the races as described in this chapter.

6. Check the steering stem for cracks and check its races for damage or wear; replace if necessary.

Assembly

Refer to **Figure 33** for 1985-1986 models or **Figure 34** for 1987-on models for this procedure.

1. Make sure both steering head bearing outer races are properly seated in the steering head tube.

2. Apply a coat of cold grease to the upper bearing outer race and to the upper bearing.

3. Install the upper bearing into the upper bearing outer race.

4. Apply a coat of cold grease to the lower bearing inner race and to the lower bearing.

5. Install the lower bearing over the steering stem and onto the lower bearing inner race.

6. Install the steering stem into the steering head tube and hold it firmly in place.

7. Install the top bearing inner race (**Figure 39**).

8. Install the bearing adjustment nut (**Figure 38**) and tighten to 23-27 N•m (17-20 ft.-lb.). Then turn the steering stem back and forth a few times to seat the bearings.

9. Retighten the bearing adjustment nut to the torque specification in Step 8.

10. Install a new bearing adjustment nut lockwasher. Bend two of the lockwasher tabs (opposite from each other) into the bearing adjustment nut grooves.

> *NOTE*
> *Step 11 and Step 12 must be performed in this order to assure proper upper and lower fork bridge to fork alignment.*

11. Install the fork tubes in the lower fork bridge and continue to slide the fork tubes into position. Align

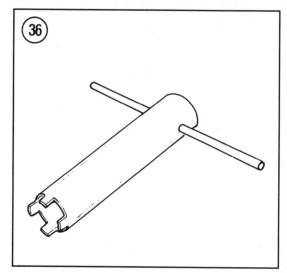

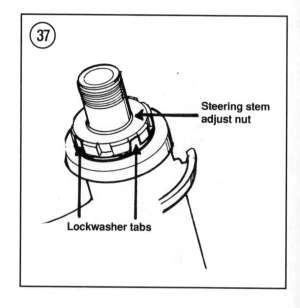

Steering stem adjust nut

Lockwasher tabs

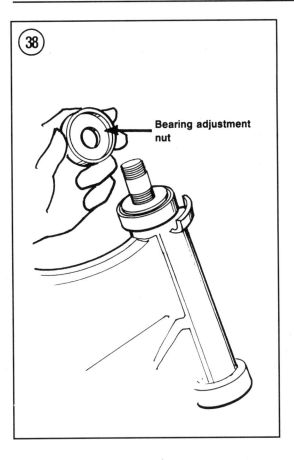

(38)

Bearing adjustment nut

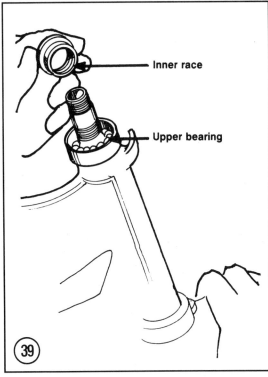

(39)

Inner race

Upper bearing

the top of each fork tube so it is flush with the top surface of the upper fork bridge.

12. Tighten these items in the following order.

    a. Lower fork bridge bolts.

    b. Stem nut.

    c. Upper fork bridge bolts.

Tighten all items to the torque specifications listed in **Table 1**.

13. Install the hydraulic brake 3-way hose connector onto the lower portion of the steering stem assembly.

14. On 1985-1986 models, install the horns and connect the electrical connector to the horn.

15. Install the ignition switch, headlight assembly and the instrument cluster or speedometer as described in Chapter Eight.

16. Install the handlebar as described in this chapter.

17. Complete the installation of the front forks as described in this chapter.

STEERING HEAD BEARING RACES

The headset and steering stem bearing races are pressed into place. Because they are easily bent, do not remove them unless they are worn and require replacement.

The top and bottom bearing races are not the same size. The bottom race is the slightly larger of the two. Be sure that you install them in the proper ends of the frame steering head tube.

Steering Head Bearing Outer Race Replacement

To remove the headset race, insert a hardwood stick or soft punch into the head tube (**Figure 40**) and carefully tap the race out from the inside. After it is started, tap around the race so that neither the race nor the steering head tube are damaged. To install the steering head bearing race, tap it in slowly with a block of wood, a suitable size socket or piece of pipe (**Figure 41**). Make sure that the race is squarely seated in the steering head race bore before tapping it into place. Tap the race in until it is flush with the steering head surface.

10

Steering Stem Lower Bearing and Race and Grease Seal Removal/Installation

NOTE
Do not remove the steering stem lower bearing race unless it is going to be replaced with a new bearing race. Do not reinstall a bearing race that has been removed as it is no longer true to alignment.

1. To remove the steering stem lower bearing inner race, try twisting and pulling it up by hand. If it will not come off, carefully pry it up from the base of the steering stem with a screwdriver; work around in a circle, prying a little at a time. Remove the bearing inner race, dust seal and dust seal washer.
2. Slide on a new dust seal washer and dust seal over the steering stem.
3. Slide the lower bearing inner race over the steering stem.
4. Tap the race down with a long piece of metal pipe that fits the inner race diameter or use a piece of hardwood; work around in a circle so the bearing and inner race will not be bent. Make sure it is seated squarely and is all the way down.

FRONT FORKS

The front suspension uses spring controlled, hydraulically damped, telescopic forks with air assist.

Before suspecting major trouble, drain the front fork oil and refill with the proper type and quantity; refer to Chapter Three. If you still have trouble, such as poor damping, a tendency to bottom or top out or leakage around the rubber seals, follow the service procedures in this section.

To simplify fork service and to prevent the mixing of parts, the legs should be removed, serviced and installed individually.

Removal

1. Remove the front wheel as described in this chapter.
2. Remove the brake caliper(s) assembly(ies) as described in Chapter Twelve.
3. On models so equipped, remove the air valve cap and bleed off *all* air pressure by depressing the valve stem.

WARNING
Always bleed off all air pressure; failure to do so may cause personal injury when disassembling the fork assembly.

NOTE
Release the air pressure gradually. If released too fast, fork oil will spurt out with the air. Protect your eyes and clothing accordingly.

4. Remove the bolts securing the front fender (A, **Figure 42**) and remove the fender.
5. On 1985-1986 models, perform the following:
   a. Remove the chrome cover caps.

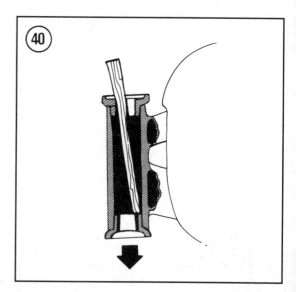

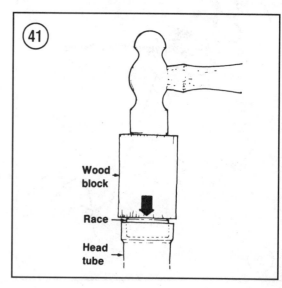

b. Remove the Allen bolts securing the fork brace and remove the fork brace.

6. If the fork assemblies are going to be disassembled, loosen, but do not remove, the fork top cap bolts (**Figure 43**).

7. Loosen the upper and lower fork bridge bolts (B, **Figure 42**).

8. Remove the fork tubes (C, **Figure 42**). It may be necessary to rotate the fork tubes slightly while pulling them down and out.

Installation

1. Insert the fork tubes up through the lower and upper fork bridges.

2. Align the top of the fork tube with the top surface of the upper fork bridge.

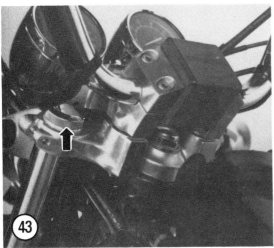

3. Tighten the upper and lower fork bridge bolts loosely at this time—just enough to hold them in place.

4. Tighten the upper and lower fork bridge bolts to the torque specifications in **Table 1**.

5. On 1985-1986 models, install the fork brace and tighten the Allen bolts to the torque specifications listed in **Table 1**. Install the trim caps into the bolt heads.

6. Install the front fender and tighten the bolts securely.

7. Install the front wheel as described in this chapter.

8. Install the front brake caliper assembly(ies) as described in Chapter Twelve.

> *WARNING*
> *Never use any type of compressed gas as an explosion may be lethal. Never heat the fork assembly with a torch or place it near an open flame or extreme heat, as this will also result in an explosion.*

> *CAUTION*
> *Never exceed an air pressure of 3.0 kg/cm^2 (43 psi) as damage may occur to internal components of the fork assembly.*

9. On 1985-1986 models, make sure the front wheel is off the ground and inflate the forks to 0-40 kPa (0-6 psi). Do not use compressed air, only use a small hand-operated air pump.

10. Take the bike off of the centerstand, apply the front brake and pump the forks several times. Recheck the air pressure and readjust if necessary.

Disassembly

Refer to **Figure 44** for 1985-1986 models or **Figure 45** for 1987-on models during the disassembly and assembly procedures.

1. Clamp the slider in a vise with soft jaws.

> *NOTE*
> *The Allen bolt has been secured with a thread locking compound and is often very difficult to loosen and remove because the damper rod will turn inside the slider. It sometimes can be loosened with an air impact driver. If you are unable to loosen the bolt, take the fork*

tubes to a dealer and have the screws removed.

2. Loosen the Allen bolt at the base of the slider.

3. Remove the Allen bolt at the base of the slider.

4. Hold the upper fork tube in a vise with soft jaws and loosen the fork top cap bolt, if it was not loosened during the fork removal sequence.

> **WARNING**
> *Be careful when removing the fork top cap bolt as the spring is under pressure. Protect your eyes accordingly.*

5. Remove the fork top cap bolt from the fork.

6. Remove the fork tube spacer, the spring seat and the fork spring.

7. Remove the fork from the vise, pour the fork oil out and discard it. Pump the fork several times by hand to expel most of the remaining oil.

8. Remove the dust seal from the slider.

9. Using circlip pliers, remove the internal snap ring from the slider.

10. Install the fork slider in a vise with soft jaws.

> **NOTE**
> *On this type of fork, force is needed to remove the fork tube from the slider.*

11. There is an interference fit between the bushing in the fork slider and the bushing on the fork tube. In order to remove the fork tube from the slider, pull hard on the fork tube using quick in and out strokes. Doing this will withdraw the bushing, backup ring and oil seal from the slider.

> **NOTE**
> *It may be necessary to slightly heat the area on the slider around the oil seal prior to removal. Use a rag soaked in hot water; do not apply a flame directly to the fork slider.*

12. Withdraw the fork tube from the slider.

> **NOTE**
> *Do not remove the fork tube bushing unless it is going to be replaced. Inspect it as described in this chapter.*

13. Turn the fork tube upside down and slide off the oil seal, backup ring and slider bushing from the fork tube.

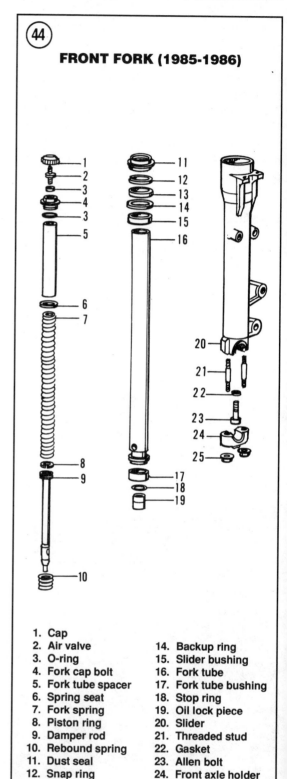

(44)

FRONT FORK (1985-1986)

1. Cap
2. Air valve
3. O-ring
4. Fork cap bolt
5. Fork tube spacer
6. Spring seat
7. Fork spring
8. Piston ring
9. Damper rod
10. Rebound spring
11. Dust seal
12. Snap ring
13. Oil seal
14. Backup ring
15. Slider bushing
16. Fork tube
17. Fork tube bushing
18. Stop ring
19. Oil lock piece
20. Slider
21. Threaded stud
22. Gasket
23. Allen bolt
24. Front axle holder
25. Nut

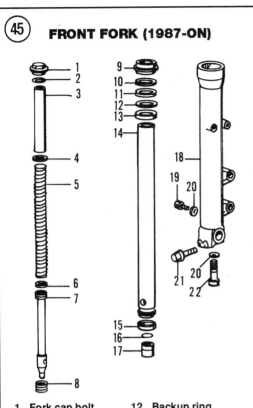

45 **FRONT FORK (1987-ON)**

1. Fork cap bolt
2. O-ring
3. Fork tube spacer
4. Spring seat
5. Fork spring
6. Piston ring
7. Damper rod
8. Rebound spring
9. Dust seal
10. Snap ring
11. Oil seal
12. Backup ring
13. Slider bushing
14. Fork tube
15. Fork tube bushing
16. Stop ring (1987-1990)
17. Oil lock piece
18. Slider
19. Drain bolt
20. Sealing washer
21. Bolt
22. Allen bolt

NOTE
Do not discard the slider bushing at this time. It will be used during the installation procedure.

14. Remove the oil lock piece, the damper rod and rebound spring.

15. Inspect the components as described in this chapter.

Inspection

1. Thoroughly clean all parts in solvent and dry them. Check the fork tube for signs of wear or scratches.

2. Check the damper rod for straightness. **Figure 46** shows one method. The rod should be replaced if the runout is 0.2 mm (0.008 in.) or greater.

3. Carefully check the damper rod and piston ring for wear or damage (**Figure 47**).

4. Check the upper fork tube for straightness. If bent or severely scratched, it should be replaced.

5. Check the lower portion of the slider for dents or exterior damage that may cause the upper fork tube to hang up during riding. Replace if necessary.

6. Measure the uncompressed length of the fork spring (not rebound spring) as shown in **Figure 48**. If the spring has sagged to the service limit dimensions listed in **Table 3**, the spring must be replaced.

7. Inspect the slider and fork tube bushings (**Figure 49**). If either is scratched or scored, they must be replaced. If the Teflon coating is worn off so that the copper base material is showing on approximately 3/4 of the total surface, the bushing must be replaced. Also check for distortion on the check points

10

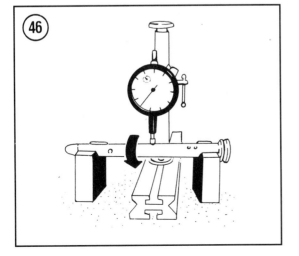

46

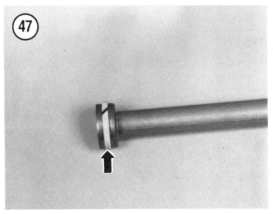

47

of the backup ring; replace as necessary. Refer to **Figure 50**.

8. Any parts that are worn or damaged should be replaced. Simply cleaning and reinstalling unserviceable components will not improve performance of the front suspension.

Assembly

1. Coat all parts with fresh DEXRON automatic transmission fluid or fork oil prior to installation.

2. If removed, install a new fork tube bushing (**Figure 51**).

3. Install the rebound spring onto the damper rod and insert this assembly into the fork tube (**Figure 52**).

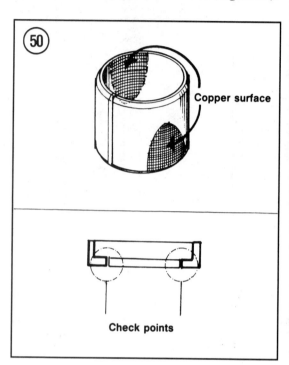

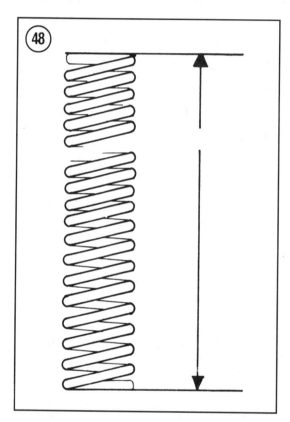

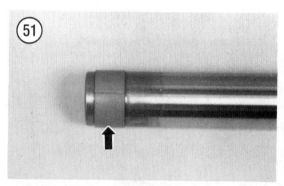

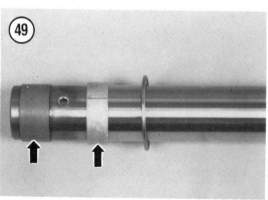

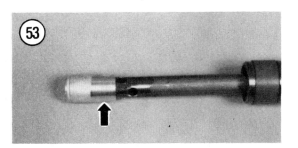

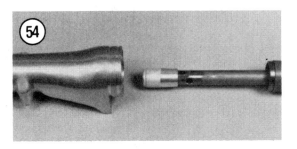

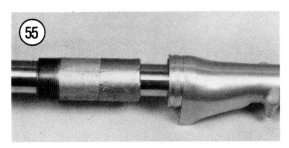

4. Temporarily install the fork spring, spring seat, spacer and fork top cap bolt. This will help hold the damper rod in place.

5. Install the oil lock piece onto the damper rod (**Figure 53**).

6. Install the upper fork assembly into the slider (**Figure 54**).

7. Slide the fork slider bushing down the fork tube and rest it on the slider.

8. Slide the fork slider backup ring (flange side up) down the fork tube and rest it on top of the fork slider bushing.

9. Place the old fork slider bushing on top of the backup ring. Drive the bushing into the fork slider with Honda special tool Fork Seal Driver (part No. 07947-KA50100) and attachment (part No. 07947-KF00100). Drive the bushing into place until it seats completely in the recess in the slider. Remove the installation tool and the old fork slider bushing.

NOTE
*A piece of 2 in. galvanized pipe can also work as a tool. If both ends are threaded (a close nipple pipe fitting), wrap one end with duct tape (**Figure 55**) to prevent the threads from damaging the interior of the slider.*

10. Coat the new seal with DEXRON automatic transmission fluid. Position the seal with the marking facing upward (**Figure 56**) and slide it down onto the fork tube (**Figure 57**). Drive the seal into the slider with Honda special tool Fork Seal Driver (part No. 07947-KA50100) and attachment (part No. 07947-KF00100); refer to **Figure 58**. Drive the oil seal in until the groove in the slider can be seen above the top surface of the oil seal.

NOTE
The slider seal can be driven in with a homemade tool as described in the NOTE following Step 9.

11. Install the snap ring with the sharp side facing up. Make sure the snap ring is completely seated in the groove in the fork slider (**Figure 59**).

12. Make sure the gasket is on the Allen bolt (**Figure 60**).

13. Apply red Loctite (No. 271) to the threads of the Allen bolt prior to installation.

14. Install it into the fork slider and tighten to the torque specification listed in **Table 1**. If you are

10

unable to tighten the bolt to the correct torque specification, finish tightening the bolt after the fork tube is reinstalled in the bike's frame.

15. Remove the fork top cap bolt, the fork tube spacer, the spring seat and the fork spring.

16. Fill the fork tube with the correct quantity of DEXRON automatic transmission fluid or fork oil as listed in **Table 4**.

17A. On 1985-1986 models, install the fork spring with the closer wound coils toward the bottom end of the fork.

17B. On 1987-on models, install the fork spring with the closer tapered end coils toward the bottom end of the fork.

18. Install the fork seat and the fork tube spacer (**Figure 61**).

19. Slide the dust seal (**Figure 62**) down and into place on the fork slider.

20. Inspect the O-ring seal (**Figure 63**) on the fork top cap bolt; replace if necessary.

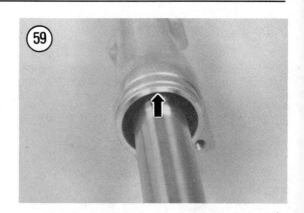

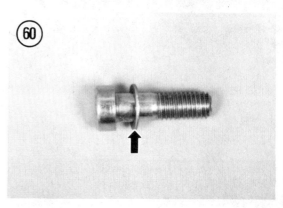

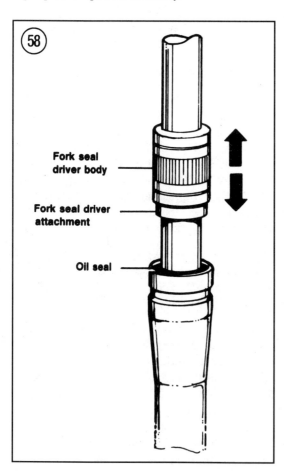

Fork seal driver body

Fork seal driver attachment

Oil seal

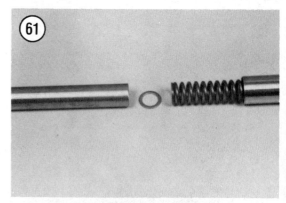

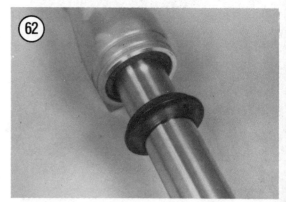

21. Install the fork top cap bolt (**Figure 64**) while pushing down on the spring. Start the bolt slowly, don't cross-thread it.

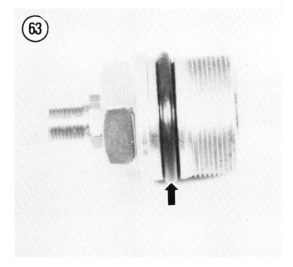

22. Place the slider in a vise with soft jaws and tighten the top fork cap bolt to the torque specification listed in **Table 1**.

23. Repeat for the other fork assembly.

24. Install the fork assemblies as described in this chapter.

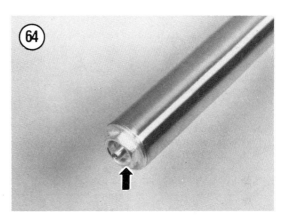

Tables are on the following page.

10

Table 1 FRONT SUSPENSION TORQUE SPECIFICATIONS

Item	N·m	ft.-lb.
Front axle	55-65	40-47
Holder nut	27-33	20-24
Front axle pinch bolt		
(1987-on)	30	22
Brake disc bolts		
1985-1990*	40	29
1992-on	43	31
Handlebar holder bolts	20-30	14-22
Steering stem		
Nut	80-120	58-87
Bearing adjust nut	23-27	17-20
Fork bridge bolts		
Upper	9-13	7-9
Lower	45-55	33-40
Fork top cap bolt	15-30	11-22
Fork brace Allen bolts	10-14	7-10
Fork slider Allen bolt	15-25	11-18

*Lightly coat threads with grease or oil prior to installation.

Table 2 TIRE INFLATION PRESSURE (COLD)

	Air pressure	
Tire size	Normal	Maximum load limit*
1985-1986		
Front		
110/90-18 61H	32 psi (225 kPa)	32 psi (225 kPa)
Rear		
140/90-15 70H	32 psi (225 kPa)	40 psi (280 kPa)
1987-on		
Front		
110/90-19 62H	33 psi (225 kPa)	33 psi (225 kPa)
Rear		
170/80-15 77H	33 psi (225 kPa)	40 psi (280 kPa)

*Up to maximum load limit of 200 lb. (89 kg) including total weight of motorcycle with accessories, rider(s) and luggage.

Table 3 FRONT SUSPENSION SPECIFICATIONS

	Standard	Service limit
Front fork spring length		
1985-1986	455.7 mm (17.94 in.)	446.6 mm (17.58 in.)
1987-1990	420.7 mm (16.56 in.)	412.3 mm (16.23 in.)
1992-on	459.4 mm (18.09 in.)	450.2 mm (17.72 in.)
Fork tube runout	—	0.2 mm (0.008 in.)

Table 4 FRONT FORK OIL CAPACITY*

1985-1986	415 cc (14 oz.)
1987-1990	442.5-447.5 cc (14.99-15.16 oz.)
1992-on	446.5-451.5 cc (15.10-15.27 oz.)

*Capacity for each fork leg.

CHAPTER ELEVEN

REAR SUSPENSION AND FINAL DRIVE

This chapter includes repair and replacement procedures for the rear wheel, rear suspension components and the final drive unit.

Power from the engine is transmitted to the rear wheel by a drive shaft and the final drive unit.

Tire changing and wheel balancing is covered in Chapter Ten.

Refer to **Table 1** for rear suspension torque specifications. **Table 1** and **Table 2** are located at the end of this chapter.

REAR WHEEL

Removal/Installation

1. Place the bike on the centerstand or block up the engine so that the rear wheel clears the ground.
2. Completely unscrew the rear brake adjusting nut (A, **Figure 1**).
3. Depress the brake pedal and remove the brake rod from the pivot joint in the brake arm. Remove the pivot joint from the brake arm and install the pivot joint and the adjusting nut onto the brake rod to avoid misplacing them.
4. To remove the brake torque link from the brake panel, perform the following:
  a. Remove the cotter pin from the bolt (B, **Figure 1**).
  b. Remove the bolt, nut and washer.
  c. Swing the brake arm down and out of the way.
5. Loosen the axle pinch bolt (A, **Figure 2**).
6. Remove the rear axle self-locking nut (**Figure 3**).
7. Insert a drift or screwdriver into the hole in the end of the rear axle and withdraw the axle (B, **Figure 2**) from the right-hand side.
8. Slide the wheel to the right to disengage it from the hub drive splines and remove the wheel.

9. Don't lose the spacer (**Figure 4**) on the right-hand side between the brake panel and the swing arm.

Inspection

Measure the axial and radial runout of the wheel with a dial indicator as shown in **Figure 5**. The maximum axial and radial runout is 2.0 mm (0.08 in.). If the runout exceeds this dimension, check the wheel bearing condition.

If the wheel bearings are okay, the wheel will have to be replaced, as it cannot be serviced. Inspect the wheel for signs of cracks, fractures, dents or bends. If it is damaged in any way, it must be replaced.

> *WARNING*
> *Do not try to repair any damage to an alloy wheel as it will result in an unsafe riding condition.*

Check axial runout as described under *Rear Hub Inspection* in this chapter.

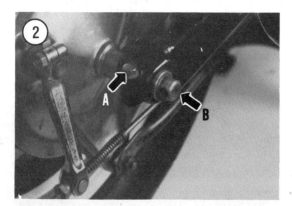

Installation

> *NOTE*
> ***Figure 6*** *is shown with the final drive unit removed for clarity.*

1. The distance collar within the final drive unit may move out during axle and wheel removal. If so, push it back into place. If the distance collar falls out, reinstall it into the hub with the narrow end in first (**Figure 6**).

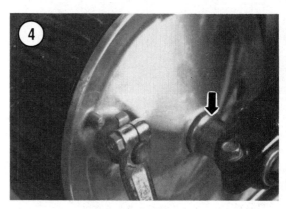

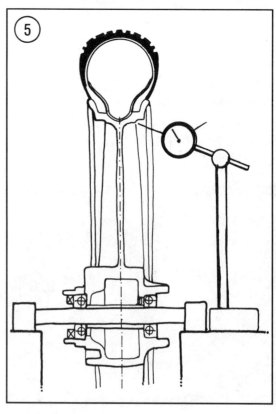

2. Apply a light coat of grease (lithium based NLGI No. 2 grease with molybdenum disulfide) to the final driven flange spline and to the rear wheel ring gear (**Figure 7**).

3. Loosen the final drive case (**Figure 8**) mounting nuts.

4. Position the rear wheel so that the splines of the final driven flange and the final drive align. Slowly move the wheel back and forth and push the wheel to the left until it completely seats.

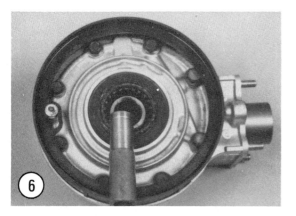

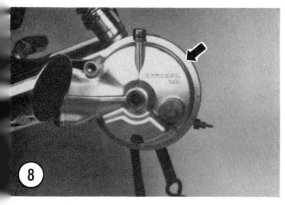

5. Position the spacer (**Figure 4**) on the right-hand side between the brake panel and the swing arm.

6. Install the rear axle from the right-hand side and install the axle nut only finger-tight.

7. To install the brake torque link, perform the following:

   a. Swing the brake arm up and into position.

   b. Install the bolt from the backside and install the washer and nut. Tighten the bolt and nut to the torque specification listed in **Table 1**.

   c. Install a new cotter pin and bend the ends over completely.

8. Insert a drift into the hole in the axle to keep the axle from turning.

9. Tighten the rear axle nut to the torque specification listed in **Table 1**.

10. Tighten the final drive gear case nuts, then the axle pinch bolt to the torque specifications listed in **Table 1**.

11. After the wheel is installed, completely rotate it and apply the brake several times to make sure it rotates freely and that the brakes work properly.

12. Adjust the rear brake free play as described in Chapter Three.

REAR HUB

Inspection

Inspect each wheel bearing prior to removing it from the wheel hub.

> *CAUTION*
> *Do not remove the wheel bearings for inspection as they will be damaged during removal. Remove wheel bearings only if they are to be replaced.*

1. Perform Step 1 and Step 2 of *Disassembly* in this chapter.

2. Turn each bearing by hand (**Figure 9**). Make sure the bearings turn smoothly.

3. On non-sealed bearings, check the balls for evidence of wear, pitting or excessive heat (bluish tint). Replace the bearings if necessary; always replace as a complete set. When replacing the bearings, be sure to take your old bearings along to ensure a perfect match.

> *NOTE*
> *Fully sealed bearings are available from many bearing specialty shops.*

Fully sealed bearings provide better protection from dirt and moisture that may get into the hub.

4. Check the axle for wear and straightness. Use V-blocks and a dial indicator as shown in **Figure 10**. If the runout is 0.2 mm (0.01 in.) or greater, the axle should be replaced.

5. Inspect the splines of the final driven flange. If any are damaged, the flange must be replaced.

Disassembly

Refer to **Figure 11** for this procedure.

1. Remove the rear wheel as described in this chapter.

2. Remove the O-ring seal from the final driven flange.

3. Pull straight up and remove the final driven flange (**Figure 12**) from the hub.

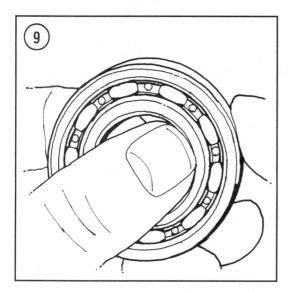

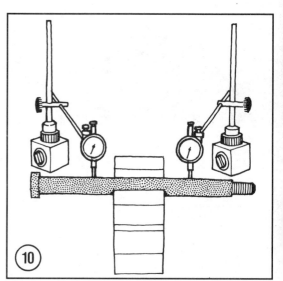

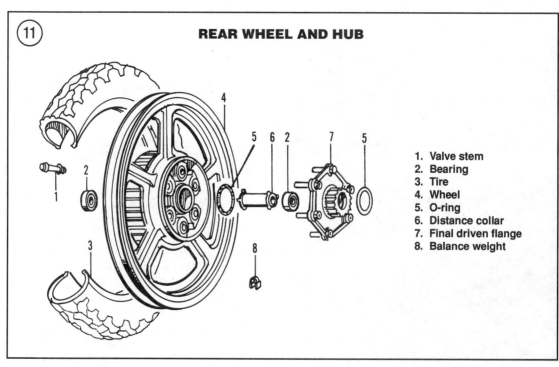

REAR WHEEL AND HUB

1. Valve stem
2. Bearing
3. Tire
4. Wheel
5. O-ring
6. Distance collar
7. Final driven flange
8. Balance weight

4. Before proceeding further, inspect the wheel bearings as described in this chapter. If they must be replaced, proceed as follows.

5A. A special Honda tool set-up can be used to remove the wheel bearings as follows:

    a. Install the 20 mm bearing remover head (Honda part No. 07746-0050600) into the right-hand bearing.

    b. Turn the wheel over (left-hand side up) on the workbench so the bearing remover is touching the workbench surface.

    c. From the left-hand side of the hub, install the bearing remover expander shaft (Honda part

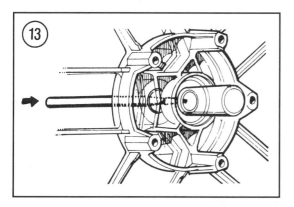

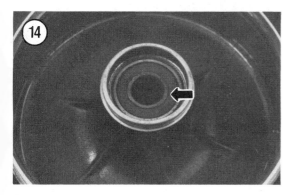

No. 07746-050100) into the bearing remover head. Using a hammer, tap the expander into the bearing remover.

    d. Stand the wheel up to a vertical position.

    e. Tap on the end of the expander (**Figure 13**) and drive the right-hand bearing out of the hub. Remove the bearing and the distance collar.

    f. Repeat for the left-hand bearing.

5B. If special tools are not available, perform the following:

    a. To remove the right- and left-hand bearings and distance collar, insert a soft aluminum or brass drift into one side of the hub.

    b. Push the distance collar over to one side and place the drift on the inner race of the lower bearing.

    c. Tap the bearing out of the hub with a hammer, working around the perimeter of the inner race.

    d. Repeat for the other bearing.

6. Clean the inside and the outside of the hub with solvent. Dry with compressed air.

7. Clean the inside and the outside of the final driven flange with solvent. Remove and discard the O-ring seal at the base of the splines. Dry with compressed air.

Assembly

1. On non-sealed bearings, pack the bearings with a good-quality bearing grease. Work the grease in between the balls thoroughly; turn the bearing by hand a couple of times to make sure the grease is distributed evenly inside the bearing.

2. Blow any dirt or foreign matter out of the hub prior to installing the bearings.

> *CAUTION*
> *Install non-sealed bearings with the single sealed side facing outward.*

3. Pack the hub with multipurpose grease.

4. Press the distance collar into the hub from the left-hand side.

> *CAUTION*
> *Install the standard bearings (they are sealed on one side only) with the sealed side facing out (**Figure 14**). Tap the bearings squarely into place and tap on*

11

the outer race only. Use a socket (Figure 15) that matches the outer race diameter. Do not tap on the inner race or the bearing might be damaged. Be sure that the bearings are completely seated.

5. Install the right-hand bearing into the hub.
6. Install the left-hand bearing into the hub.
7. Install the final driven flange into the rear hub.
8. Install a new O-ring seal onto the base of the splines on the final driven flange.
9. Install the rear wheel as described in this chapter.

FINAL DRIVE UNIT AND DRIVE SHAFT

Removal

1. Remove the rear wheel (A, **Figure 16**) as described in this chapter.
2. Drain the final drive unit oil as described in Chapter Three.
3. Remove the lower bolt or nut (B, **Figure 16**) securing the left-hand shock absorber to the final drive unit. Pivot the shock absorber up and out of the way and secure it to the frame with a Bungee cord.
4. Remove the nuts securing the final drive unit (**Figure 8**) to the swing arm.
5. Pull the final drive unit and drive shaft straight back until it is disengaged from the splines on the universal joint.

Disassembly/Inspection/ Assembly

The final drive unit requires a considerable number of special Honda tools for disassembly and assembly. The price of all of these tools could be more than the cost of most repairs or seal replacement by a dealer.

All of the internal components of the final drive unit are shown in **Figure 17** for 1985-1986 models or **Figure 18** for 1987-on models.

1. Using a circular motion, carefully pull the drive shaft from the final drive unit.
2. Check that the dust cover flange bolt (**Figure 19**) is in place and is tight.
3. Inspect the splines on the final driven ring gear (**Figure 20**). If they are damaged or worn, the ring gear must be replaced.

NOTE
If these splines are damaged, also inspect the splines on the rear wheel final driven flange; it may also need to be replaced.

4. Inspect the splines on the final driven primary joint (A, **Figure 21**). If they are damaged or worn, the primary joint must be replaced. If these splines are damaged, also inspect the splines on the drive shaft; it may also need to be replaced.
5. Make sure the bearing retainer adjust lock and bolt (B, **Figure 21**) are in place and tight.
6. Inspect the splines on the universal joint end of drive shaft (**Figure 22**). If they are damaged or worn, the drive shaft must be replaced. If these splines are damaged, also inspect the splines on the universal joint; it may also need to be replaced.

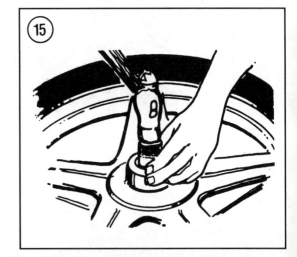

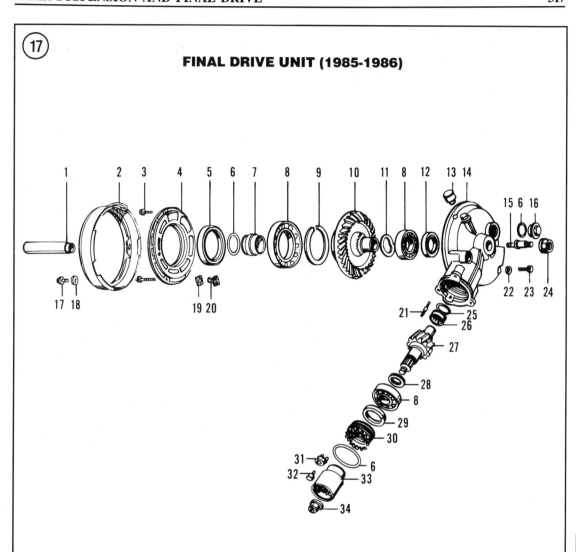

FINAL DRIVE UNIT (1985-1986)

1. Distance collar
2. Dust guard plate
3. Bolt
4. Gear case cover
5. Oil seal
6. O-ring seal
7. O-ring seal holder
8. Bearing
9. Spacer
10. Gear set (part of No. 27)
11. Wave washer
12. Oil seal
13. Breather cap
14. Case
15. Threaded stud
16. Cap
17. Bolt
18. Washer
19. Nut
20. Pin
21. Threaded stud
22. Sealing washer
23. Drain bolt
24. Axle nut
25. Clip
26. Needle bearing
27. Gear set (part of No. 10)
28. Thrust washer
29. Thrust washer
30. Bearing retainer
31. Nut
32. Bolt
33. Primary joint
34. Nut

11

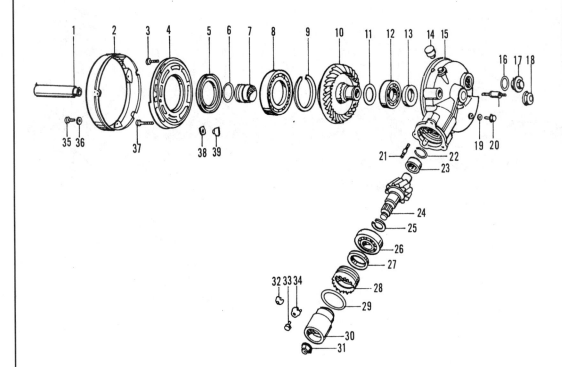

FINAL DRIVE UNIT (1987-ON)

1. Distance collar
2. Dust guard plate
3. Bolt
4. Gear case cover
5. Oil seal
6. O-ring seal
7. O-ring seal holder
8. Bearing
9. Spacer
10. Gear set (part of No. 24)
11. Wave washer
12. Bearing
13. Oil seal
14. Breather cap
15. Case
16. O-ring seal
17. Cap
18. Nut
19. Washer
20. Drain bolt
21. Threaded pin
22. Clip
23. Needle bearing
24. Gear set (part of No. 10)
25. Shim
26. Bearing
27. Oil seal
28. Bearing retainer
29. O-ring seal
30. Primary joint
31. Nut
32. Bearing adjust lock
33. Bolt
34. Bearing adjust lock
35. Bolt
36. Nut
37. Bolt
38. Nut
39. Pin

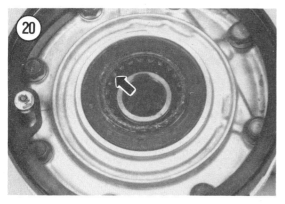

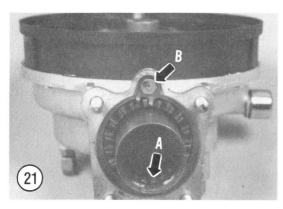

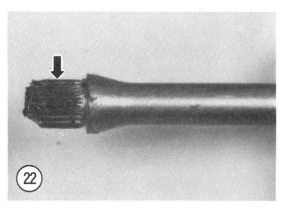

7. Inspect the splines on the final drive unit end of drive shaft (A, **Figure 23**). If they are damaged or worn, the drive shaft must be replaced. If these splines are damaged, also inspect the splines in the final drive unit; it may also need to be replaced.

8. Check the damper spring (B, **Figure 23**); replace if necessary.

9. Replace the oil seal (C, **Figure 23**) on the drive shaft. The oil seal must be replaced every time it is removed from the drive shaft.

10. Remove the stopper ring (D, **Figure 23**) from the groove in the end of the drive shaft splines. Discard the stopper ring.

11. Check that gear oil has not been leaking from either side of the unit (ring gear side or pinion joint side). If there are traces of oil leakage, take the unit to a dealer for oil seal replacement.

12. Make sure the damper spring (B, **Figure 23**) is installed in the end of the drive shaft.

13. Install a new stopper ring into the groove in the end of the drive shaft splines. Make sure it is correctly seated in the groove.

Installation

1. Apply a light coat of molybdenum disulfide grease (NGLI No. 2) to the splines of the drive shaft and install the drive shaft into the final drive unit. Using a soft-faced mallet, tap on the end of the drive shaft to make sure the drive shaft is completely seated into the final drive unit splines.

2. Apply a light coat of molybdenum disulfide grease (NGLI No. 2) to the final driven spline.

3. Install the final drive unit and drive shaft into the swing arm. It may be necessary to rotate the final driven spline slightly back and forth to align the splines of the drive shaft and the universal joint.

11

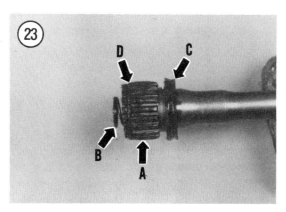

4. Install the final drive unit's mounting nuts only finger-tight at this time. Do not tighten the nuts until the rear wheel and rear axle are in place.

5. Install the rear wheel as described in this chapter.

6. Tighten the final drive unit nuts to the specifications listed in **Table 1**.

7. Install the shock absorber lower washer and bolt or nut and tighten to the torque specifications listed in **Table 1**.

8. Refill the final drive unit with the correct amount and type of gear oil. Refer to Chapter Three.

UNIVERSAL JOINT

Removal/Inspection/ Installation

1. Remove the swing arm as described in this chapter.

2. Remove the universal joint from the engine output shaft.

3. Clean the universal joint in solvent and thoroughly dry with compressed air.

4. Inspect the universal joint pivot points for play (**Figure 24**). Rotate the joint in both directions. If there is noticeable side play, the universal joint must be replaced.

5. Inspect the splines at each end of the universal joint (**Figure 25**). If they are damaged or worn, the universal joint must be replaced.

> *NOTE*
> *If these splines are damaged, also inspect the splines in the final drive unit and the engine output shaft; they may also need to be replaced.*

6. Apply a light coat of molybdenum disulfide grease (NGLI No. 2) to both splined ends.

7. Install the universal joint onto the engine output shaft.

8. Install the swing arm as described in this chapter.

SWING ARM

In time, the roller bearings will wear and will have to be replaced. The condition of the bearings can greatly affect handling performance and if worn parts are not replaced, they can produce erratic and dangerous handling. Common symptoms are wheel hop, pulling to one side during acceleration and pulling to the other side during braking.

A Honda special tool is required for loosening and tightening of the pivot adjusting bolt locknut. The tool is the Swing Arm Pivot Locknut Wrench (Honda part No. 07908-4690001). This tool is required for proper and safe installation of the swing arm. If this locknut is not tightened to the correct torque specification, it may allow the adjusting bolt to work loose. This could result in the swing arm working free from the right-hand side of the frame causing a serious accident.

Refer to **Figure 26** for 1985-1986 models or **Figure 27** for 1987-on models for this procedure.

Removal

1. Place the bike on the centerstand and remove the seat.

2. Remove the exhaust system as described in Chapter Seven.

3. Remove the rear wheel as described in this chapter.

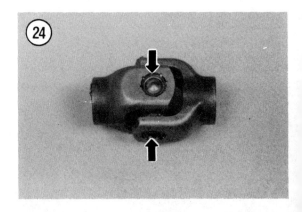

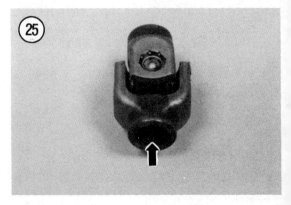

4. Remove the final drive unit and drive shaft as described in this chapter.

5. Remove the lower mounting bolt and nut securing the right-hand shock absorber.

NOTE
It is not necessary to remove the shock absorber unit, just pivot the unit up and out of the way with a Bungee cord.

6. On 1985-1986 models, remove the right-hand rear foot peg assembly as described in Chapter Thirteen.

7. Grasp the rear end of the swing arm and try to move it from side to side in a horizontal arc. There should be no noticeable side play. If play is evident and the pivot adjusting bolt is tightened correctly, the bearings should be replaced.

8. Remove the trim cap on both pivot bolts.

9. Use the special tool, Swing Arm Pivot Locknut Wrench (Honda part No. 07908-4690001), and loosen the right-hand pivot bolt locknut (**Figure 28**).

10. Use a 17 mm Allen wrench and remove the right-hand adjusting bolt (**Figure 29**).

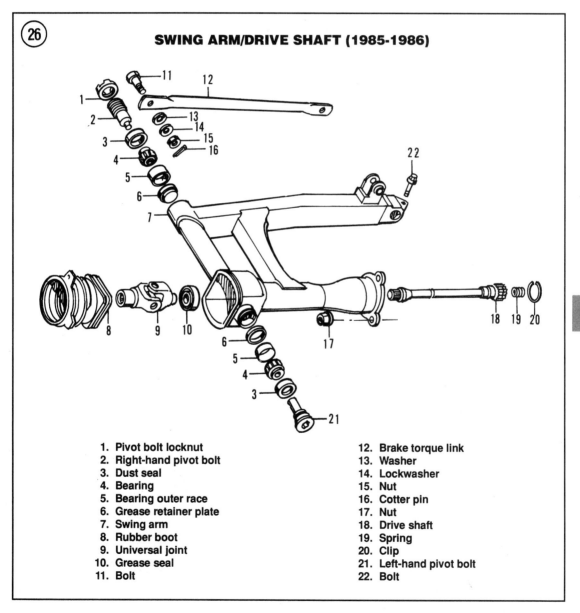

㉖ SWING ARM/DRIVE SHAFT (1985-1986)

1. Pivot bolt locknut
2. Right-hand pivot bolt
3. Dust seal
4. Bearing
5. Bearing outer race
6. Grease retainer plate
7. Swing arm
8. Rubber boot
9. Universal joint
10. Grease seal
11. Bolt
12. Brake torque link
13. Washer
14. Lockwasher
15. Nut
16. Cotter pin
17. Nut
18. Drive shaft
19. Spring
20. Clip
21. Left-hand pivot bolt
22. Bolt

11

11. Use a 17 mm Allen wrench and remove the left-hand pivot bolt (**Figure 30**).

12. Pull back on the swing arm, free it from the frame and remove it from the frame.

13. Leave the universal joint on the engine output shaft.

Installation

1. Make sure the universal joint is installed on the engine output shaft.

2. If removed, install the rubber boot on the drive shaft side of the swing arm with the "UP" mark facing up.

3. Position the swing arm into the mounting area of the frame. Align the holes in the swing arm with the holes in the frame.

4. Apply a light coat of grease to the inner end of both the right- and left-hand pivot bolts. Install the right- and left-hand pivot bolts.

5. Make sure the swing arm is properly located in the frame and then tighten the left-hand pivot bolt to the torque specifications listed in **Table 1**.

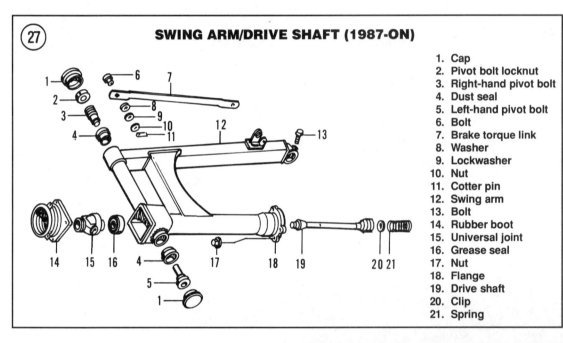

SWING ARM/DRIVE SHAFT (1987-ON)

1. Cap
2. Pivot bolt locknut
3. Right-hand pivot bolt
4. Dust seal
5. Left-hand pivot bolt
6. Bolt
7. Brake torque link
8. Washer
9. Lockwasher
10. Nut
11. Cotter pin
12. Swing arm
13. Bolt
14. Rubber boot
15. Universal joint
16. Grease seal
17. Nut
18. Flange
19. Drive shaft
20. Clip
21. Spring

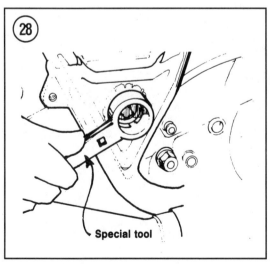

Special tool

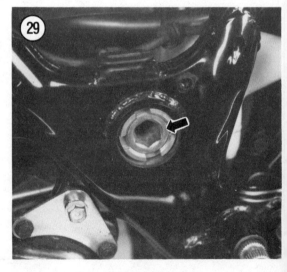

6A. On 1985-1986 models, tighten the right-hand pivot bolt to 20 N•m (14 ft.-lb.), then loosen it and retighten it to the torque specification listed in **Table 1**.

6B. On 1987-on models, tighten the right-hand pivot bolt to 12 N•m (9 ft.-lb.), then loosen it and retighten it to the torque specification listed in **Table 1**.

7. Move the swing arm up and down several times to make sure all components are properly seated.

8. Retighten the right-hand pivot bolt to the correct torque specification.

9. On the right-hand side, perform the following:

  a. Hold onto the right-hand pivot bolt with a 17 mm Allen wrench to make sure the pivot bolt does not move while tightening the locknut.

  b. Use special tool, Swing Arm Pivot Locknut Wrench (Honda part No. 07908-4690001) (**Figure 31**), and tighten the locknut to the torque specification listed in **Table 1**.

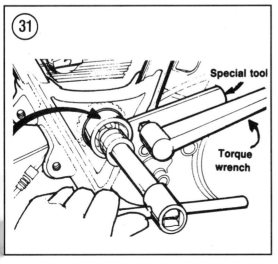

10. Install the final drive unit and drive shaft assembly as described in this chapter.

11. Install the rubber boot onto the rear of the engine. Make sure it is correctly installed on both the engine and swing arm. This is necessary to keep out dirt and water.

12. Install the rear shock absorbers as described in this chapter.

13. Install the rear wheel as described in this chapter.

14. Install the exhaust system as described in Chapter Seven.

Bearing Replacement

The swing arm is equipped with a roller bearing at each end. The inner race and roller bearing will come right out. No force should be needed. After the grease seal is removed, the bearing outer race is pressed in place and has to be removed, so don't remove it unless the bearing is going to be replaced.

The bearing outer race must be removed and installed with special tools that are available from a Honda dealer. The special tools are as follows:

  a. Bearing remover: Honda part No. 07936-4150000.

  b. Slide hammer weight: Honda part No. 07936-3710200.

  c. Driver handle: Honda part No. 07936-3710100.

  d. Outer bearing driver: Honda part No. 07749-0010000.

  e. Attachment, 37 × 40 mm: Honda part No. 07746-0010200.

1. Remove the swing arm as described in this chapter.

2. Remove the dust seal and bearing assembly from each side of the swing arm.

3. Secure the swing arm in a vise with soft jaws.

NOTE
The special tools used on 1985-1986 models grab the outer race and then withdraw it from the swing arm with the use of a tool similar to a body shop slide hammer.

4A. On 1985-1986 models, remove the right-hand bearing race first (**Figure 32**) as follows.

  a. Drill a 13 mm (1/2 in.) hole through the grease retainer plate on each side.

b. Remove the attachment from the end of the bearing remover.

c. Slide the bearing remover shaft through the hole in the bearing race and install a 29 mm OD washer or equivalent attachment onto the end of the shaft.

d. Slide the weight on the hammer upward several times and remove the bearing race.

e. Remove the grease retainer plate and discard it.

f. Repeat for the left-hand bearing.

4B. On 1987-on models: remove the grease retainer plates and bearing races as follows.

a. Drill a 3/8 in. hole through the right-hand grease retainer plate.

b. Insert the 1/4 in. steel rod through the hole in the right-hand retainer plate and knock the left-hand outer race and grease retainer plate out of the swing arm. See **Figure 33**.

c. Repeat for the right-hand grease retainer plate and bearing race.

5. Thoroughly clean out the inside of the swing arm with solvent and dry with compressed air.

6. Apply a light coat of waterproof grease to all parts before installation.

7. Install new grease retainer plate(s) into the bearing receptacle.

NOTE
Either the right- or left-hand bearing race can be installed first.

8. To install the new roller bearing outer race, place the outer bearing driver over the bearing race and drive the race into place with the driver handle and a hammer (**Figure 34**). Drive the race into place slowly and squarely. Make sure it is properly seated.

CAUTION
Never reinstall a bearing outer race that has been removed. During removal it becomes slightly damaged and is no longer true to alignment. If installed, it will damage the roller bearing assembly and create an unsafe riding condition.

9. Repeat Step 8 for the other bearing race.

10. Install a new roller bearing and dust seal on each end of the swing arm.

11. Install the swing arm as described in this chapter.

SHOCK ABSORBERS

The shock absorbers are spring controlled and hydraulically dampened. Spring preload can be ad-

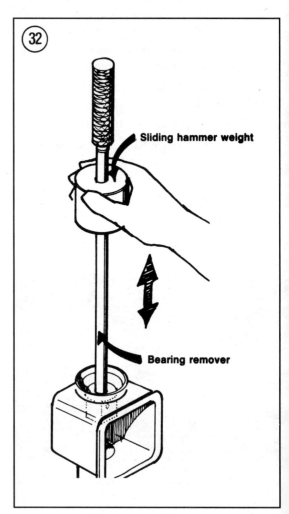

Sliding hammer weight

Bearing remover

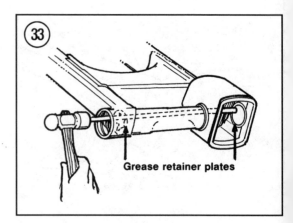

Grease retainer plates

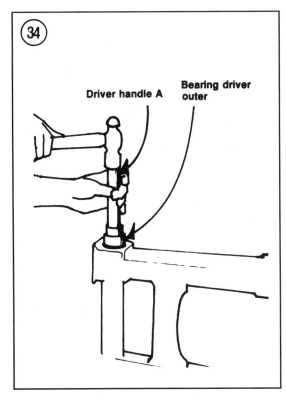

Driver handle A   Bearing driver outer

justed by rotating the spring lower seat at the base of the spring (**Figure 35**) *clockwise* to increase pre-load and *counterclockwise* to decrease it.

> *NOTE*
> *Use the wrench furnished in the factory tool kit.*

Both spring lower seats must be indexed on the same detent. The shocks are sealed and cannot be rebuilt. Service is limited to removal and replacement of the hydraulic unit or the spring.

Removal/Installation

Removal and installation of the rear shocks is easier if done separately. The remaining unit will support the rear of the bike and maintain the correct relationship between the top and bottom shock mounts.

1. Place the bike on the centerstand and remove the seat.
2. Adjust both shocks to their softest setting, completely *counterclockwise*.
3. On 1985-1986 models, remove the trim cap from the upper mount.
4. Remove the upper and lower nut or bolt and washer (**Figure 36**) securing the shock absorber to the frame and swing arm or final drive unit.
5. Pull the unit straight off the upper mount and remove it.
6. Install by reversing these removal steps. Tighten the upper and lower mounting nut or bolt and washer to the torque specifications listed in **Table 1**.
7. Repeat for the other side.

Preliminary Inspection

1. Check the damper unit (**Figure 37**) for leakage and make sure the damper rod (**Figure 38**) is straight.

> *NOTE*
> *The damper unit cannot be rebuilt; it must be replaced as a unit.*

2. Inspect the rubber bushings in the upper and lower joints (**Figure 39**). Replace if necessary.
3. Inspect the rubber stopper. If it is worn or deteriorated, remove the locknut and slide off the rubber stopper. Replace with a new one.

Disassembly/Assembly

Refer to **Figure 40** for 1985-1986 models or **Figure 41** for 1987-on models for this procedure.

The shock is spring-controlled and hydraulically damped. The shock damper unit is sealed and cannot be serviced. Service is limited to removal and replacement of the damper unit and the spring.

The shock must be disassembled with the use of special tools that are available from a Honda dealer. They are described in this procedure.

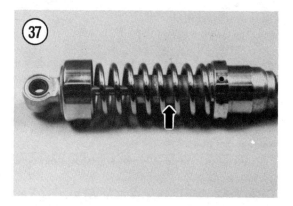

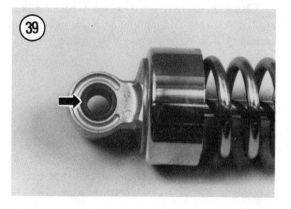

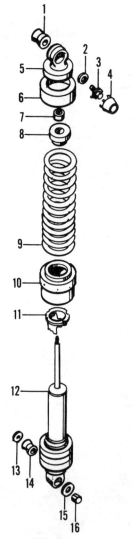

**SHOCK ABSORBER
(1985-1986)**

1. Bushing
2. Washer
3. Bolt
4. Cap
5. Upper joint
6. Spring cover
7. Nut
8. Rubber stopper
9. Spring
10. Spring lower seat
11. Spring adjuster
12. Damper unit
13. Washer
14. Bushing
15. Washer
16. Nut

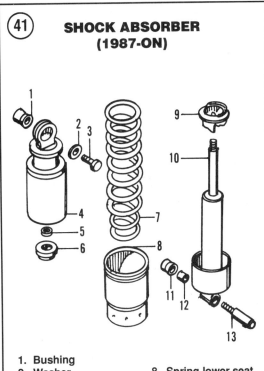

SHOCK ABSORBER (1987-ON)

1. Bushing
2. Washer
3. Bolt
4. Spring upper cover
5. Nut
6. Rubber stopper
7. Spring
8. Spring lower seat
9. Spring adjuster
10. Damper unit
11. Bushing
12. Collar
13. Special bolt

WARNING
Without the proper tool, this procedure can be dangerous. The spring can fly loose, causing injury. For a small bench fee, a dealer can do the job for you.

1. Install the shock absorber in a compression tool: Honda part No. 07959-3290001 for 1985-1986 models or Honda part No. 07GME-0010000 for 1987-on models as shown in **Figure 42**.

NOTE
The shock compressor tool must be modified to accommodate this particular shock absorber safely. Two additional components have to be added to the basic compressor tool. Replace the base and guide of the compressor tool with a set of attachments (Honda part No. 07959-MB-1000). Also place a collar (Honda part No. 52486-463-0000) in the shock absorber's lower joint prior to installing the shock absorber into the compressor tool.

2. Compress the spring just enough (approximately 30 mm) to gain access to the locknut under the upper joint.

3. Place the upper joint in a vise with soft jaws and loosen the locknut (**Figure 43**).

4. Completely unscrew the upper joint. This part may be difficult to break loose as a thread locking compound was applied during assembly.

11

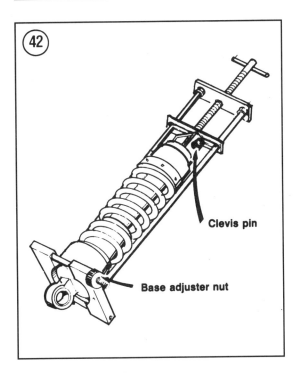

Clevis pin

Base adjuster nut

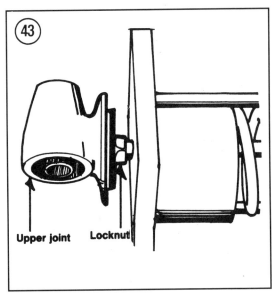

Upper joint   Locknut

5. Release the spring tension and remove the shock from the compression tool.

6. Remove the spring cover, spring guide, spring, spring lower seat and spring adjuster from the damper unit.

7. Measure the spring free length (**Figure 44**). The spring must be replaced if it has sagged to the service limit listed in **Table 2** or less.

8. Assembly is the reverse of these disassembly steps. Note the following.

9. If the locknut was removed, apply red Loctite (No. 271) to the threads of the damper rod prior to installing the locknut. Screw the locknut all the way down to the end of the threads.

10. Apply red Loctite (No. 271) to the threads of the damper rod prior to installing the upper joint. Screw the upper joint on all the way. Secure the upper joint in a vise with soft jaws and tighten the locknut along with the damper rod against the upper joint.

> *NOTE*
> *The damper rod should rotate with the locknut when the locknut is tightened against the bottom surface of the upper joint.*

> *NOTE*
> *After the locknut is tightened completely, the locknut must be against the bottom surface of the upper joint and against the end of the threads on the damper rod.*

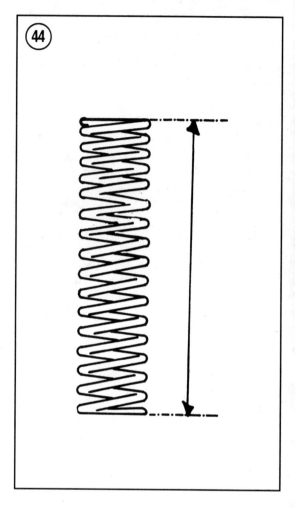

11. Align the upper spring seat with the upper joint when releasing the spring compressor tool.

Table 1 REAR SUSPENSION TORQUE SPECIFICATIONS

	N·m	ft.-lb.
Rear axle nut	80-100	58-72
Rear axle pinch bolt	24-30	17-22
Shock absorber damper locknut		
1985-1990	33	24
1992-on	48	35
Shock absorber nuts (1985-1986)		
Upper	24-30	17-22
Lower	30-40	22-29
Shock absorber bolts (1987-on)		
Upper	27	20
Lower (left)	23	17
Lower (right)	35	25
Final drive unit nuts	60-70	43-51
Swing arm		
Left-hand pivot bolt	90-120	65-87
Right-hand pivot bolt	10-20	7-14
Right-hand pivot bolt locknut		
Actual	100-130	72-94
Indicated	91-118	66-85

Table 2 REAR SHOCK ABSORBER SPRING FREE LENGTH

	Standard	Service limit
1985-1986	227.4 mm (8.95 mm)	222.9 mm (8.78 in.)
1987-1990	201.9 mm (7.94 in.)	197.9 mm (7.79 in.)
1992-on	200.8 mm (7.91 in.)	196.8 mm (7.75 in.)

11

CHAPTER TWELVE

BRAKES

The front wheel brake system consists of dual disc brakes on 1985-1986 models or a single disc brake on 1987-on models. All models are equipped with a drum brake on the rear.

The front wheel disc brakes are actuated by hydraulic fluid and are controlled by a hand lever connected to the master cylinder. As the brake pads wear, the brake fluid level drops in the reservoir and automatically adjusts for wear. The rear wheel drum brake is actuated mechanically by a rotating camshaft and is controlled by a foot pedal.

When working on hydraulic brake systems, it is necessary that the work area and all tools be absolutely clean. Any tiny particles of foreign matter and grit in the caliper assembly or the master cylinder can damage the components.

Consider the following when servicing the front brake systems.

1. Disc brake components rarely require disassembly, so do not disassemble them unless necessary.

2. Use only DOT 4 brake fluid from a sealed container.

WARNING
Do not intermix silicone based (DOT 5)
brake fluid as it can cause brake com-
ponent damage leading to brake system
failure.

3. Do not allow disc brake fluid to contact any plastic, painted or plated surfaces or surface damage will occur.

4. Always keep the master cylinder reservoir cover closed to prevent dust or moisture from entering.

5. Use only DOT 4 brake fluid to wash parts. Never clean any internal brake components with solvent or any other petroleum based cleaners. Solvents will cause the seals to swell and distort and require replacement.

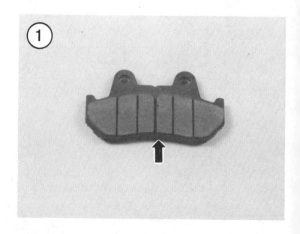

6. Whenever *any* component has been removed from the brake system the system is considered "opened" and must be bled to remove the air bubbles. Also if the brake feels "spongy," this usually means there is air in the system and it must be bled. For safe brake operation, refer to *Bleeding the System* as described in this chapter.

> *WARNING*
> *When working on the brake system, do **not** inhale brake dust. It may contain asbestos, which can cause lung injury and cancer. Wear a disposable face mask and wash your hands thoroughly after completing the work.*

If there is any doubt about your ability to correctly and safely carry out major service on the brake components, take the job to a dealer or brake specialist.

Refer to **Table 1** for brake specifications and **Table 2** for torque specifications. **Table 1** and **Table 2** are located at the end of this chapter.

FRONT BRAKE PAD REPLACEMENT

The front disc brakes are actuated by hydraulic fluid and are controlled by a hand lever on the master cylinder. As the brake pads wear, the brake fluid level drops in the reservoir and automatically adjusts for wear.

There is no recommended mileage interval for changing the friction pads in the disc brake. Pad wear depends greatly on riding habits and conditions. The pads should be checked for wear every 6,400 km (4,000 miles) and replaced when the wear indicator reaches the edge of the brake disc. To maintain an even brake pressure on the disc, always replace both pads in the caliper at the same time.

> *CAUTION*
> *Check the pads more frequently when the wear line (**Figure 1**) approaches the disc. On some pads, the wear line is very close to the metal backing plate. If pad wear happens to be uneven for some reason, the backing plate may come in contact with the disc and cause damage.*

Refer to **Figure 2** for this procedure.

1. Loosen the pad pin retainer bolt.

2. Remove the caliper mounting bolt (**Figure 3**) securing the caliper assembly to the caliper bracket.

3. Pivot the caliper assembly up and slide it off of the brake disc. Then slide the caliper assembly off of the caliper bracket.

4. Remove the pad pin retainer bolt (A, **Figure 4**).

5. Lift the pad pin retainer (B, **Figure 4**) off of the caliper assembly.

6. Pull the 2 pad pins out of the caliper.

7. Lift the inboard and outboard brake pads out of the caliper.

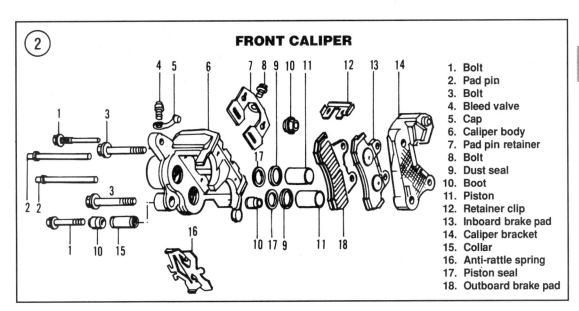

FRONT CALIPER

1. Bolt
2. Pad pin
3. Bolt
4. Bleed valve
5. Cap
6. Caliper body
7. Pad pin retainer
8. Bolt
9. Dust seal
10. Boot
11. Piston
12. Retainer clip
13. Inboard brake pad
14. Caliper bracket
15. Collar
16. Anti-rattle spring
17. Piston seal
18. Outboard brake pad

12

8. If necessary, remove the pad spring (**Figure 5**).

> *WARNING*
> *When working on the brake system, do **not** inhale brake dust. It may contain asbestos, which can cause lung injury and cancer. Wear a disposable face mask and wash your hands thoroughly after completing the work.*

9. Clean the pad recess and the end of the pistons with a soft brush. Do not use solvent, a wire brush or any hard tool which would damage the cylinders or pistons.

10. Carefully remove any rust or corrosion from the disc.

11. Lightly coat the ends of the pistons and the backs of the new pads *(not the friction material)* with disc brake lubricant.

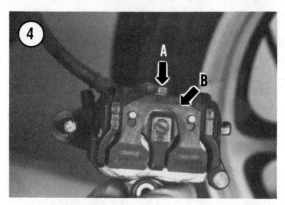

> *NOTE*
> *When purchasing new pads, check with your dealer to make sure the friction compound of the new pad is compatible with the disc material. Remove any roughness from the backs of the new pads with a fine-cut file.*

12. When new pads are installed in the caliper, the master cylinder brake fluid will rise as the caliper pistons are repositioned. Perform the following:

   a. Clean the top of the master cylinder of all dirt and foreign matter.

   b. Remove the top cover (**Figure 6**), set plate and diaphragm from the master cylinder and slowly push the caliper pistons into the caliper. Constantly check the reservoir to make sure brake fluid does not overflow. Remove fluid, if necessary, before it overflows.

   c. The pistons should move freely. If they don't and there is evidence of them sticking in the cylinder, the caliper should be removed and serviced as described in this chapter.

13. Push the caliper pistons in all the way to allow room for the new pads.

14. If removed, install the anti-rattle spring as shown in **Figure 5**.

15. Insert the outboard pad (**Figure 7**) into the caliper.

16. Align the outboard pad pin hole with the bore of the caliper and push the upper pin through the outboard pad (**Figure 8**).

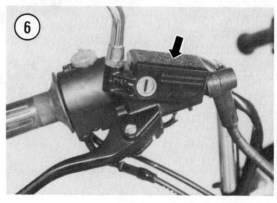

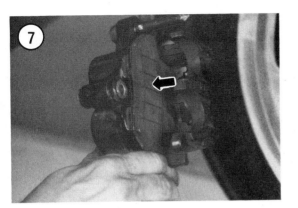

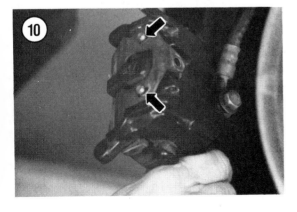

17. Install the inboard pad (A, **Figure 9**) into the caliper.

18. Push the upper pin through the inboard pad and caliper (B, **Figure 9**). Push the pin in until it bottoms out.

19. Push down on both brake pads and install the lower pad pin through both brake pads and the caliper. Push the pin in until it bottoms out.

20. Align the pad pin retainer with the pad pins. Push the pin retainer down and make sure it engages completely with each pin (**Figure 10**).

21. Install and tighten the pad pin retaining bolt (A, **Figure 4**) to the torque specification in **Table 2**.

22. Make sure the retainer clip is positioned on the caliper bracket.

23. Lubricate the caliper upper pivot bolt and pivot boot on the caliper bracket with silicone grease.

24. Insert the upper caliper pivot pin into the caliper bracket. Then swing the caliper assembly down and onto the brake disc. Be careful not to damage the leading edge of the pads during installation.

25. Install the caliper mounting bolt and tighten to the torque specifications in **Table 2**.

26. Place wood blocks under the engine or frame so that the front wheel is off the ground. Spin the front wheel and activate the brake lever as many times as it takes to refill the cylinder in the caliper and correctly locate the pads.

27. Refill the master cylinder reservoir, if necessary, to maintain the correct fluid level. Install the diaphragm, set plate and top cover.

12

WARNING
Use brake fluid from a sealed container clearly marked DOT 4. Other types may vaporize and cause brake failure. Always use the same brand name. Do not intermix as many brands are not compatible. Do not intermix silicone based (DOT 5) brake fluid as it can cause brake component damage leading to brake system failure.

28. Bed the pads in gradually for the first 80 km (50 miles) by using only light pressure as much as possible. Immediate hard application will glaze the new friction pads and greatly reduce the effectiveness of the brake.

FRONT MASTER CYLINDER

Removal/Installation

1. Remove the rear view mirror (A, **Figure 11**) from the master cylinder.

> *CAUTION*
> *Cover the fuel tank and instrument cluster or speedometer with a heavy cloth or plastic tarp to protect them from accidental brake fluid spills. Wash*

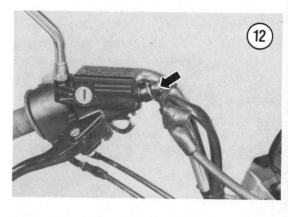

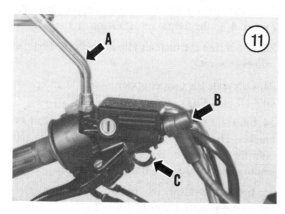

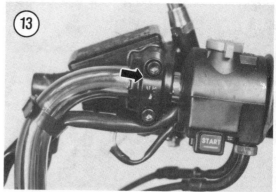

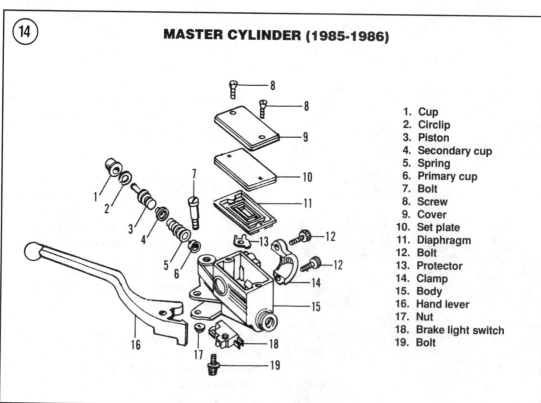

MASTER CYLINDER (1985-1986)

1. Cup
2. Circlip
3. Piston
4. Secondary cup
5. Spring
6. Primary cup
7. Bolt
8. Screw
9. Cover
10. Set plate
11. Diaphragm
12. Bolt
13. Protector
14. Clamp
15. Body
16. Hand lever
17. Nut
18. Brake light switch
19. Bolt

brake fluid off any painted or plated surfaces immediately, as it will destroy the finish. Use soapy water and rinse completely.

2. Pull back the rubber boot (B, **Figure 11**) and remove the union bolt (**Figure 12**) securing the brake hose to the master cylinder.

3. Remove the brake hose and tie the loose end up and cover the end to prevent the entry of foreign matter.

4. Disconnect the electrical connector (C, **Figure 11**) from the brake switch.

5. Remove the clamping bolts and clamp securing the master cylinder to the handlebar and remove the master cylinder.

6. Install by reversing these removal steps while noting the following.

7. Install the clamp with the "UP" arrow (**Figure 13**) facing up. Align the face of the clamp with the punch mark on the handlebar. Tighten the upper bolt first, then the lower to the torque specification listed in **Table 2**.

8. Install the brake hose onto the master cylinder. Be sure to place a sealing washer on each side of the fitting and install the union bolt. Tighten the union bolt to the torque specification listed in **Table 2**.

9. Bleed the brake as described in this chapter.

Disassembly

Refer to **Figure 14** for 1985-1986 models or **Figure 15** for 1987-on models for this procedure.

1. Remove the master cylinder as described in this chapter.

2. Remove the screws securing the top cover (**Figure 16**).

3. Remove the top cover, set plate (**Figure 17**) and diaphragm (**Figure 18**).

4. Pour out the hydraulic fluid and discard it. *Never reuse hydraulic fluid.*

5. Remove the pushrod and end piece.

6. Remove the rubber boot (**Figure 19**) from the area where the hand lever pushrod actuates the internal piston.

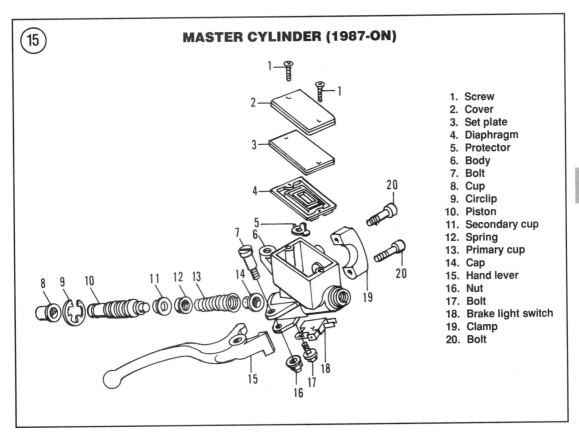

MASTER CYLINDER (1987-ON)

1. Screw
2. Cover
3. Set plate
4. Diaphragm
5. Protector
6. Body
7. Bolt
8. Cup
9. Circlip
10. Piston
11. Secondary cup
12. Spring
13. Primary cup
14. Cap
15. Hand lever
16. Nut
17. Bolt
18. Brake light switch
19. Clamp
20. Bolt

12

7. Using circlip pliers, remove the internal circlip and washer (**Figure 20**) from the body.

8. Remove the secondary cup and the piston assembly.

9. Remove the primary cup and spring.

10. If necessary, remove the screw and remove the clutch switch (**Figure 21**).

11. Remove the pivot bolt and nut securing the brake lever and remove the lever (**Figure 22**).

Inspection

1. Clean all parts in denatured alcohol or fresh brake fluid. Inspect the cylinder bore and piston contact surfaces for signs of wear and damage. If either part is less than perfect, replace it.

2. Check the end of the piston (**Figure 23**) for wear caused by the hand lever pushrod. Replace the piston if necessary.

3. Check both the primary and secondary cup (**Figure 24**) for damage. Replace as necessary. Replace the piston if the secondary cup requires replacement.

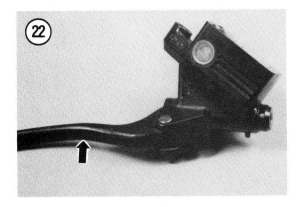

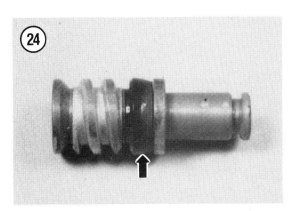

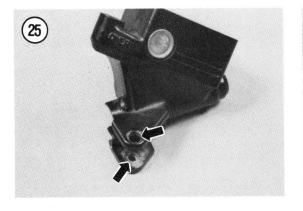

4. Check the hand lever pivot bore (**Figure 25**) in the brake master cylinder. If worn or elongated, the master cylinder must be replaced.

5. Inspect the pivot bore (**Figure 26**) in the hand lever. If worn or elongated it must be replaced.

6. Make sure the passages in the bottom of the fluid reservoir are clear.

7. Check the reservoir top cover, set plate and diaphragm (**Figure 27**) for damage and deterioration and replace as necessary.

8. Inspect the threads in the bore for the fluid line (**Figure 28**).

9. Inspect the cylinder bore (**Figure 29**) for scratches or damage. Replace the master cylinder if necessary.

10. Measure the cylinder bore (**Figure 30**). Replace the brake master cylinder if the bore exceeds the specifications given in **Table 1**.

11. Measure the outside diameter of the piston as shown in **Figure 31** with a micrometer. Replace the piston assembly if it is less than the specifications given in **Table 1**.

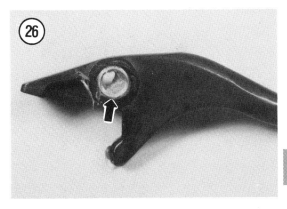

12

Assembly

1. Soak the new cups in fresh brake fluid for at least 15 minutes to make them pliable. Coat the inside of the cylinder with fresh fluid prior to assembly of parts.

> *CAUTION*
> *When installing the piston assembly, do not allow the cups to turn inside out as they will be damaged and allow brake fluid leakage within the cylinder bore.*

2. Install the spring, primary cup and piston assembly into the cylinder together (**Figure 32**).

> *NOTE*
> *Be sure to install the primary cup with the open end in first, toward the spring.*

3. Push the piston assembly down as far as it will go (**Figure 33**).

4. Install the washer and the circlip (**Figure 20**); make sure the circlip seats firmly in the groove (**Figure 34**).

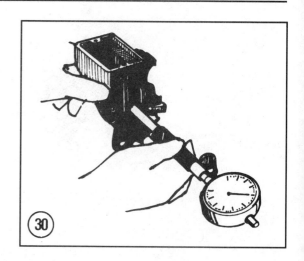

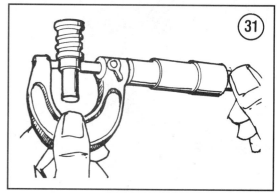

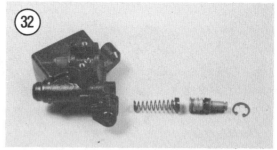

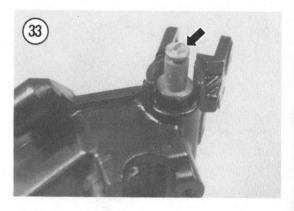

5. Slide in the rubber boot (**Figure 35**), the pushrod and the pushrod end piece.

6. Install the diaphragm, set plate and top cover. Do not tighten the cover screws at this time as fluid will have to be added later.

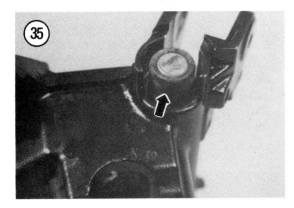

7. Install the lever onto the master cylinder body. Install and tighten the pivot bolt and nut securely

8. If removed, install the brake switch and tighten the screw securely.

9. Install the brake master cylinder and bleed the brake system as described in this chapter.

FRONT CALIPER

Removal/Installation

Refer to **Figure 36** for this procedure.

CAUTION
Do not spill any brake fluid on the painted portion of the front wheel. Wash off any spilled brake fluid immediately, as it will destroy the finish. Use soapy water and rinse completely.

WARNING
Dispose of this fluid according to local EPA regulations—never reuse brake fluid. Contaminated fluid can cause brake failure.

1. Place a container under the brake line at the caliper. Remove the union bolt and sealing washers (**Figure 37**) securing the brake line to the caliper assembly. Remove the brake line and let the brake fluid drain out into the container. Dispose of this brake fluid—never reuse brake fluid. To prevent the

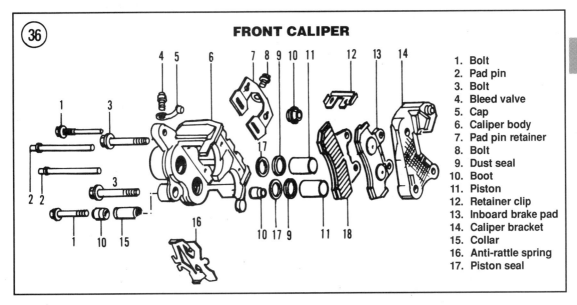

FRONT CALIPER

1. Bolt
2. Pad pin
3. Bolt
4. Bleed valve
5. Cap
6. Caliper body
7. Pad pin retainer
8. Bolt
9. Dust seal
10. Boot
11. Piston
12. Retainer clip
13. Inboard brake pad
14. Caliper bracket
15. Collar
16. Anti-rattle spring
17. Piston seal

12

entry of moisture and dirt, cap the end of the brake line and tie the loose end up to the forks.

2. Loosen the caliper mounting bolt (A, **Figure 38**) and caliper shaft bolt (B, **Figure 38**) gradually in several steps. Push on the caliper while loosening the bolts to push the pistons back into the caliper.

3. Remove the caliper mounting bolt and caliper shaft bolt. Pivot the caliper assembly up and off the disc and remove the caliper assembly.

4. On 1985-1986 models, repeat Steps 1-3 for the other caliper assembly.

5. Lubricate the caliper upper pivot bolt and pivot boot with silicone grease.

6. Install by reversing these removal steps while noting the following.

7. Carefully install the caliper assembly onto the disc. Be careful not to damage the leading edge of the pads during installation.

8. Tighten the caliper mounting bolt and caliper shaft bolt to the torque specifications listed in **Table 2**.

9. Install the brake hose, with a sealing washer on each side of the fitting, onto the caliper. Install the union bolt and tighten to the torque specification listed in **Table 2**.

10. Bleed the brake as described in this chapter.

> *WARNING*
> *Do not ride the motorcycle until you are sure that the brakes are operating properly.*

Caliper Rebuilding

If the caliper leaks, the caliper should be rebuilt. If the pistons stick in the cylinders, indicating severe wear or galling, the entire unit should be replaced.

Refer to **Figure 36** for this procedure.

> *WARNING*
> *When working on the brake system, do **not** inhale brake dust. It may contain asbestos, which can cause lung injury and cancer. Wear a disposable face mask and wash your hands thoroughly after completing the work.*

1. Remove the caliper assembly as described in this chapter.

2. Remove the caliper pivot pin bolt (**Figure 39**).

3. Unscrew and remove the bolt (A, **Figure 40**) securing the pad pin retainer (B, **Figure 40**) and remove the retainer from the caliper.

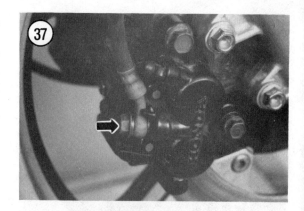

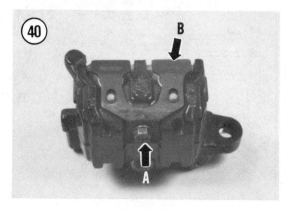

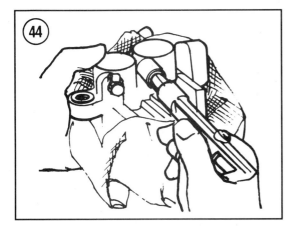

4. Unscrew and remove the bleed screw and cap.

5. Withdraw both pad pins (**Figure 41**) from the caliper.

6. Remove the brake pads (**Figure 42**) from the caliper.

7. Remove the anti-rattle spring (**Figure 43**) from the caliper.

8. Place a shop cloth or piece of soft wood over the ends of the pistons.

9. Perform this step over and close down to a workbench top. Hold the caliper body with the piston facing away from you.

WARNING
*In the next step, the pistons may shoot out of the caliper body like bullets. Keep your fingers out of the way. Wear shop gloves and apply air pressure gradually. Do **not** use high pressure air or place the air hose nozzle directly against the hydraulic hose fitting inlet in the caliper body. Hold the air nozzle away from the inlet allowing some of the air to escape during the procedure.*

10. Apply the air pressure (**Figure 44**) in short spurts to the union bolt hole (**Figure 45**) and force the pistons out of the caliper. Use a service station air hose if you don't have an air compressor.

CAUTION
In the following step, do not use a sharp tool to remove the dust and piston seals from the caliper cylinders. Do not damage the cylinder surfaces.

11. Use a piece of plastic or wood and carefully push the dust seals and the piston seals in toward the caliper cylinder and out of their grooves. Remove

12

the dust and piston seals from the cylinders and discard both seals.

12. Inspect both seal grooves (**Figure 46**) in each cylinder in the caliper body for damage. If damaged or corroded, replace the caliper assembly.

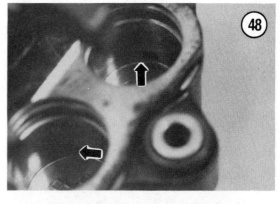

> *NOTE*
> *The caliper body cannot be replaced separately. If it is damaged in any way, the entire caliper assembly must be replaced.*

13. Inspect the caliper body (**Figure 47**) for damage, replace the caliper body if necessary.

14. Inspect the brake fluid passageways (**Figure 48**) in the base of each cylinder bore. Make sure they are clean and open. Apply compressed air to the openings and make sure they are clear. Clean out if necessary with fresh brake fluid.

15. Inspect the cylinder walls (**Figure 49**) and the pistons (**Figure 50**) for scratches, scoring or other damage. If either is rusty or corroded, replace either the pistons or the caliper assembly.

16. Measure the outside diameter of the pistons with a caliper (**Figure 51**). Replace the piston(s) if the

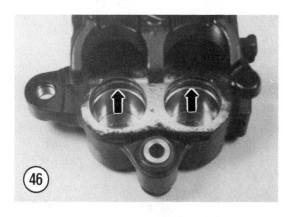

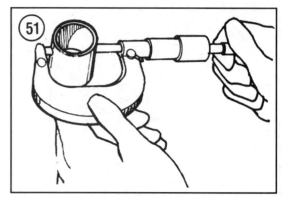

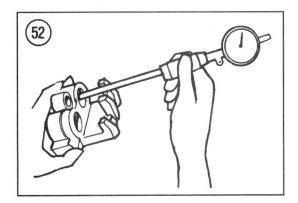

dimension is less than the specifications given in **Table 1**.

17. Measure each cylinder bore (**Figure 52**). Replace the caliper assembly if the bore exceeds the specifications given in **Table 1**.

18. Inspect the caliper mounting bolt holes. If worn or damaged, replace the caliper assembly.

19. Inspect the rubber boots (**Figure 53**) for damage or deterioration. Replace if necessary.

20. Make sure the hole in the bleed screw (**Figure 54**) is clean and open. Apply compressed air to the opening and make sure it is clear. Clean out if necessary with fresh brake fluid.

21. If serviceable, clean the caliper body with rubbing alcohol and rinse with clean brake fluid.

NOTE
Never reuse a dust seal or piston seal that has been removed. Very minor damage or age deterioration can make the seals useless.

22. Coat the new dust and piston seals with fresh DOT 4 brake fluid.

23. Carefully install the new piston seals (**Figure 55**) and new dust seals (**Figure 56**) into the grooves in the caliper cylinders. Make sure the seals are properly seated in their respective grooves.

24. Coat the pistons and the caliper cylinders with fresh DOT 4 brake fluid.

25. Position the pistons with the *open end facing out* toward the brake pads and install the pistons into the caliper cylinders (**Figure 57**). Push the pistons in until they bottom out (**Figure 58**).

26. Install the bleed screw and cap.

27. Install the anti-rattle spring (**Figure 43**) into the caliper.

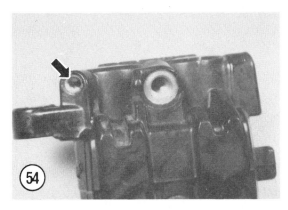

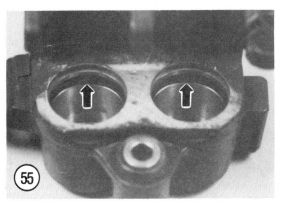

28. Install both brake pads (**Figure 42**) and push them down on the anti-rattle spring.

29. Install the pad pins (**Figure 41**) into the caliper and through the holes in the outboard pad.

30. Install the pad pin retainer (B, **Figure 40**) onto the ends of the pad pins. Push the retainer down and make sure it seats completely on the groove in each pad pin. Tighten the pad pin bolt (A, **Figure 40**) to the torque specification listed in **Table 1**.

31. Install the brake caliper as described in this chapter.

FRONT BRAKE
HOSE REPLACEMENT

There is no factory-recommended replacement interval but it is a good idea to replace all brake hoses every four years or when they show signs of cracking or damage.

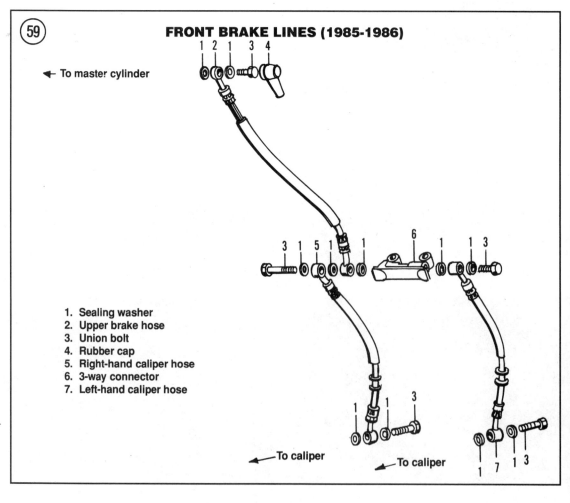

FRONT BRAKE LINES (1985-1986)

← To master cylinder

1 2 1 3 4

3 1 5 1 1 6 1 1 3

1. Sealing washer
2. Upper brake hose
3. Union bolt
4. Rubber cap
5. Right-hand caliper hose
6. 3-way connector
7. Left-hand caliper hose

1 1 3

← To caliper

← To caliper

1 7 1 3

Refer to **Figure 59** for 1985-1986 models or **Figure 60** for 1987-on models.

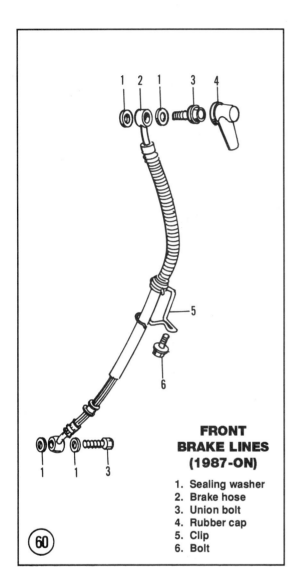

FRONT BRAKE LINES (1987-ON)

1. Sealing washer
2. Brake hose
3. Union bolt
4. Rubber cap
5. Clip
6. Bolt

CAUTION
Cover the front wheel, fender and fuel tank with a heavy cloth or plastic tarp to protect it from accidental spilling of brake fluid. Wash brake fluid off of any painted or plated surface immediately, as it will destroy the finish. Use soapy water and rinse completely.

1. Place a container under the brake hose at the caliper. Remove the union bolt and sealing washers (**Figure 61**) securing the brake hose fitting to the caliper assembly.

2. Remove the brake hose from the clip on the fork leg. Remove the brake hose and let the brake fluid drain out into the container (**Figure 62**). Apply the front brake lever as many times as necessary to force the brake fluid out of the brake hose.

3. To prevent the entry of moisture and dirt, plug the brake hose inlet in the caliper.

WARNING
Dispose of this brake fluid according to local EPA regulations—never reuse brake fluid. Contaminated brake fluid can cause brake failure.

4. On 1985-1986 models, repeat Steps 1-3 for the other caliper.

5. Remove the rubber boot (**Figure 63**) from the union bolt.

6. Remove the union bolt and sealing washers (**Figure 64**) securing the brake hose to the master cylinder and remove the hose and sealing washers.

7. On 1985-1986 models, perform the following:
   a. Remove the union bolt and sealing washers (A, **Figure 65**) securing the left-hand brake hose to the 3-way connector.

12

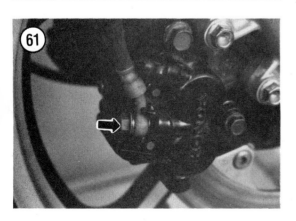

b. Remove the union bolt and sealing washers (B, **Figure 65**) securing the upper hose and the right-hand lower hose to the 3-way joint and remove them and the sealing washers.

8. Install new hoses, sealing washers and union bolts in the reverse order of removal. Be sure to install new sealing washers in the correct positions. Refer to **Figure 59** for 1985-1986 models or **Figure 60** for 1987-on models.

9. Tighten all union bolts to torque specifications listed in **Table 2**.

10. Refill the master cylinder with fresh brake fluid clearly marked DOT 4 only. Bleed the brake as described in this chapter.

> *WARNING*
> *Use brake fluid from a sealed container clearly marked DOT 4. Other types may vaporize and cause brake failure. Always use the same brand name. Do not intermix, as many brands are not compatible. Do not intermix silicone-based (DOT 5) brake fluid as it can cause brake component damage leading to brake system failure.*

> *WARNING*
> *Do not ride the motorcycle until you are sure that the brakes are operating properly.*

FRONT BRAKE DISC

Removal/Installation

1. Remove the front wheel as described in Chapter Ten.

> *NOTE*
> *Place a piece of wood or vinyl tube in the calipers in place of the disc. This way, if the brake lever is inadvertently squeezed, the pistons will not be forced out of the cylinders. If this does happen, the caliper might have to be disassembled to reseat the pistons and the system will have to be bled. By using the wood or vinyl tube, bleeding the system is not necessary when installing the wheel.*

> *CAUTION*
> *Do not set the wheel down on the disc surface, as it may get scratched or*

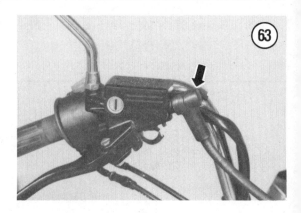

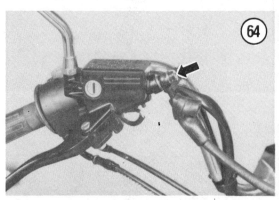

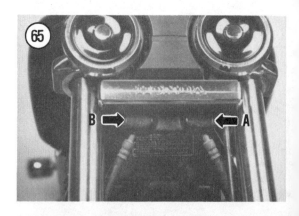

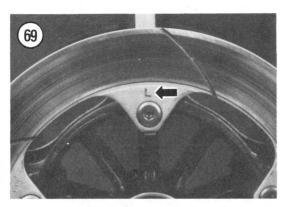

*warped. Set the wheel on 2 blocks of wood (**Figure 66**).*

2A. On 1985-1986 models, perform the following:

    a. Hold the left side of the axle with a wrench.

    b. Loosen and remove the right-hand axle nut (A, **Figure 67**).

    c. Remove the axle (A, **Figure 68**) from the left-hand side.

    d. Remove the speedometer gear box (B, **Figure 68**) from the left-hand side.

    e. Remove the side collar (B, **Figure 67**) from the right-hand side.

2B. On 1987-on models, perform the following:

    a. Remove the side collar from the right-hand side.

    b. Remove the speedometer housing from the left-hand side.

NOTE
*On 1985-1986 models, the brake discs are marked with a "R" (right-hand side) and "L" (left-hand side) (**Figure 69**). The brake discs must be reinstalled on the correct side for proper brake operation.*

3. Remove the bolts (**Figure 70**) securing the brake disc(s) to the hub and remove the discs.

4. On dual disc models, if necessary, repeat Step 4 for the disc on the other side of the wheel.

5. Install by reversing these removal steps while noting the following.

6. On 1985-1990 models, apply a light coat of grease or oil to the brake disc bolts.

7. Tighten the disc mounting Allen bolts to the torque specifications listed in **Table 2**.

12

Inspection

It is not necessary to remove the disc from the wheel to inspect it. Small marks on the disc are not important, but radial scratches deep enough to snag a fingernail reduce braking effectiveness and increase brake pad wear. If these grooves are found, the disc should be replaced.

1. Measure the thickness of the disc at several locations around the disc with a micrometer or vernier caliper. The disc must be replaced if the thickness in any area is less than that specified in **Table 1**.

2. Make sure the disc bolts are tight prior to running this check. Check the disc runout with a dial indicator as shown in **Figure 71**. Slowly rotate the wheel and watch the dial indicator. If the runout exceeds that listed in **Table 1**, the disc(s) must be replaced.

3. Clean the disc of any rust or corrosion and wipe clean with lacquer thinner. Never use an oil-based solvent that may leave an oil residue on the disc.

BLEEDING THE SYSTEM

This procedure is not necessary unless the brakes feel spongy, there has been a leak in the system, a component has been replaced or the brake fluid has been replaced.

On dual disc models, when bleeding the front brakes, bleed one caliper at a time.

Brake Bleeder Process

This procedure uses a brake bleeder that is available from motorcycle or automotive supply stores or from mail order outlets.

1. Remove the dust cap from the bleed valve on the caliper assembly.

2. Connect the brake bleeder to the bleed valve (**Figure 72**) on the caliper assembly.

> *CAUTION*
> *Cover the front wheel with a heavy cloth or plastic tarp to protect it from the accidental spilling of brake fluid. Wash any brake fluid off of any plastic, painted or plated surface immediately; as it will destroy the finish. Use soapy water and rinse completely.*

3. Clean the top of the master cylinder of all dirt and foreign matter.

4. Remove the screws securing the master cylinder cover (**Figure 73**) and remove the cover, set plate and diaphragm.

5. Fill the reservoir almost to the top lip; insert the diaphragm, set plate and the cover loosely. Leave the cover in place during this procedure to prevent the entry of dirt.

> *WARNING*
> *Use brake fluid from a sealed container marked DOT 4 only (specified for disc brakes). Other types may vaporize and cause brake failure. Do not intermix*

different brands or types as they may not be compatible. Do not intermix a silicone based (DOT 5) brake fluid as it can cause brake component damage leading to brake system failure.

6. Open the bleed valve about one-half turn and pump the brake bleeder.

> *NOTE*
> *If air is entering the brake bleeder hose from around the bleed valve, apply several layers of Teflon tape to the bleed valve. This should make a good seal between the bleed valve and the brake bleeder hose.*

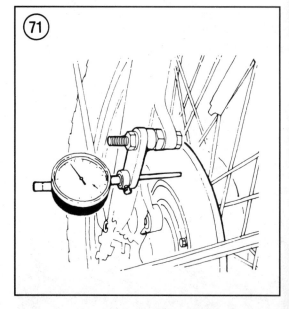

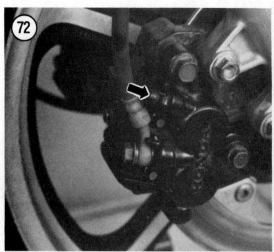

7. As the fluid enters the system and exits into the brake bleeder the level will drop in the reservoir. Maintain the level at about 9.5 mm (3/8 in.) from the top of the reservoir to prevent air from being drawn into the system.

8. Continue to pump the lever on the brake bleeder until the fluid emerging from the hose is completely free of bubbles. At this point, tighten the bleed valve.

NOTE
Do not allow the reservoir to empty during the bleeding operation or more air will enter the system. If this occurs, the entire procedure must be repeated.

9. When the brake fluid is free of bubbles, tighten the bleed valve, remove the brake bleeder tube and install the bleed valve dust cap.

10. If necessary, add fluid to correct the level in the reservoir. It should be to the upper level line.

11. On dual disc models, repeat Steps 1-10 for the other front caliper assembly.

12. Install the diaphragm, set plate and cover (**Figure 73**) and tighten the screws securely.

13. Test the feel of the brake lever. It should be firm and should offer the same resistance each time it's operated. If it feels spongy, it is likely that there is still air in the system and it must be bled again. When all air has been bled from the system and the fluid level is correct in the reservoir, double-check for leaks and tighten all fittings and connections.

WARNING
Dispose of used brake fluid according to local EPA regulations—never reuse

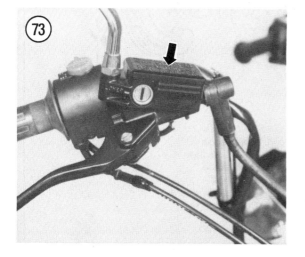

brake fluid. Contaminated brake fluid can cause brake failure.

WARNING
Before riding the bike, make certain that the brake is operating correctly by operating the lever several times.

14. Test ride the bike slowly at first to make sure that the brakes are operating properly.

Without a Brake Bleeder

1. Remove the dust cap from the bleed valve on the caliper assembly.

2. Connect a piece of clear tubing to the bleed valve on the caliper assembly (**Figure 72**).

CAUTION
Cover the front wheel with a heavy cloth or plastic tarp to protect it from the accidental spilling of brake fluid. Wash any brake fluid off of any plastic, painted or plated surface immediately; as it will destroy the finish. Use soapy water and rinse completely.

3. Clean the top of the master cylinder of all dirt and foreign matter.

4. Remove the screws securing the master cylinder cover (**Figure 73**) and remove the cover, set plate and diaphragm.

5. Fill the reservoir almost to the top lip; insert the diaphragm, set plate and the cover loosely. Leave the cover in place during this procedure to prevent the entry of dirt.

6. Place the other end of the tube into a clean container. Fill the container with enough fresh brake fluid to keep the end submerged. The tube should be long enough so that a loop can be made higher than the bleed valve to prevent air from being drawn into the caliper during bleeding.

WARNING
Use brake fluid from a sealed container marked DOT 4 only (specified for disc brakes). Other types may vaporize and cause brake failure. Do not intermix different brands or types as they may not be compatible. Do not intermix a silicone based (DOT 5) brake fluid as it can cause brake component damage leading to brake system failure.

12

7. Fill the reservoir almost to the cover lip; insert the diaphragm, set plate and the cover loosely. Leave the cover in place during this procedure to prevent the entry of dirt.

8. Slowly apply the brake lever several times as follows:

   a. Pull the lever in. Hold the lever in the applied position.

   b. Open the bleed valve about one-half turn. Allow the lever to travel to its limit.

   c. When this limit is reached, tighten the bleed valve.

9. As the fluid enters the system, the level will drop in the reservoir. Maintain the level at about 9.5 mm (3/8 in.) from the cover of the reservoir to prevent air from being drawn into the system.

10. Continue to pump the lever and fill the reservoir until the fluid emerging from the hose is completely free of bubbles.

NOTE
Do not allow the reservoir to empty during the bleeding operation or more

air will enter the system. If this occurs, the entire procedure must be repeated.

11. Hold the lever in, tighten the bleed valve, remove the bleed tube and install the bleed valve dust cap.

12. If necessary, add fluid to correct the level in the reservoir.

13. On dual disc models, repeat Steps 1-11 for the other front caliper assembly.

14. Install the diaphragm, set plate and cover (**Figure 73**) and tighten the screws securely.

15. Test the feel of the brake lever. It should be firm and should offer the same resistance each time it's operated. If it feels spongy, it is likely that there is still air in the system and it must be bled again. When all air has been bled from the system and the fluid level is correct in the reservoir, double-check for leaks and tighten all fittings and connections.

WARNING
Dispose of used brake fluid according to local EPA regulations—never reuse

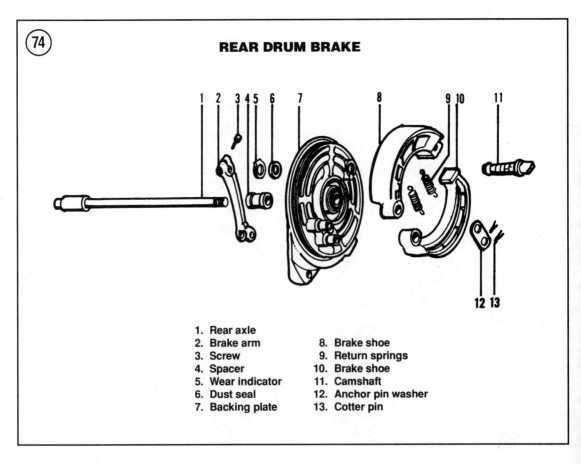

REAR DRUM BRAKE

1. Rear axle
2. Brake arm
3. Screw
4. Spacer
5. Wear indicator
6. Dust seal
7. Backing plate
8. Brake shoe
9. Return springs
10. Brake shoe
11. Camshaft
12. Anchor pin washer
13. Cotter pin

brake fluid. Contaminated brake fluid can cause brake failure.

WARNING
Before riding the bike, make certain that the brakes are operating correctly by operating the lever or pedal several times.

16. Test ride the bike slowly at first to make sure that the brakes are operating properly.

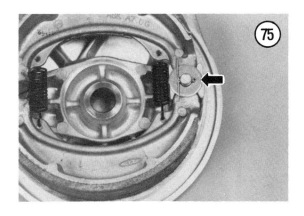

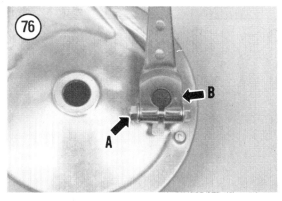

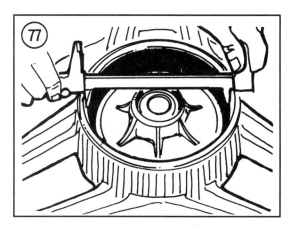

REAR DRUM BRAKE

Pushing down on the brake foot pedal pulls the rod which in turn rotates the camshaft. This forces the brake shoes out into contact with the brake drum.

Pedal free play must be maintained to minimize brake drag and premature brake wear and maximize braking effectiveness. Refer to Chapter Three for complete adjustment procedure.

Disassembly

Refer to **Figure 74** for this procedure.

WARNING
*When working on the brake system, do **not** inhale brake dust. It may contain asbestos, which can cause lung injury and cancer. Wear a disposable face mask and wash your hands thoroughly after completing the work.*

1. Remove the rear wheel as described in Chapter Eleven.

2. Pull the brake assembly straight up and out of the brake drum.

3. Remove the cotter pin and washer from the brake backing plate (**Figure 75**).

4. Remove the bolt and nut (A, **Figure 76**) securing the brake arm and remove the brake arm, wear indicator and dust seal. Withdraw the camshaft from the backing plate.

5. Using needlenose pliers, remove the return spring (next to the camshaft) from the brake linings. Remove the other return spring in the same manner.

Inspection

1. Thoroughly clean and dry all parts except the brake linings.

2. Check the contact surface of the drum for scoring. If there are grooves deep enough to snag your fingernail, the drum should be reground.

3. Measure the inside diameter of the brake drum with a vernier caliper (**Figure 77**). If the measurement is greater than the service limit listed in **Table 1**, the rear wheel must be replaced (the brake drum is an integral part of the wheel).

4. If the drum can be turned and still stay within the maximum service limit diameter, the linings will

12

have to be replaced and the new ones arced to conform to the new drum contour.

5. Measure the brake linings with a vernier caliper (**Figure 78**). They should be replaced if the lining portion is worn to the service limit dimension or less. Refer to specifications listed in **Table 1**.

6. Inspect the linings for imbedded foreign material. Dirt can be removed with a stiff wire brush. Check for any traces of oil or grease; if they are contaminated they must be replaced.

7. Inspect the cam lobe and pivot pin area of the backing plate (**Figure 79**) for wear or corrosion. Minor roughness can be removed with fine emery cloth.

8. Inspect the brake shoe return springs for wear. If they are stretched, they will not fully retract the brake shoes. Replace as necessary.

Assembly

1. Grease the camshaft with a light coat of molybdenum disulfide grease. Install the cam into the backing plate from the backside (**Figure 80**).

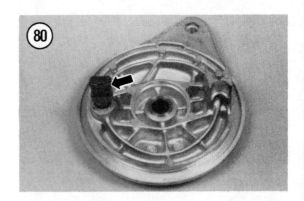

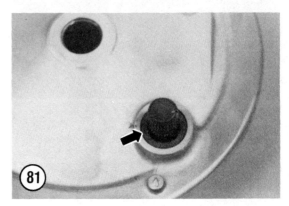

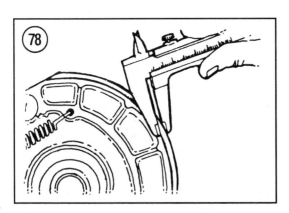

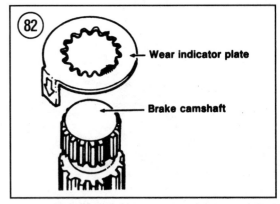

Wear indicator plate

Brake camshaft

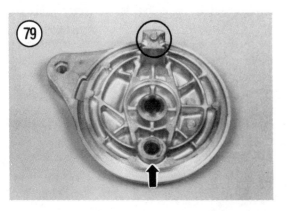

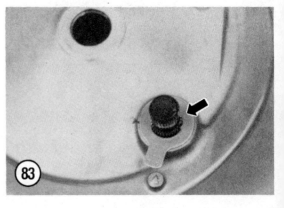

2. From the outside of the backing plate, install the dust seal (**Figure 81**).

3. Align the wear indicator to the camshaft as shown in **Figure 82** and push it down all the way to the backing plate (**Figure 83**).

4. When installing the brake arm onto the camshaft, be sure to align the dimples on the two parts (B, **Figure 76**). Tighten the bolt and nut to the torque specification listed in **Table 2**.

5. Grease the camshaft and pivot post with a light coat of molybdenum disulfide grease; avoid getting any grease on the brake backing plate where the brake linings may come in contact with it.

6. Hold the brake shoes in a "V" formation with the return springs attached and snap them into place on the brake backing plate. Make sure they are firmly seated on it (**Figure 84**). Install the double lock-washer and new cotter pins. Bend the ends over completely.

7. Install the brake panel assembly into the brake drum.

8. Install the rear wheel as described in Chapter Eleven.

9. Adjust the rear brake as described in Chapter Three.

REAR BRAKE PEDAL

Removal/Installation (1985-1986)

Refer to **Figure 85** for this procedure.

1. Completely unscrew the adjustment nut (**Figure 86**) on the brake rod.

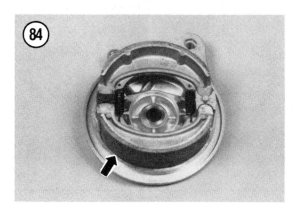

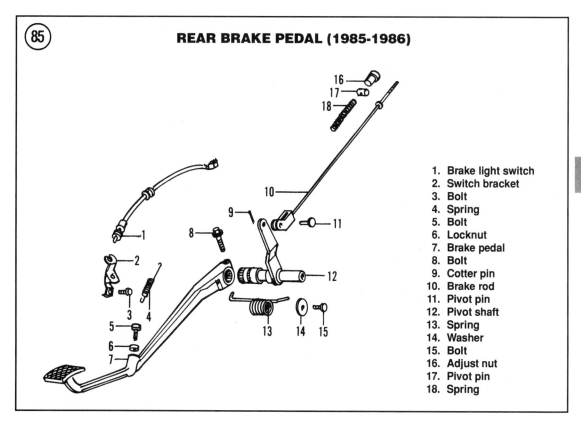

REAR BRAKE PEDAL (1985-1986)

1. Brake light switch
2. Switch bracket
3. Bolt
4. Spring
5. Bolt
6. Locknut
7. Brake pedal
8. Bolt
9. Cotter pin
10. Brake rod
11. Pivot pin
12. Pivot shaft
13. Spring
14. Washer
15. Bolt
16. Adjust nut
17. Pivot pin
18. Spring

12

2. Push down on the brake pedal and remove the brake rod from the pivot joint in the brake arm. Install the pivot joint onto the brake rod and reinstall the adjustment nut to avoid misplacing the small parts.

3. Disconnect the brake light switch return spring and the brake pedal return spring from the brake pedal.

4. Remove the clamping bolt (A, **Figure 87**) and remove the brake pedal (B, **Figure 87**) from the pivot shaft.

5. Remove the right-hand footpeg assembly as described in Chapter Thirteen.

6. Remove the cotter pin and pivot pin securing the brake rod assembly to the pivot shaft arm.

7. Remove the bolt and washer securing the brake pedal assembly to the frame. Remove the brake pedal.

8. Disconnect the return spring from the pivot shaft arm.

9. Remove the pivot arm shaft from the frame.

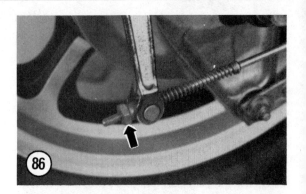

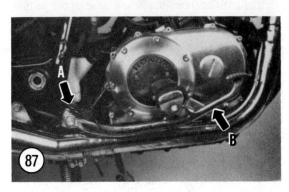

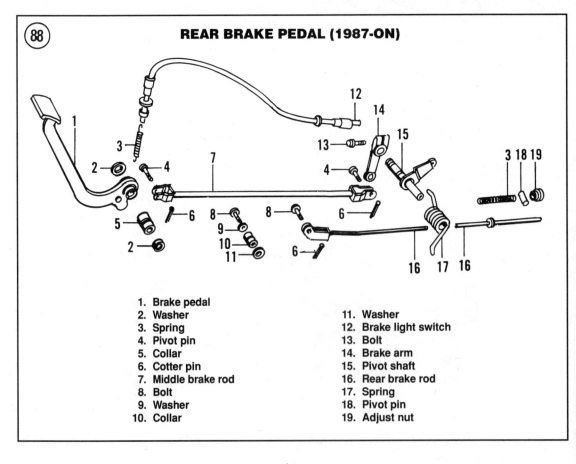

REAR BRAKE PEDAL (1987-ON)

1. Brake pedal
2. Washer
3. Spring
4. Pivot pin
5. Collar
6. Cotter pin
7. Middle brake rod
8. Bolt
9. Washer
10. Collar
11. Washer
12. Brake light switch
13. Bolt
14. Brake arm
15. Pivot shaft
16. Rear brake rod
17. Spring
18. Pivot pin
19. Adjust nut

10. Install by reversing these removal steps while noting the following.

11. Apply a light coat of multipurpose grease to all pivot areas prior to installing any components.

12. Install the brake pedal. Align the punch marks on the brake pedal and the brake pivot shaft.

Removal/Installation
(1987-on)

Refer to **Figure 88** for this procedure.

1. Completely unscrew the adjustment nut (**Figure 86**) on the rear brake rod.

2. Push down on the brake pedal and remove the rear brake rod from the pivot joint in the brake arm. Install the pivot joint onto the rear brake rod and reinstall the adjustment nut to avoid misplacing the small parts.

3. Disconnect the brake light switch return spring and the brake pedal return spring from the brake lever.

4. Remove the cotter pin and pivot pin securing the middle brake rod assembly to the pivot shaft arm.

5. Remove the bolts securing the brake pedal/front footpeg assembly to the frame. Remove the brake pedal and middle brake rod assembly.

6. Remove the cotter pin and pivot pin securing the rear brake rod assembly to the pivot shaft arm. Remove the rear brake rod assembly.

7. Disconnect the return spring from the pivot shaft arm.

8. Remove the pivot arm shaft from the frame.

9. Install by reversing these removal steps while noting the following.

10. Apply a light coat of multipurpose grease to all pivot areas prior to installing any components.

11. Install the brake pedal. Align the punch marks on the brake pedal and the brake pivot shaft.

Tables are on the following page.

12

Table 1 BRAKE SPECIFICATIONS

Item	Specification	Wear limit
Master cylinder		
Cylinder bore ID		
1985-1986	15.870-15.913 mm	15.93 mm
	(0.6248-0.6265 in.)	(0.627 in.)
1987-on	12.70-12.74 mm	12.75 mm
	(0.500-0.501 in.)	(0.502 in.)
Piston OD		
1985-1986	15.827-15.854 mm	15.82 mm
	(0.6231-0.6242 in.)	(0.623 in.)
1987-on	12.66-12.68 mm	12.65 mm
	(0.498-0.499 in.)	(0.498 in.)
Front caliper		
Cylinder bore ID	30.230-30.280 mm	30.290 mm
	(1.1902-1.1922 in.)	(1.1925 in.)
Piston OD	30.148-30.198 mm	30.140 mm
	(1.1869-1.1889 in.)	(1.1866 in.)
Front brake disc thickness	4.5-5.2 mm	4.0 mm (0.16 in.)
	(0.18-0.20 in.)	
Disc runout	—	0.3 mm (0.12 in.)
Rear brake drum ID	180 mm (7.09 in.)	181.0 mm (7.13 in.)
Rear brake shoe thickness	5.0 mm (0.20 in.)	2.0 mm (0.08 in.)

Table 2 BRAKE TORQUE SPECIFICATIONS

Item	N·m	ft.-lb.
Brake hose union bolts	25-35	18-25
Front master cylinder		
Cover screws	1-2	0.7-0.9
Clamp bolts	10-14	7-10
Brake caliper		
Mounting bolt	20-25	14-18
Pin bolt	25-30	18-22
Pad pin retainer bolt	8-13	6-9
Brake disc mounting bolts		
1985-1990*	40	29
1992-on	43	31

*Lightly coat threads with grease or oil prior to installation.

FRAME AND REPAINTING

This chapter includes replacement procedures for miscellaneous components attached to the frame.

This chapter also describes procedures for completely stripping the frame. Recommendations are also provided for repainting the stripped frame.

KICKSTAND (SIDESTAND)

Removal/Installation

1. Place a wood block(s) under the frame to support the bike securely.

2. Raise the kickstand and disconnect the return spring from the pin on the frame with Vise-grip pliers.

3. From under the frame, remove the bolt and nut (A, **Figure 1**) and remove the kickstand (B, **Figure 1**) from the frame.

4. Install by reversing these removal steps. Apply a light coat of multipurpose grease to the pivot surfaces of the frame tab and the kickstand yoke prior to installation.

5. Tighten the bolt and nut securely.

CENTERSTAND

Removal/Installation
(1985-1986)

> *NOTE*
> *The 1987-on models are not equipped with a centerstand.*

1. Place a wood block(s) under the frame to hold the bike securely in place.

13

2. Raise the centerstand and use Vise-grip pliers to unhook the return spring for the centerstand.

3. Unscrew the bolt on each side securing the centerstand to the frame.

4. Remove the centerstand from the frame.

5. Remove the pivot collar from each pivot area on the centerstand.

6. Install by reversing these removal steps while noting the following.

7. Apply multipurpose grease to the pivot collar and to the pivot area of the centerstand where the pivot collar rides.

FOOTPEGS

Refer to **Figure 2** for these procedures.

Individual Footpeg Replacement

1. Remove the cotter pin and washer securing the footpeg to the bracket on the frame. Remove the pivot pin (**Figure 3**) and footpeg.

2. Make sure the spring is in good condition and not broken. Replace as necessary.

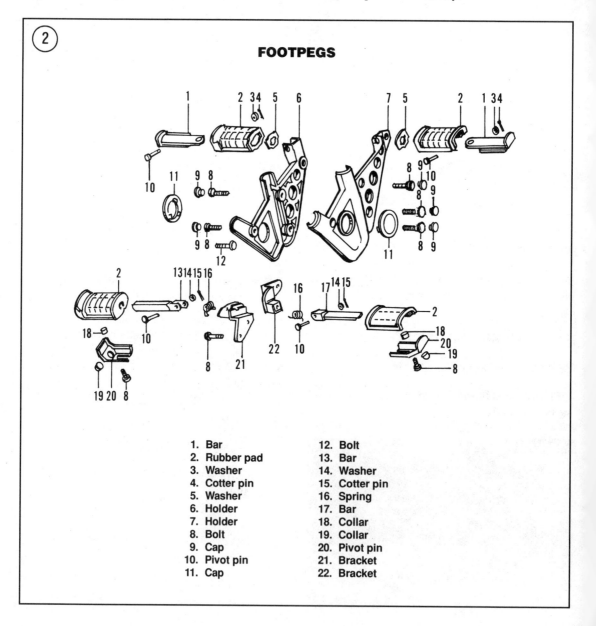

(2)

FOOTPEGS

1. Bar	12. Bolt
2. Rubber pad	13. Bar
3. Washer	14. Washer
4. Cotter pin	15. Cotter pin
5. Washer	16. Spring
6. Holder	17. Bar
7. Holder	18. Collar
8. Bolt	19. Collar
9. Cap	20. Pivot pin
10. Pivot pin	21. Bracket
11. Cap	22. Bracket

3. Lubricate the pivot point and pivot pin prior to installation. Install a new cotter pin and bend the ends over completely.

Footpeg Assembly Removal/Installation

1. Remove the bolts (**Figure 4**) securing the front assembly to the frame and remove the assembly.

2. Remove the bolts securing the rear assembly (**Figure 5**) to the frame and remove the assembly.

3. Install by reversing these removal steps while tightening the bolts securely.

SEATS

Removal/Installation (1985-1986)

Refer to **Figure 6** for this procedure.

1. Remove the nuts securing the pillion seat (**Figure 7**).

2. Pull up on the rear of the pillion seat and unhook it from the retainer on the front seat.

3. Remove the nuts (**Figure 8**) securing the front seat to the rear fender.

4. Pull the front seat toward the rear and remove it.

5. Install by reversing these removal steps.

Removal/Installation (1987-on)

Refer to **Figure 9** for this procedure.

1. Remove the nuts securing the pillion seat back and remove the seat back.

2. To remove the pillion seat, perform the following:
   a. Remove the nut securing the seat at the rear.
   b. Pull the pillion seat backwards and remove it.

3. To remove the main seat, perform the following:
   a. Remove the nuts securing the seat at the rear.
   b. Pull the main seat backwards and remove it.

4. Install by reversing these removal steps. Tighten all mounting nuts securely.

FRONT FENDER

Removal/Installation

1. Remove the front wheel (A, **Figure 10**) as described in Chapter Ten.

2. Remove the bolts securing the front fender (B, **Figure 10**) and remove the front fender.

3. Install by reversing these removal steps while noting the following.

4. Be sure to install the speedometer cable stay on the rear left-hand bolt.

5. Tighten all mounting bolts securely.

13

REAR FENDER AND GRAB RAIL

Removal/Installation (1985-1986)

Refer to **Figure 11** for this procedure.

1. Remove the seats (A, **Figure 12**) as described in this chapter.

2. Remove the rear wheel (B, **Figure 12**) as described in Chapter Eleven.

3. Remove the bolt and collar securing the covers (A, **Figure 13**) on each side of the grab rail. Remove both covers.

4. Remove the bolt securing the upper grab rail to the lower grab rails. Remove the upper grab rail (C, **Figure 12**).

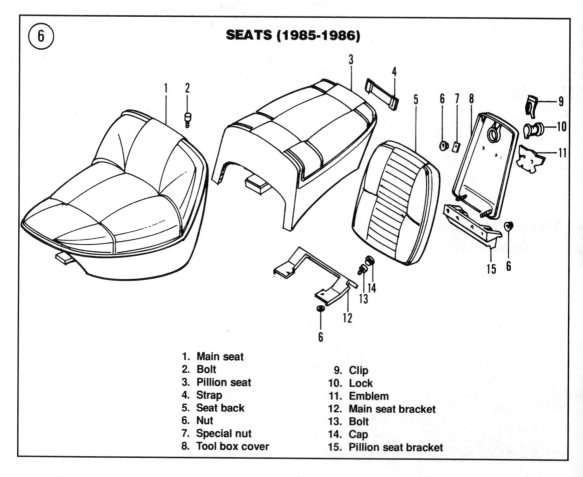

SEATS (1985-1986)

1. Main seat
2. Bolt
3. Pillion seat
4. Strap
5. Seat back
6. Nut
7. Special nut
8. Tool box cover
9. Clip
10. Lock
11. Emblem
12. Main seat bracket
13. Bolt
14. Cap
15. Pillion seat bracket

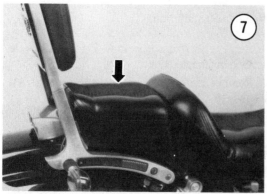

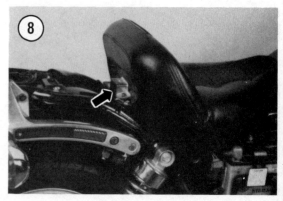

5. Disconnect the electrical connectors (B, **Figure 13**) to both rear turn signals and the taillight/brake light.

6. Carefully remove the trim caps from the front bolt hole (D, **Figure 12**) on the lower portion of the grab rail.

7. Remove the bolts securing the lower portion of the grab rail (E, **Figure 12**) on each side and remove both grab rails.

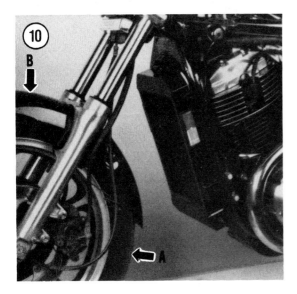

8. Remove the cap nuts securing the rear fender and mud guard to the frame and remove the rear fender from the frame.

9. Install by reversing these removal steps.

Removal/Installation (1987-on)

Refer to **Figure 14** for this procedure.

1. Remove the seats as described in this chapter.

2. Remove the rear wheel as described in Chapter Eleven.

3. Remove the bolts and washers securing the upper grab rail to the lower grab rails. Remove the upper grab rail. These bolts also secure the rear fender to the frame.

4. Disconnect the electrical connectors to both rear turn signals and the taillight/brake light.

5. Remove the bolts securing the lower portion of the grab rail and rear fender, on each side, and remove both grab rails.

6. Remove the rear fender from the frame.

7. Install by reversing these removal steps.

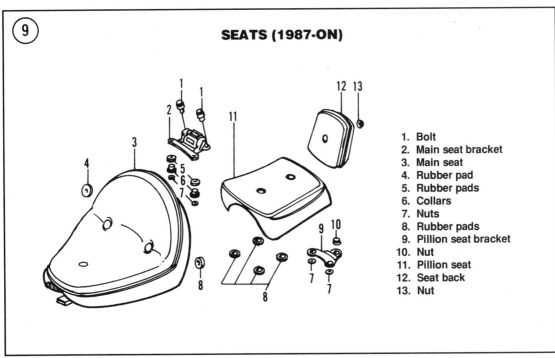

SEATS (1987-ON)

1. Bolt
2. Main seat bracket
3. Main seat
4. Rubber pad
5. Rubber pads
6. Collars
7. Nuts
8. Rubber pads
9. Pillion seat bracket
10. Nut
11. Pillion seat
12. Seat back
13. Nut

13

FRAME

The frame does not require routine maintenance. However, it should be inspected immediately after any accident or spill.

Component Removal/Installation

1. Remove the seat, side cover panels and fuel tank.

2. Remove the engine as described in Chapter Four.

3. Remove the front wheel, steering head and front forks as described in Chapter Ten.

4. Remove the rear wheel, shock absorber and swing arm as described in Chapter Eleven.

5. Remove the battery as described in Chapter Three.

6. Remove the wiring harness.

7. Remove the kickstand and footpegs as described in this chapter.

8. On 1985-1986 models, remove the centerstand as described in this chapter.

9. Remove the steering head races from the steering head tube as described in Chapter Ten.

10. Inspect the frame for bends, cracks or other damage, especially around welded joints and areas that are rusted.

11. Assemble by reversing these removal steps.

Stripping and Painting

Remove all components from the frame. Thoroughly strip off all old paint. The best way is to have it sandblasted down to bare metal. If this is not

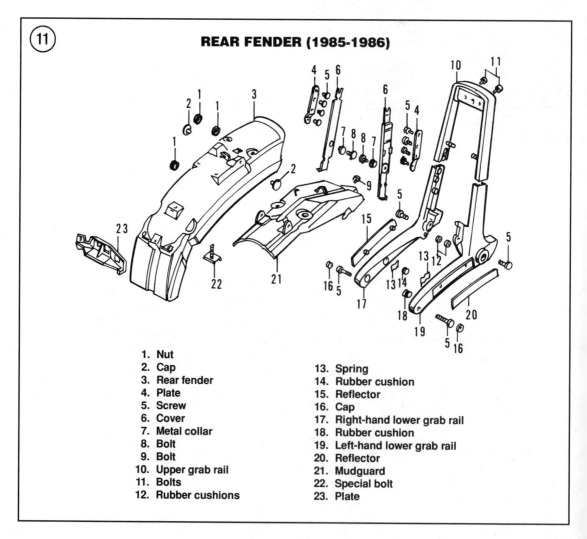

REAR FENDER (1985-1986)

1. Nut
2. Cap
3. Rear fender
4. Plate
5. Screw
6. Cover
7. Metal collar
8. Bolt
9. Bolt
10. Upper grab rail
11. Bolts
12. Rubber cushions
13. Spring
14. Rubber cushion
15. Reflector
16. Cap
17. Right-hand lower grab rail
18. Rubber cushion
19. Left-hand lower grab rail
20. Reflector
21. Mudguard
22. Special bolt
23. Plate

possible, you can use liquid paint remover, steel wool and a fine, hard wire brush.

CAUTION
Some of the fenders, side covers, frame covers and air box are molded plastic. If you wish to change the color of these parts, consult an automotive paint supplier for the proper procedure. Do not use any liquid paint remover on these *components as it will damage the surface. The color is an integral part of some of these components and cannot be removed.*

When the frame is down to bare metal, have it inspected for hairline and internal cracks. Magnaflux is the most common and complete process.

Make sure that the primer is compatible with the type of paint you are going to use for the finish color.

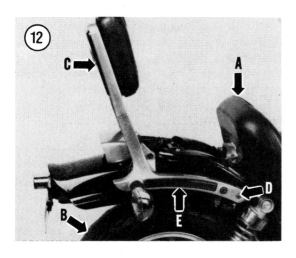

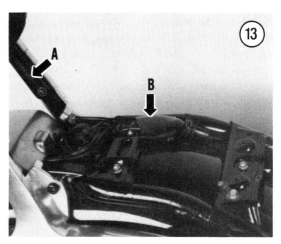

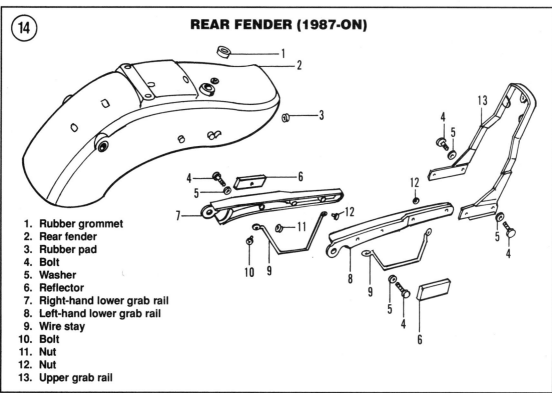

REAR FENDER (1987-ON)

1. Rubber grommet
2. Rear fender
3. Rubber pad
4. Bolt
5. Washer
6. Reflector
7. Right-hand lower grab rail
8. Left-hand lower grab rail
9. Wire stay
10. Bolt
11. Nut
12. Nut
13. Upper grab rail

13

Spray on one or two coats of primer as smoothly as possible. Let it dry thoroughly and use a fine grade of wet sandpaper (400-600 grit) to remove any flaws. Carefully wipe the surface clean and then spray a couple of coats of the final color. Use either lacquer or enamel base paint and follow the manufacturer's instructions.

A shop specializing in painting will probably do the best job. However, you can do a surprisingly good job with a good grade of spray paint. Spend a few extra dollars and get a good grade of paint as it will make a difference in how good it looks and how long it will stand up. It's a good idea to shake the can and make sure the ball inside the can is loose when you purchase the can of paint. Shake the can as long as is stated on the can. Then immerse the can **upright** in a pot or bucket of **warm** water (not hot—not over 120° F).

WARNING
*Higher temperatures could cause the can to burst. Do **not** place the can in direct contact with any flame or heat source.*

Leave the can in the water for several minutes. When thoroughly warmed, shake the can again and spray the frame. Be sure to get into all the crevices where there may be rust problems. Several light mist coats are better than one heavy coat. Spray painting is best done in temperatures of 70-80° F (21-26° C); any temperature above or below this will cause problems.

After the final coat has dried completely, at least 48 hours, any overspray or orange peel may be removed with a *light* application of Dupont rubbing compound (red color) and finished with Dupont polishing compound (white color). Be careful not to rub too hard or you will go through the finish.

Finish off with a couple coats of good wax prior to reassembling all the components.

It's a good idea to keep the frame touched up with fresh paint if any minor rust spots or scratches appear.

INDEX

A

Air filter case 223
Alternator 242-244
Alternator rotor, starter clutch
   assembly and starter gears 137-147

B

Basic hand tools 13-18
Battery 37-41
Bleeding the clutch 179-180
Brakes 33
   bleeding 348-351
   front brake pad replacement 331-333
   front caliper 339-344
   front disc 346-348
   front hose replacement 344-346
   front master cylinder 334-339
   rear drum 351-353
   rear pedal 353-355
Break-in procedure 147

C

Cable replacement
   choke 224-226
   throttle 223-224

Carburetor
   adjustments 220-223
   operation 208
   service 208-220
Centerstand 357-358
Charging system 240-242
Choke cable replacement 224-226
Clutch 32, 153-168
   bleeding 179-180
   diode 255
   hose replacement 175-176
   hydraulic system 169-170
   master cylinder 170-174
   oil pressure check 180-181
   oil relief valve 168-169
   slave cylinder 176-179
Connecting rods 131-134
Coolant hoses 284
Coolant pipes 283-284
Cooling fan 278
Cooling system
   check 274
   radiator 274-277
   thermostat 278-280
   water pump 280-283
Crankcase 120-128
   breather hose (U.S. models only) 37
   breather system (U.S. only) 233
Crankshaft 128-130
Cylinder 105-108

14

Cylinder (continued)
    head cover and camshaft 74-89
    heads 89-91

E

Electrical system
    alternator 242-244
    charging system 240-242
    clutch diode 255
    components 268-271
    ignition coil 248-249
    ignition system 245-248
    lighting system 255-263
    pulse generator 249-250
    spark unit 248
    starter 251-255
    starter solenoid 255
    starting system 250-251
    switches 263-268
    voltage regulator/rectifier 244-245
Emission control and battery decals 13
Engine 71-74
    alternator rotor, starter clutch
        assembly and starter gears 137-147
    break-in procedure 147
    camshaft 74-89
    connecting rods 131-134
    crankcase 120-128
    crankshaft 128-130
    cylinder 105-108
    cylinder head cover 74-89
    cylinder heads 89-91
    hydraulic tappets 103-105
    hydraulic valve adjuster system 69-71
    noises 32
    oil pressure relief valve 119
    oil pump 116-119
    oil pump drive sprockets
        and drive chain 113-115
    output gear unit 134-137
    performance 31-32
    piston, piston pin and piston rings 108-113
    primary drive gear 119-120
    principles 69
    rocker arm assemblies 99-103
    serving in frame 71
    starting troubleshooting 30-31
    valves and valve components 91-99

Evaporation emission control
    (California models only) 37
Evaporative emission control system
    (California models only) 233
Excessive vibration 32
Exhaust system 234-238
Expendable supplies 11-12
External shift mechanism 183-188

F

Fasteners 7-10
Final drive unit and drive shaft 316-320
Footpegs 358-359
Frame 362-364
Front brake disc 346-348
Front brake hose replacement 344-346
Front brake pad replacement 331-333
Front caliper 339-344
Front fender 359
Front forks 302-309
Front hub 288-292
Front master cylinder 334-339
Front suspension and steering 33
Front wheel 286-288
Fuel
    filter 227-228
    pump 228-229
    shutoff valve 226-227
    tank (1987-on) 232-233
    tanks (1985-1986) 229-232

H

Handlebar 295-297
Hose replacement 175-176
Hydraulic
    tappets 103-105
    valve adjuster system 69-71

I

Ignition
    coil 248-249
    system 33
    system 245-248
Internal shift mechanism 202-204

K

Kickstand (sidestand) 357

L

Lighting system 255-263
Lubricants 10-11
Lubrication, periodic 41-48

M

Maintenance, periodic 48-57
Mechanic's tips 22

O

Oil
  pressure relief valve 119
  pump 116-119
  pump drive sprockets and drive chain . . 113-115
Operating requirements 29
Output gear unit 134-137

P

Parts replacement 12-13
Periodic lubrication 41-48
Periodic maintenance 48-57
Piston, piston pin and piston rings 108-113
Pre-checks 35-36
Precision measuring tools 18-20
Primary drive gear 119-120
Pulse generator 249-250

R

Radiator 274-277
Rear brake pedal 353-355
Rear drum brake 351-353

Rear fender and grab rail 360-361
Rear hub 313-316
Rear wheel 311-313
Riding safety 22-24
Rocker arm assemblies 99-103
Routine checks 34-35

S

Safety first 2-3
Seats 359
Service
  hints 3-5
  intervals 36
Servicing engine in frame 71
Shock absorbers 324-328
Sidestand (kickstand) 357
Slave cylinder 176-179
Spark unit 248
Special tools 21-22
Starter 251-255
  solenoid 255
Starting
  difficulties 30
  engine 29-30
  system 250-251
Steering
  head and stem 297-301
  head bearing races 301-302
Supplies, expendable 11-12
Swing arm 320-324
Switches 263-268

T

Thermostat 278
Throttle cable replacement 223-224
Tire
  changing 293-295
  repairs 295
Tires and wheels 36-37
Tools
  basic 13-18
  precision 18-20
  special 21-22
  troubleshooting instruments 29
Torque specifications 6-7
Transmission 33, 188-201

14

Troubleshooting
   brakes 33
   clutch 32
   engine noises 32
   engine performance 31-32
   excessive vibration 32
   front suspension and steering 33
   ignition system 33
   instruments 29
   operating requirements 29
   starting difficulties 30
   starting the engine 29-30
   transmission 33
Tune-up 57-64

U

Universal joint 320

V

Valves and valve components 91-99
Voltage regulator/rectifier 244-245

W

Washing the bike 5-6
Water pump 280-283
Wheel balance 292-293

WIRING DIAGRAMS

1985 VT1100

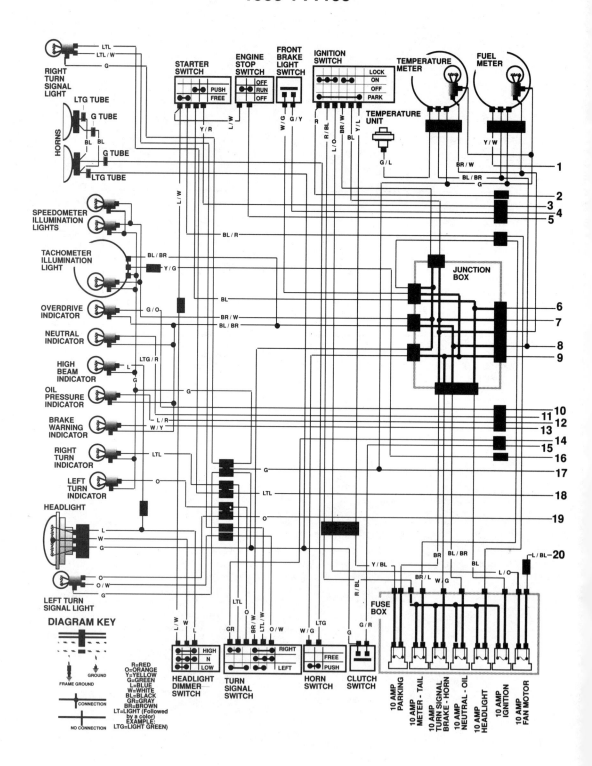

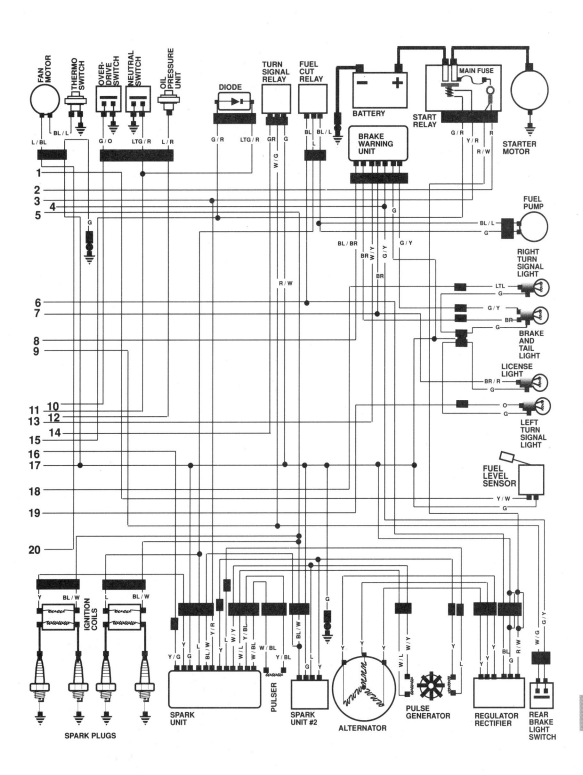

15

1986 VT1100

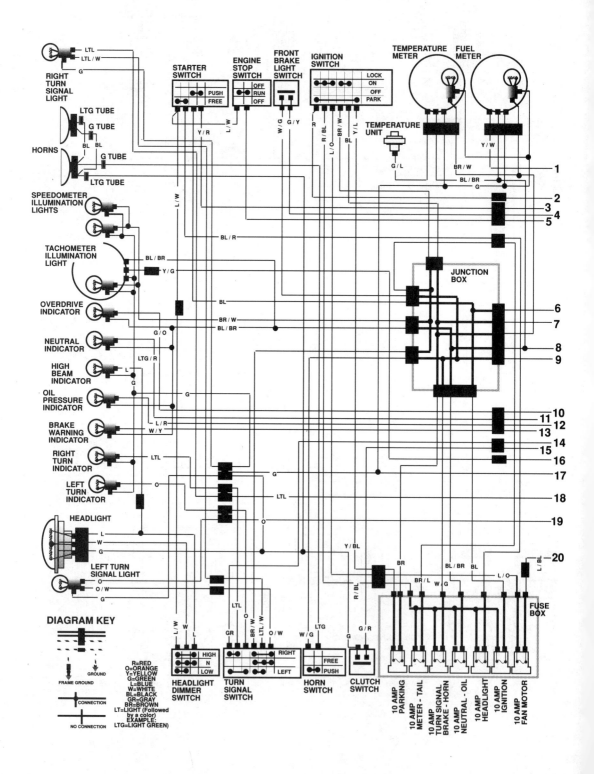

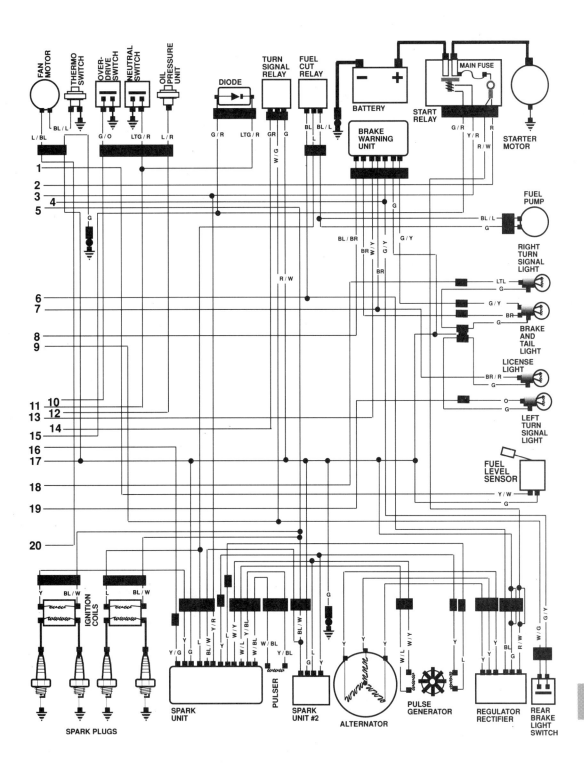

1987-1988 VT1100

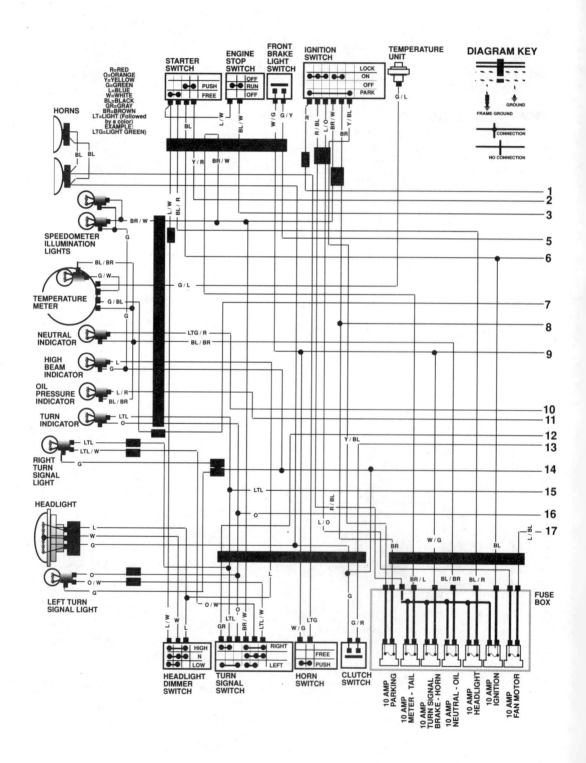

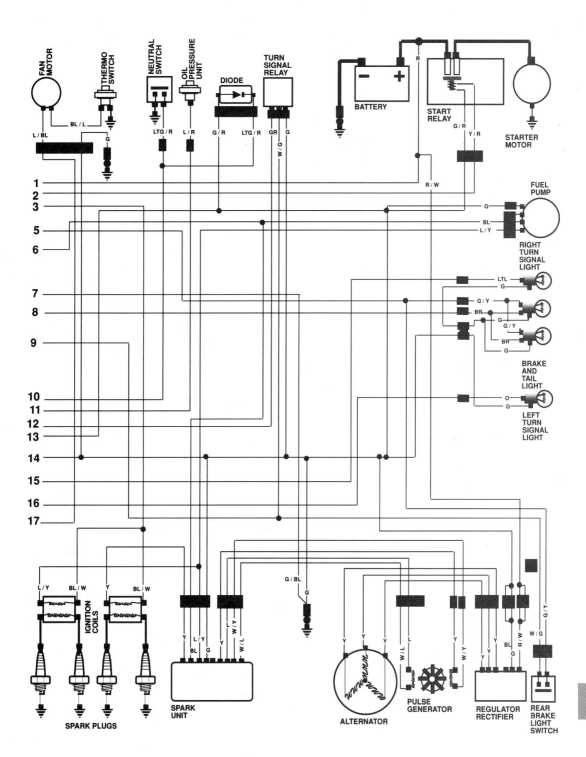

1989-ON VT1100

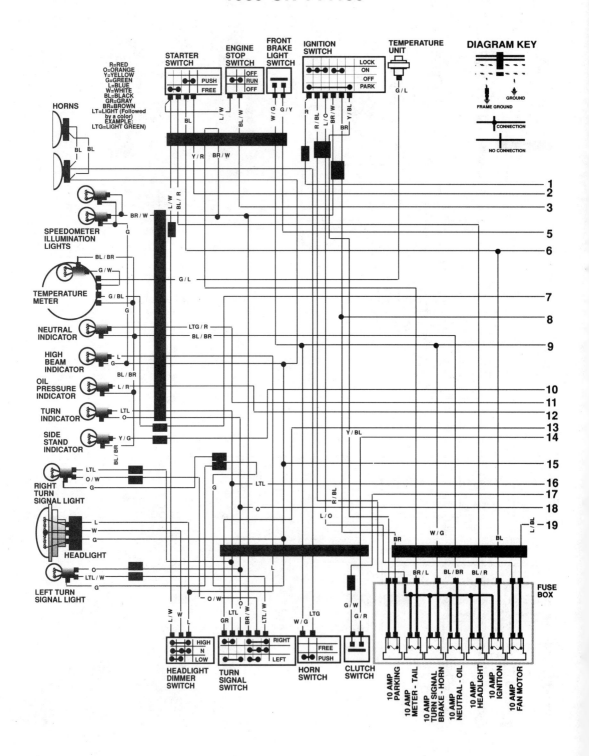

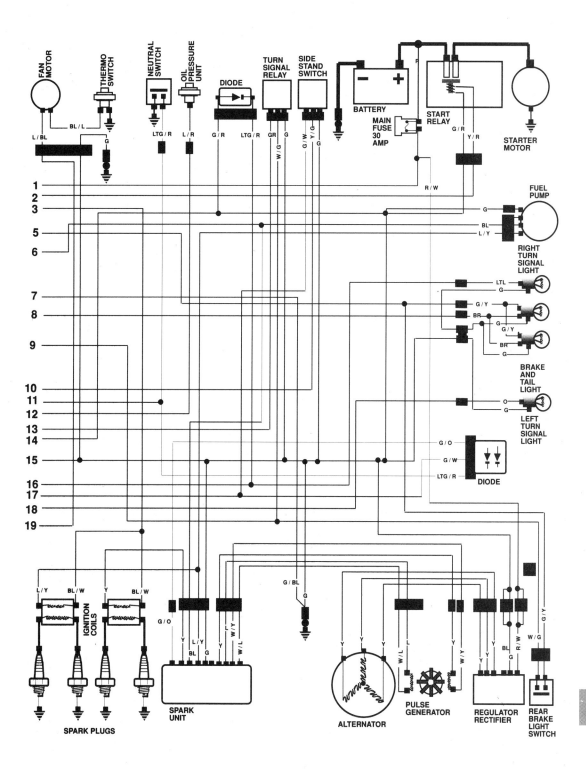

15

NOTES

NOTES

MAINTENANCE LOG

Service Performed	Mileage Reading				
Oil change (example)	2,836	5,782	8,601		